The Actor's Art

The
Actor's
Art

Conversations with Contemporary American Stage Performers

**Edited by Jackson R. Bryer
and Richard A. Davison**

RUTGERS UNIVERSITY PRESS
New Brunswick, New Jersey, and London

Library of Congress Cataloging-in-Publication Data
The actor's art : conversations with contemporary American stage performers / edited by
Jackson R. Bryer and Richard A. Davison.
    p. cm.
Includes bibliographical references and index.
ISBN 0-8135-2872-0 (alk. paper) — ISBN 0-8135-2873-9 (pbk. : alk paper)
1. Actors—United States—Interviews.   I. Bryer, Jackson R.   II. Davison, Richard Allan.

PN2285 .A23 2000
792'.028'0922—dc21

00-039035

British Cataloging-in-Publication data for this book
is available from the British Library.

Manufactured in the United States of America

Contents

Introduction

Most of the seventeen actors interviewed in this book will be honoring the stage well into this new century; by 2027, their combined careers will have spanned one hundred years of acting history. Jessica Tandy made her stage debut in 1927, around the time sound came to movies, near the end of the decade that has been labeled variously the Lost Generation, the Roaring Twenties, and the Jazz Age, two years before the stock market crash of 1929. It was also a time when an increasing number of actors who could both speak convincingly and look photogenic were being wooed from Broadway to Hollywood.

When the youngest actor in this book, Nathan Lane, first appeared on Broadway in 1982, he had already worked in television and off-Broadway productions. Actors nowadays can move more easily back and forth from stage to film to television. Even though Broadway and Hollywood remain three thousand miles apart, television work, nonexistent until the late 1940s, now thrives on both coasts. But for these interviews we and the actors interviewed have put the greatest emphasis on the stage, because, unlike those performances preserved on film or videotape, most stage performances are lost to all save memory. And although professional theaters offering repertory experience are less available to actors today than to Jessica Tandy and her generation, who cut their teeth on it, most of the actors in this book sharpened their skills in companies where they had the chance to play many roles.

As the number of plays opening each season in New York dramatically diminishes, actors today have fewer opportunities to play on Broadway, where traditionally much was gained even when an actor appeared in a play that flopped. As Hume Cronyn recalls, "You were in failure after failure after failure and you learned and you learned and you learned." All the actors featured here have acted with sustained brilliance in successes and failures on and off Broadway. We chose them partly because critics and historians of acting have ranked them among the best of the best, but mainly because we have seen many of their performances, and what we have seen and heard has taught and delighted us. The high quality of their art made the choices easy. Their collective comments provide a superb history of the finest and most representative acting of the last seven decades of the twentieth century.

Jessica Tandy made her professional acting debut in London in 1927 only four years after John Barrymore had concluded a legendary, record-breaking run of *Hamlet* in New York. In 1927 New York was in the midst of a peak season, with over 260 productions, which would represent the highest number of plays ever on Broadway.* That year the original *Show Boat* boasted a cast of ninety-six and a top ticket price of $5.50; the 1994 revival had a cast of sixty-eight and a top ticket price of $75.00. In Tandy's Broadway debut year, 1930, the New York season included more than 180 different plays performed in Broadway's sixty legitimate theaters. By 1934, the year of Hume Cronyn's Broadway debut, the number of annual productions had dropped to 161. The 98 productions during the 1938–39 season represented the first dip below 100 in thirty-five years. Still, during the 1920s and 1930s, plenty of work was available in Broadway theaters, less off-Broadway, much in repertory theater and in film, none as yet in television. Live theater was flourishing despite heavy competition for audiences from Hollywood.

Shortly after World War I, the recently founded Theatre Guild was already producing an important share of Broadway plays, attracting top actors and directors. By 1931 (with Sarah Bernhardt dead for eight years, Katharine Cornell making Candida her favorite role, and Katharine Hepburn eight years away from her greatest stage success in *The Philadelphia Story*), the Guild had been joined as an important production organization by the Group Theatre, which put on plays with its own company of actors, directors, and playwrights (among them, Clifford Odets, Sidney Kingsley, and William Saroyan), many of whom had on-the-job training during the politically driven 1930s. In 1947, Group Theatre members Robert Lewis and Elia Kazan founded the Actors Studio to develop further the skills of young actors, including Marlon Brando, Montgomery Clift, Julie Harris, Steven Hill, Cloris Leachman, Anne Jackson, Patricia Neal, Maureen Stapleton, Eli Wallach, and James Whitmore. They invited Lee Strasberg to teach some of the classes.

Always a cheaper place to produce a play, and often allowing more artistic freedom, off-Broadway began early in the twentieth century to provide an alternative training ground for actors. Katharine Cornell performed with the off-Broadway Washington Players during pre–World War I years, before they became Broadway's Theatre Guild and she became a Broadway star. Companies that formed after World War I and stayed off-Broadway included the Provincetown Players (best known for performing Eugene O'Neill's and Susan Glaspell's early plays), the Neighborhood Players, the Cherry Lane Theatre, the Negro Players, the Brooklyn Rep, and Eva Le Gallienne's Civic Repertory Theatre. In the middle to late 1930s, the Federal Theatre Project under the Works Progress Administration employed many actors and directors (including John Houseman and Orson Welles) and became the platform for the Mercury Theatre, producing the controversial "Voodoo" *Macbeth* and *The Cradle Will Rock* before its funding was cut in 1939.

*Most of the statistics that follow are gleaned from the *New York Times*, *Variety*, and Gene Brown's *Show Time* (1997).

After World War II, with actors who had been in the service looking for work, off-Broadway theaters got a major boost; by the late 1950s, off-Broadway was moving toward the high number of stages and new productions it claims today. In the 1950s, off-Broadway showcased actors in new experimental plays alongside productions of Chekhov, O'Casey, Brecht, Thornton Wilder, and Shakespeare, at such theaters as the Phoenix, Circle in the Square, and Joseph Papp's New York Shakespeare Festival. Both veteran and apprentice performers worked under nurturing, albeit not lucrative, conditions. Actors such as Jason Robards, Geraldine Page, Julie Harris, James Earl Jones, Colleen Dewhurst, and George C. Scott also did radio and live television work in the 1950s to help subsidize their theater work. By 1960–61, off-Broadway had launched playwrights like Jean Genet (in English), Jack Gelber, and Edward Albee. By the 1960–61 season, the ninety-five off-Broadway shows, many at new theaters such as the Living Theatre, Caffe Cino, and La MaMa, were more than double the number of shows that opened on Broadway.

Memories and stories of legendary performances from the 1930s, 1940s, and 1950s were inspirations for both seasoned and neophyte actors throughout the 1960s. Many of the performers in this volume speak passionately of being inspired by such artists as Laurette Taylor in *The Glass Menagerie;* Gielgud in *Hamlet;* Olivier in *Oedipus Rex* and *The Entertainer;* Ethel Waters in *The Member of the Wedding;* Cornell in *Candida* and *Antony and Cleopatra* (the 1947 production with fledgling actors Charleton Heston, Tony Randall, Maureen Stapleton, and Eli Wallach); Ralph Richardson's Falstaff in *Henry IV;* Alfred Lunt and Lynn Fontanne in *The Visit;* Claudia McNeil in *A Raisin in the Sun;* Jason Robards in both *The Iceman Cometh* and *Long Day's Journey into Night;* and Kim Stanley in *Bus Stop.* Over the next four decades, they would add their own work to this list of great performances: Shirley Knight in *Kennedy's Children;* Ruby Dee in *Boesman and Lena;* Zoe Caldwell in *The Prime of Miss Jean Brodie;* James Earl Jones in *The Great White Hope;* Stacy Keach in *Indians;* Hume Cronyn and Jessica Tandy in *The Gin Game;* Julie Harris in *The Belle of Amherst;* Maureen Stapleton in *The Gingerbread Lady;* Jason Robards in *A Moon for the Misbegotten;* Nathan Lane in *Guys and Dolls;* Eli Wallach and Anne Jackson in *Luv;* Cherry Jones in *The Heiress;* Eileen Heckart in *Butterflies Are Free;* Blythe Danner in *A Streetcar Named Desire;* and George Grizzard in *A Delicate Balance.*

By the 1970–71 New York season, the old had met the new: at seventy-two, the classically rooted Judith Anderson played Hamlet, and a young Diana Rigg, exhibiting the new political and artistic freedom that had become increasingly evident in New York theater during the late 1960s, had a nude scene in *Abelard and Heloise.* A more liberal view toward race-blind casting allowed George C. Scott to cast black actors as Willy Loman's neighbors in a 1975 Broadway production of *Death of a Salesman.* The early 1970s were also marked by the deaths of Noël Coward and Katharine Cornell. Film actress

Lauren Bacall came to Broadway and won a Tony for *Applause*. Zero Mostel reinvented his 1958 role in *Ulysses in Nighttown,* this time with a nude Molly Bloom. Irene Worth won a Tony for *Sweet Bird of Youth,* and Tennessee Williams discussed his homosexuality in his memoirs. Twenty years later Stephen Spinella would receive a Tony for his deeply moving portrayal of a gay protagonist in *Angels in America.* By 1978–79 the top price for nonmusical plays was twenty dollars, for musicals twenty-five dollars. The top ticket for *Cats* in 1982–83 would be forty dollars.

Mae West, Gower Champion, Lynn Fontanne, Ethel Merman, and Tennessee Williams died in the early 1980s. British actor Ian McKellen won a Tony for *Amadeus,* and Lauren Bacall won her second Tony for the musical *Woman of the Year.* Theater costs continued to rise, and British theater continued to influence Broadway. By 1983–84, the number of new Broadway productions had decreased to thirty-six, while the number of Equity actors increased to thirty thousand, double the number of 1974–75. Orson Welles and Yul Brynner died on the same day, October 10, 1985, in the midst of a season whose thirty-one productions represented a new low. However, by 1986, largely due to four imported British musicals, *Cats, Les Misérables, Starlight Express,* and *Me and My Girl,* the declining Broadway audience figures rose for the first time in five years. But then, in part because of the longevity of the musical blockbusters, the 1988–89 Broadway season experienced another record low of only twenty-nine new productions. Off-Broadway and off-off-Broadway continued to control most of the New York market for new plays and smaller-budget musicals, which by now employed more Equity actors than did Broadway productions. Nineteen eighty-nine was also the year of the loss of one of the greatest actors of the century, Laurence Olivier.

That the 1990–91 Tony Award for best actor in a musical went to Jonathan Pryce in *Miss Saigon* was an appropriate sign of the continuing domination of British imports, especially musicals, into the early 1990s. That same season, the top American musical actress, Mary Martin, died, followed by the loss in 1991–92 of the largest number of representatives of the substance and glory of Broadway theater from the 1920s to the 1990s, the old guard and the not-so-old: Eva Le Gallienne, Judith Anderson, Molly Picon (at ninety-four), José Ferrer, Colleen Dewhurst, and Joseph Papp. Also that season, the Pulitzer Prize was awarded to *The Kentucky Cycle,* which had premiered at the Seattle Repertory Theatre, another indication of the movement of new productions away from Broadway to regional theaters. Tony Randall's National Actors Theatre made its debut with a revival of *The Crucible* in 1991 (appropriately at the venerable Belasco Theatre, which dates back to 1903) and continues to maintain a national repertory theater. It joined the other remaining nonprofit theater companies producing on Broadway to the benefit of actors and audiences alike: Circle in the Square (which had moved uptown in 1972), the Lincoln Center company (dating from the early 1960s), and the Roundabout Theatre Company (founded off-Broadway in the mid-1960s).

By the 1993–94 season, Helen Hayes was gone, and Broadway was down to thirty-seven theater houses from sixty in the 1920s. There are now over thirty theaters off-Broadway and well over two hundred off-off-Broadway. In 1994–95, Broadway attendance climbed to more than nine million for the first time in thirteen years, with blockbuster musicals again largely responsible for the increase. There were now more than a hundred thousand Equity actors in New York competing for eight hundred jobs on Broadway. Regionally trained Cherry Jones won the Tony for *The Heiress,* and the British actor Ralph Fiennes won it for *Hamlet,* in 1994–95. In 1995–96, George Grizzard's and Nathan Lane's Tony Awards for the revivals of *A Delicate Balance* and *A Funny Thing Happened on the Way to the Forum* pointed up the influx of tried-and-true productions of the past. Such revivals would increasingly reduce the number of new plays on Broadway while offering prime roles for prime actors. In 1999, such outstanding revivals on Broadway as *Death of a Salesman, The Iceman Cometh, The Price, Waiting in the Wings,* and *Amadeus* often built their productions around celebrated actors, while award-winning new plays like *Wit* and *Side Man,* which opened off-Broadway, brought lesser-known actors into the spotlight.

With the exception of summer Shakespeare festivals (which offer some repertory experience), the repertory stock companies, so vital during the first half of the century, had all but vanished by its end. Regional theaters have filled the gap to some extent. Skilled artists now find homes all across the country at places like the Alley Theatre in Texas, the Arena Stage in Washington, D.C., the Actors Theatre of Louisville, and the Seattle Repertory Theatre.

All of the actors interviewed in this book have had valuable experience in repertory and/or summer stock theater companies. Another thing these seventeen actors have in common, along with talent, is a unique presence onstage that belies and transcends any label that might be given to a so-called product of an acting school, or program, or method, or guru. They have all continually given us the gift of their native talents and transmuted their stage and life experiences into performances that are transcendent and unique.

Whether playing fragile or domineering, earthy or elegant women, Jessica Tandy clothed herself in a talent that shone onstage for almost seventy years. Hume Cronyn bristles with talent whether playing wickedly gnomelike terrible liars, charmingly debonair fathers and grandfathers, or feisty, doting husbands to Jessica Tandy. Eli Wallach can still register wickedness, lechery, merriment, and romance in his eyes and body whether he is (at eighty) recreating his role of a fifteen-year-old-boy flying a kite in *This Property Is Condemned* or playing an eighty-year-old widower padding across the stage to answer his apartment doorbell in *Visiting Mr. Green.* Eileen Heckart has used her distinctive voice and impeccable timing to help immortalize characters such as the sexually inhibited sister in *The Dark at the Top of the Stairs,* heroines like Eleanor Roosevelt and Margaret Sanger, and, most recently, the Alzheimer's-stricken grandmother in *The Waverly Gallery.* Jason Robards, who first brought Hickey to life in José Quintero's Circle in the Square production of *The Iceman Cometh,* went on to electrify Broadway in such plays as *The Disenchanted, Long Day's Journey into Night,* and *A Moon for the Misbegotten* before he brought Hickey to Broadway some thirty years later. Ruby Dee is shrewdly intelligent and poignantly affecting whether kneeling on the side of a riverbank and calling out her man's name in *Boesman and Lena* or standing behind an ironing board and observing her troubled family in *A Raisin in the Sun.* Maureen Stapleton, touching, acerbic, witty, and hilarious in *The Rose Tattoo* and *Plaza Suite,* indefatigably tragic in *Mother Courage,* always seems real, believable, and never actorish, even when her character is called on to go over the top. Julie Harris (nominated for ten Tony Awards and winner of five) consistently gives superbly authentic performances, ranging from the free-spirited Sally Bowles in *I Am a Camera* to the free-minded Emily Dickinson in *The Belle of Amherst.*

With a smile wrapped around intelligence and energy, Anne Jackson can play the nuances of an adolescent girl in *This Property Is Condemned* (as she recently did with her husband, Eli Wallach, in *Tennessee Williams Remembered*) even better now than she played them so brilliantly over fifty years ago. George Grizzard's energy, sometimes joyful, sometimes fierce, is always ebullient; even when his face and body seem at rest, something is always happening. His long-overdue Tony, for *A Delicate Balance,* is recent evidence that he has maintained and perhaps even gone beyond the brilliance he displayed as Shep Stearns in *The Disenchanted.* The riveting presence of James Earl Jones onstage in *The Great White Hope* and in *Fences* more than matches the resonant power of his voice. Zoe Caldwell remains a master talent whether she is playing a vengeful Medea, arguably truer than Judith Anderson's, or a master teacher in *Master Class,* re-creating the magic of Maria Callas. Shirley Knight is always indelibly believable, whether playing a Marilyn Monroe–like movie star in *Kennedy's Children* or a matronly housewife in *Young Man from Atlanta.* When a twenty-one-year-old Stacy Keach sailed his plumed hat into the wings and sold Mercutio's Queen Mab speech to a spellbound crowd at the Oregon Shakespeare Festival, he launched a brilliant acting career in which he seems at his best onstage, whether in the title role of *Macbeth* or in his multiple roles in *The Kentucky Cycle.* Blythe Danner is always a class act, always true to her character, from her early role as a girlfriend of a blind boy in *Butterflies Are Free* to her more recent ones as many-nuanced housewives in *Moonlight* and *The Deep Blue Sea.* Although she modestly calls herself "a worker bee," she can play the queen to perfection. Cherry Jones, whose stage presence emanates a golden glow, is equally electrifying when standing still and looking at another actor in *Pride's Crossing* or when sprinting up a long flight of stairs in *The Heiress.* Nathan Lane captivates, whether quiet and reflective or physically and verbally alive, in comedy or drama. He would make a wonderful Tom in *The Glass Menagerie,* a perfect James Tyrone Jr. in *Long Day's Journey into Night,* roles he told us that he very much wants to play.

Most of the actors in this book know one another. In talking about their own performances, they all have much to say about their fellow actors, past and present. Many of the performers interviewed in this book have worked together; their admiration of one another surely lays to rest the frequently expressed belief that the acting profession is permeated with petty jealousies and feuds. These interviews indicate that, at the highest levels of the profession at least, this is not the case. And their comments about contemporaries not represented in this volume are similarly positive. Names that recur as inspirations include Eileen Atkins, Marlon Brando, Morris Carnovsky, Colleen Dewhurst, Judi Dench, Edith Evans, John Gielgud, Uta Hagen, Rosemary Harris, Hal Holbrook, Fredric March, Laurence Olivier, Ralph Richardson, Paul Scofield, George C. Scott, Kim Stanley, Elaine Stritch, Laurette Taylor, Meryl Streep, and Irene Worth. Maureen Stapleton thinks herself a better actress when playing with Jason Robards or George C. Scott and would "go anywhere to see Julie Harris and Colleen Dewhurst and Zoe Caldwell." Julie Harris says of Olivier's acting: "Everything he ever did was an inspiration to me." Many of these actors' insights are drawn from or supported by firsthand and anecdotal observations of other admired performers. Certain directors' names reappear throughout this volume as well, indicating that they have been able to impress actors of varying styles and temperaments, a sure testimony to their directing skills. They include Harold Clurman, Gerald Gutierrez, Tyrone Guthrie, Elia Kazan, Joshua Logan, Mike Nichols, José Quintero, and Gene Saks.

That the observations and opinions of these seventeen actors and actresses are drawn from their personal careers, which often span several decades, gives them added force and credibility. These observations frequently affirm the main ingredients of superior acting outlined in the writings of one of the best of modern drama critics, Stark Young, whose statements on acting in *The Flower in Drama* seem as a result even more accurate:

> Acting is not art until it ceases to be life. It is not art until it takes what it portrays and recreates that in its own terms and adds to it something that was not there before. . . . Great actors remain themselves.

> To talk of flashes of inspiration and thrills and devastating magnetism is not to discuss acting, but only certain heavenly by-products of the art. . . . Acting has an honest groundwork of essentials and certain hard fundamentals on which it stands.

> That the sensibility and intelligence . . . of an actor, his gift, his soul, his music, his miracle of talent, are what measures his achievement, is indisputable. . . . But no matter how great this self of the actor's may be, he cannot express it until he develops an adequate technique. . . . An actor who

has not found for himself technical machinery one way or
another, is like a man without a tongue.

These interviews certainly belie Samuel Johnson's definition of actors as
merely "dancing dogs." What these actors have to say about their art is invari-
ably intelligent and thoughtful. They make clear that acting is very hard work,
not just something that happens spontaneously and naturally. But, at their
finest, they do not let the mechanism show; they are never caught acting.
They borrow the best from other artists and incorporate what works for them
into their own performances. They speak clearly and audibly, remain in the
moment, and make each moment part of the rhythm of a seamless performance. They neither fret about what they have just done the moment before
nor telegraph what they will do next in the scenes to come. They know that
the fluidity of an entire performance is essential, that it must seem to flow
without artifice. In a recent interview with Mel Gussow in the *New York
Times,* Uta Hagen said that her "whole goal as an actress" was "the spontaneity that comes without planning." This requires using finely honed tools to enhance an innate talent. She is describing what all the actors who saw and
heard Laurette Taylor's Amanda Wingfield in the original production of *The
Glass Menagerie* once, twice, or a dozen times experienced. Actors and directors, including Hagen (who saw Taylor's classic performance ten times), never
caught her acting, never caught her telegraphing her next move. How they
achieve this appearance of spontaneity and fluidity through study and hard
work is what many of the actors in this book try to explain. As with most artistic geniuses who produce masterpieces, whether in literature, music, painting, or theater, it is often difficult for them to explain how they do it. But their
attempts to do so are fascinating to hear.

What the actors in this volume have in common with Laurette Taylor,
along with innate talent, is a strong personality at the core of their work. As
their responses indicate, very few of these actors can be pigeonholed as either
a technique actor (who works from the outside in) or a Method actor (who
works from the inside out). They all begin and end with a superior blend of
the two and then some. With superior technique, they have strengthened the
human qualities so essential to great acting. They have done their homework,
and what they have learned they have practiced painstakingly. They have
learned control of manner, voice, diction, movement, and gesture, so that
body, mind, and spirit are one, Having mastered their craft, they can create
for us the magic of "the first time" at each performance, whatever the length
of the play's run.

Because we wanted to see what answers would be common to several performers as well as which would evoke totally different responses, we asked
some of the same questions in each interview. We were gratified by the variety of insightful responses we received and the felicity with which they were
expressed. Thus, Ruby Dee talks of how an actor must "process the informa-

tion that comes out of the atmosphere . . . people . . . colors . . . music . . . anything." Cherry Jones describes the actor's goal as "an ease, utter ease," such as Elaine Stritch's (in *A Delicate Balance*) "brilliant marriage of physicality and just utter believability." Zoe Caldwell highlights the importance of the script: "I am a conduit for the writer." Jason Robards says that an actor must "obey the rules of the character, not the rules that you think." Nathan Lane says an actor "should have an action, but sometimes you should trust that you come out and say the lines, and if they're good lines, it'll work." Hume Cronyn believes that an actor should "have a sense of technique that goes beyond a constant poring over your emotional entrails. . . . The bank of your memory of awareness and your physical capacities . . . make up your instrument." George Grizzard observes that "what you have to do is have this mystery to lure an audience in order for them to do part of your work, to involve them. Don't do it all for them." Blythe Danner quotes Edith Evans on acting: "I never think of being great, but only about being true," and adds, "If you're not moved to laughter or tears in the theater, it's sort of a waste of time." With all this variety of responses, however, certain themes pervade these conversations: being truthful onstage, serving the playwright, and, above all, taking risks in the selection of new roles.

In discussions of their own creative processes as artists, F. Scott Fitzgerald, Ernest Hemingway, and Lorraine Hansberry make observations that apply to the essentials of outstanding acting. In "The Rich Boy," Fitzgerald writes, "Begin with an individual, and before you know it you have created a type; begin with a type, and you find that you have created—nothing." Hemingway in an *Esquire* interview on writing could also be talking about the discipline that goes into great acting:

> Watch what happens. . . . If you get a kick out of it . . . see what the action was that gave you the emotion . . . the excitement. Then write it down making it clear so the reader will see it too and have the same feeling that you had. . . . Listen now. When people talk, listen completely. Don't be thinking what you're going to say. Most people never listen. Nor do they observe. You should be able to go into a room and when you come out know everything that you saw there and not only that. If that room gave you any feeling you should know exactly what it was that gave you that feeling.

Speaking of playwriting and *A Raisin in the Sun,* Hansberry declares, "I believe that one of the soundest ideas in dramatic writing is that in order to be universal you must pay great attention to the specifics." At its best, the actor's art is like the writer's art: one true gesture equals one true sentence, and the whole of the performance is equal to more than the sum of its parts.

Great actors, like great writers, are all practicing the specifics of an art, not a slavish adherence to nature or so-called real life. Heeding Hamlet's advice to the players, they hold the mirror up to nature and perfect the mirror image, the *representation* of nature. They embody Alexander Pope's definition of art in the creation and realization of their performances: the art of their acting is ". . . nature to advantage dress'd, / What oft was thought, but ne'er so well expressed." They are doing what the American novelist Frank Norris describes in "Fiction Is Selection" as the goal of his own art, creating what "*seems* real not what *is* real" (our italics). Great actors enhance our willing suspension of disbelief so that we are so charged by the electricity between actor and audience that details of the experience remain seared in our memories.

Acting may be the most fleeting, the most ephemeral, of the arts. This book is an attempt to help preserve the details, the nuances, the moments, the rhythms inherent in performances that otherwise will be lost with the persons who created those performances and with the audiences who savored them. We are delighted to be part of the process that preserves their memories for posterity. What follows is a series of insights spanning seventy-five years of acting in the American theater. We are proud to have assembled this outstanding cast of seventeen. Even, and sometimes especially, in the comments of the actors most reluctant to talk about how they do what they do so well, the words are choice.

For significant help in the preparation of this book, we wish to thank Marc Singer and Drew Eisenhauer for their work on the transcriptions of the interviews; Linda Stein for research assistance; Debbie Lyall for secretarial services; Milena Davison for expert editing; India Cooper for her meticulous copyediting of the manuscript; and Marilyn Campbell and Leslie Mitchner of Rutgers University Press for their patience and expertise.

February 14, 2000
College Park, Maryland
Newark, Delaware

About the Interviews

Seven of the interviews originated as sessions in the series "The Smithsonian Celebrates Broadway's 100th Birthday!" which was sponsored by the Smithsonian Institution's Campus on the Mall, and took place in Washington, D.C., in the fall of 1993 as follows:

The principal questioner for the interview with Hume Cronyn and Jessica Tandy was Hap Erstein, drama critic of the *Palm Beach* (Fla.) *Post*.

The principal questioner for the interview with Zoe Caldwell was Bob Mondello, theater critic of the *City Paper* (Washington, D.C.) and frequent reviewer and commentator for National Public Radio's *All Things Considered*.

The principal questioner for the interview with George Grizzard was Robert Prosky, stage and film actor and longtime member of the acting company at the Arena Stage in Washington, D.C.

The principal questioner for the interview with Eileen Heckart was the late Richard L. Coe, theater critic emeritus of the *Washington Post*.

The principal questioner for the interview with Stacy Keach was Michael Kahn, artistic director of the Shakespeare Theatre (Washington, D.C.) and director of the drama division of the Juilliard School.

The principal questioner for the interview with Shirley Knight was Linda Sherbert, deputy editor of *Atlanta Magazine*.

The principal questioner for the interview with Jason Robards was Hap Erstein.

Additional questions were addressed to each of the guests in the Smithsonian series by members of the audience.

The other interviews in the volume took place under the following circumstances:

The interview with Blythe Danner was conducted in the dining room of the Hotel DuPont in Wilmington, Delaware; the interviewers were Jackson R. Bryer and Richard A. Davison. Additional questions were addressed to Danner in a follow-up telephone interview by Bryer.

The interview with Ruby Dee was conducted backstage at the Sylvia and Danny Kaye Playhouse at Hunter College in New York City; the interviewers were Jackson R. Bryer and Richard A. Davison.

The interview with Julie Harris was conducted at the Wyndham Hotel in New York City; the interviewers were Jackson R. Bryer and Richard A. Davison. Additional questions were addressed to Harris in a follow-up telephone interview by Davison.

The interview with Cherry Jones was conducted at Rafiella's restaurant in New York City; the interviewers were Jackson R. Bryer and Richard A. Davison.

The interview with James Earl Jones was conducted via telephone; Jones was in Boston. The interviewer was Penelope Niven, author of *Carl Sandburg: A Biography* (1991) and *Steichen: A Biography* (1997) and coauthor, with James Earl Jones, of *James Earl Jones: Voices and Silences* (1993).

The interview with Nathan Lane was conducted at Good Enough to Eat restaurant in New York City; the interviewers were Jackson R. Bryer and Richard A. Davison.

The interview with Maureen Stapleton was conducted at her home in Lenox, Massachusetts; the interviewer was Jackson R. Bryer.

The interview with Eli Wallach and Anne Jackson was conducted at the auditorium of the Smithsonian Institution's National Museum of American History in Washington, D.C.; the interviewers were Jackson R. Bryer and Richard A. Davison.

The Actor's Art

Zoe Caldwell

Photo courtesy Zoe Caldwell

Zoe Caldwell was born in Hawthorn, Victoria, Australia, on September 14, 1933. She made her acting debut as an original member of the Union Theatre Repertory Company in Melbourne in 1953, her London debut as Ismene in Antigone *(1960), and her New York debut as the Prioress in* The Devils *(1965). Her other early roles include Bianca (with Paul Robeson),* Othello; *Cordelia (with Charles Laughton),* King Lear; *and Helena,* All's Well That Ends Well, *all three at Stratford-on-Avon, England (1958–59). She has worked with Canada's Stratford Festival and Tyrone Guthrie's Minneapolis theater, where she played Rosaline,* Love's Labours Lost *(1961); Frosine,* The Miser *(1962); Natasha,* The Three Sisters *(1963); Cleopatra (with Christopher Plummer),* Antony and Cleopatra; *Lady Anne,* Richard III; *and Mrs. Page,* The Merry Wives of Windsor *(all in 1967). Other roles include Pegeen Mike,* Playboy of the Western World *(1961); title role,* Saint Joan *(1962); title role,* Mother Courage and Her Children *(1964); Countess Aurelia,* The Madwoman of

Chaillot *(1964); Millamant,* The Way of the World *(1965); Orinthia,* The Apple Cart *(1966); Lena Szezepanowska,* Misalliance *(1966); Polly,* Slapstick Tragedy *(1966; Tony Award); title role,* The Prime of Miss Jean Brodie *(1968; Tony Award); Emma Hamilton,* A Bequest to the Nation *(1970); Eve,* The Creation of the World and Other Business *(1972); Alice,* The Dance of Death *(1974); Mary Tyrone,* Long Day's Journey into Night *(1976); title role,* Medea *(1982; Tony Award); Lillian Hellman,* Lillian *(1986); Katharine Brynne,* A Perfect Ganesh *(1993); and Maria Callas,* Master Class *(1996; Tony Award).*

Her directorial credits in the theater include An Almost Perfect Person *(1977),* Richard II *(1979),* These Men *(1980),* Othello *(1981),* The Taming of the Shrew *(1985),* Hamlet *(1986),* Park Your Car in Harvard Yard *(1991), and* Vita and Virginia *(1994). She appeared in the film* The Purple Rose of Cairo *(1985) and on television in* Lantern Hill *(1990).*

She received the John Gielgud Award for Excellence in the Dramatic Arts in 1998.

This interview took place on December 6, 1993.

•————————————————————————————•

Interviewer: Let's start at the beginning. You were raised in Australia, and your first performance, I understand, was at the age of nine. Then you had a radio show by the time you were eleven. What did your folks think about the theater?

Caldwell: I was a professional by the time I was nine. I'd played Slightly Soiled in *Peter Pan;* that was the name of the character I played. Then I did, at the age of eleven, have a program called *News and Interviews.* I interviewed visiting celebrities who came into Melbourne. Strangely enough, I really wasn't precocious. I should have been, with all that going on. I have a son who when he was three was diagnosed as having a small motor skills disability, and I was told of it as though it was some terrible dire thing. When we took him to the great guru of motor skills disabilities, Katrina de Hirsch in New York, she tested him for six weeks and said, "Yes, he does, but he comes by it honestly." My husband, Robert Whitehead, said, "Well, it isn't me," and I said, "I think it's me." She said, "That's very interesting. What form did it take?" I said, "Well, I couldn't count or know my left from my right." Writing or doing needlework was difficult, but my large motor skills were very good. I needed to communicate, as all human beings do, and so I found very quickly that I could articulate. I could sing, dance, and tell stories, and so it was survival. I think that's why I wasn't precocious; it was just that I had to do it to communicate, to survive. My mum and dad were bright enough to realize that I should be given every opportunity to develop whatever skills I wanted to employ, so they had me taught dancing, movement, and elocution. That's what it was called when I was a little girl. I think it now would have some fancy name. It would be speech or something like that. From the age of seven to the age of eighteen I was lucky to have a most extraordinary teacher. So I was very, very fortunate to be given the gift of survival very early. Wouldn't it be thrilling if everybody in our whole world could be given that early? In no time at all the world would have no problems with crime and violence.

Interviewer: You had the opportunity to leave Australia somewhat before you did. You had a chance to go to London with *Summer of the Seventeenth Doll.* Why didn't you go? Why did you decide to stay in Australia for a little bit longer? Was it to be a big fish in a small pond? Was it to develop skills before you went?

Caldwell: No, I was mad as a hatter that I wasn't going, but I'd been very fortunate throughout my life to have a lot of Jean Brodies. The first Jean Brodie was Winifred Moverly Browne, who taught me, through scholarship— I never paid any tuition from the age of seven to the age of eighteen—and gave me a voice, which is a very handy thing to have if you're an actor. She also took me to galleries and introduced me to reading. She was a true Jean Brodie. Then, at a certain age, there was a woman called Elsie Beyer, who was the head of the Australian Elizabethan Theatre Trust, of which I was an original member. When *The Summer of the Seventeenth Doll* was going to London and I was the original Bubba in it, I thought naturally I'd go. I was terrific as Bubba—and I was suddenly using my own Australian sounds, and that was very potent and powerful. Elsie Beyer said, "No, dear, you're not going yet, dear. If you go now and do an Australian part in an Australian play, they'll only think of you as an Australian actress who can do nothing but Australian parts, and I want you to be a great classical actress, dear, so you wait." That's why I waited.

Interviewer: Is there a difference between London acting and Australian acting?

Caldwell: Yes. It's very difficult, I think, to have to keep a little bit of your sounds back. I now have a kind of bastard accent, which contains many, many, many sounds. I have a lot of sounds; I choose the sounds that I keep. In those days if you were an Australian actress, you went to London and you worked as a waitress and then of a night you went and attempted to play in a slightly foreign voice. I teach Shakespeare to Americans, and I tell them primarily you must use your own sounds, your own voice. George III gave us all a lot of trouble, but George III happened to be a German, so the sounds he made became the King's English. Actually, the sounds that most American actors are using, if they use their own sounds, are much nearer to the sounds that Shakespeare actually wrote for.

Interviewer: While we're on the subject of American actors, are they different from British actors? I was trying to articulate to a friend not so long ago what is actually the conventional explanation that British actors are somehow more intellectual in their approach to a part and that there is something muscular and emotional about American actors. Is that valid at all?

Caldwell: I don't think "intellectual" is the right word, but they do work from a slightly different discipline. Freud and Marx and Chekhov and Stanislavsky and Lee Strasberg had a big, big influence on American actors. So American actors work from their own selves and their own sense memories. That is sometimes very limiting, because if you're only working from your own self and your own sense memory, then how the hell do you play Cleopatra or Richard II? You're limited by your own sense of self. I always think that if we could take the training that most American actors get and give it to English actors and take the training that most English actors get and give it to American actors, we would have a whole Atlantic full of great, great, great actors! Please God they can swim. There are great actors on both sides of the Atlantic. Sometimes they just work differently.

Interviewer: Can you describe how you get into a part? How do you get inside a character?

Caldwell: How do I personally? Because there are no rules. I get very well, physically very well, so that anything that I am required to do I *can* possibly do. I try to get as mentally well and as emotionally well too, so again I am a conduit for the writer. I have inordinate respect for the writer. I feel that the actor is like a priest or priestess, the channel through which the word is passed to the audience. Once having cleared the decks for action, I do as much research as it's possible for me to do if I'm playing somebody who actually lived. I do a lot of research. If I have to play someone with a special accent that I don't have, then I go to a person who will teach me that accent, so that by the time the rehearsal comes I'm not wasting everybody's time trying to learn an accent. Then I rely on what the writer tells me. That means following his score—following his or her commas, following the exclamation marks, following the period full-stops, following the semicolons, the colons. That is a writer's score. And too often, I'm afraid, actors are not trained to the discipline of really following what the writer wants. Then I rely on what is fed to me by the other actors, by the way the designer wants me to look, and by what the director is attempting to tell me. If it is in direct contrast to what the writer is telling me, I'll go with the writer, not with the director; so sometimes I'm a troublemaker. Does that answer your question?

Interviewer: Yes, absolutely. There is an example of my own from watching you in *Medea*. You said a letter in the word "annihilation" that I had never heard, the *h*, and I wondered if that was the accent. You talk about playing the entire score of a writer. You broke "annihilation" up by syllables; every syllable of it became a different note somehow. It was an astonishing moment. Is that what you're talking about?

Caldwell: No, that was my conceit. There was an *h* and I thought, "Why not use it?"

Interviewer: Let me move on to your Broadway debut, which I understand was a very interesting one. You went on midperformance for Anne Bancroft. What is it like to enter a part that is already being played by someone else?

Caldwell: Well, it was tough for the audience because I played it totally differently. It was Sister Jean in *The Devils*. Before I married Robert and had kids and dogs and all that stuff, I was just a working actress. I didn't marry Robert until I was thirty-five, so I was a working actress from nine to thirty-five. I just simply took the next job, whatever the next job; it never occurred to me to say, "Is it the right part? Is it the right play? Is it the right director?" No, I said, "Next job." So I was never out of work. I played parts that I was not ready for, but it didn't matter. I think it's very healthy really. I was working at the Guthrie, and they asked me would I come to New York to play Varya in *The Cherry Orchard*, which Michael Kakyonus was going to do with Lila Kedrova on Broadway. I said, "Oh sure, I'll start straightaway," and they said, "No, you're going to have to hang around New York for a couple of months." I said, "Oh no, I couldn't do that. I'll take the next job that's offered." And they said, "If we can find you a job in New York, will you stay?" And I said, "Sure." So they said, "Would you consider standing by" (not understudying; they had an understudy) "for Anne Bancroft in *The Devils*?" I said, "Sure," and they asked me to come down and see the performance.

I came to New York, saw the play, and thought every single person involved in that production had got it all wrong. Jason Robards, who is a thrilling actor, is not a sensual actor; Christopher Plummer is a sensual actor. Jason was playing Grandier, and the night I saw it he walked on, got his lace caught in the crucifix, and ripped it apart; he tore all the lace. Grandier would have very, very carefully undone the lace not to tear it. Anne, who is a brilliant and marvelous and exciting actress, was playing Sister Jean a little bit like Bernadette but with a slight back problem. Sister Jean in *The Devils* is a brilliant young high-born woman with curvature of the spine. I was staying with Hume [Cronyn] and Jessica [Tandy] at the time, and I said, "Do either of you know anybody who had curvature of the spine?" "Yes," said Jessica, she'd gone to school with somebody, and I said, "What was she like?" She said, "She was continually bent low, and just to hold her head up was terribly, terribly, terribly difficult." They lived at 75th Street, and I walked one block to the Broadway Theatre as my own self, and then the next block I would walk as Jean. What I wanted to know was not only how did it feel, but I also walked past windows so I could see my reflection. That's not a reassuring thing when you see the reflection of yourself like that. Also, I wanted to see what other people did when they saw me, and how they reacted to me and then how they reacted to someone with curvature of the spine. That informed me greatly in the part.

So I played this extraordinary Jean, and there was Anne playing Bernadette. It didn't really matter, because she was going to go down to the islands with Mel Brooks for a holiday for three weeks at Christmas and I was going to take over; but, suddenly, I was having supper somewhere, having had some wine and spaghetti and a really swell time, and they rang and they said, "Anne has hurt her back. Would you come immediately to the Broadway and take over—in the middle of the show." I'd never rehearsed, and I had never ever clapped eyes on Jason Robards. We didn't have any scenes together; at the end of *The Devils* Grandier is thrown—crippled, broken, with his hair all torn off—at the feet of Jean, and she says, seeing him, "They told me you were beautiful and they were right." That's the first time she claps eyes on him. It was the first time I'd ever clapped eyes on Jason Robards when I said those lines; but it was sort of an electric, extraordinary experience and a terrific way to enter Broadway because I didn't have any real responsibility. I just had to keep the show open, and it was a thrilling way to do my first part on Broadway. It was shocking for the audience, but at the end we all had a good time; they stood and cheered, and I cheered them, and we had a great time.

Interviewer: In fact, I have here a review of that performance from the *Toronto Globe,* which said that people were disappointed they weren't seeing Bancroft at first but when you spoke your first lines, "you could hear the startling hush."

Caldwell: Well, of course, because I was so different. They thought a different Jean had come on!

Interviewer: This brings me to a question that I'm hesitant to ask of actresses and actors simply because I am a critic. To what extent can critics be useful to you? Do you read them, and have they ever contributed anything to your performance? Have they ever influenced anything that you've done?

Caldwell: Well, I used to read them, and they used to influence me greatly. It's very, very, very difficult to have something really horrendous that you are doing pointed out to you. On the other hand, it's just as destructive to have something absolutely exquisite that you are doing pointed out to you, because you can never do it again. As soon as it goes up into your head, forget it; you can never do it again. So I learned not to read them. I stopped reading them after Harold Clurman died, because I *would* change a part radically for Harold Clurman. But Harold Clurman was not a "critic," he reviewed the plays. Harold Clurman, of course, was a theater philosopher. Are you a theater philosopher?

Interviewer: I try, but I'm not in his league.

Caldwell: Well, you're younger than he, but you care. We don't quite have a theater philosopher anymore. He wrote, he lived, he directed, he taught, he reviewed plays; he was a total theater man. That's where his passion was; that's where his life was. For Harold I would totally alter clothes, hair, manner, everything; but that's because my respect for Harold was so total. If I don't read them now, of course, then, I don't change my performance.

Interviewer: Do they affect the way a performance plays? After the review comes out, does it change the way an audience responds?

Caldwell: Yes. It's mainly the audience's response that is changed, because the audience views the play either as a success or a failure, unfortunately. Critics should simply review it as a play that has a little problem here, a little problem there, or has no problems at all. That's a very civilized way of dealing with theater. What we're dealing with is the *New York Times* and the sort of ridiculous power that we've given to whoever it is. When Clive Barnes was there, Clive Barnes was the most important voice in American theater because he either kept your show running or he closed it. Now we have David Richards, who is writing very, very well for the Sunday *Times.* I remember when David was writing in Washington for the *Post.* In fact, he wrote for another paper before he wrote for the *Post,* the *Washington Star.* He was very sort of chipper when he wrote for the *Star,* then he became the *Washington Post* and he changed his writing. Then he came to the *Times,* and I think his reviews for the Sunday *Times* are really marvelous, really good. We're all very excited about having a real reviewer again. Frank Rich is a brilliant writer, but he always seemed to me to be writing his baccalaureate with each review, telling you how much he knew, which wasn't a great help to anybody.

Interviewer: We're getting close chronologically to *The Prime of Miss Jean Brodie.* That show made you a star in the United States in a way that you had not been before. Did that change the way you selected parts? Did it do something to the way you operated?

Caldwell: No. What changed my way of operating was that I got married to Robert and got pregnant with Sam while I was playing in *The Prime of Miss Jean Brodie.* Those two gentlemen changed my way of looking at theater because I had a greater priority. Because I was old to be a first-time wife and a first-time mum and I found it so thrilling, that's where I wanted to be, not in the theater. Of course, I'll always be in the theater in some form; but now there's another young man called Charlie, and they take up the slack.

Interviewer: How do you decide what is the right role for you?

Caldwell: Since I've had Robert and Sam and Charlie, I only take things that I really think, "I have no idea how to do that." Like a little university course, I go and explore and see. That's why I did Mary Tyrone, because I had never understood Eugene O'Neill. And there was danger that I wouldn't until Harold Clurman came along and took over the production! It's why I did *Lillian.* It's why I did the latest play that I just did. After seven years' absence, I did a new play of Terrence McNally's called *A Perfect Ganesh.* The Manhattan Theatre Club asked me to do it. I said, "Send me a script." They never sent a script, and I went to the reading without ever reading the play. (People can't believe that this is so; I must be an idiot. No, I think I'm not an idiot; I think I'm just very sure of myself.) I was the only person at the table who had never read the play. I read it appallingly, so at the end of the reading I had to say, "If you still want me, I will do it." That I found thrilling because it was new territory and I learned so much. I'm only interested when I can learn. I learn a lot by teaching; that's why I truly love teaching. I learn a lot by directing; that's why I like to direct. But acting, I don't have that strange sort of ambition anymore. Well, at sixty, I shouldn't. That's how old I am.

Interviewer: The first time you directed was with Colleen Dewhurst in *An Almost Perfect Person*. Why did you begin doing that?

Caldwell: They sent the play to me—it was called *Winning Is Better,* by Judith Ross—and I liked the character, but I said, "No, no, no, I don't want to do the play." They said, "Okay." Then they rang the next day and said, "Would you direct it?" So often I'd thought that actors are not helped enough by directors. I'd never spoken out loud in rehearsals, but I'd thought about it a lot, and I thought, "Well, this is a chance for me to see if I know what I'm talking about." I said, "Sure I will, but only if I can get the right woman to play the part." Colleen was going through a sort of a funny depressing time—I think she was going through menopause—and she was feeling blue. I said, "Come with me and I'll take you out of that blueness and we'll discover this together." Colleen was great at being Mother Earth, so she was always asked to be Mother Earth; but I knew she was a ditsy pussycat, a deliciously feminine pussycat. I thought, "If I can just let her be that onstage it'll be terrific for the audience and terrific for Colleen." It was. I dressed her up and I made her do her hair and have her nails done, and her feet done and she loved it. It was good.

Interviewer: It sounds as if you take on assignments that you think are difficult in one way or another. The point of doing them perhaps is to scare yourself a little bit. What is the toughest task that you've taken on—or is it always just the next one?

Caldwell: Well, they're tough in different ways.

Interviewer: What's the toughest performance that you've ever decided to give?

Caldwell: To give? Hands down, *Lillian*. That's because Lillian Hellman was a very tough woman, which I didn't really realize when I took it on. I just loved her writing and I thought, "This is such marvelous writing. I'd love to explore that woman." What I didn't realize is that I had to take her into my bloodstream. You try taking Lillian Hellman into your bloodstream; it doesn't make you a well person. I smoked nonstop, I drank a lot of vodka, I was desperately lonely and deeply unhappy. That was the toughest thing ever; it put me off acting. That's why I didn't act for seven years.

Interviewer: I can imagine that, but the answer surprises me because Mary Tyrone is hardly a joyride and I can't imagine that Medea was easy to play.

Caldwell: No, Medea was easy.

Interviewer: It was?

Caldwell: Yes, Medea was easy.

Interviewer: Why?

Caldwell: It's so marvelously written. Robinson Jeffers has given you such a clean, good script. I'd played in it when I was a very young woman, with the Australian Elizabethan Theatre Trust before I went to England. I'd played Second Woman of Corinth when Judith Anderson had come out to play it. I knew I didn't want to play it—and couldn't play it—like Judith played it, but I wanted to find my own way, and I did. Judith eventually allowed me to, and found great joy in relinquishing the part to me. It was as though she suddenly learned what it was to be a parent, because she wanted me to wear her wig, her dress, her sandals. I said, "Judith! My head is too big, my body has given birth to kids, and my feet are too big." She said, "Just try them all on and see." I tried them all on and they all fit perfectly, except I started saying, "Deeeeeaaath, deeeaaath," like Judith. I said, "I can't, Judith." It was her idea that I play Medea. I said, "You've chosen the bridegroom, you want me to wear the wedding dress that you wore, you want me to wear the same wreath and veil and the same bridal bouquet. No, a good parent says, 'It's your wedding, my darling. I'll be behind you.' " She was, and it was thrilling, thrilling. A big-time, big-time extraordinary thing being on the stage with that lady who was eighty-three and better than she'd ever been, simpler than she'd ever been. It was extraordinary. Extraordinary for her too because she learned how to give. Judith had never been a big giver, and she'd never had children, so she didn't know about real giving.

Interviewer: She sounds as if she was a big influence in a way.

Caldwell: She was a big influence. I'll tell you why she was a big influence. When I was twenty-one playing the Second Woman of Corinth, Judith came from America, and she was this great, great star who opened the Australian Elizabethan Theatre Trust as Medea, and she was extraordinary. Then every night when the curtain came down, she went to her hotel room and drank herself into oblivion because she had no husband—she'd had husbands, but by this time she had no husband—no children, no life, only what was on the stage. She taught me the lesson: don't, I beg you, don't allow theater to be everything; you must have a life—with any luck a marriage, and if you're deeply lucky, children. There's a marvelous photograph of the opening of the Australian Elizabethan Theatre Trust in Canberra, which is our political capital. Everybody is bowing. Judith is in the front bowing, and I'm just down the way a piece and I'm looking at Judith. Judith said, "You devil. I know what you were thinking. Look at her, ambition written all over her. You know what she was thinking? 'Someday all this will be mine.'" I could never tell her, "No, Judith, what I was saying is, 'Don't be that lonely.'" But she did help me; she was extraordinary. I loved her.

Interviewer: Who would you say is the stage artist who has been most influential on your life?

Caldwell: Actor?

Interviewer: Or director.

Caldwell: Or director? Harold Clurman, director. Tony Guthrie, director. I was very lucky to have those two big, big powerhouse men. Acting? Edith Evans, Maureen Stapleton, and Ralph Richardson.

Interviewer: Let's start with Maureen Stapleton. In what way?

Caldwell: Maureen pretends to be a silly old Irish drunk. Maureen is a great artist. Maureen is a true artist. She doesn't have to seek around in sense-memory terms for the human connection; it's there. She is an artist. She has very much, strangely enough, the same bottom-line humanity that Ralph Richardson has. When Maureen does something, you are aware of all humanity's pain. The same with Ralph. That's big-time artist. Ralph, while seeming very stylized, had the same human connection. I remember seeing him play *The Complaisant Lover* in London, in which he played a dentist. A silly ridiculous dentist who played practical jokes—whoopee cushions under his guests' seats and really dumb-ass jokes like that. He did nothing. He didn't pretend to be a dentist—he was just a person—but because of that performance I have a kind of compassion for all dentists. That's big-time artist. That's what real artists do: they let you in and broaden your vision. That's what that little yellow chair in the van Gogh painting does. You don't look at a little yellow rush-colored chair ever again without seeing it in that way.

Tennessee Williams did it in spades. I was in a play called *The Gnädiges Fräulein,* which was the next part I was offered after *The Devils.* It was done in New York. It was part of a double bill by Tennessee. This was at the end of Tennessee's writing time, when anything that Tennessee did everybody said, "It's no good. Who does he think he is? Forget Tennessee Williams." That's before he died. Now of course everything's fine again. With the first play, called *The Mutilated,* he'd been there before, and I think he'd been there better. The second play was called *The Gnädiges Fräulein.* It was set in the Florida Keys, and it demanded that [set designer] Ming Cho Lee do a little clapboard house that was blown at a slant by the Gulf winds. It was a transient house. On the veranda, there were two little wooden rocking chairs. The transient house consisted of the woman who ran the transient house, an opera singer, a sailor, an American Indian, a gossip columnist who came on to observe life at the transient house, and a cocaloony bird, played by a man, with big eyes and a big beak. The women were all in whiteface. I had to play this ridiculous part. I had to learn to do pratfalls, and Kate Reid and I sat in these two little rocking chairs, and we smoked pot, "Mary Janes," all through. I mean pretend Mary Janes. Sometimes we got mad and we rocked our rocking chairs out of unison. Sometimes we were perfectly marvelously in harmony and rocked in unison. Sometimes we stood on our rocking chairs; but whatever we did we stayed there. That's the way Tennessee orchestrated it. We wore clown shoes. Clown shoes are the normal size in back, but they just stick out too much at the front. It was directed by Alan Schneider, who was a marvelous director but didn't know how to do this particular play. Alan's big suit was not humor, and Tennessee had written the most extraordinary black comedy. Alan had asked me to do things that I didn't see written by Tennessee. Tennessee came every day, but by the time he came to rehearsals, he was just high and smiling, and I knew he wasn't to be trusted—but his text was to be trusted. So I just went through the text and I did every single thing he asked me to do. Everything; no matter how difficult, I did it. I won a Tony, and the play lasted nine days. I didn't win a Tony because I was brilliant; I won a Tony because I did exactly what that extraordinary artist had asked.

Then I did other things. I married Robert and got pregnant with Sam, and in 1969 we went down to the Florida Keys for our honeymoon. Everyone had said, "What a ridiculous play! It's so surrealistic. All his imagery is so surrealistic." The opera singer played by Maggie Leighton at the beginning was blind in one eye and eventually blind in two, because she used to compete with the cocaloony birds down at the wharf for fish and they'd pecked out her good eye. She'd fallen in love with a seal trainer and she had stood on the rolling ball to compete with the seals. I mean wild stuff. There was this sailor with a very tight bum, and there was this marvelous, marvelous Indian. We go down to Key West and what do we see? A lot of little clapboard houses slightly off-kilter. On the veranda what do we see? Two, usually, little weathered rocking chairs. Go into the bars and what did we see? Sailors with very tight bums, because it's a naval center; a lot of hippies dressed like Indians—bands, long hair; strange, strange women who have been trapped at a certain time in their lives. Because Key West is very hot, they put a lot of powder on. So what do they seem to have? White faces. Then when they put on a lot of green eye shadow, or mauve I should say, and a lot of red lipstick, and they dye their hair gold or lavender, what do they look like? Because they're still wearing the shoes that they thought they looked great in—only their legs now are thin and strange—the shoes look strangely like clown shoes. All Tennessee was doing was writing what he saw. But because he was an artist he revealed to us who are not artists a truth, and we can never see it the same way again. That's what van Gogh did with the chair, that's what musicians do, and with any luck, that's what actors do.

Interviewer: Is acting all about truth then?

Caldwell: I suppose. I don't know.

Interviewer: I'm just curious about it because it's always struck me that the stage is about enlarging truth somehow, that it is about making it bigger. And you're telling me that it's really just capturing it.

Caldwell: No. Truth—I mean, small-time truth is when you and I meet at a bar later on and we have a little conversation. Just the fact that we are here on a stage with a proscenium and a whole lot of people are gathered together and they become unified and you and I are separate: naturally it can be truth, but it's got to obviously be a larger presentation of the truth. But if it isn't rooted in truth, beware!

Interviewer: Movies?

Caldwell: Oh no, I'm not a movie actress.

Interviewer: As far as I know, you have been in *Purple Rose of Cairo,* as the Countess.

Caldwell: That's it. That's my one film—and that was a mistake. No, no, it wasn't a mistake when I eventually did it. I have been offered films, and I look at a script and I think, "There's nothing for me to play. Why do they want me for this? I don't understand it." I love films. I love watching them. I love good film acting, but I can't do it. Robert and I were skiing up in the Laurentians, and Juliet Taylor, who's the casting director for a lot of people, including Woody Allen, rang and said, "Zoe, would you like to be in Woody's new movie?" I said, "Sure! Send me the script." She said, "Woody doesn't send scripts," and I said, "In that case, no. Thanks and Happy New Year and all that stuff. Good-bye, Juliet." Robert said, "Who was that?" and I explained. He said, "Ring her back! This is your opportunity. Every time you're offered a script and you read it, you say, 'What is there for me to play in this?' This time you won't get a chance to read it. Just say yes, you'll do it." So I rang back and I said, "Juliet, I'll do it." She said, "Oh, terrific," and I said, "What's the part?" She said, "It's a countess" and I said, "Oh, terrific! A European countess?" She said "No, it's just a countess," and I said, "An American countess?" She said, "No, just a countess," and I said, "Ah, ha. Okay, when do you want me?" She said, "Monday." This was Sunday night. I said, "Who got sick?" She said, "Eve Arden's husband." I said, "You want me to play a part that's right for Eve Arden's husband?" She said, "No, no, no. Eve Arden's husband got sick and she had to go back to Los Angeles, so would you play the part that Eve Arden was going to play?" And I said, "Okay, fine."

So I went along to Paul Huntley to get fitted for a wig, and it was a great sort of marvelous Mae West kind of strawberry blond mad wig. I said, "Paul, what is the part?" He said, "Don't know, dear, don't know. Just told it was a countess, dear." Then I went to the man who did the clothes and I said, "What is the part? What is the part?" He said, "Oh, it's a countess. It's so marvelous. It's so funny." Then he put me in this strange costume and a lot of monkey fur and gloves up to here. That night, under the door, I got one side— a side is one page—from Woody Allen. Hot off the press. I looked and there wasn't a joke in it. I thought, "Well, I don't see anything funny in this." Early next morning I went to the studio, and I was made up and dressed and went onto the set. I was playing with Van Johnson and a lot of well-known people. My first lines were "Where is everybody? Weren't we meeting at the Copacabana?" So dressed like this I said, "WHERE IS EVERYBODY? WEREN'T WE MEETING AT THE COPACABANA?" There was a terrible pause. The whole set froze, and Woody Allen shuffled up to me and said, "A little less theatrical." I said, "What?" He said, "A little less theatrical." I said, "I'm sorry, I don't know what you're saying." He said, "A little less theatrical." I said, "Oh, great." So I said, "Where is everybody? Weren't we meeting at the Copacabana?" "A little less theatrical." I did it three times to "a little less theatrical," and then I said, "Look, I'm dressed like a fellow in drag here. I'm supposed to be playing a part that's right for Eve Arden. You haven't sent me the script. You've never spoken to me. Give me a line reading." He gave me a line reading and I did the part. And I had a good time.

Interviewer: How did he want you to say that line?

Caldwell: A lot less than I was saying. Eventually as we all warmed up—not Woody, he never warmed up, but the rest of the people (Van Johnson just made jokes all the time and he was very funny)—we all got mad because we didn't know what we were playing. We were all dressed up, and we were supposed to be playing characters in a movie out of which one of the characters had stepped into the audience, but how were we to know? Anyway, that's my one film.

Interviewer: I'm trying to think what I've seen you direct. I saw *Park Your Car in Harvard Yard* with Jason Robards and Judith Ivey in Baltimore.

Caldwell: In Baltimore? Oh, my God! That was terrible, terrible, terrible; but we got very, very good. The whole thing, which was about three and a half hours, we cut down to one hour and forty minutes.

Interviewer: This is a woman who really respects the work of the writer! Tell me about cutting a three-hour play down to one hour and forty minutes.

Caldwell: The audience is always a good guide. If they're walking out or falling asleep you know you have to cut. Even the writer knew he had to cut, so we cut. But we had a terrible time in Baltimore, because he was rewriting and we were putting in rewrites. Those two actors were nearly going mad, but eventually we got it right and then they were very, very, very good. Boy, they were good. They are such marvelous actors, Jason Robards and Judith Ivey. Two characters and a cat, a marvelous cat.

Interviewer: Do you approach directing differently because you're an actress? Is it different from, say, the way Tyrone Guthrie approached directing?

Caldwell: No, not like Tony, no. I do keep the energy level high in rehearsals because I think that that's important. I think everybody has to feel engaged in some way. It's no good if some of the actors are off reading the newspaper or falling asleep. That takes energy from the rehearsal, which isn't good, which isn't productive. Like Tony, I do try to keep the ball in the air. But no, I think I'm very influenced by being an actor and very influenced by being a woman.

Interviewer: How does being a woman affect your directing?

Caldwell: I think I am not afraid of feminine sensibilities. A really marvelous director of either sex is not afraid of feminine sensibilities. Michael Bennett was the most brilliant director who was not afraid of feminine sensibilities. That doesn't mean you're afraid of masculine ones either; I think I have easy access to both, but anybody who's good does—and I am good.

Interviewer: How did you come to teaching, and where do you teach?

Caldwell: I never set out to teach. I just waited until I was asked, and Joe Conaway from Florida Atlantic University asked me to come and sit in the Eminent Scholar's chair for two months, and I said, "I will if I can teach Shakespeare." I really adore teaching Shakespeare, and I adore helping American actors have ease with Shakespeare. They said, "Sure." They had wanted Hume Cronyn, but he got a movie, so they took me as a sort of second. Then they found out what a rich, rich jewel they had, and I've been the Eminent Scholar ever since! I go down for February and March, which is very bright of me because we live in Pound Ridge and you feel that spring is never going to arrive in February and March; so I go down to Boca Raton and I have the best learning and exhilarating time with marvelous young bright people. I do think that's so thrilling, the young people of today. The younger they are the more thrilling they are; of course, they're what it's all about.

Interviewer: One of the most magical moments that we've all seen in theater is your Medea. Would you tell us why that was not difficult to prepare for and how you prepared for it?

Caldwell: As well as becoming very well, I became purposely anorexically thin. Medea is in such a state of desolation that she says she doesn't eat, she doesn't drink; so I became anorexically thin. Robert and I, for one year before, did a little private university course on ancient Greece: we read, read, read, read, looked, looked, looked, went to Greece, and I studied all the movements and studied all the goddess world. Then I did my usual stuff with text design and other actors, and I found it thrilling.

Interviewer: You seemed so tall in that play.

Caldwell: I was in flat sandals, no heel at all.

Interviewer: Miss Caldwell is five foot two.

Caldwell: Two and a half.

Interviewer: How do you do tall onstage?

Caldwell: Judith Anderson looked tall. Look at Al Pacino. Don't you always think of him as a big man? He's a little, little man, but his presence is big. I think that's what does it.

Interviewer: What Shakespeare heroine would you like to play and why?

Caldwell: Well, I played her—Cleopatra. She is the greatest role for a woman, bar none. She is everything, and I played her. I wish I hadn't, because then I could have a go again, but now I'm too old. I had Christopher Plummer as my Antony, so I was jolly lucky, and I had Michael Langham as my director, so I was thrice blessed.

Interviewer: Is there a part you'd like to be offered now?

Caldwell: I always thought I'd make a terrific Gertrude because I was always unsatisfied with the Gertrudes, but then I saw a definitive Gertrude. If ever I see any actress play a part definitively, then I have no desire to play it. I think, "It's done. For our time that's done." Maggie Smith—definitive Millamant. Nobody in our time will be a Millamant like that. I'd seen a lot of actresses play Gertrude, and they'd always been the leading actress. The closet scene was the great scene that they were going to do, and they always had a marvelous negligee with a flowing train designed for them and a wonderful wig. David Warner did a Hamlet at the Royal Shakespeare Company with an actress who wasn't their leading actress. She is a great and glorious actress called Elizabeth Spriggs. If ever you get a chance to see her anywhere, run. She is a big woman, and she came on with her hair parted just flat with a plait; she had a white cotton nightie and she was ready for bed. She sat on that bed and she watched Hamlet and looked at him and looked at him, and looked at him, and looked at him, and looked at him, and looked at him. When he said, "Look, look. My father. See how he steals away. Do you not see?" she didn't look. She looked at Hamlet and said, "No, nothing at all, yet all there is I see. Oh, Hamlet." You knew that she knew that she had failed her son, deeply and irrevocably failed her son. Of course, there wasn't a dry eye in the house, but that's the way it should have been played. She did it— so I can't play Gertrude now.

Interviewer: Have you ever done any British TV?

Caldwell: Yes, when I was very young I did. I did a series called *Rogue Herries* by Hugh Walpole, and fifteen years ago I did Arkadina in Chekhov's *The Seagull.* I did quite a lot actually when I was young. I don't think I was very good, but I was okay. I did a lot in Canada for the CBC. They had at one point, for about ten years, extraordinary television. I went to Stratford and they said, "Would you come down and play Lady Macbeth to Sean Connery's Macbeth?" and I said, "Sure." So I went there and I played for about a year—all great roles—on CBC. That was a thrilling experience. Sean Connery was a very, very good Macbeth, strangely enough. Well, not strangely enough. He's a Scot and he'd had training and been at the Bristol Old Vic doing Shakespeare. He'd just done Hotspur in the big series for BBC. At that point, he hadn't been James Bond yet. When he left us, he had a fiendish cold, and he went down to New York to see that guy to audition for James Bond. His wife, Diane Cilento, had just left him, he was feeling blue, and he had this really bad cold. He said, "They want me to come down and audition for 007. Stupid, stupid." I said, "Well, good luck anyway." That was the last I saw of him!

Interviewer: How would you compare acting for the stage, for television, and for movies?

Caldwell: I think at the base of it, it's all the same. The truth is the same. It's just that, deep in my bloodstream, I am a theater actor. That's what I really thrive on, but it's a marvelous discipline for me to be smaller for television or for film. Maybe I'll be marvelous when I'm eighty. I'll suddenly come into my own because I'll be so tired, all my energy will have gone, and they'll say, "My God, she's so marvelous on film. She does just enough."

Interviewer: Is there a difference between performing in a Broadway house, on a proscenium stage with the largeness of a Broadway house, and performing in a regional theater in a small or alternative-type space or stage? Is there a difference in the way you perform?

Caldwell: I think you perform slightly differently because you're affected by it if it's a thrust, if it's proscenium, if it's enormous. I played *Lillian* around the country with a body mike (a good one) in those old cinemas with three or four thousand people. A little person sitting at a table. With *Lillian,* I just had a table, a cup of coffee, a thermos, a bag, and cigarettes and a lighter; but I played that. It's the thing that made me need to move and dance and sing and talk. If you really want to communicate with that gentleman right at the back, then, boy, that's where you communicate. It's the need, I think, so it doesn't matter. If that gentleman was sitting down front, I would communicate with him in a slightly different way. But the basis is the same, I think.

Interviewer: Another thing about regional theaters is that they have acting companies that have been together. Does that affect the way that you as a visiting artist or as a company member play? If you're doing the same thing over and over and over again with performers that you have been performing with, does that make it different?

Caldwell: That question is a very good one. I'm a very good company member because that's how I was trained—in all these what they call institutional theaters. It's a terrible name; it sounds as though you're in a straitjacket! I never did play with one company two consecutive years, because I felt a certain layer of fat and ease grew up between us. I always wanted to feel when I came into a company that there was a danger. That danger was diminished if you hung around too long and your kids went to their kids' school, you hung out at the same bar, or you knew everything about everybody. There was no mystery, and also you did then tend to play the same kind of role all the way through. You're either the leading lady or the character; whereas I like to have no rules and a lot of danger because that's the way you grow, I think. That's the way I grow. Does that make sense?

Interviewer: Yes, totally. With all that danger, what is the most terrifying thing that has ever happened to you onstage?

Caldwell: Too many to tell! I know someone who was a very big influence— Charles Laughton. I played Cordelia to Charles Laughton's Lear at Stratford. We didn't like one another at all. He really disliked me a lot, and I wasn't keen on him—but I found he was extraordinary. Unfortunately, with his head and with his emotions, he understood Lear totally (and I say that very rarely); but by the time he played it, he was physically so out of condition that he couldn't do it. To play any of those great Shakespearean roles you have to be in such shape, incredible physical condition like a great, great athlete—and he wasn't. So, every single night, I watched every single performance that he gave, because every single night, one scene would be played definitively. It was never the same scene, so you had to be there to catch it. Every night before the day that I would play Cordelia—I was a slim little wisp of a thing, but I wanted to be as slim as I could for him because he had to carry me on—I would take a lot of laxatives to purge myself so I would be as little as I could possibly be. It was good actually for Cordelia not to like the fellow who played Lear. It has a resonance. He taught me a great deal, so I'd better give him credit.

Interviewer: There are a number of new playwrights, like Mamet, who use questionable language. What do you think of that?

Caldwell: We've all gone hog wild with all sorts of words. It's in our everyday speech—not in *our* everyday speech, yours and mine. If it is valid for the character, terrific; if it's there because they want to be modern, that does not make for a very good playwright, or indeed it makes for a rotten play and therefore of course it's silly. When certain women now feel that they have to say, "Oh fucking this and fucking that," because it seems very in, it's so boring because it's not meant to be. But when you hear some kids in Harlem say, "Motherfucker! Motherfucker! Motherfucker!" it breaks your heart. If it's valid it's fine. There are some stunning playwrights today. There's Tony Kushner, for example. *Perestroika* is stunning. He uses a lot of expletives, but they're right. Every single one is absolutely right for that character at that time. Boy, is he writing for now! David Mamet is a wonderful writer, but David is very stylized. He's a thrilling writer. Sam Shepard's got a new play coming. When I was teaching down in Florida the first year, I had one cynical girl who did not believe a word of what I was saying and thought I was just trying to bring in some rigidity of my own to rule the roost. She was doing Sam Shepard's *Lie of the Mind* in the night, and she asked if I would come and see her and give her a critique. I said, "Sure," so I went, and she was appalling. She played the brain-damaged girl, and she all but turned her toes in to prove that she was brain-damaged. The next day in class she said, "Miss Caldwell, you saw *Lie of the Mind*. What did you think?" I said, "I thought certain performances were just marvelous, better than the New York production. Yours was appalling." She said, "Why?" I said, "Well, you were telling me so loudly that you were brain-damaged that I didn't believe that you were brain-damaged for an instant." "Really?" Three days later, she came in and she said, "Miss Caldwell, I've got to tell you. I looked at my part last night with the punctuation. I found one word, full stop, two words, full stop, one word, full stop, four words, full stop, one word, full stop. If you only have the capacity for one word in a thought before you stop, you are clearly brain-damaged." Sam Shepard had given it all to her. She said, "Will you come back and see me?" and I said, "Yes." I went back, and she just stood there with her own marvelous body, and marvelous voice, and marvelous face, and spoke Sam Shepard's lines with the full stops where they were, and she broke your heart.

Interviewer: Has the theater changed since you got into it?

Caldwell: Yes.

Interviewer: How?

Caldwell: I think there's more fear. There's not enough theater. My husband always quotes Harold Clurman, who said, "The history of the theater is the history of flops." What he meant was if you have a great body of work, you're going to have twenty flops, five okay, four pretty good, three very good, and—with any luck—one of them might be great. That's the one that goes into the anthologies. If you have four plays coming in, you haven't got enough room for flops and you sure as hell haven't got enough room for greatness. So it engenders fear. Audiences used to go and spend their hard-earned money, but not so much of their money, so they could afford to say, "What the hell, we'll go and see a show. Put on your coat, we'll go and see a show." Nowadays you have to plan—work it out, work out the baby-sitter, work out where you're going to park the car. Are you going to park the car or are you going to take a bus? How are you going to get there, who's going to come, who's going to be worth paying fifty, seventy bucks? It's too difficult. Theater should be free and easy. Look at those Greeks; they all got in for free all day: kids, slaves, women—not all sitting in the same area of the theater, mark you, but in the theater—all races, all ages. That's what we should have available; then the actors wouldn't be afraid. The actors shouldn't be saying, "Should I go to California? Should I do this soap? I should do the soap. I shouldn't hang about waiting for a play." That's fear! If we are the great hope and make people feel and know that they're human together, it's no good sitting in your own room watching a video. That's like masturbation. Theater is the thrilling thing. Experienced together. This is called love. If we're afraid, then it's not going to come off and we're going to be lacking a whole lot of hope. It's big-time. Theater is big-time, properly done.

Interviewer: How can we make theater more accessible as a career option for young people?

Caldwell: We don't have to. Theater is not a career option. It's a necessity to make you whole. It has to do with the society as a whole. It has to do with what's happening to us as a society. We've been asleep for quite a few years as a society. We've been a noncaring, noninvolved society, so we're going to have to change our ways. I'll tell you, the time is coming—I think it's just about going to happen now—when a real resurgence of theater is going to happen.

Interviewer: Did you see *The Kentucky Cycle,* and did you like it?

Caldwell: Yes, I saw it. I went on the opening day and night, and I adored it. I thought, my goodness, Broadway has a whole day and a night of *Kentucky Cycle* at the Royale Theatre—with an American writer, American actors, American designer, American composer; and at another theater, the Walter Kerr, a whole day and a night of *Angels in America*—with an American writer, American director, American designer, American composer, and American actors. I'd say we're doing pretty well here!

Hume Cronyn
and Jessica Tandy

Hume Cronyn was born in London, Ontario, Canada, on July 18, 1911. He studied acting at the New York School of the Theatre, with Harold Kreutzberg at the Mozarteum in Salzburg, Austria, and at the American Academy of Dramatic Arts. He made his professional debut in Up Pops the Devil *(1931) and his Broadway debut playing a janitor and understudying Burgess Meredith in* Hipper's Holiday *(1934). Among his other Broadway stage roles are Erwin Trowbridge,* Three Men on a Horse *(1936); Leo Davis,* Room Service *(1937); Steve,* Escape the Night *(1938); Andrei Prozoroff,* The Three Sisters *(1939); Lee Tatnall,* Retreat to Pleasure *(1940); Harley L. Miller,* Mr. Big *(1941); Jodine Decker,* The Survivors *(1948); Michael,* The Fourposter *(1951); Julian Anson,* A Day by the Sea *(1955); Oliver Walling,* The Man in the Dog Suit *(1958); Doctor,* Portrait of a Madonna *(1959); Jimmie Luton,* Big Fish, Little Fish *(1961). At the Guthrie Theater he played Harpagon in* The Miser, *Tchebutykin in* The Three Sisters, *Willy Loman in* Death of a Salesman *(all in*

1963), the title role in Richard III, *Yephikodov in* The Cherry Orchard, *and* Harpagon *in* The Miser *(all in 1965). Back on Broadway he played Polonius in* Hamlet *(1964; Tony Award), Tobias in* A Delicate Balance *(1966), and Grandfather and Willie in* Promenade, All! *(1972). At Stratford, Ontario, he played Shylock in* The Merchant of Venice *and Bottom in* A Midsummer Night's Dream *(both in 1976). Other Broadway roles include Weller Martin,* The Gin Game *(1977); Hector Nations,* Foxfire *(1980); General Sir Edmund Milne,* The Petition *(1986); and Ghost of Christmas Past,* A Christmas Carol *(1990).*

His many films include Shadow of a Doubt *(1943),* The Phantom of the Opera *(1943),* Lifeboat *(1944),* Main Street After Dark *(1944),* The Seventh Cross *(1944),* Ziegfeld Follies *(1945),* The Postman Always Rings Twice *(1946),* The Beginning or the End *(1947),* Brute Force *(1947),* People Will Talk *(1951),* Crowded Paradise *(1956),* Sunrise at Campobello *(1960),* Cleopatra *(1963),* Hamlet *(1964),* Gaily, Gaily *(1964),* The Arrangement *(1969),* There Was a Crooked Man *(1970),* Conrack *(1974),* The Parallax View *(1974),* Honky Tonk Freeway *(1981),* Rollover *(1981),* The World According to Garp *(1982),* Impulse *(1984),* Brewster's Millions *(1985),* Cocoon *(1985),* Batteries Not Included *(1987),* Cocoon: The Return *(1988),* The Pelican Brief *(1993),* Camilla *(1994), and* Marvin's Room *(1996).*

On television, he has appeared in The Bridge of San Luis Rey *(1958),* A Doll's House *(1959),* The Moon and Sixpence *(1959),* Juno and the Paycock *(1960),* The Gin Game *(1981),* Foxfire *(1987),* Day One *(1989),* A Month of Sundays *(1989),* Age-Old Friends *(1990; Emmy Award),* Christmas on Division Street *(1991),* Broadway Bound *(1992; Emmy Award),* To Dance with the White Dog *(1993; Emmy Award),* An African Love Story *(1996),* Alone *(1997),* Twelve Angry Men *(1997),* Seasons of Love *(1998),* Sea People *(1999),* Santa Claus and Pete *(1999), and episodes of* Alfred Hitchcock Presents, Hawaii Five-O, Alcoa Hour, United States Steel Hour, Kaiser Aluminum Hour, *and* Philco Television Playhouse.

He received the Brandeis University Creative Arts Award in 1978, the Kennedy Center Honors in 1986, the National Medal of the Arts in 1990, and a Lifetime Achievement Tony Award in 1994. He was elected to the Theater Hall of Fame in 1979.

Jessica Tandy was born Jessie Alice Tandy in London, England, on June 7, 1909. She trained for the stage at the Ben Greet Academy of Acting in London. She made her stage debut as Sara Manderson in The Manderson Girls *in London in 1927. Other roles in England include Alicia Audley,* Lady Audley's Secret; *Titania,* A Midsummer Night's Dream *(both in 1933); Viola,* Twelfth Night; *Anne Page,* The Merry Wives of Windsor; *Ophelia, John Gielgud's* Hamlet *(all three in 1934); Pamela March,* Honour Thy Father *(1936); Viola and Sebastian,* Twelfth Night; *Katharine,* Henry V *(both in 1937); Cordelia, John Gielgud's* King Lear; *and Miranda,* The Tempest *(both in 1940). She made her Broadway debut as Toni Rakonitz in* The Matriarch *(1930). Other Broadway roles include Cynthia Perry,* The Last Enemy *(1930); Kay Conway,* Time and the Conways *(1938); Nora Fintry,* The White Steed *(1939); Blanche DuBois,* A Streetcar Named Desire *(1947; Tony Award); Agnes,* The Fourposter *(1951); Martha Walling,* The Man in the Dog Suit *(1958); and Louise Harrington,* Five Finger Exercise *(1959). At the Guthrie Theater she played Olga,* The Three Sisters; *Gertrude,* Hamlet; *Linda Loman,* Death of a Salesman *(all in 1963); Lady Wishfort,* The Way of the World; *Madame Ranevskaya,* The Cherry Orchard; *and Mother-in-law,* The Caucasian Chalk Circle *(all in 1965). Back on Broadway she played Agnes,* A Delicate Balance *(1966); Marguerite Gautier,* Camino Real *(1970); Marjorie,* Home *(1971); The Wife,* All Over *(1971); Winnie,* Happy Days, *and The Mouth,* Not I *(1972); Fonsia Dorsey,* The Gin Game *(1977; Tony Award); Annie Nations,* Foxfire *(1982; Tony Award); Amanda Wingfield,* The Glass Menagerie *(1983); and Elizabeth Milne,* The Petition *(1986).*

She made her movie debut in The Indiscretions of Eve *(1933). Her other films include* Murder in the Family *(1938),* The Seventh Cross *(1944),* Dragonwyck *(1946),* Forever Amber *(1947),* September Affair *(1950),* The Desert Fox *(1951),* The Light in the Forest *(1958),* Adventures of a Young Man *(1962),* The Birds *(1964),* Butley *(1974),* Honky Tonk Freeway *(1981),* Still of the Night *(1982),* Best Friends *(1982),* The World According to Garp *(1982),* The Bostonians *(1984),* Cocoon *(1985),* Batteries Not Included *(1987),* The House on Carroll Street *(1988),* Cocoon: The Return *(1988),* Driving Miss Daisy *(1989; Academy Award),* Fried Green Tomatoes *(1991),* Used People *(1992),* Nobody's Fool *(1993),* Century of Cinema *(1994), and* Camilla *(1994).*

On television, she appeared in The Marriage *(1954),* The Fourposter *(1955),* The Moon and Sixpence *(1959),* Foxfire *(1987; Emmy Award),* The Gin Game *(1981),* The Story Lady *(1991),* To Dance with the White Dog *(1993), and* An African Love Story *(1996).*

She was inducted into the Theater Hall of Fame in 1979 and received the Kennedy Center Honors in 1986, the National Medal of Arts in 1990, and a Lifetime Achievement Tony Award in 1994. She died on September 11, 1994.

This interview took place on October 18, 1993.

• ── •

Interviewer: You have been onstage for more than six decades, filling it with great grace and intelligence, and for the most part I'll be confining my questions to the years "BC"—before *Cocoon.* You had film careers early on and then incredible stage careers and then film careers again. For the most part, I'm going to confine my questions to the stage careers. Hume, I realize that you wrote an autobiography called *A Terrible Liar,* so I'm not sure I can fully believe anything you say—but let me start by asking you to tell a story from that autobiography: it's a little-known fact that you began your professional career in Washington at the National Theatre. Could you tell us that story?

Cronyn: I was supposed to be studying law at McGill in Montreal, and I was incapacitated. I was a boxer, but I wasn't a good enough boxer, so I was in the hospital for a while. My doctor was a great theater buff, and he was having a fling with the leading lady of the Cochran Stock Company, which was playing at the National Theatre in Washington. He said, "Come on, Hume, you can't go back to school yet. Come on down with me. I'll introduce you to Nancy, I'll introduce you to the director, and they'll give you a job." I came down, I met Nancy, I met the director, and he did give me a job at fifteen dollars a week. That was my first time on the professional stage. It was in a play aptly titled *Up Pops the Devil*. With fifteen bucks a week I couldn't make it, so I had to write home and say, "Money, please." My father was very ill at that time, so my eldest brother was deputized to act for him. There are some words you never forget. He wrote back and said something like, "If you have decided to make the theater your profession, you would probably be wise to seize the bull by the horns and take this opportunity; but let me tell you you've gone about it in the most damnably stupid fashion imaginable." Those words were seared into my head; but I got the fifty bucks. Is that the story you wanted?

Interviewer: That's the story I wanted. Jessica, your background is very different from Hume's. Do you recall what your stage debut was like?

Tandy: It was in a little theater in London, in the West End, but off-off-Shaftesbury Avenue. In fact, it was an upstairs room; it was called Playroom Six, and I think it held about fifty people in the audience. I played a very fashionable young lady, the ingenue, who had wonderful clothes. I had to provide them on two pounds a week, so I did a lot of sewing. I did do very well, however. That was my beginning, and then one thing led to another, I guess.

Interviewer: But it was not obvious from your first starts that this would be a profitable business.

Tandy: No, no, not at all! It takes a little while before you really get your foot in the door.

Interviewer: Because you two have worked together so well and so often, bringing out qualities in each other, it is interesting that your approaches to a role are really quite opposite. It may be an oversimplification, but it is said that, Jessica, for the most part you work from the inside out, and Hume from the outside in. Could you explain?

Cronyn: Let's take outside in. That's me. When I've read a part and it sounds like something I'd like to attempt, that I might possibly be able to do, I find myself concerned about externals. What sort of a hat does he wear? What's the shape of his nose? How does he walk? How does he use his hands? The costume is important to me. What am I wearing? Can I be comfortable in it? How can I use the clothing? How many pockets has the jacket got? I just finished making a film within the last few weeks where for the most part I wear

jeans and a shirt. I'm playing a nurseryman down in Georgia. And I have to
have glasses, not the kind that hang around my neck, but ones that would fit
in my pocket. Then I needed another pocket on the side because the character is described as having a turnip watch on a leather thong, so that would
have to go on the other side. All the shirts that were produced had only one
pocket. Wardrobe had to cut off the tails of every shirt to make me an extra
pocket, with the result that my shirt never tucked in properly. There's an honorable tradition for externals. I directed Freddie March once in a play. He was
a wonderful actor, but the very first thing he talked about was his costume,
his wardrobe. I remember going backstage to see Larry Olivier when he was
doing *Othello,* and he couldn't wait to show me his lenses for his eyes. He had
lenses made so that his eyes were dark brown. From the third row you
couldn't tell what color they were, but they helped him. Every little thing you
can adopt—believe in—I think builds toward that security which is every actor's prayer. It also helps to learn the words. Jessie will, as she frequently does,
contradict me. I think we end up pretty much in the same place. Jess
wouldn't dream of first considering costume, hats. There's a wonderful saying—this is for the actor: "Don't ask how you do it, ask why." Why does the
character behave in that fashion? Why does he always keep his legs crossed?
Why does he always slump? Why? Why? Why? What are the innate charac-
teristics? I think you can go in the front door or go in the back door; the thing
is to possess the house. Over to you.

Tandy: Well, he's said it; he's told you my side too. It does and it doesn't
matter which way you go. I think every actor has to find his own way to the
result, and as long as you all end up speaking to each other, that's just fine.

Interviewer: But in the way that Hume was talking about a costume turning
on little lights over his head, what is it for you? Can you give us some examples or generalize about how you get to a role?

Tandy: I think I try to delve into the script, because actually I believe it's all
there if only I can dig it out. One awful trap sometimes is that other characters in a play will say things about your character—but it's their opinion.
Sometimes you get led astray and you think, "Oh, I'm like that, am I? I must
play that." No. No. No. You have to know who you are. Then I think, if you
can, don't act it but be it. Then I think you've won.

Interviewer: When you took *The Gin Game* to Russia, the head of the
Moscow Art Theatre said, "They're showing us what the Stanislavsky Method
is all about." That's a lovely compliment, but I wonder whether it's an accurate one. Do you consider yourselves Method actors in the sense that it's usually meant?

Tandy: Yes, of course. Stanislavsky had a company of very, very experienced
actors, and what he set about doing was finding out and writing down what it

was they all did to arrive at the point where they were. Well, there are all kinds of catch phrases in the Stanislavsky Method like "affective memory." When I read about "affective memory," I said to myself, "Oh, but of course. We've been doing that for years." We didn't call it "affective memory," but we knew what it was.

Interviewer: But what about the aspect of the Method that has been brought over here—the notion of looking into yourself and finding the parts of your own personality that are like the character?

Tandy: I believe that that is kind of narrowing, because whoever it is you're playing is not yourself. It's somebody quite different.

Cronyn: May I?

Tandy: Absolutely! Why not?

Cronyn: It's one thing to look into yourself to use all the strength of your own experience. At the beginning of Act II, you murder somebody; but you've had no experience in that—hopefully. What is that kind of passion and that kind of violence like? You have to search out in your own life something that you feel might have actually led you to an act of such desperation. From that point of view, it's inevitable; I don't care what label you put on it. I think actors from the time they've used the spoken word onwards have always done that. I don't think there's any great revelation there. The trouble is that there's been more nonsense written about Stanislavsky and the Stanislavsky Method than you'd want to have to wade through. You must use all your inner resources. If an actor isn't constantly aware from the time he's very young, he will not build up a bank of experience (even though most of it is vicarious) on which he can draw later. From that point of view, going inward is terribly important; but what happens with a lot of Method actors is they're acting in here. There's an audience! It has to go out there! You do have to have a sense of technique that goes beyond a constant poring over your emotional entrails. The Method is responsible for some very bad acting, and it's inclined to be exclusionary.

Interviewer: Let me ask you to think of the role that you've done which is most like your own personality.

Tandy: Oh, there isn't one.

Cronyn: No, I hope not.

Interviewer: Let me cross that one out, then.

Cronyn: The further you can get away from that the better. You try to get away from you, and yet "you" is everything that your emotional bank and your physical capacities allow you to bring. It's the power of your imagination, the bank of your memory of awareness, and your physical capacities that make up your instrument.

Interviewer: Let's talk a little about your rehearsal technique. You've said, Hume, that Jessica often is there to contradict and to correct. And you've often said that, in rehearsal, you each, much to the amazement of the other actors, will give the other some feedback. Isn't that right?

Tandy: Yes, I think we feel free to do that, which is a wonderful ability, to be welcome to do that.

Interviewer: And rare? Is it not rare?

Tandy: Well, I wouldn't dream of doing it to someone I didn't know very, very well. Because it might be taken wrong; it might be misunderstood. Yet it isn't criticism; it's meant to be helpful.

Interviewer: It is just curious to me, with your two different methods and approaches, that you're still able to get inside his head, understand what he's trying to do.

Cronyn: Oh, she can't do that.

Tandy: Thank God. Hume has had the grace to say that there have been times in rehearsal when he's worried about me because he's forging ahead—he's doing very well indeed, he knows exactly what he's about—and he looks behind his shoulder and I'm way back there. He thinks, "Come on! Come on! Come on!" And then about a week later he looks up and I'm way out there.

Interviewer: This is one of the great love stories; you have been married for fifty-one years. So let's pop that bubble too. I want you to tell me the story about your first dinner date.

Cronyn: Well, it was a ghastly failure. The first time I ever met Jessie was, where else, backstage. I had gone back to see a friend, and Jessie was in the company. She was the leading lady, and with great pride he introduced me to the leading lady. My story is that later that night we went out to supper. This actor friend of mine was interested in Jessie, and I was distinctly odd man out. Jessie was English, and I made what I thought were some amusing remarks about the foibles of English character. There was considerable silence from the lady on my right, and then she turned to me very deliberately and she said, "You are a fool." That's the way that started. Later on, a couple of weeks later, I managed to get her out for dinner on her own, with just the two of us, and I spent almost the entire dinner describing an apartment which I meant to buy and which I was going to live in with my about-to-be-wife. She didn't say, "You are a fool," but she was again oddly silent through all this. I've now opened a can of peas that I can't close.

Interviewer: The lovely lady next to you has been shaking her head.

Cronyn: I was engaged to be married when we met, and for that matter you were married and had a child, right? So we're both a disgrace to the whole institution.

Interviewer: Jessie, you were shaking your head a little bit as he was telling this.

Tandy: I'm sure I never said, "You are a fool." I may have thought it, of course.

Cronyn: This time you gave it voice. Those are not things you make up or forget.

Interviewer: Perhaps Hume was just being very intuitive about what you were thinking.

Tandy: Could be.

Interviewer: Let's go through some of the performances of your great careers. Let's start, Jessica, with *A Streetcar Named Desire*. You originated the role of Blanche DuBois, and you got the role when Tennessee Williams and Elia Kazan came out to California to see you in a one-act Tennessee Williams play that Hume had directed. Tell us about meeting them, about being offered the role, about what you asked, about everything.

Tandy: It was like suddenly a great big door opened to me, because I had felt that in Hollywood, although I was under contract to Fox, I was not being used as I could be. I wasn't being given anything challenging to do. The stage, after all, was my first love, and this was a play which was a groundbreaker. There was no question but that this was a very wonderful play, and to be given the opportunity to play it was terrific. That I owe to Mr. Cronyn, who saw the possibilities.

Cronyn: In you?

Tandy: In me, yes, and doing that other play of Williams's helped me to that moment.

Cronyn: And in that other play of Williams's she was bloody wonderful. I think I was the first person to ever put Tennessee Williams's work under option. In fact, I know I was. I had the option on nine one-act plays, and I just couldn't get them on. After the option expired, I carried it on an extra year at the behest of Audrey Wood, who was Tennessee's agent. This is such a long-winded story that I'm not going to go through it all, but I did finally get one of those nine on in California. I was under contract to MGM, Jessie at Fox, and we were both homesick for the theater and the stage. There was a wonderful small theater in Hollywood in those days called the Actors' Lab, and Joe Papirofsky (that's Joe Papp) was one of my students. There were some other very distinguished ones. Anyway, we did that play, which was called *Portrait of a Madonna.* Jessie was actually much too young for it, but it made a great stir. That's what brought Tennessee and Irene Selznick, the producer, and Kazan out to California to see it.

Interviewer: Jessica, do you remember the night that you knew they were in the audience watching you?

Tandy: Oh yes. I thought everything went wrong, that it was the worst performance I had ever given. As a matter of fact, the next day I just went out walking. Nobody could find me, because they were calling, they wanted to talk to me. But I wasn't home.

Interviewer: You were trying to hide?

Tandy: Yes.

Interviewer: They handed you this script, you read *A Streetcar Named Desire,* and your feeling was what?

Tandy: What a gift! What a gift! It was a wonderful experience, and I enjoyed it enormously. Kazan was a very sensitive, wonderful director who managed to get the best out of everyone he worked with, I think.

Interviewer: I understand that many of Tennessee Williams's plays changed a great deal from a draft to the final product. To some extent, were you a part of that process? How did you affect the final product?

Tandy: It didn't change at all from the beginning. No, there were no changes.

Cronyn: I stood outside the Shubert Theatre, where the play opened, with Tennessee and Kazan, and I ventured that the play was too long. I said it would be stronger if it was fifteen minutes shorter. Chutzpah! Tennessee absolutely seriously turned to me and said, "Okay, you cut it." And he wasn't kidding. I holed up in the hotel the next day, and I managed to cut about ninety seconds. This is quite accurate; you couldn't take one of the bricks out of the wall without something else shifting. It just didn't work. That was not true of all Tennessee's work.

Interviewer: In the range of the various roles that you each have originated, I guess I'm looking for those romanticized stories of the actor and the playwright and director collaborating on the evolution of the script. Were there examples of that that come to mind? With *A Delicate Balance, The Gin Game,* others?

Tandy: I can't think of one. I know of one, but I was not concerned. It was *The Gin Game,* which was first done in Hollywood by a group of actors who were workshopping. In the original script of *The Gin Game,* at the end of the first act, the man beat her over the head and she had a wig with blood in it so that it was all bloody and gory. That was the end of the first act. The second act apparently was a monologue by the man. In working this material, the actors and the director began to show the author what he had written and what wonderful humor there was as well as all the painful truths. So it changed and the script that we started with on the first day of our rehearsals was the script that they had finished. So it has happened.

Interviewer: I've always felt that you two and Mike Nichols really earned part of the Pulitzer Prize that that play won. It was at least as much the production.

Tandy: I think Mike certainly did. He's a very good director and was very aware of the humor, which was essential. You can't have a play about two old, forgotten, miserable people in a nursing home and have a good evening; but there *was* humor there, and he winkled it out.

Interviewer: Did it not also seem a potentially static, wordy play, two people sitting at a table?

Tandy: It was very difficult because there were fourteen games of gin—all the same and all a little bit different—so how to remember it was a big problem. We finally said to Mike, "Mike, please go away for three days. Just go away until we know it, and then you can come back." He said, "If you get it all right, what have you done? All you've done is get it all right. That's not enough." He said, "Why don't you give yourselves a crib?" A crib? He said, "You've got a table there in front of you. Why don't you write down something on it that will give you a cue as to which game you're in?" Against all our feelings, we did it, and it was a great help because we didn't have to wonder about what was coming next. We knew what was coming next and could play the play, although one night Hume cut out three games. He didn't know it and denied it, but it's true.

Cronyn: I remember Mike saying during rehearsals, "You'll never get it with clenched heads."

Interviewer: Hume, it's curious that that would be a difficult play for you to memorize. You've done *Krapp's Last Tape*. Does it have its own internal logic that makes it in ways easier to memorize?

Cronyn: They're all hard to memorize. They're all agony to memorize. I can't really draw distinctions. You asked, "Wasn't *The Gin Game* static?" Being static doesn't necessarily mean you're stuck on opposite sides of the table when there's so much that is going on inside those people. I was doing a very brief lightning tour for the National Endowment for the Arts. They sent me around to about eight or ten regional theaters just to see what was going on, to talk to the artistic directors, and then to write a report. When I got to the Actors Theatre in Louisville, Jon Jory, the artistic director, said, "I've got a play here that would be wonderful for you and Jess; we're going to do it in about five or six months. Will you read it?" I said, "Sure, if I can take it on the airplane." I read it between Louisville and Los Angeles, and I went to a pay phone in the airport in Los Angeles. The author's name and telephone number were on the first page. I called him and said, "I'd like to buy your play." Obviously, something in the reading had caught me.

Interviewer: One of my favorites is certainly *A Delicate Balance,* and it strikes me that that could not be an easy one to quickly get a handle on.

Cronyn: No, it wasn't.

Interviewer: Were there questions you asked Albee or Alan Schneider? How did you unlock the secrets of that play to be able to be Agnes and Tobias?

Tandy: Well, he wrote it and he wrote it very well. The mere way he puts his sentences together for that particular character gives such a clear picture of the sort of person that she is. He wrote it superbly. I didn't have to ask him about that one.

Cronyn: I did.

Tandy: The next one, *All Over,* I did, and he couldn't answer me.

Cronyn: An author sometimes won't answer. There's a lovely story which Ralph Richardson told about Beckett. When he read *Waiting for Godot,* Ralph said, "Now, old boy, could you tell me what this is all about?" And Beckett simply said, "I'm sorry but I can't answer any of your questions." I remember Ralph saying, "Well, I thought that was rather shirty of him." You ask a painter sometimes, if you're forward enough to do it, "What is it? What did you see? What did you hope it would convey?" Very often they will say, "What you see. What you understand. What you take from it." "But I don't take anything!" "Well then, you have a problem, don't you?" In *A Delicate Balance,* I had one of the most emotional scenes I've ever played in the theater. I knew I didn't have it right. Alan Schneider was Beckett's disciple, but he was also very close to Edward; but you had to protect Alan. He was a dear man and in my opinion a very good director, but you had to protect Alan's feelings very carefully. It was a strange reversal: instead of the director being very careful about his actors, the actors had to be very careful about this director. At least, that was always my feeling; you had to keep reassuring him. I had asked Alan about this scene, and he had explained it and explained it and explained it, and it made no difference. So I thought, "I have to talk to Edward. I have to ask Edward." I went to Alan and said, "Have you any objection to my sitting down with Edward and talking about that scene? Perhaps he'll use different words." Alan, his dignity preserved, said, "Yes, go ahead. Of course, by all means." We met very early one morning in the theater before rehearsal, and I remember Edward drawing a scale of the orgasm.

Interviewer: Excuse me, did you say . . . ?

Cronyn: Yes, I did. That's just the word you heard. It sounds almost mystical. It wasn't. He was quite exact, and let me tell you it was in no way prurient. He led me through the whole climax of the sex act with a graph. He drew it, musically, really. That did it. I got it.

Interviewer: He was charting the scene?

Cronyn: Yes, he was charting the emotional intensity of the scene, and he made it very clear.

Interviewer: It's not surprising that he now likes to direct his own work.

Cronyn: Right.

Tandy: Yes, I think he should.

Cronyn: I don't.

Tandy: You don't?

Cronyn: I don't. This is a generality, but I don't think writers should direct their own stuff, I don't think actors should try to direct themselves. I've done it numbers of times, and that's how I learned not to do it.

Interviewer: When I was thinking about doing this interview, I sort of isolated in my mind a couple of moments that you have done onstage which to me typify the thrill that you've given me. I suspect, or I fear, that you may come back and say to me that these are mere gimmicks. I want to throw them out to you and ask you what you should never ask an artist, to explain.

Cronyn: Wait a minute. Before you even go in and dig a pit: there is no such thing as a gimmick if it works.

Interviewer: Thank you. And these two worked. Jessica, there is a moment in *Foxfire* when Annie Nations, aged Annie Nations (much older than you were when you acted the role), whirls and whirls and suddenly when she comes out of that whirl she is seventeen years old. I believed that you were seventeen years old.

Tandy: Well, you see, first of all, I believed it. That's a given. That scene didn't work on screen. On the stage you heard the music in the background of the people dancing at the corn-husking. The lights changed, the music came in, and I felt as though I was seventeen years old. Then all the things that were said in that following scene were only things that would be said by seventeen- or eighteen-year-old people. So the writer had done it.

Cronyn: Thank you.

Interviewer: And the lighting designer helped?

Tandy: And the lighting designer and the music and the whole thing.

Cronyn: When Susan Cooper and I were writing that, we were beholden to the introduction of the characters. All the characters were fictional, but they'd been formed really from the *Foxfire* books and from our very careful research down there with that wonderful man Eliot Wigginton, who has gone through a bad couple of years. But the whole story was one that Susan and I had to make up, and I remember Susan saying, "You should see the proposal." You should see the proposal? I was in my seventies, and Jessie—a girl of sixteen or seventeen? "Come on, Susan." "It'll work. It'll work." And it certainly did! The other one was when I said, "I think you must see her in labor later on when the character's son is being born." We brought both these scenes to Jessie, and Jessie thought we'd both gone over the edge. They worked marvelously. If you play with conviction, the audience will go with you every time. That's why there is so much nonsense about typecasting. Let's not get into that.

Interviewer: There are a couple of moments in *The Gin Game* where Weller Martin gets furious, and the entire amount of blood in your body goes to your face. How do you do that?

Cronyn: Well, it's a gimmick. There is a physical trick involved. I've only done it twice in the theater: once in *Coward in Two Keys,* which had a long and honorable run; once in *The Gin Game.* Just physiologically, what I did not do was hold my breath. It's somewhat limiting if you have to speak. You can tense the muscles of your neck and throat in a way that gets the blood to your head and face, but it doesn't return without destruction to the heart. You will turn very red and eventually purple. I wouldn't do it anymore. It's sort of a self-strangulation thing. I could do it right here and now.

Tandy: But you won't, will you?

Cronyn: No, I won't; but it's actually a physical thing you can learn to do.

Interviewer: For all the emotion that was going on in that play, are you bothered by people saying, "He made his face go red"? That's probably the thing that many people did take away.

Cronyn: Yes, there was even a piece about it in *Time* magazine. But I hope you said, "He was in a passion."

Interviewer: Indeed. We've talked about some of these extraordinary plays and you think, "Well, of course, they would choose to be in these plays." What is it that you look for in a role? How do you choose the roles that you do? Is it a gut reaction? Is it a rational analysis?

Tandy: I think it's a gut reaction.

Cronyn: I read for the first time always as an audience. I can visualize it and see it. I may not see it the way the author wrote it, but I know whether it catches me or not. Yes, I suppose it's a gut reaction. There are other elements that enter in. When I played, particularly in films, I didn't care what it was as long as it was a good part for me. I didn't think about it much. The last ten years or so (I think it's true of both of us), without ever carrying a banner or getting on a soapbox, I think we have been very attracted by things that were affirmative, things that said something positive about life no matter how sad they might have been. It's all I can do to take the front page of the newspaper. I was asked recently to appear in a film about prison life. It is a particularly vivid and brutal film. It doesn't matter what they wanted me to do. I wasn't actually involved in the scene that I'm about to describe, but there was a rape scene. It was sodomy. You have a feeling one way or another about anal intercourse. I didn't balk at all about the moral implications; what I hated was the violence of it, because it wasn't consensual sex between two males. It was an act of ravishment, of violence, of rape, and I just thought, "I can't do that." Not out of any sort of moral stand at all.

We've just finished a film for television [*To Dance with the White Dog*], which comes on December fifth for Hallmark, which we consider a sort of Tiffany of the television shows. It's a lovely story written, again, by Susan Cooper. I actually sent the book to her and asked her to adapt it. She doesn't like doing television, but she said she would do this. Then I persuaded Jessie to play in it. It's a very important part but not a very big part. She said she'd do it, and that's what put the package together. When I first read the book, I sent it to Hallmark and they passed. It wasn't until I could get the right elements together that they accepted it. It's a story in which people face death and die. It sounds grim. Not at all; it's very affirmative. You get to be our age and one of the things that's very disappointing about your friends is that they die. It leaves a big hole in your life, and they shouldn't do that. So one thinks about it.

Interviewer: One would think, though, that whatever Hume Cronyn and Jessica Tandy wanted to do on television there would be eager executives saying, "Yes, when do we start?"

Tandy: Not necessarily.

Cronyn: Not necessarily. We don't have that clout. We are not big film stars. We're not "bankable." Sometimes I'm very glad we're not.

Interviewer: It brings to mind the theater and how easily or uneasily one gets a play on these days. Talk a bit about how the theater has changed—I mean the business of the theater—in the course of your careers.

Cronyn: You want me to be affirmative?

Interviewer: And answer that question? Okay. It's difficult.

Tandy: The only affirmative thing about it is that there are so many other alternatives to Broadway. There are a great many places which are not in the mainstream that do very good work with new writers and are contributing to the theater. About affirmative, if I can just talk for myself for a moment. When I go to the movies or to a play and come out hating the fact that I belong to the human race, I'm absolutely miserable. When I go to a play or movie which shows the possibility of the best side of the nature of man, I come out walking on air, glad to be a member of the human race, and that's what I would like the theater to be—a power to make us all the best of ourselves.

Interviewer: Wonderfully said! I wonder whether you can give us the name of a movie you've seen recently that has given you that feeling. You each get a chance.

Tandy: *Enchanted April.*

Cronyn: There are numbers of them; there isn't a paucity of them. By affirmative, we don't mean happy, happy, happy.

Tandy: No, no, no.

Cronyn: Sometimes what's affirmative is deeply moving and disturbing but is revelatory in some fashion so that you come out enriched or having learned something or having been made to face something that you've never really looked at before carefully.

Tandy: I believe there is an audience for that, and I think it's all wrong that people really want violence. I don't think that's true.

Cronyn: If you take *Cocoon*—I'm talking about films now exclusively—and to some extent *Fried Green Tomatoes,* and I hope this one we just made, which has the strange title of *To Dance with the White Dog,* and one Jessie's made that will come out in February [*Camilla*] and even the last television shows I've done, they were positive. They weren't all very happy, but there were revelations in all of them of at least the flashes of magnificence which can appear in the human spirit.

Interviewer: I have to add a movie title. Jessica was in this film that nobody else saw, and I'm not exactly sure why, except some critics didn't much care for it. If you get a chance, rent a film called *Used People.* Jessica, in his autobiography, Hume said that you rehearse in the bathtub and it drives him a bit mad. It's time for rebuttal. What are his rehearsal habits or other habits that drive you a bit crazy?

Tandy: Everything he does is perfect.

Interviewer: You know that's never going to sell.

Cronyn: Now you know why the marriage has lasted!

Tandy: I drive him crazy because he likes to come away from rehearsal and forget it for now and go back to it tomorrow. I never stop, so in the bathroom, on the bus, wherever it is, I'm thinking about it.

Cronyn: I'm surprised she hasn't been arrested.

Tandy: Are you making a mock of me?

Interviewer: Jessica, in *Fried Green Tomatoes*, there's a bit of ambiguity as to which of the two younger characters you play. Which would you choose?

Tandy: I can't. When I said I would do it and read the script first of all, I was going to play Ninny. If you remember, in the book, Ninny was a sort of peripheral character who had been taken in by that family. I think she was an orphan, and so she observed that whole family and admired Idgie enormously. Early on, before we even started rehearsals, the director said, "I have a brilliant idea. What it's going to be is that you are really going to be not Ninny, but Idgie grown old." So I went through the script and I said, "Ah, well, it says here I married her brother. Is that all right?" We got all those things out so that it all fitted. Then he changed his mind and he said, "I want you to wear dark eyes so you match her eyes but you're going to go back to Ninny." If I had been playing Idgie as an old woman, I would have dressed differently. First of all, Idgie would never have married. I would have been consistent. I would also have watched Mary Stuart Masterson very carefully to see what little things I could bring into my performance that would reflect hers. But I didn't do that, because he said, "No, no, you're not that character," until the last day of shooting, when he said there was something ambiguous so that he thought for a moment I really was—which I didn't buy for a moment. I was very confused, as you may have noticed.

Interviewer: Which one would you have wanted to be?

Tandy: I would have wanted to have been Ninny. I think that would be the one she should be, the one who observed all those people and could tell about them.

Interviewer: Has either one of you talked the other out of doing a particular role?

Tandy: No. I talked him into playing Polonius, and quite rightly, because he was brilliant. He didn't want to do it.

Interviewer: What was the reticence?

Cronyn: Oh dear, I had played Hamlet, not very well, and I have seen numbers of *Hamlet*s, and Polonius always struck me as a rather comic caricature and rather tiresome. Indeed, Shakespeare speaks of him as being decidedly tiresome. But there is a whole other side to him. He was prime minister during three administrations; this man could be no fool. I was working at the

Guthrie Theater and I got a cable from John Gielgud saying, "Burton and I would like you to play Polonius." I thought, "I don't want to play Polonius." But Jessie said, "You have to play it." And she was quite right.

Interviewer: It was an extraordinary production (mainly for Polonius, if I may say), with Richard Burton as Hamlet, in rehearsal clothes for the most part. Hume, talk about *Hamlet* and playing opposite Richard Burton.

Cronyn: I don't know that I can say anything very interesting, which does not mean I'm hiding something derogatory. Richard was a Welsh "boyo" of enormous talent. He was one of those actors—there are not very many of them—who have the finger of God on them: the voice, the presence, the manner, the intelligence. And he was very fortunate in the schooling of Philip Burton. Richard's proper name was Jenkins, and he took Philip's name. He just had it all. But there were things that interested Richard and things that interested Marlon that took them away from their craft, and so these were great losses. I did two things with Richard. I did *Hamlet,* and I also did the film *Cleopatra.* I knew him well, and I liked him a lot. I don't want to go on.

Interviewer: I think we hear you. When other actors play the roles you originated, how does that make you feel?

Tandy: Oh, bully for them, that's great. That's fine. I don't think it belongs to me at all. I also object to this word "originated." Or sometimes people say, "You created the role"—I never created the role. The writer created the role. I hopefully interpret what he wrote; so it's not a creative process, it's an interpretive process.

Cronyn: Darling, you're not talking to the Authors League here. You don't have to be so careful! I'm teasing you because it sounds like writer propaganda.

Interviewer: Are there future prospects for seeing you onstage?

Tandy: I don't think so. Eight times a week, twice on Saturday, twice on Sunday: that takes a very great deal of energy. I'm not sure I have it. He's got it, but I'm not sure that I have. At least, when you make a movie, it's a certain number of weeks. That's very hard work, too, and very concentrated work, but at least you see a light at the end of the tunnel. Whereas you can rehearse a play for four weeks, preview for two weeks, and close on Saturday. That's one scenario. You can also be a big hit and have a long sentence ahead of you.

Interviewer: Many people would like that sentence, but I understand what you are saying.

Cronyn: Of course, you like that sentence from the point of view of financial security, but the best of all worlds is to play in rep where you're playing a number of things. But that is not really a viable commercial undertaking, at least not on Broadway.

Interviewer: Wait a minute, that would solve this eight-performances-a-week problem. What if we got you a rep company?

Tandy: I loved playing in a rep company. The happiest times of my life were those at the Old Vic and at Minneapolis and at Stratford, Ontario, where maybe I would play three times a week but it would be three different roles, three different plays; so it was very stimulating, wonderful.

Cronyn: You wanted us to say something rather solemn about the theater and its future. It ain't going to go away, but its form will change and is changing. We're going through a particularly painful period now.

Interviewer: The serious play being crowded out?

Cronyn: Exactly. You do see serious plays, but you have to seek them out in little highways and byways. The market seems to be entirely toward musicals. When I was in the learning process—I mean my last couple of years of university, my first years in New York, first as a student and then as a young actor—there were seventy-five theaters operating. There were fifteen or twenty straight plays, more perhaps, in one season. You were in failure after failure after failure and you learned and you learned and you learned. I think what's tough now for young actors and actresses is to get the kind of training and experience that is absolutely essential. In the most wonderful school, you can go just so far. You have to go out there and do it and do it again and do it differently, and that opportunity, it seems to me, really doesn't exist.

Interviewer: But in the days you are talking about with so many plays, the universe of theater was between 42nd Street and 60th Street in New York. Now it is the entire nation.

Tandy: Yes, yes.

Cronyn: There was also a considerable network of summer theaters that are no more. That provided a training ground. Now we have something that's richer, in the regional theaters, which when I was young didn't exist at all. It's true there have been some trade-offs; but the bottom line is it's so hard to pay the rent on what an actor can earn in the theater that television and commercials and, to a lesser extent, feature films are magnets that can't be ignored.

Interviewer: What was it like, Jessica, working with young Marlon Brando?

Tandy: It was wonderful. There was no question that he was an extremely talented actor. He is an extremely talented actor. I had seen him before we started those rehearsals in another play, *Truckline Cafe*, where he was really good. He was marvelous as Stanley; I don't think there's ever been another one since. He has given some wonderful performances onscreen. I wish he had stayed in the theater a little longer, but he didn't.

Interviewer: I don't mean this facetiously, but did you ever fear for yourself during some of those scenes with him?

Tandy: No, I only feared for myself when Jack Palance played it for a few performances a week or when Marlon was off. He was so strong I thought my ribs would break when he picked me up! It was like being in a vise.

Interviewer: It is curious that the title *Driving Miss Daisy* has not come up yet in the conversation. I think we were all terribly moved by that film and that performance. Could you talk a little bit about the filming of it and how your friendship with Morgan Freeman grew?

Tandy: Well, first of all, I saw the play with Frances Sternhagen, and she was never out of my mind when I was playing it. I thought she was perfection. I didn't see Morgan play it onstage, but of course he is a consummate actor. He had the background to know all about living in the South, which I didn't have. I'm not southern, I'm not Jewish; but I knew that lady very well. As a matter of fact, she was a little bit like my mother. So I had observed a great deal that fitted, and I thought it was a wonderful play, a wonderful story. We had a director who was brilliant—very sensitive, very responsive to actors. It was a joy to make from beginning to end; and to work with Morgan was perfection.

Interviewer: As excited as I was to hear that you were going to do this role, I worried for this film. Were there ever times you had to fight them not to hype up this movie, to turn it into a "movie movie"? Was that ever the battle?

Tandy: No, I don't remember that. How would that come about? Would that not come about in marketing it? No, no. It was Richard and Lily Zanuck's baby, and they loved it and they gave it everything. It was very, very difficult to get made at all, because no one would give them any money. Nobody thought it was going to be a success, until after it was a success, and then everybody who turned it down said, "Well, I knew that." They were very good. They hired the author of the play to write the screenplay, which was one of the best things they ever did, because he wrote it so well.

Interviewer: How do you make the transition from the stage to the screen as an actor?

Tandy: I don't think I've ever done it except for *Foxfire,* and that was for television. You have to learn that less is more. You don't have to project; you don't have to reach the back of the room. The camera will do a great deal. I'm really not very experienced at playing movies, so I'm not an authority.

Cronyn: I made a lot of them. I made a lot of them back in the forties and fifties, and then there was a long period where I didn't make any. Now I've been making them more recently. I don't find the transition difficult at all. Jessie has used the key phrase that you have to watch—less is more. You get that camera up six inches from your face, just looking at your eyes, you'd better think it because there's nothing else that you can do. From this front row, they can hardly see my eyes. If I tried to use in front of the camera the communication I use in the theater, it would be hopeless. I would be so wildly overboard. Something I have to watch in film a lot is that I'm really theater-trained. Sometimes I've watched actors, very skilled actors, who seem in front of the camera to do nothing; they seem to do absolutely nothing, and then you see them on the screen and you are suddenly aware that what they were doing is very alive because they are thinking it and it shows in the twitch of an eyebrow, in a glance—something that wouldn't register in the theater at all. So you do learn to modify the performance and at the same time, hopefully, not to lose the essential energy. It isn't energy when I'm close to shouting. That's just projecting! But there's an inner energy which activates every thought, every little gesture, everything that you say, so that you feel it's alive, it's alive, it's alive. That is essential on the stage, but it also is very helpful carried over into film—but contained, contained, contained.

Blythe Danner

Blythe Danner was born in Philadelphia, Pennsylvania, on February 3, 1943. After studying drama at Bard College (B.A., 1965), she made her professional debut as Laura in The Glass Menagerie *(1965). She made her Broadway debut as Jill Tanner in* Butterflies are Free *(1969; Tony Award). Other professional roles include Elise,* The Miser *(1969); title role,* Major Barbara *(1971); Viola,* Twelfth Night *(1972); Nina,* The Seagull *(1974); Isabel,* Ring Round the Moon *(1975); Cynthia Karslake,* The New York Idea *(1977); Lisa,* Children of the Sun *(1979); Tracy Lord,* The Philadelphia Story *(1980); Elvira,* Blithe Spirit *(1987); Blanche DuBois,* A Streetcar Named Desire *(1988); Beatrice,* Much Ado About Nothing *(1988); Melissa,* Love Letters *(1989); Arkadina,* The Seagull *(1994); Kate,* Sylvia *(1995); Bel,* Moonlight *(1995); Hester Collyer,* The Deep Blue Sea *(1998); and Jane,* Ancestral Voices *(1999).*

She has been featured in many films: To Kill a Clown *(1972),* 1776 *(1972),* Lovin' Molly *(1974),* Hearts of the West *(1975),* Futureworld *(1976),* The

Great Santini *(1979)*, Man, Woman, and Child *(1983)*, Brighton Beach Memoirs *(1986)*, Another Woman *(1988)*, The Prince of Tides *(1991)*, Husbands and Wives *(1992)*, To Wong Foo, Thanks for Everything *(1995)*, Homage *(1996)*, The Myth of Fingerprints *(1997)*, Mad City *(1997)*, The Farmhouse *(1998)*, The Proposition *(1998)*, No Looking Back *(1998)*, Forces of Nature *(1999)*, The Love Letter *(1999)*, Meet the Parents *(2000)*, *and* Invisible Circus *(2000)*.

Her television shows include Dr. Cook's Garden *(1970)*, To Be Young, Gifted, and Black *(1972)*, Columbo: Etude in Black *(1972)*, The Scarecrow *(1973)*, Adam's Rib *(1973)*, Sidekicks *(1974)*, F. Scott Fitzgerald and "The Last of the Belles" *(1974)*, Eccentricities of a Nightingale *(1976)*, The Court-Martial of George Armstrong Custer *(1977)*, A Love Affair: The Eleanor and Lou Gehrig Story *(1977)*, Are You in the House Alone? *(1978)*, You Can't Take It with You *(1979)*, Too Far to Go *(1979)*, Inside the Third Reich *(1982)*, In Defense of Kids *(1983)*, Helen Keller: The Miracle Continues *(1984)*, Guilty Conscience *(1985)*, Tattinger's *(1989)*, Money, Power, Murder *(1989)*, Judgment *(1990)*, Never Forget *(1991)*, Getting Up and Going Home *(1992)*, Cruel Doubt *(1992)*, Lincoln *(1992)*, Oldest Living Confederate Widow Tells All *(1994)*, Leaves of Absence *(1994)*, A Century of Women *(1994)*, A Call to Remember *(1997)*, Saint Maybe *(1998)*, Murder, She Purred: A Mrs. Murphy Mystery *(1998)*, *and guest appearances on* M*A*S*H, St. Elsewhere, The X-Files, *and* Tales from the Crypt.

This interview took place on August 25, 1997, and June 24, 1999.

• ——————————————————————— •

Interviewer: How did you get interested in the theater?

Danner: When I was seventeen, my closest friend and her parents took me to see a matinee of Chekhov's *The Seagull* at the Bucks County Playhouse in Pennsylvania. Ellis Rabb's company, the APA [Association of Producing Artists], which was then considered the finest repertory company in the country, was there for the summer season, and Rosemary Harris played Nina in *The Seagull*. It was extraordinary. I didn't know what hit me. I was transported into a world I'd never known before. I would be devoted to Chekhov for the rest of my life. A few years earlier, I had seen the original company of *West Side Story* on Broadway when I was about fourteen. That, too, was an emotional experience. I loved the passion of the piece. No musical I have seen since has moved me as deeply.

Interviewer: Was your family interested in theater?

Danner: Yes, very much so. Actually, everyone in my family was and is quite artistic. My father was known as "the singing banker" in Philadelphia. He had a beautiful tenor voice and sang a lot of oratorios with the Philadelphia

Chamber Orchestra. My oldest brother, William Moennig, is a renowned violinmaker in Philadelphia; and my brother Harry was at the Met Studio in New York as a young tenor and is now an actor.

Interviewer: The Met as in the Metropolitan?

Danner: Right. I remember my mother singing and performing *Hansel and Gretel* for me almost from the time I was born. She too had a beautiful voice, and she and Dad were the perennial stars of the PTA shows in Springfield, a suburb of Philadelphia where we lived. So I was surrounded by talented people. Actually, I had always wanted to be a nurse. Whenever we—my cousins and I—would play-act, that's the role I would choose; but I hated the sight of blood, so that took care of that. Ha!

Interviewer: When you went to college at Bard, were you already thinking of being in the theater?

Danner: Yes, there was a wonderful drama program at the high school I went to, the George School in Bucks County; that was really my first time onstage. Then, after George School, I was an exchange student for a year in Berlin, the year the wall was built. You know, the wall was built because approximately two thousand people fled East Berlin every day, crossing the border to the West; so the Communist government clamped down and built the wall. They patrolled it with armed policemen who shot and killed many refugees trying to escape, but they still continued to risk their lives to flee to the West. Many would come to Amerika House for refuge, and those people were sent into the auditorium to wait while their documents were being processed. I had joined a little troupe that performed musicals there, so we were onstage singing and dancing numbers like "I'm Just Wild About Harry," twirling our umbrellas, while the people who had just escaped with their lives were in the auditorium watching us. There they sat with all their worldly goods on their laps, some sobbing, some smiling, for having made it across the border. It was truly bizarre. What must they have thought—watching us mindlessly frolicking about, seemingly oblivious to what they had just been through. It certainly wasn't the most appropriate welcome, but it was an extraordinary experience for all of us.

Interviewer: Did you act in college in the summers as well?

Danner: I apprenticed at a few theaters, and at the end of my senior year at Bard I got my Equity card. One of my teachers, Charlie Kakatsakis, was associated with a theater in Fishkill, New York, run by Lonnie Chapman. Charlie directed the production of *Glass Menagerie* in which I got my Equity card playing Laura opposite Elena Karam, an actress who was associated with Elia Kazan.

Interviewer: Then, after you finished at Bard, how did you get into the professional theater?

Danner: The Theater Company of Boston was run by David Wheeler, a brilliant man who drew many of the greats to his theater. When I went to take a look at the company in hopes of working there, Bob Duvall, Al Pacino, Jon Voight, and Dustin Hoffman were all in the company. I met with David, who just happened to have a part for a girl who spoke German and had to be skinny, from starvation during World War II. They said I was the only skinny German-speaking girl who showed up at the audition, so my auspicious beginning was by default, I guess.

Interviewer: That Berlin year came in very handy, didn't it?

Danner: Yes, it sure did.

Interviewer: How did you get from Boston to New York and into the New York theater?

Danner: The Theater Company took that production I just spoke of, called *The Infantry,* into New York, off-Broadway, and sadly it was a very short run. *Butterflies Are Free,* my first Broadway play, came soon after that. When I first read it, I thought it was charming but rather lightweight. I wanted to be a serious actress, and in this play I had to run around in my underwear at one point. I wasn't in love with that idea, so when I met with Milton Katselas, the director, I said I really didn't think this was for me. Milton asked me to reconsider and said, "I think we really can make something of this." He was right. It was a charming, heartwarming night of theater, and we were a huge success. I was especially happy for the playwright, Leonard Gersh, an extremely lovely man.

The night after I won the Tony Award for that role, a strange thing happened. I made my entrance as usual, which as I remember it was somewhat acrobatic, and it always got a good laugh. Timing was everything with this entrance, and I was proud of it. But because I had won the Tony Award the night before, unexpectedly, for me, I got a huge hand, which completely threw off the timing. I remember thinking, "This is ridiculous; the audience is ruining my whole entrance." I was furious. I remember thinking at that moment, "This is not going to become the most important thing in my life." I think because success came so quickly at such a young age, in the early stage of my career I didn't appreciate it. Up until that point I hadn't worked all that long or hard yet to deserve a Tony Award, and I think I had a bit of disdain for all the hoopla. It isn't until recently, some thirty years later, that I have come to realize how much it all means to me. I used to feel that what I did wasn't important, but over the years I've had people tell me that I've made a difference somehow in their lives with a performance. (Every actor I know has had that happen.) I've made them look differently at their lives or changed them in some way, and that, of course, one can't take lightly.

Interviewer: Now that you're established, or since you've been established, how do you go about choosing roles?

Danner: I just try to select the best material available. It comes along so seldom, and I'm very appreciative when it does. There was a time when the children were growing up that a wonderful role would come along and I wouldn't take it because I didn't want to leave them. When I did a project, I'd try and take them along to England or Germany, so they too would have an adventure. But now that they're grown up and doing very well on their own, I go just about anywhere and do almost anything, small or large roles. Indeed, they have done well. My son is twenty-three and is directing and writing and being very well received in the film world; and my daughter, Gwyneth Paltrow, of course, won an Oscar this year for her performance in *Shakespeare in Love*. I'm certainly very proud of her, but what makes me even more proud is that, on the heels of her great success, she has chosen this summer to return to Williamstown, to the theater festival where she spent almost every summer of her life growing up, and play Rosalind in *As You Like It*. That thrills me no end, knowing that she knows that it's the work that is the most important thing and not the fame and the glory, as Chekhov says.

Interviewer: I understand there's some sort of wonderful tie-in between Gwyneth's role in *Shakespeare in Love* and an earlier event in your career.

Danner: Yes, as a matter of fact, early on in my pregnancy with Gwyneth I was playing Viola in *Twelfth Night* at Lincoln Center, and of course in *Shakespeare in Love* she plays Violet de Lessup, the character in the film that is based on Viola in *Twelfth Night*. So that is particularly poignant for me.

Interviewer: You say that now you'll do just about anything and go just about anywhere; but surely you've turned down plays and you've turned down films. Now that you're free to do them in terms of your domestic situation, why do you turn them down?

Danner: I just turned down one that was about husbands cheating on their wives. If it's real drivel, I won't do it. (Of course, don't tempt me with a trip to Bora Bora; I might say yes.) It's usually the role. Even if the piece isn't extraordinary—because there are so few pieces that are today—if it's a great role and a challenge and something that will take me somewhere I haven't been before, both literally and figuratively, I'll do it.

Interviewer: You mentioned that Rosemary Harris's performance in *The Seagull* was one of the early plays that got you excited about theater. Do you find that Chekhov has some special challenges? Do you do different kinds of preparation for Chekhov than for a lighter play?

Danner: I think the great plays just wash over you and take you with them. You have to allow them to envelop you. Trust Mr. Chekhov. Something spiritual happens. If you are open to any challenge, if you are free of tension, the great plays lift you up and let you soar, fly. For the lesser plays you have to labor more intensively to provide for yourself the connecting tissue that isn't there, that the great writers give you in spades.

Interviewer: You trust the material.

Danner: You trust the material. We were doing Pinter's *Betrayal* on Broadway with Raul Julia and Roy Scheider, and I remember thinking every night as the curtain went up, "I'm playing for every woman in the audience who has lived the inner life of Emma," the woman I was playing. It opened me up emotionally every night. It's important to be mindful and just allow everything that's happening around you to affect you. Tension is, I think, your worst enemy as an actor.

Interviewer: Can you say more about how you prepare for a role, say, for Chekhov? *The Seagull,* for instance, seems to recur in your life: you saw it with Rosemary Harris; you did it; some twenty years later you did it with your daughter. Your daughter did the role you had done twenty years before. Was there a difference in your preparation for the earlier one and the later one?

Danner: I was very nervous the first time. It takes courage to play Chekhov honestly and boldly, which is what our director, Nikos Psacharopoulos, demanded. Emotionally, Nina is a demanding role and rarely played by actresses as young as Chekhov indicates. Nikos, the founder of the Williamstown Theatre Festival, was Greek, and his passionate nature was a good marriage with Chekhov. You couldn't hide from him. I was terrified. I realized I was going to have to make a leap into waters I had never been in before.

Interviewer: How did you do it?

Danner: Nikos pushed me to the brink. I was luckily working with a great group of actors, most of whom had worked on Chekhov before; so I was very fortunate. They were a great help.

Interviewer: Do you work on a role from the inside out or the outside in— or is it whatever works?

Danner: It's so hard to talk about that, because every role and piece is different. I hear that British actors, for the most part, start from the outside and work in. I think we as a group, American actors, usually do the opposite. But I think it's come to the point now, now that we're so many years away from the inception of the Method, there are so many varied approaches that actors can now choose from.

Interviewer: What about working with different kinds of directors? How do you distinguish between directors you've worked with? What kinds of directors do you like to work with? You can name names or not as you see fit. What works best for you?

Danner: A director who loves me—or at least convinces me he does. Ha! Peter Hall, who directed *Betrayal,* is also a classical musician. He's very, very precise. I learned an awful lot about timing and holding back and keeping emotion within, using the language to convey the emotion—the English approach. All of that was a real lesson. I loved working with Nikos, who constantly pushed us to go deeper and deeper and become fuller and fuller. When you feel the director loves your work and respects you, you give your best. I enjoy working with a variety of different approaches as long as I feel my opinion is valued. I've worked with a lot of directors who say, "Stand there and say the lines." Immediately you find yourself closing down, I think, because we're like children in a lot of ways. The directors are like our fathers. The more they reach out to us and embrace us, the more we're willing to give. I think most actors are like that unless they're extremely self-confident and nothing throws them.

Interviewer: Aren't there actors who come in there with a pretty good understanding and want to do it their way? You're an actor who wants a director to help you.

Danner: I'm basically a company person. I always am most comfortable in a repertory situation. Chekhov is the perfect example because there are always wonderful roles for everybody. There are no small parts. Certainly in Chekhov even the small parts are glorious.

Interviewer: Are there great differences between acting in films and acting onstage? Obviously in film you don't shoot it sequentially, but as an actor do you draw upon the same resources or use different resources? Is it a different process for you?

Danner: I think you work basically the same way; you just use a different set of muscles. In the film I'm working on now [*The Farmhouse*] we're in a cornfield in a house that's dilapidated and falling down. That's the set. It's a wonderful ambience in which to create this character. It adds a dimension one doesn't have onstage—the real thing. I love doing low-budget films because you work with young people who are learning about filmmaking. All the crew is alert and interested. When you're working with these young kids it's a joy, because they're so enthusiastic. They're your audience. You can hear a pin drop when the work is good, and when it's not you hear them get restless and you think, "Something's not quite right there." They're a wonderful barometer. I find working on a low-budget film also gives you more freedom, because you know that as the clock is ticking away you're not spending a million dollars a minute, and that tends to be more relaxing.

Interviewer: Actors often say that when you act in a film, because the camera is right on top of you—as opposed to a theater, where obviously most of the audience is at a greater distance—everything is magnified. Are you conscious of that as an actor?

Danner: Yes, and I used to hate it. I never felt comfortable working on film until recently because I was so conscious of that. I love the stage because of the physical freedom. I'm a very physical person, so it was very difficult for me to learn to pull it in and not move around so much.

Interviewer: Everyone says that you have a wonderful voice. Did it come from genes, training, or what? How have you perfected it?

Danner: Thank you, but the way the huskiness crept in was actually not intended. When I was doing *Butterflies Are Free,* I had not so long before come back from Germany, where I had studied singing lieder; and I had a very high-pitched clear voice. The girl I played, Jill Tanner, was supposed to be a free spirit, comfortable in her own skin. I felt that my voice should be different, have a deeper or more relaxed sound. I started doing a gravelly voice not really being conscious of it. I thought, "Oh, this is kind of good for the role," but not realizing that I was doing permanent damage. I went to a voice teacher who couldn't solve my dilemma. That was pretty much the end of my singing career; I lost the flexibility of my vocal cords. I've learned over the years to be more careful. Now I do extensive warm-ups. I do a lot of yoga. When I worked with Kevin Kline in *Much Ado About Nothing,* every night Kevin did his stretching exercises before he went onstage. His voice was bigger and more relaxed as a result, and I copied him. I also started working with a wonderful vocal teacher, Ralph Proodian, in New York, who I think can correct any vocal problem.

Interviewer: Speaking of Shakespeare, and you've done a bit of Shakespeare, how do you handle the blank verse? This has been a problem with some "American" actors. Do you consciously try to get the sense but retain the rhythm, strike some balance? Or do you just forget it's blank verse and just say it?

Danner: Having been raised in a musical household, I think I have some sort of idea of the music. Peter Hall used to talk about that. He said that one's sense of inner musicality was a tremendous help; but I've always longed to study with a great Shakespearean coach and learn how it's done.

Interviewer: You've done a lot of classical roles, but occasionally—*Butterflies Are Free,* for example, and with *Sylvia*—you've done a role that had never been done before, an original play. Is that process any different?

Danner: It depends on the quality of writing. Those two examples were very well written as we went into rehearsal; they were polished. But I've worked on some new plays where it was agony because the map wasn't well drawn. Each time there was a very good core but so much work had to be done and, unfortunately, everyone wasn't always on the same wavelength.

Interviewer: Are you saying by implication that you're more comfortable in a situation where you can trust the material and you don't have to be part of the process?

Danner: I like being part of the process, but only if there is a strong, insightful director with a good grasp of the material who can be helpful with the changes needed. And of course it helps to have a writer who is not married to every word and is open to cuts and changes, to making it better. A lot of writers cannot be objective about this.

Interviewer: The way your career has gone, it would seem as if you more often than not have opted to be in plays that have had many productions and are classical. Is that accidental or is that conscious?

Danner: I don't think it's been conscious. I've rejected a lot of plays that just weren't good. I knew the input, the kind of work that would have to be done to get them right. It requires a lot of time and commitment. I'd have to be very much in love with it in its raw stage for me to go through that again.

Interviewer: What is a part that you've never played that you would love to play?

Danner: All the Chekhovs that I have not played. Madame Ranevskaya in *The Cherry Orchard.* Colleen Dewhurst played her at Williamstown. I played the maid. I first saw Irene Worth play her at Lincoln Center. It was the first time I saw Meryl Streep. I was doing a play at BAM [the Brooklyn Academy of Music] called *The New York Idea,* and I went, on my day off, to see *The Cherry Orchard* with Meryl and Irene Worth. I remember Meryl's entrance, this dazzling girl falling onto the stage, and going through my menu as I call it, my program, saying, "Who is this incredible person? What a presence!"

Interviewer: Colleen Dewhurst, in her autobiography, has some nice words to say about you, but not about Nikos Psacharopoulos.

Danner: Oh no. They really didn't hit it off at all.

Interviewer: Was it chemistry or what?

Danner: I don't know. They went away and talked privately. I assume it was their different ways of working. Many actors loved working with Nikos because he would push people to places where they hadn't gone or were frightened of. He wanted me to play Masha in *The Three Sisters* the year after *The Seagull.* I said, "Nikos, there's no way I can do this. It's just much too difficult. I don't have the depth. I can't do it." He wouldn't take no for an answer. He said, "This is ludicrous. You're doing it." I was never so grateful in all my life, because it was one of the most extraordinary experiences.

Interviewer: Not everybody would respond the same way to that kind of pushing. Are you saying that some people would fight it?

Danner: Yes, of course we all did at some point. When Rosemary [Harris] was directed by Nikos in *A Month in the Country* she adored him because she felt that she had certain mannerisms that were safe—as we all do. These are places that we can go to if we're feeling shaky; we go to what's familiar, what we think will work. He would say, "Don't do that. No, no." She loved it because, she said, "He got me away from those habits." He did that for all of us. But he had a strange way of working; it wasn't even articulate a lot of times. If you got it, you got it. If you didn't, you didn't.

Interviewer: You loved it enough to go back again and again to Williamstown.

Danner: Yes. We never stopped learning from Nikos. He was an extraordinary teacher-director. But there were times I wanted to choke him, and we would all have really rowdy arguments. That's what I loved about it, because, being brought up in Philadelphia to be sort of a proper young lady, it was wonderful to be thrown into this massive chaotic passionate situation. I loved it. It was something I hadn't experienced before.

Interviewer: Have you ever directed?

Danner: No, I never have.

Interviewer: Is it something that interests you?

Danner: I wouldn't want to do a film, because there's so much involved technically, but I am interested in directing in the theater. The wonderful thing about Williamstown is that, for the most part, everyone knows one another well enough so if you have a good idea, all will say, "Let's try it." If you're working with people you don't know, that openness is not always welcomed. When we did *Streetcar*, Sigourney Weaver, Chris Walken, and I played Stella, Stanley, and Blanche. Chris was remarkable. He was full of ideas, even for the scenes he wasn't in, and Sigourney and I appreciated it. That was a great experience, and a great production. If the director is open and confident and has a free way of working, that's fine. If not, you make the best of it and you get on with it. Once you've opened the play and he's not around, you can have a little more fun and more freedom.

Interviewer: But doesn't the director come back and visit the production from time to time? What happens when he or she sees what you've done?

Danner: Well, usually they're very happy and they think they've made the improvements! That's been my experience.

Interviewer: So you get away with it?

Danner: Well, yes, and we've made it better because we've gotten so familiar with it and have played it night after night.

Interviewer: And then they take credit for it?

Danner: Yeah. Why not? Whatever works, right? We're all in this together. The fact is that every piece is evolving until closing night. You never stop working, finding something fresh. No one cares who gets the credit, I think, as long as the work becomes richer. Everyone contributes.

Interviewer: But if you're interested in directing, why haven't you directed?

Danner: There just hasn't been the time or the inclination yet, but I'm hoping I will be directing eventually.

Interviewer: What are some of the other roles that you want to do? You mentioned Chekhov. What else?

Danner: I'd like to do some Noël Coward. Ever since I saw Colleen [Dewhurst] and Jason [Robards] do *A Moon for the Misbegotten*, I've wanted to try O'Neill. Now there's an example of one's life being changed forever. I got up to leave the theater and had to sit down again for half an hour—to weep.

Interviewer: What was the most challenging role you ever did?

Danner: I think probably Blanche in *Streetcar*. I might also say Masha in Chekhov's *Three Sisters* and Nina in *The Seagull*.

Interviewer: Why were they particularly challenging?

Danner: Emotionally, I had to go places where I hadn't gone before. I wasn't sure I had the courage to go there. In those roles you can be seduced into trying to do a turn; but my before-show mantra every night was "Let the play wash over me and let me be true." Actors really are so brave, I think, because they have to suffer the slings and arrows of outrageous fortune. No matter what anyone says, you carry on. I love the story of Ruth Gordon, who was playing in *Mrs. Warren's Profession* several years ago. She got dreadful notices; they just took her over the coals. The next night she came in and said, "Thank God that's over. Now let's go to work." She didn't mope or feel sorry for herself. That's really what an actor has to do. You can't be thin-skinned. You have to take it on the chin and go on.

Interviewer: How do you feel about critics? Do you read them? Do you care?

Danner: I don't read them anymore. I try not to care, although I'm human, of course. The only way you know if you don't read them is when someone calls and says, "I'm sorry for that awful review"—or you pick up on the backstage behavior if everyone avoids the subject completely. For a long time when I began I was spoiled because I always got great reviews. Then I got a couple of real doozies and I said, "Oh good, I survived that and it didn't kill me." If you're not careful, you believe them, and that goes for the audience too. We can all be such sheep. If a critic says something's great, we'll go. Some of my biggest disappointments have been plays that got raves. A review is, after all, only somebody's opinion. Of course, they usually dictate whether you'll run or not, but I really do believe that as an artist you can't pay them much mind, because you *have* to get on with it. Another thing is that a lot of performers get much stronger as the play gets further into its run. I remember reading about Lynn Fontanne and Alfred Lunt. The critics were so respectful of them. They knew that Lynn was always nervous on opening night, so the critics would come a few times before they wrote their reviews. Wouldn't it be wonderful if that happened today? That's why I loved working for Joe Papp, because his shows would run a long time before the critics came. It's still that way at the [New York Shakespeare] Festival, thank goodness.

Interviewer: When you go to the theater as an audience member, do you see a play differently because you're an actress? Are you looking for or appreciating different things?

Danner: Of course. The joke in our business is the costume designer can only see the costumes, the choreographer only the dancing, the lighting man the lights; so of course we actors are scrutinizing the acting. I don't look for fireworks, but for the truth in the playing, and in the writing. The truth is the most important thing. I believe it was Edith Evans who said, "I never think about being great, but only about being true." Sometimes when I know I haven't filled a moment truthfully on a given night, I lose sleep over it. It's disappointing to me today that so much that is considered great is what I think is over the top. It really annoys me. It doesn't seem that the truth matters as much to audiences anymore, even to the critics. They want to be dazzled, but not necessarily with truthful performances. One sees it all the time now, in the movies and in the theater.

Interviewer: Did you ever not take a role that you regretted not taking?

Danner: Oh yes, a couple. But, again, I was busy mothering. I never had dreams of being a star, so it was never that I thought, "That would have been the one." I never ever felt that way.

Interviewer: Choose a performance where you think you did your best work. I hope you think you've done the best all the time, but what is the one performance you'd like people to remember?

Danner: I think it would be Blanche. When we did it at Williamstown I think it was all our finest work—Chris Walken and Sigourney Weaver and myself. It's a very difficult play, but glorious to play.

Interviewer: What about it makes you proudest of it?

Danner: As a group we banded together and explored one of the greatest plays ever written, in my opinion. Also, there were nights when I forgot who I was. I completely escaped into Blanche; I inhabited her.

Interviewer: And that hasn't happened to you often?

Danner: It doesn't happen often. If you're lucky, it happens maybe six or eight times in your career.

Interviewer: Why do you think it happens?

Danner: Because you've grown together with the character. It always happens for me late in the run. You just have no shackles. You're completely free and you fly somewhere where the character lives and you, the actor, are left behind. Those are the nights you never want to go to sleep.

Interviewer: Can you predict in terms of a particular role where you feel you're getting into it sufficiently and it might happen?

Danner: When you read a great play and you have a physical response (that's usually the key), you just know that something is there that profoundly moves you, speaks to you.

Interviewer: Would you like to bottle it and use it the next night?

Danner: Oh, sure! Then of course you try to re-create it and you can't. It will come again but differently.

Interviewer: Were there times when the people on stage realized that something was different?

Danner: Sometimes. Yes. I've had actors come up to me and say, "You really were there tonight." I felt it too. Of course, what's ironic is that the opposite can happen too; you think you're terrific and they don't. That's what makes the whole process mystifying—the element of never knowing whether you'll fall on your face or not. It's dangerous and very seductive.

Interviewer: What kinds of actors do you like to work with? What is the ideal actor-actor relationship on stage?

Danner: The ideal actor-actor relationship is like throwing a ball and knowing that the other person, no matter where you throw it, will catch it and return it. I remember that with Raul Julia when we did *Betrayal*. I felt that with Kevin; I felt that with Chris Walken. They're all very different actors. The problem comes when you work with actors who have huge egos and are not as giving. But if you're a member of a company and you're all working toward the same end—which is revealing the truth of the play and not yourself—it's very gratifying. You have to be willing to lose what you think is a great moment for the good of the play.

Interviewer: Ideally, then, what you want is a situation where all of you could lose yourself in the play and lose your sense of ego and have the play become more important than anything, including who you are.

Danner: Yes, as Shakespeare said, the play is the thing. It's why Chekhov is so wonderful to play also. I don't like actors who work to a metronome. There are those actors for whom you have to come in exactly when you came in the night before or else they won't talk to you. I've worked with a few like that. That's not a lot of fun. You want to know that you can make a mistake and after all it may not be a mistake. Sometimes something new will be revealed that you hadn't thought of, and you'll accidentally find something that's better than you'd planned. The improvisatory nature of it makes it very exciting.

Interviewer: Speaking of other actors, do you have role models, actors whom you specifically have admired?

Danner: Well, there's Meryl [Streep], and of course Vanessa [Redgrave]. We all worship at their altars. They're extraordinary. They just are. They go places where I think very few actors go.

Interviewer: You've said that you like actors who have great soul.

Danner: Doesn't everybody? It's usually in the eyes that you see that. It's spiritual. The actor must take the audience on a spiritual journey, depending on the play of course.

Interviewer: You've acted in New York on and off Broadway, and you've done regional theater. Is there any difference between New York and elsewhere? Or is it all acting?

Danner: It's more stressful, of course. In New York you know that you're going to have all the New York critics there, and so everybody's always a little nervous about that, I think. Once you're open and running you're fine.

Interviewer: Is there a different feel? A lot of actors and playwrights say that in a regional theater, where it's a subscription audience, you're going to run for four or five weeks no matter what. They say it's a very different feel than it is in New York, where your future is determined by the critics and there is a certain open-endedness to the run.

Danner: Most of the New York theater I've done, except for a few Broadway and off-Broadway plays, has been with subscription theaters, like the Manhattan Theatre Club, the Roundabout, Lincoln Center, and the New York Shakespeare Festival; you feel very protected. You have a guaranteed run, which is fabulous, but you're not committed to a play for a long run—which is great too.

Interviewer: What's the last thing you saw in the theater as an audience member that really thrilled you? It can be a performance or it can be a play.

Danner: Well, the one that will always live in my heart is, as I mentioned earlier, Colleen and Jason in *A Moon for the Misbegotten.* I think that was the one that packed the biggest wallop. I'll never forget it. That was about as good as it gets, I think. It was just magic. If you're not moved to laughter or tears in the theater, it's sort of a waste of time. That's why we're all in this, I think, as actors and audiences. We want to be transported. We want to be really moved to the core.

Interviewer: Kazan in his autobiography talks about valuing actors who are dangerous. There are certain kinds of actors—Brando, Montgomery Clift, George C. Scott, for example—that when you see them you don't know what the next thing they're going to do might be. They might do anything. How do you feel about that? Is that something that excites you?

Danner: Absolutely! Bobby Duvall is just that kind of actor; so is Chris Walken. You feel you're walking on the edge of a cliff when you're acting with them. It's hair-raising in the best sense. Every muscle, every fiber of your mind and body, is at attention. It's thrilling to be in such an actor's company. The great ones are like that—and what's more, they are so generous. You know if you should trip and fall off that cliff, they will risk their lives to catch you.

Ruby Dee

Ruby Dee was born Ruby Ann Wallace in Cleveland, Ohio, on October 14, 1923. She studied at Hunter College, at the American Negro Theatre, with Morris Carnovsky, and at the Actors Workshop with Paul Mann and Lloyd Richards. She made her Broadway debut in 1943 in the drama South Pacific, *and went on to play, among other roles, Libby George in* Jeb *(1946) and the title role in* Anna Lucasta *(1946). She created the role of Ruth Younger in* A Raisin in the Sun *in 1959. For the American Shakespeare Festival in 1965 she played Cordelia in* King Lear *and Kate in* The Taming of the Shrew. *Other major roles include Lena,* Boesman and Lena *(1970); Julia Augustine,* The Wedding Band *(1972); Gertrude,* Hamlet *(1975); Amanda Wingfield,* The Glass Menagerie *(1989); and her one-woman show,* My One Good Nerve *(1996 and 2000).*

Her films include The Fight Never Ends *(1947),* What a Guy *(1947),* That Man of Mine *(1947),* The Jackie Robinson Story *(1950),* No Way Out *(1950),* The Tall Target *(1951),* Go, Man, Go! *(1954),* Edge of the City

(1957), St. Louis Blues *(1958)*, Our Virgin Island *(1959)*, Take a Giant Step *(1959)*, A Raisin in the Sun *(1961)*, The Balcony *(1963)*, Gone Are the Days *(1963)*, The Incident *(1967)*, Up Tight! *(1968)*, Buck and the Preacher *(1972)*, Countdown at Kusini *(1976)*, Cat People *(1982)*, Do the Right Thing *(1989)*, Jungle Fever *(1991)*, Cop and a Half *(1993)*, Just Cause *(1995)*, A Simple Wish *(1997)*, A Time to Dance: The Life and Work of Norma Canner *(1998)*, *and* Baby Geniuses *(1998)*.

Among her television appearances are The Guiding Light *(1967)*, Peyton Place *(1968–69)*, Deadlock *(1969)*, The Sheriff *(1971)*, To Be Young, Gifted, and Black *(1972)*, It's Good to Be Alive *(1974)*, I Know Why the Caged Bird Sings *(1979)*, All God's Children *(1980)*, Ossie and Ruby! *(1980)*, Go Tell It on the Mountain *(1984)*, The Atlanta Child Murders *(1985)*, Windmills of the Gods *(1988)*, Lincoln *(1988)*, The Court-Martial of Jackie Robinson *(1990)*, Decoration Day *(1990; Emmy Award)*, The Ernest Green Story *(1993)*, The Stand *(1994)*, Mr. & Mrs. Loving *(1996)*, Captive Heart: The James Mink Story *(1996)*, Porgy and Bess: An American Voice *(1998)*, Passing Glory *(1999)*, Having Our Say: The Delany Sisters' First 100 Years *(1999)*, Storm in the Summer *(2000)*, *and* Finding Buck McHenry *(2000)*, *and guest appearances on* The Fugitive, Spenser: For Hire, China Beach, The Golden Girls, Great Performances, Promised Land, *and* Cosby.

She was elected to the Theater Hall of Fame in 1988 and received the National Medal of the Arts in 1995.

This interview took place on March 1, 1998.

• ———————————————————————————— •

Interviewer: How did you first get interested in theater, and what made you decide to be an actress?

Dee: I think I was born on that track, a track to express yourself. As early as I can remember, I've been reciting something. I remember myself on platforms, even as a little child. My mother—my stepmother really—had been a teacher, and she really wanted to educate the whole family, including my father. She had wanted to be an actress too. So I think it came to me with the territory, this tendency to express myself. When I was eleven, I remember, my mother took some poems I'd written and sent them to the *Amsterdam News*. I still have them. My sister had the same interests—my older sister. I've been encouraged since I can remember to be a word person. I think my mother had hoped I would sing, but I could never sing. But music has been very much a part of my life in terms of rhythm and cadence, even with the spoken word. I've been looked upon as a dramatic actor all my life and known as such. I rarely wrote anything after I started growing up. I began to write things in humor, then I began to write musicals although I didn't know music—I'd taken piano lessons—so I was happy to express myself in all those ways.

Interviewer: How did you get from Cleveland to New York and the American Negro Theatre?

Dee: I grew up in Harlem.

Interviewer: You were born in Cleveland, though, weren't you?

Dee: I was born in Cleveland, but I was about nine months old when I came to New York.

Interviewer: Did you go to the theater as a young person at all?

Dee: No, not really. It wasn't until I was about fifteen or something like that that I met a boy whose sister belonged to the American Negro Theatre. They were looking for somebody to play the debutante in a piece called *On Strivers' Row* written by Abram Hill. He was one of those people who had opened the spaces for the new talent. I'm forever grateful to these kinds of people.

Interviewer: Had you had any acting experience at that point?

Dee: Harlem was a very active place. I remember being on picket lines or at political rallies and assemblies at churches—breaking down segregation, marching with picket signs with my mother. I remember being on a platform with Adam Clayton Powell. In a sense, I grew up in the drama of the times, listening to the speeches, watching the pickets, and hearing people in the trucks up and down Seventh Avenue protesting this or announcing a meeting and that kind of thing. All of that, I think, is fuel to the imagination of a child.

Interviewer: The American Negro Theatre experience was the first time you'd ever worked in a real theater?

Dee: Yes.

Interviewer: Then you worked for them for a number of years, didn't you?

Dee: Yes. Outside of being in school plays and things like that—I remember playing a boy—the American Negro Theatre was my first experience in theater.

Interviewer: How many different shows did you do? How long were you with them?

Dee: Oh my goodness, I would say about five years on and off, while I was in school. There was a great controversy between my mother and my father, about all those late hours.

Interviewer: What sort of experience was it? Was that where you got your early important formative training?

Dee: I'll tell you the truth; of course, we tend to romanticize as we get older and as we look back. But it was one of the most exciting, meaningful times in my whole life, that experience in Harlem that I grew up in. It was tough, it was dramatic, it was encouraging, it was dangerous, it was safe, it was loving, it was nurturing—I would give anything in the world for it.

Interviewer: Did you play a variety of parts?

Dee: In the theater and in Harlem, yes, I had a variety of parts. I started by doing all the young leads in the American Negro Theatre up until the time they did *Anna Lucasta*. Then I was in school, trying to get my degree, which my mother insisted on; all those things happened at once.

Interviewer: How did Hunter College figure in with your acting career?

Dee: I went to junior high school at P.S. 136 in Harlem. A friend's mother who looked white found out that the black schools were not being encouraged to have their children compete for entrance into Hunter High School. So she did all kinds of things and got students from Junior High School 136 to take the test for Hunter High School. More of us entered and more of us proportionately succeeded in getting into Hunter High School than in the whole city of New York. Our teachers were mostly white, but they were a rooting section that I had never encountered. They kept us after school for a year preparing us to get to Hunter High School, because it was so difficult. We took tests, they drilled us, and they took a bunch of us that were in the rapid classes and they schooled us. When our tests came back, they congregated in the halls and hugged each other. I never will forget it. It was an extraordinary time in my life.

Interviewer: Then you went from the high school directly into college?

Dee: Right.

Interviewer: All this time you were also acting professionally?

Dee: Yes.

Interviewer: That's a lot of work. *Anna Lucasta* started at the American Negro Theatre and then was taken downtown to Broadway?

Dee: Oh yes.

Interviewer: The whole production?

Dee: The whole production. As a matter of fact, it was a very important thing in the arts, the American Negro Theatre. It was the beginning of the end of us, too, because we had not prepared to be this tremendous success. We got integrated. We'd been having teachers and people come in from all over the country, and from Russia; we had writing and speech and movement. Nobody has written about it, but I think the American Negro Theatre was as vital a part of the theater movement as anything in this country. But after *Anna Lucasta,* it became "Oh, do you want to get to Broadway?"

Interviewer: Its innocence was gone because now it was all about getting to Broadway.

Dee: That's right.

Interviewer: But you did things at American Negro Theatre after *Anna Lucasta,* didn't you?

Dee: Yes. But most of the things that I did were before, I think—like *Starlight* and *Natural Man.*

Interviewer: Once *Anna Lucasta* was done on Broadway, you then became recognized as a major young acting talent, didn't you?

Dee: Yes. But even before that, in Harlem, I remember feeling recognized, feeling special in a way. It was that kind of community. I was singled out. They made me know that I was going to be an actor. When the government came to cast its propaganda film for the GIs—it was about VD; I didn't know it!—I was late for this audition. When I got there, they were about to leave, but they waited and they spoke to me, and indeed I did get the part. I was the nice girl who had it.

Interviewer: You didn't know, though, when you were auditioning what it was about! Was the situation for Negro actors very difficult in the mainstream American theater at the time of *Anna Lucasta?*

Dee: Oh yes.

Interviewer: It was a very segregated theater.

Dee: Yes, very. I remember having dreams of going to be an actor, going to be a star out in Hollywood. I was disabused of that notion. That would not happen to me as a black girl. It happens to you, the realization of the fact that because you are black certain things won't happen for you. First I thought I was going to do cartoons for Disney.

Interviewer: Voice-overs?

Dee: No, do cartoons, drawings, because I could draw. That intrigued me. And then I just knew I was going to go out to Hollywood and be a starlet. But then it hits you. It occurs to you at a certain time in your life—

Interviewer: Do you remember when that happened?

Dee: I'd been writing letters to studios all over. It was somebody in the library, because my mother used to send us to the library where the theater books were—upstairs. On Saturdays, they had poetry-writing contests. I won a box of jelly beans for a story I wrote. So it was someone there, Roberta Bosley, someone who didn't want me to get hurt. Or something like that. Because I just knew that I was going to Hollywood; but she told me.

Interviewer: But not long after that you played nontraditional roles. You played Cordelia in *King Lear* at the Shakespeare festival in Stratford in 1965. That wasn't an all-black cast, was it?

Dee: No, but that was much later in my life.

Interviewer: Was that the first nontraditionally black role that you played?

Dee: No, I don't think so, but I don't have a very good memory about things in my past. So I don't remember. Surely the most significant was doing *Taming of the Shrew* and Cordelia.

Interviewer: That was in 1965 too. Was that a major difference for you, to be able to do those roles usually played by a white actress in an established, well-known company?

Dee: Yes, but what got me there was working much earlier with [Howard] Da Silva and [Morris] Carnovsky, who were my teachers. We went up to Crystal Lake and did *The World of Sholem Aleichem.* That was around the time of the McCarthy period and the consciousness of racism and that kind of thing. I met a group of people because we were politically active. I made a speech for the Rosenbergs at Carnegie Hall—against them being killed. I remember thinking, "Why are we doing this?" We were doing it because all of our lives were involved with racial injustices and lynchings and fund-raisers and this and that and the other. That's always been part of my life. Always there were whites in the hall, always there were Jews in the hall. When I was asked to speak for the Rosenbergs, it wouldn't have ever occurred to me to say no. I was shocked when somebody suggested that I should not speak for the Rosenbergs. So I just did it because that's what we did. We'd known all these people all of our lives.

Interviewer: They were not all black. Rather, many of the people that you had been politically active with were white.

Dee: They were white, a lot of them were Jews, a lot of them were Communists. But that never made any difference. As I look back on it now, oh my God, it was an exciting time. I just didn't happen to be a joiner of anything, because my mother wasn't. But I was always involved, connected.

Interviewer: And that political activism led directly to Carnovsky?

Dee: That led me to Carnovsky, Da Silva, Marge Nelson, Phoebe Brand, that whole crowd that had gotten out of Hollywood. They showed me a way of being an actor without going to Hollywood. They introduced us to special writing for causes, for people. They introduced us to all of that because we hadn't known that. It was an astonishing time for us. I'm sorry it was so terrible for so many people who lost their jobs, their sanity, their lives.

Interviewer: Carnovsky played Lear in that Stratford production, didn't he?

Dee: My teacher. I never will forget that, watching my teacher. It was an exciting time for me. I had gone to his classes, so I was enormously pleased to be working with him in *Lear*. I never got over the fact that I was playing with Morris; all these people filled me with awe and great respect. I remember one day I was standing backstage waiting for his entrance because I came in soon after he did. I kept peeking into his dressing room. The light was on and he was back there and people were talking and he was smoking a cigarette. I said, "Oh my God, he's going to be on in less than two minutes." When was he going to prepare as he had instructed us to prepare? I got so nervous for him I was going to stop him and let him know when his cue was going to come up. Thank God I didn't. I just stood there and watched him. I didn't think he was going to make the cue. When he came out, somebody put his robe on him, he put out the cigarette, walked to the edge of the stage, and walked out. He was a whole different guy. I couldn't imagine that, a few seconds ago, he was back there in that dressing room. I saw him become Lear just instantly.

Interviewer: Can you do that?

Dee: Now I can do it, thanks to Paul Mann, who taught me. I learned so many things. Now I can appreciate the fact that we don't know how we learn. We don't know how we bring out that which we already have. Who unlocks us? What unlocks us? You never know. That moment with Morris was one thing. I had to put that into perspective later, though, after I had worked with Paul Mann. Mann showed me how to get access through everything that you see, touch, and reason with. He taught me how to process the information that comes out of the atmosphere. It comes from people, it comes from colors, it comes from music, it comes from anything. That's what I got from Paul, not that he literally set it down. I suppose one of the things that I do remember most about Paul that brought me to an understanding of the craft was he brought in a newspaper and sat there reading an editorial and talking to us. Then we went to a scene which applied to what he had just read. He showed me something about preparing the territory for the moment that I hadn't known before. How did you get from point A to point B in yourself? Paul showed me how to track a path. That's what Paul showed me how to do. If you keep going in that route, it gets easier to get from point A to point B. That's what Paul did for me. You can't say to somebody exactly, "This is how you go there." From that newspaper article to that scene: anything is liable to trigger the agitation from the essence, as Morris used to say, what agitates the essence.

Interviewer: Do you think that's a very individual thing? Did you just happen to respond well to what he told you?

Dee: I think it's essential for every actor, but we each come to it differently. The very person of Paul taught me so much, even when I wouldn't do some things he asked me to do.

Interviewer: That's been the most interesting thing for us, as we've interviewed people for this book: so many different marvelous actors come at the craft from different approaches.

Dee: But you do come to it.

Interviewer: How do you come at it? When you have a new role to do, how do you prepare for it? Do you approach it intellectually? Do you approach it in terms of the things on the stage with you?

Dee: Now I don't worry it like I used to. When I did Cassandra in the *Agamemnon,* for hours I would pray and I would sing. I would prepare myself and prepare myself for so long. Now, like Morris, I don't need much time. I can be there because Paul, Morris, and, to some extent, Lloyd Richards showed me how to just get what I need from all these things that surround an actor—hair, eyes, the vibrations, aunts, uncles, the size of the room. What do I need for this moment? Now I don't sweat it like I used to. A few months ago I did a reading with Uta Hagen; I was so happy. I had never worked with Uta. She hadn't been in my realm of people. I found I didn't have to worry about reading the thing—because I was so busy and I didn't have time to read it. Because of the techniques that I've picked up, I can now just pick up the words off the page, and we draw it through us, we drag it through ourselves. On the way, we make the connections we need to make. Does that make sense?

Interviewer: Of course. What you're talking about, though, too, is experience, isn't it? You've been doing it for many years.

Dee: Everything becomes food for the moment.

Interviewer: You also played Gertrude in *Hamlet* for Joe Papp. What do you remember about that performance and that production?

Dee: Let me tell you something. For all that I've just now told you, there are challenges. Sometimes I just can't find it. Gertrude was one of those parts that I had a rough time finding. Maybe it was because of Joe's high expectations for me; I really don't know. I never felt that I clicked in, like the piece fits in the puzzle and it's there and you don't have to worry about it. It's just like the degrees that happen in a performance. To the extent that you connect, you can relax; you can't do any more. You're there. But there are some nights when you don't quite fit in, when you have to keep nudging yourself in to fit. That's how I felt about Gertrude; I never really felt I got that character. Whether it was the arrogance, the elegance, something was missing for me; some subconscious block was going on.

Interviewer: Do you think that if you had had a longer time to do it, you might have gotten it?

Dee: I think I might have done it better later.

Interviewer: Do you find that sometimes difficult roles improve in the course of a run when you have had the luxury of doing them for a while?

Dee: That's right. Also, people come with preconceived notions. For instance, everybody has expectations about certain black characters—the granny, the auntie. You've got to find something special about that person; because of who you are, the character becomes different. You have to buck all those things that people expect you to say. That character's become a stereotype, a shorthand for all the very specific people. It's just like the maid or the hooker; there's all kinds. When Lorraine Hansberry came up with *The Sign in Sidney Brustein's Window,* I was amazed at how critically she was put down.

Interviewer: It wasn't what they expected.

Dee: Yes, how dare you be a black girl and not talk about your troubles and being black and mean old white folks and poor Negroes and stuff like that? How dare you not do this? I can't blame the whole of America, the mental process being kind of American in the first place. You really have to deal with racism in your psyche. Even the most marvelous of people are teethed on racism. This is a racist country, for all of its marvelous things. It's exciting, it's conscious, it's aware, it talks about it, it acknowledges it to an extent. You get these stereotyped white folks in the black plays. I remember this because there would always be the mea culpa white folks in the plays. Then white people would call it a great play, because you were castigating white folks.

Interviewer: Now that you have a choice of roles, on what basis do you select what you want to do?

Dee: I really like to do things that I feel excited about when I read them on the page. Characters that don't appeal to me are those types that have been written over and over. I've been doing Ruth from *Raisin in the Sun* so much— the colored woman behind the ironing board. When Lloyd [Richards] talked to me about doing *Raisin,* I so much wanted to do Beneatha.

Interviewer: You would rather have done Beneatha than Ruth?

Dee: I begged him. I had no idea that he was even thinking about me as Ruth. He hadn't told me to read Ruth; he just told me to read the play. I assumed I was going to do Beneatha, because that's the part I wanted. After I saw Diana Sands, I could understand his choice. Also, I'm a good backgrounder. I'm a good canvas; you can paint all over me. I wasn't aware of that in myself at that time. But Lloyd was. He said, "Ruby, I need you to do Ruth." That's what he said; I never will forget it.

Interviewer: He was right, wasn't he?

Dee: Yes, but I was indignant at the time. I wanted to be in that play.

Interviewer: Talk a little bit about that production. Was it exciting to be part of it?

Dee: Oh yes; but at first, here I was onstage so much, with everything happening in front of me. Background. But you get to appreciate that role also. In every culture there's that woman who's there—against which everything else happens. Were she not there, things couldn't go on. There would be a hole. That's what *Raisin* showed me in marvelous detail for the year that I played it night after night after night.

Interviewer: How was it working with Claudia McNeil? I'll never forget that performance.

Dee: Neither will I, because Claudia, first of all, had the most magnificent contralto voice I ever heard. I know Sidney Poitier was very unhappy because for the audiences at curtain time Claudia was the center; Claudia received the raves. It took me years to find out why. It was because Claudia is that part of the American cultural scene that is very necessary to white America. She's Mama, Mammy, keeping the black folks in, keeping that wild boy calm. She's making the difference to the peace of mind for the majority of the population. That was Claudia, and that was why she was so marvelously accepted.

Interviewer: But can't that character be seen today as much more ambivalent than that? She holds Walter back in many ways. Can't she be seen as a very selfish person in certain ways?

Dee: Well, to tell you the truth, it took me a long time to deal with this piece because I thought of Claudia as a modern-day referee between black society and white society. White society could feel comfortable as long as Mama was on the scene. It was the New Day nanny.

Interviewer: What role does Ruth play in that dynamic?

Dee: She is trying to make this young black spirit responsible and an upstanding citizen and do the right thing. She's helping Mama in a sense. Part of me is convinced that it was a hit because there were two women trying to get Walter Lee to act right, to be an acceptable member of society. I felt so sorry for Sidney. Also, as I look back on it, although Lorraine's family was in real estate, the idea that it was some great triumph because you're moving to a white neighborhood has always rubbed me the wrong way. Somebody asked me when I moved to Westchester, "Why do you want to move over there? That's already integrated. Why don't you come over here, where it's not integrated? We need some blacks." Suddenly I felt guilty and, at the same time, afraid of something in myself. I don't really want to live among anybody that I have to be on my best behavior for. I don't want to prove myself at home. I wouldn't want to move into a neighborhood where I was the first one.

Interviewer: You were also in the film of *Raisin*—and you've done a lot of other films. What is the difference between stage acting and film acting?

Dee: I think on the stage you're exploring the limits of yourself. How loud and how strong and how big and how wide is the human entity? How much are we like giants and kings? Can we touch the sky in the arts? In film, I think we're taking pictures of thoughts—and that's intriguing.

Interviewer: How do you mean that?

Dee: Well, for example, if you look at me in a certain way I can almost tell what you're thinking. When one eyebrow goes up, that's a whole page of literature. The camera can catch that.

Interviewer: You can't do that on the stage.

Dee: There are subtleties onstage, but I think the camera can photograph the soul. It's maximums through minimums.

Interviewer: Do you find film acting enjoyable, challenging, or is it just different from stage acting?

Dee: I think one also depends on the other. Because once you know dimensions, once I know how wide I can stretch my arms, I can then know when I have to make a small gesture. I can know the proportion, what on stage equals what on film. I can just sit there and think for five minutes. I think the stage is remarkable to the extent that we can touch soul to soul. We can affect other people and know it. There's a tangible thing that happens. That's no different than carrying a wireless telephone so that I can connect with you. Just as I can connect through my cell phone, I believe that human beings can connect with each other.

Interviewer: Because it's a live art?

Dee: The same thing is true in film, but I *know* it when I'm on the stage. I can feel it.

Interviewer: How important are the other actors onstage? If as Gertrude you had had a different actor playing Claudius or Hamlet, might it have been dramatically different, or not?

Dee: Yes, I think it might have been. The most marvelous thing about being an actor is that, at the best moments, you can relax so much that you can open and let people come in and you can let them out.

Interviewer: What are some memorable productions that you recall, other than Carnovsky's Lear?

Dee: Oh, I think about Alice Childress's *Wedding Band*. I think about *Boesman and Lena,* the Athol Fugard piece I did.

Interviewer: Are those two of your favorite roles?

Dee: Dramatic roles, yes. Of course, I loved doing *Long Day's Journey into Night* also. When I've been efficient enough to allow myself to relax, and then come in when I need the moment, then I feel that it's successful. Or relaxed enough to really tune in to somebody else, to really tune in. I'm not worrying about my next line. That's why I like to learn my lines right away, so I don't have to think about them.

Interviewer: What made those three roles that you've just mentioned so important to you as you look back?

Dee: What has been most satisfying is when I've thought I've been here for them, there in the moment, as if I really am. In *Boesman and Lena,* I felt like I really was Lena. It was a four-layered character, at least four layers. She was acting at so many levels. You would like to know these paths that I told you about so you can relax. When that happens, that's the most satisfying— when I can really let this person come in and walk me. Do you know what I'm saying? It can be dangerous also. I think Peter Sellers was one of those actors that was dangerous. I don't know why. But you can do that. When those people take you away, but you're in control; you don't want to close up your gates.

Interviewer: I can still remember Lena calling the name of Boesman. I can still hear you calling the name. What did you do with your voice by way of training it?

Dee: Do you know what that voice business is? Oh, that's another whole subject. They don't do this anymore, but at Hunter I studied phonetics and voice and all that—because I was a speech and drama major at first. I changed that after I discovered I would never be a star and never go to Hollywood. I became a language major. I studied literature, and I did phonetics— how sounds are made and that kind of thing. Then, my mother insisted that I take music lessons; she wanted me to be a singer. I could never sing. There's this whole thing of placement and voice. You can score the human voice, and an actor must be able to go anyplace with the voice, just as a singer can. The characters you play are going to have to use those ranges and rhythms.

Interviewer: You've also directed. Are there advantages or disadvantages to being an actor trying to tell other actors how to act? Do you feel you have an advantage?

Dee: I do know this one thing, as an actor I'm very directable. But I see actors and I do know something about them. I can help them go someplace with themselves.

Interviewer: Because you're an actor?

Dee: Yes. I think I know how to get them from one point of themselves to another. But I haven't practiced it enough to be sure. For example, I always have to be reminded that the actors need a break now. It's like a piece of clay you're working with or dough or something; it just is making a form, but you've got to take a break. I've had intimations of this when I've said to an actor, "You're giving me somebody we've already heard before. Let's just forget about that. Let's move from one point to the other." They're about to break through, or to move into some other space. It's like a symphony. I think I could be a good coach. I think I could tell actors about rhythms and colors and pitch and how words have character and emotion and how nothing is static. I'm full of all this, and I wish I could find some way to document it. I think I could make a tape of an actor speaking. Then I could go through the tape with the actor and talk about how you get the character to inform the word. Not only the way that it's pitched, but the rhythm, because words are very alive. Words are just as alive to actors as notes are to musicians, and until we realize that we're missing something. I think English actors know it. An actor like Jack Lemmon: he's one of them. Alan Arkin is another one. I'm trying to think of these actors who know that you can score their speech in terms of the rhythm and the meaning and the moment. I don't want to be mystical at all, but I think it's part of something that's very dynamic that we as actors are in danger of overlooking and forgetting. I think we're being made to be ashamed of words and intellect and things like that.

Interviewer: Just do it. It's the notion that you just get up there and do it. You don't have to think about it; you don't have to have anybody help you.

Dee: So we're all sounding alike.

Interviewer: The whole emotional range of *Boesman and Lena* was in the various ways in which you would say his name. Was that deliberate?

Dee: Well, it was deliberate in this sense: not because I was hearing the pitch, but something informed the pitch. Do you understand? The pitch is informed. When I get onstage, if, for example, the information doesn't hit right and the pitch is wrong, it throws the rest of the thing off for me. I didn't get where I was supposed to get. Something happened in here and I didn't get what I was supposed to get—so it throws everything else off.

Interviewer: As an actor, you've worked with a lot of different directors. What is the ideal actor-director relationship from your point of view as an actor? What do you want from a director?

Dee: I think I want a director to keep the big picture in view, because I might not have it. I love a conductor. I love a director who knows what the hell he's doing. Please don't have me tell you what this is. I can do something about the specifics, but only he knows what it's for. This is especially so in films, because only the director has the big picture—and he knows how I fit. I have not studied all these other characters. He has to marry the opposites. I like the director to feel that he knows that. Then I'm comfortable. He can ask me to do anything and I'll do it. I'll do it even if it's wrong, you understand. So I have to have faith that he's telling me what is right. I'm the kind of actor that I'll do it if he tells me, even if it's wrong. I'm a director's actor.

Interviewer: What is a role that you've never done that you would love to do?

Dee: Well, number one, what I've always wanted to do—now I'd just be happy to see it done and filmed, and it would be a marvelous film—is Zora Neale Hurston's Janie. I'd love to do that. Of course, now I've missed that—for my age group. There are some writers I want to look at. I wanted to do Merle Kinbona in Paule Marshall's *The Chosen Place, the Timeless People.* I spent two years of my life breaking down that novel. Nobody asked me. I met a director I thought was going to be able to do that. It was a marvelous book, still is. I'm into "Books with Legs." I've been doing that at Crossroads Theatre. That's where I mount a book much like *Nicholas Nickleby.* The major thing I did like that was *The Disappearance* by Rosa Guy, a murder mystery. The guy who did the sets for *Nicholas Nickleby* did the sets for her book too, and I put a score to it. I had some marvelous interest in it; but I hadn't done my paperwork right, the business things. Everybody wondered, where was I getting all this money? It was out of my piggy bank, my own money. I bought the music; I had to do everything.

Interviewer: Are there any classical roles that you'd like to do?

Dee: I regret very much that I turned down a couple of roles.

Interviewer: What were they?

Dee: Emlyn Williams asked me to do the black version of *Wilhelmina* years ago. I wasn't interested because I'd just fallen in love with all of these black playwrights whose universality I felt was in question. I thought they were as universal as Shakespeare or anything. It was all these authors that I wanted to see done. I regret not doing these things, because I would have positioned myself so I might have been able to call the shots now. I might have been able to have done Janie or some of the characters in, say, for instance, Toni Morrison. I'm electrified by her; she's very much influenced by [Jean] Toomer too, you know, and Hurston.

Interviewer: Where do you fall in the recent debate between Robert Brustein and August Wilson? Wilson objects to all-black casts for traditionally white plays. You were in the black *Glass Menagerie* at Arena. You mentioned the black *Long Day's Journey* you did. Do you feel that it was good for black theater to do those?

Dee: Oh yes, yes. I'm so sorry that I turned down things I did. You go from point to point, or for some political reason you don't do that. It's a whole other subject, do you know what I'm saying? It's a whole other subject, this development as an actor. I've regretted turning down some roles. I have some letters I've written to directors for some bad reasons. I've found that directors are very malleable, they're suggestible. They'll listen. I remember one movie I did. I didn't want to do this part in Baldwin's *Go Tell It on the Mountain,* and I said, "I'll do it if you'll listen to me." I said, "Look at all the stereotyped things you have in the script." You know what, they listened to me and they cut those things out.

Interviewer: When you say you turned down these opportunities to play roles that were traditionally white roles, you did it because you felt you should be doing something for black theater?

Dee: Yes, because I wanted to do something for the black writers.

Interviewer: But later on you came to realize that, and that's why you did *Glass Menagerie* and *Long Day's Journey,* because you realized that these were roles that you could do.

Dee: Yes, oh yes. I want to say that, too, to August Wilson: by God, if we cannot do these roles for each other we're cutting each other off at the knees. If we're sensitive artists, we should be able to do anything, within reason. If it's a story about a giant, that's not going to work.

Interviewer: That limits black actors today—to say that they can't do James Tyrone.

Dee: Oh yes, oh yes.

George Grizzard

George Grizzard was born George Cooper Grizzard in Roanoke Rapids, North Carolina, on April 1, 1928. He graduated from the University of North Carolina and studied with Sanford Meisner, Philip Burton, and Alan Schneider. His stage debut was as Miner in The Corn Is Green *in 1944. His Broadway debut was as Hank Griffith in* The Desperate Hours *in 1955. Other Broadway roles include Shep Stearns,* The Disenchanted *(1958); Harold Rutland Jr.,* Face of a Hero *(1960); Ronnie Johnson,* Big Fish, Little Fish *(1961); and Nick,* Who's Afraid of Virginia Woolf? *(1962). At the Guthrie Theater he played the title role, Hamlet; Clerk,* The Miser; *Solyony in* The Three Sisters *(all in 1963); title role,* Henry V; *Mosca,* Volpone; *and The Dauphin,* Saint Joan *(all in 1964). Back on Broadway he played Tom,* The Glass Menagerie *(1965); Jack Barnstable, Salesman, Herbert,* You Know I Can't Hear You When the Water's Running *(1967); Vincent,* The Gingham Dog *(1969); Julius Rosenberg,* Inquest *(1970); Bernie Dodd,* The Country Girl *(1972); Lucifer,* The Creation of the World and*

Other Business *(1972)*; *Tony Cavendish*, The Royal Family *(1975)*; *Billy, Sidney, Stu*, California Suite *(1976)*; *John Tanner*, Man and Superman *(1978)*; *John*, The Beach House *(1988)*; *Henry Harper*, Another Antigone *(1988)*; *Tobias*, A Delicate Balance *(1996; Tony Award)*; *Cap'n Andy*, Show Boat *(1998)*, *and Eddie's Grandfather*, Ancestral Voices *(1999)*.

His films include From the Terrace *(1960)*, Advise and Consent *(1962)*, Warning Shot *(1967)*, Happy Birthday, Wanda June *(1971)*, Comes a Horseman *(1978)*, Firepower *(1979)*, Seems Like Old Times *(1980)*, Wrong Is Right *(1982)*, Bachelor Party *(1984)*, Wonder Boys *(2000)*, *and* Small Time Crooks *(2000)*.

Mr. Grizzard's television shows include A Case of Libel *(1968)*, Teacher, Teacher *(1969)*, Travis Logan, D.A. *(1970)*, Pueblo *(1973)*, The Stranger Within *(1974)*, The Adams Chronicles *(1976)*, The Night Rider *(1979)*, The Oldest Living Graduate *(1980; Emmy Award)*, Attica *(1980)*, Not in Front of the Children *(1982)*, The Shady Hill Kidnapping *(1983)*, Midas Valley *(1985)*, International Airport *(1985)*, Embassy *(1985)*, Robert Kennedy: His Times *(1985)*, Under Siege *(1986)*, That Secret Sunday *(1986)*, The Deliberate Stranger *(1986)*, Perry Mason: The Case of the Scandalous Scoundrel *(1987)*, David *(1988)*, Studio 5-B *(1989)*, False Witness *(1989)*, An Enemy of the People *(1990)*, Caroline? *(1990)*, L'Amérique en otage *(1991)*, Not in My Family *(1993)*, Simple Justice *(1993)*, Queen *(1993)*, Triumph over Disaster: The Hurricane Andrew Story *(1993)*, Scarlett *(1994)*, Sisters and Other Strangers *(1997)*, *and guest appearances on* Goodyear Television Playhouse, United States Steel Hour, Alfred Hitchcock Presents, The Twilight Zone, Spenser: For Hire, The Golden Girls, The Five Mrs. Buchanans, *and* Law and Order.

This interview took place on November 15, 1993.

•———————————————————————•

Interviewer: Where is your hometown, and where did you get your schooling? Did you have any kind of formal education in theater and acting?

Grizzard: I was born in North Carolina. I grew up in Washington, D.C., where I went to Alice Deal Junior High and to Woodrow Wilson High School. Then I spent four wonderful years in Chapel Hill at the University of North Carolina. I studied advertising. I went there to study drama, and I joined a fraternity. I got in a play right away. The dress rehearsal night was the same night as the formal pledge ceremony at the fraternity house; so, of course, I went to the dress rehearsal. The next day this man came to me and said, "Now, George, you're going to have to make up your mind whether you're going to be a KA or a faggot." I was scared to death. I was seventeen and I had never been away from home; so I became a rah-rah fraternity man for four years. I did another play on the day I graduated, and I worked at advertising in

Washington for a year until I went to work at the Arena Stage. I didn't study acting really until I got to New York. I studied with Sanford Meisner at the Neighborhood Playhouse. I kept going back to him when I would come back and forth between Washington and New York. He was a wonderful teacher, who had been in the original Group Theatre.

Interviewer: You were part of the first season at Arena Stage, weren't you?

Grizzard: It started in August of 1950. I was in the third production, so I didn't start until October. I can't believe it's been that long, but it was quite a while ago.

Interviewer: That was at the old Hippodrome, wasn't it?

Grizzard: Yes. It was down at Ninth Street. It had been a movie house, and they made it into an arena theater. The theater was there five years; I didn't stay that long. Then they went to what they called the Old Vat, the brewing company building, before they got the new theater built.

Interviewer: I still refer to it as the new theater too. That theater was built in 1960.

Grizzard: That's the new theater. I have to tell you a story. I was asked to come back one time to the Arena, and it didn't work out. I had done *Our Town* there, playing George, in about 1952. I saw they were going to do it again and I thought, "Well, wouldn't this be wonderful. I'll call and offer my services to play the Stage Manager this time." Then I read this brochure that said, "Bob Prosky will be returning with his legendary performance as the Stage Manager." I thought, "I won't bother them."

Interviewer: I came to Arena after you had left, and we were in the Old Vat at that point. But I went to look at the original theater, the Hippodrome. They had kept the configuration that Arena had built into it, but by this time it was a burlesque house and the marquee read BURLESQUE IN THE ROUND.

Grizzard: And it went downhill from there!

Interviewer: Yes, it did. That's what happens to so many legit houses. It has happened in New York, along 42nd Street. It's a shame to lose those marvelous old theaters. It doesn't happen in London and Paris as much, does it?

Grizzard: I guess not, no. The first Arena was beautiful when it opened because it was so clean. It had this gray carpet, and there were three rows on two sides and seven rows on the other two sides. There was one bathroom for men—audience and actors—and one for women. We built the sets in the lobby. Finally, they decided to spend a little money, and they rented a room on the back of the next building, which we used as a dressing room because the original dressing room was under the South Tier. There was an orange shower curtain that separated the men from the women, and we all dressed in one room. We were doing things like *School for Scandal,* with ladies in hoop skirts and big clothes. That's what makes theater wonderful. The beginnings of theaters are so exciting because after the third year people try to tear them down; so you should always try to get in on the first two or three years.

Interviewer: I've heard stories about that. There was no way of crossing back from one side of the stage to another. Quite often you had to go outside.

Grizzard: Around the block.

Interviewer: And if it was raining, somebody with an umbrella had to go with you.

Grizzard: When I was doing the witch boy in *Dark of the Moon,* I had to make that kind of entrance; I had Henry Oliver, who was a very large man, and Pernell Roberts, who was even larger, walk on either side of me around the block because it was skid row in that neighborhood. Here I was looking like a chorus boy in all black and the eyebrows up to here and I thought, "I think I'll walk with people." It was wonderful in those days, but it was just this side of amateur theater.

Interviewer: Was *Dark of the Moon* your first big role at Arena Stage?

Grizzard: Yes, *Dark of the Moon* was my first leading role at Arena. It was something, because up to that point they had only done costume dramas because they didn't have to pay royalties. You could do Shakespeare and Sheridan because the playwrights were dead. The critics in Washington kept saying, "When are you going to do something modern? Come on, this is ridiculous, stop doing all this." Ed Mangum, who started the theater, said, "All right, you want something modern?" So he did *Three Men on a Horse* and it backfired. It was the biggest hit they had ever had, and it ran for ten weeks. Everything else had run three—and you had to stretch it to get it to three. Normally, you opened at Arena on Tuesday night and then Wednesday you started rehearsal for the next play because in three weeks you had to open it; so we opened *Three Men on a Horse,* and the next day I started rehearsing *Dark of the Moon.* I rehearsed and I rehearsed and I rehearsed because we ran for ten weeks. They said that it was the most polished opening night they had ever seen! We finally took a week off about the seventh week and just rested because we were so tired of rehearsing it. It was great fun.

Interviewer: Is it difficult to go back and forth between a theater-in-the-round like the Arena and a traditional stage?

Grizzard: In theater-in-the-round you've got to keep moving so that people can see you from different places. You do have to remember that the audience is not on one side. I act a lot with my back now because I started at the Arena. It's wonderful for a young actor to start out in an arena theater because there is no hiding place. You can't go upstage and say, "What's the line?" You have to know what you are doing, and you have to work with your entire body. Some young actors will come toward you on the stage and then they will immediately take one step above you, go upstage. It's just instinct with young actors. They want to move upstage, and I used to say, "Fine, do that. I can act with my back. I'll turn my back to the audience." There are wonderful stories about when we did *Dark of the Moon*. There was a railing at the old Hippodrome; the two girl witches would come out in the dark and would lean on the railing. One night, this woman in the audience had her hand on the railing when Ethel Casey came out and went to lean. The woman said, "Oh!" pulled her hand back, and said, "How do you find your way in the dark?" Ethel didn't say anything, and the woman tapped again and said, "How do you find your way in in the dark?" Ethel said, "It's because I'm a witch." I ended up in somebody's lap in the front row one night because you had to learn to spot things and get reflections off things in order to find where you were when you came in in the dark. I'd spotted the wrong thing, and I ended up in somebody's lap. I remember the woman turning to her husband and saying, "Did you do that?"

Interviewer: In what fundamental ways is the American theater different from the time when you first began acting?

Grizzard: There was less television and more theater then. Now entertainment is given away free, so people don't pay for it as much as they used to. Even if it's very cheap, they don't go as much—because there is too much free entertainment now. Because of that, everybody is a critic now that they have all of these things coming into their living rooms. I think television has kind of stopped people from going to the live theater. A lot of people have never been to the live theater. There was no television when I started out. Television, I think, probably started in the late forties or early fifties. Not everybody on our block had a set, so you would go to the live theater or to the movie house. In those days, we went to the movies, the double features and the triple features. That's one way it's changed.

Interviewer: I think it has changed just from the actor's viewpoint. I have two sons who are actors. There is more opportunity for the actor to act today, but there is far less of an opportunity for an actor to make a living. There is a lot of work in workshop theaters and small theaters, which do very good work, yet I don't think the actors make as much. That is certainly true in New York and Los Angeles. In Los Angeles there are a hundred small-contract theaters.

Grizzard: There were no professional theaters in Washington when Arena started.

Interviewer: That's right.

Grizzard: There was amateur theater. I worked in advertising, and at night I worked with amateur theater groups. I did five plays in a year in amateur theater. Then the Arena started and I quit advertising; I was making thirty-five dollars a week as the flunkie's assistant. I stormed down to the Arena Stage and demanded (I say I demanded; I probably groveled and begged and pleaded for) an audition. They happened to have a play coming up that needed a juvenile. I auditioned the next day, on Saturday, and on Tuesday I went to work as an actor. It was a wonderful thing because I went from thirty-five dollars a week to fifteen dollars—but I was doing what I wanted to do, and that was the good part. When we played, when they let the grown-ups in, the audience, I think I got thirty-five dollars a week. After a year, Arena went Equity, which is the actors' union. Ed Mangum said, "Why don't you come back now and do one play and get your Equity card?" I did, and we got fifty-five dollars a week, which was the Equity minimum. I made that for the entire time I was at the Arena, for three years. But I saved enough to get to New York. Things didn't cost quite as much then.

Interviewer: What are the differences, if any, between acting in the regional theater and in New York on Broadway?

Grizzard: Money—and also the chance to work with more experienced people. Regional theaters are wonderful places for young people to start out and to learn the craft. By the time you get to Broadway, usually the people are more experienced and know what they are doing, so you have a much more professional arena in which to work.

Interviewer: I think that is true sometimes, but I think the reverse is true fairly often as well. I think it was more true back in the fifties and sixties; nowadays, Broadway depends on the regional theater as a source.

Grizzard: Well, I haven't done regional theater for a long time! But I'm really tired of working with bad people who don't know what they're doing. I started with Alan Schneider, who was a great disciplinarian, and I got spoiled. I really don't enjoy working with people who don't take it as seriously as I do. I'd rather not do it. I'd really rather stay in the country. I don't have that *need* to act anymore. Unless it is going to be a wonderful experience, I don't want to do it.

Interviewer: Given a few free wishes for the American theater, what would you like to see changed? I suppose it's what you just talked about. I agree as far as discipline is concerned, and Alan Schneider certainly was that sort of director. A lot of actors were frightened to death of him.

Grizzard: Yes. He expected you to work as hard as he did, and almost nobody in the world did.

Interviewer: No, they didn't.

Grizzard: He was not good with women. He didn't know much about women. He had a beautiful wife and a family, and she was a saint to put up with him. There are about five actresses I know that if you mention his name they just go screaming out of the room. I got between him and Cicely Tyson when we were doing a play together because he was crippling her. He didn't know how not to do that. It was a shame, because he had so much to offer as a director. He was a theater intellect. He had a wonderful brain about the theater, but he didn't have a public relations department at all. I started with Alan when I was sixteen. I was a high school student, and he was a graduate student at Catholic University. I was what he called "a crawl-on" in *Lute Song;* I was a Chinese beggar. I didn't even get to walk on, I had to crawl on. Later on at the Arena, we did about twelve or fifteen plays together, and then I did five plays on Broadway with him. He was a great influence in my life.

Interviewer: Can you describe your acting process? How do you get inside a character?

Grizzard: I don't think that's anybody's business. I've always thought that how much money you make, who you sleep with, and how you act are no-body's business. I think they are very private things. It's so personal that I think it's hard to share with people. Even with other actors it is difficult.

Interviewer: There is an elaborate dance, in a way, that most actors do around each other when that sort of thing comes up. When you are in the re-hearsal process, you don't go over and tell another actor, "Why don't you do it this way?"

Grizzard: Maureen Stapleton would never talk about acting; it's something she couldn't do. Finally, we were doing a play together, and we had a session with the audience after the matinee one day. It was high school students. We were doing *The Glass Menagerie,* which had by then become a classic. They kept saying, "How do you act? How do you do it?" Maureen finally said, "Well, you read the play a couple of times, and you figure out who you are and how you fit into the play, and then you play what you are at that time in your life." It's strange, but she does that, and nobody does it better. She is just bril-liant at playing Maureen, but she won't come an inch away. She won't char-acterize; she plays Maureen in every situation. When she first did *The Rose Tattoo,* she was one Serafina. The second time she did it she had gone through two divorces, a nervous breakdown, losing a hundred pounds, and she was a different Serafina; and she played Maureen at that time in her life. But it was an interesting Serafina.

Interviewer: I think actors learn in the process of doing, and that's why they can't talk too well about it. A director generally can visualize a thing and say what he wants and what his point of view of the production is. Actors have to do it, and that's how they learn how to do it, and it's different every time. Most of us are rather insecure. I don't know whether you feel this, but every time I start a play my immediate reaction is "I don't really know how to do this." Then, when you've gotten through it a little bit and it's ended up with some degree of success or what have you, the thought comes: "I've fooled them again! They haven't found out yet that I don't know how to do this." I've heard other actors say the same stuff.

Grizzard: Are we allowed to talk about television?

Interviewer: I think so.

Grizzard: I was doing a live television show one night with Diana Lynn, the lovely Diana Lynn. We opened it necking, and they were doing the countdown, "Ten, nine . . . ," and she started to laugh. I said, "What's the matter?" She said, "Suppose this is the night they find out!" We opened the show with both of us laughing and kissing, and they had no idea what caused it. All of a sudden there are going to be twenty million people and they might find out you can't do it and you never knew how to do it! We all feel that every time we start. If you go to the theater and somebody does it all for you and makes it very easy, you tend to look at the other person. What you have to do is have this mystery to lure an audience in order to make them do part of your work, to involve them. Don't do it all for them. Then it's like water running over them. Make them ask, "What is he doing?" That's what involves an audience.

Interviewer: That's what's best, I think, about theater as opposed to the other media. It's an event that is built anew every evening between the audience and the actor. Sometimes it works and, frankly, sometimes it doesn't; but it's a group effort. With a film, the film doesn't interact, but at least the audience interacts. Now we've gotten down to television where sometimes it's one person who is working with an electronic image; and we've lost something very elemental about the experience, I feel, when that happens. It's what theater should be celebrated for. Who were the strongest influences in your career?

Grizzard: Alan Schneider and Tyrone Guthrie were the greatest influences in my life. Of actors who have influenced me, Jason Robards did. I've done three plays in New York with Jason, and a movie and a television show. Most of the work I did with Alan was naturalistic theater. With Guthrie, it was the big plays—*Hamlet* and *Henry V* and *Volpone* and *Three Sisters.* He wouldn't let me be in the American plays, because he said, "You already know how to do that. You come here to grow and stretch." He was a wonderfully funny, delicious man. He said one of the great things about the critics that is so freeing for an actor. He said, "Everyone who comes to the theater has a right to his own opinion, but he doesn't have the right to have it taken seriously." That's very freeing for a young actor, even for a middle-aged actor. I don't read them much anymore, but you can't believe all of those things, good and bad, that are said about you, because you know what you are. You don't have to be told.

Interviewer: What is your opinion of theater critics?

Grizzard: I think they are very valuable for audiences and for producers. Harold Clurman and Walter Kerr are the only two critics I know who reviewed acting from a knowledgeable viewpoint, so they were the two that I read, and they've both quit writing now. The others are valuable for an audience, to pique an audience's interest, for the producer to know if he is going to run next week; but I don't think they are valuable for actors. I'm sure they're good for playwrights too—if playwrights will listen—because they can change or learn from them. I don't think they do actors any good.

Interviewer: There have certainly been a lot of plays that have been killed because of the critics' reviews, plays which could have lived a little longer— and which deserved to live. On the other hand, I don't know how we would do without them, because they also do the opposite.

Grizzard: I think that our union should fight for the word "opinion" to be printed at the top of every review that comes out. People read newspapers and they think, "This is the truth." Well, this is an opinion, and that's what I think should be at the top of every review of films, television, and plays so that people understand that it is like an editorial. It is an opinion.

Interviewer: With respect to the roles you have created, to what extent and in what ways were you allowed to be a member of the creative team in shaping the final script?

Grizzard: It depends on the playwright, I think. The good ones allow you to be a part of it because they realize that you are there to interpret what they have written. The bad ones and the young ones tend to think what they have written is written in stone, and you are there to say the words that they would say if they had the courage to stand up in front of an audience and say them. The good ones, Arthur Miller for instance, would come and work with us. With Arthur's so-called comedy, *The Creation of the World and Other Business,* in which I replaced another actor, he was rewriting all the time. He kept changing and changing. I was playing Lucifer, the serpent, the wonderful seducer of Eve. I finally said, "Arthur, look, that's just one curl of the snake's tail too many." "Fine," he said, "let's don't do it." He always would listen, as would Tyrone Guthrie. He wouldn't necessarily do it, but he would always listen. He would say, "Right. No." Or he would say, "Right. We'll do that. You're as clever as paint."

Interviewer: I watched him once. I went to see something at the Guthrie. He was directing a Greek play; I forget which one it was. He had on this old torn sweater. He was very tall, and I remember him walking back and forth down the aisle trailing cookie crumbs behind him wherever he went. He kept munching cookies all the time.

Grizzard: His feet were so far from his head that he didn't think they belonged to him, so he never wore socks—even in Minneapolis in the wintertime. He would come in and take off his galoshes, and he'd have on house slippers with no socks. He had a cold for at least six months of the year, every year. He didn't think his feet had anything to do with him at all. People have written books about him, interviewing actors and directors and designers who worked with him. They are very witty because it was kind of contagious when you were around him.

Interviewer: What was your most challenging role?

Grizzard: Hamlet. Henry V was harder because it demanded a vocal facility that I didn't have. It's one battle cry after another. It's terrible for somebody whose voice is no stronger than mine. The quiet scenes, the prayer scenes and the scenes at the camp at night, were wonderful to play; but the battle cries were just very demanding on me. When I did Hamlet (it opened the Guthrie Theatre in 1963), what was fascinating to me was the audition. I went in to meet Tyrone Guthrie. They asked me to read something, so I read a Robert Frost poem. When I got through, I looked at him and I said, "You're disappointed, aren't you?" He said, "Yes, I am rather. I expected something more rhetorical." I said, "I don't know what rhetorical means. What does rhetorical mean?" He said, "It means you talk loud, then you talk soft." I said, "I've only done one Shakespeare, so I don't know that I could do that." He said, "Well, do you think you could do it with me? I'm looking for a Hamlet." I said, "That's an interesting idea." He said, "Why don't you come back next week and we'll work on it." I went out and bought a copy of *Hamlet.* I read the play and I thought, "Oh, this is a good part." I went back and there was Douglas Campbell, who was a Scots actor, a big man with a magnificent voice, and we read the ghost scene together. I sounded like Henry Aldrich, and he had this wonderful booming voice. When we got through, Guthrie said to me, "You are a damned good actor, but you don't know anything about this, do you?" I said, "No, I don't really; but we've got a year, and I promise you I will work on it every day for a year." He said, "I think I want you to do this, but I have to talk to some people." Then he started showing me costume sketches, and I thought that was a good sign. About a week later he called or had someone call and say that yes, they would like me to come and be a part of the company and play Hamlet. I was very excited about that, and I did work on it. Every day that I didn't work on it, I thought, "Oh, next May, I'm going to really need this day." It was wonderful. I went out two weeks before the company arrived and worked with him. He answered all of my questions in about three days, I think. It was a great experience and the greatest year of my life, because I went into *Who's Afraid of Virginia Woolf?* knowing that I was going to play Hamlet. They agreed to let me out in three months, so I got to be a part of the original production of that wonderful play. Then I got to leave after three months, because it was a very painful play to be in, and run off and play a Danish prince. It was a wonderful year. It's been downhill since then!

Interviewer: How do you select a role? Does it have to strike you viscerally, or is it a more rational process?

Grizzard: It depends on how much they are paying. I'm kidding. It has to be visceral, except in television. Then I have absolutely no taste at all. I got one script once that I read and threw across the room and then I thought, "Wait a minute, there are only five people in this." So I went and picked it up again and it was awful. You probably have seen it but I thought, "I'm going to be on camera a lot because I am the husband of the leading lady and she is a very popular actress." So I did it. It was a television show called *The Stranger Within* in which Barbara Eden got knocked up by a spaceship. I was her husband, and I had had a vasectomy, and I was pretty angry because I didn't understand why she was pregnant. She took off on a spaceship at the end. They show it now; it's one of your classic bad television shows. I did that because I knew I was going to get a lot of camera. I didn't like to do television much and I thought, "If I'm going to do it, I want to be on the screen a lot." I did a movie called *Bachelor Party* against all of my agent's wishes because I wanted to go to Hollywood. I hadn't been there for about three years. I made a great deal of money as a result of the residuals that were paid on that, but it was one of the tackiest movies ever made. I was shocked that they didn't cut some of the things that I thought, "Oh well, they will cut this. They won't let this go in the theater." No, it was there. It was all there. The saving grace was that Tom Hanks was in it; it was one of Tom's first movies. He was quite wonderful. You do things for different reasons. On the stage I won't do anything unless it really means something to me, because it means too much to me. But I'll do almost anything on television—and it shows.

Interviewer: Actually, people think we sit down and make these big choices. Generally speaking, it's what is available. You don't try to "build a career." It's what's out there, what is sent to you.

Grizzard: I was a very selfish actor. I always did only what I wanted to do. I was not like the guys who said, "Look, I'm going to do this movie about hot-rodders and then I'm going to do *Hedda Gabler*." I thought, "No, you're going to do another movie about hot-rodders after that. You've got to start doing the good stuff early or you're never going to get there." My first play on Broadway was *The Desperate Hours,* which was a melodrama about convicts taking over a house. It was important because Paul Newman was in it. We played brothers. It was his second play. After that, all I got offered were screaming melodramas, and I said no. I turned down about three different plays. I was a kid but I said, "I'm holding out for a comedy." I did finally get a comedy, which should have run three days—and I played it for two years. It was a play called *The Happiest Millionaire* with Walter Pidgeon. It was a whole career change. Instead of this convict, I played a boy heir to ninety million, and it was a light, silly comedy. Then that's all I got sent for the next year and a half. You've got to say, "Wait a minute. I've done that. I don't want to do that. I want to do something else." My whole life I've tried to keep changing and doing different things, because I really became an actor for me, for my pleasure. It sounds very selfish. That's why I keep trying to change and do different things that stimulate me, because otherwise I'm going to bore you to death. As Liz Ashley used to say, "If I'm bored, they're going to be more bored." You have to keep yourself very excited about your life and what you are doing.

Interviewer: What's a role that you passed on and later regretted?

Grizzard: Edward II. It was when I was offered the season at Stratford. It was to play Benedick in *Much Ado* and to play Edward II. It was a time of great black/white strife in this country, and Lanford Wilson had written a play about a mixed marriage [*The Gingham Dog*]. I thought it was very important to do it, so I did. It ran four performances, and I turned down Edward II and Benedick in order to do it. I don't regret it, but artistically I do, because I would like to have done those two roles.

Interviewer: What is the last play which you saw as an audience member that thrilled you?

Grizzard: I saw *Miss Saigon* last week, and I loved it. I thought it was very exciting. But I love most musicals, because I can't sing.

Interviewer: Are there any roles that were written with you specifically in mind?

Grizzard: Prince Charming. Seriously, the playwright is the fountainhead, and we're there, as much as we hate to think of it, to interpret what he's written. That's what makes me turn down plays—if I don't feel that I can help the playwright interpret his play. I turned down a play by Tennessee Williams. I was so excited to be asked to be in a play of his, directed by José Quintero and starring Geraldine Page. It was one of the most exciting offers I ever got, and then I read the play [*Clothes for a Summer Hotel*]. I read it again and I just sank lower and lower and lower. I thought, "I can't be in this play. I can't help him say this." It was because I so disbelieved what he had written about Scott Fitzgerald. I had to turn it down. I regret it now, because I would have gotten to work with Geraldine and Tennessee. They're both dead now, and they were wonderful theater artists. It was just pompous of me not to do it. I should have bent myself; but I knew that I would be miserable and I would make everybody else miserable. I just didn't think I could do it. I would have been terrible in that play.

Interviewer: Do you think there is still room on Broadway for serious theater?

Grizzard: I hope so. When I saw *The Kentucky Cycle,* I thought, "Now, there's serious theater." I was fascinated and I had a wonderful time. The critics didn't have as good a time as I did, unfortunately. I thought it was big and fascinating theater. I was so hoping that it would be accepted in New York. But you can't go to New York and say, "I won the Pulitzer Prize with this play," because they'll say, "Oh, really? We'll tell you whether you're any good or not." They did it to Preston Jones's *Texas Trilogy*. Remember that? It had a wonderful run in Washington and went to New York. The *Saturday Review* on the cover said, "The New American O'Neill" or Chekhov or something, and the New York critics said, "Oh, really? We'll tell you." They just destroyed it. You have to sneak onto Broadway if you have anything important and pretend you didn't mean to really do this. You're just going to flip it off and see. Then you might get by with it. But you can't come in saying, "This play won the Pulitzer Prize without ever having played in New York"—because they will get you.

Interviewer: Have you ever done a role that you regretted doing?

Grizzard: I should not have accepted Tartuffe without knowing who was directing it, and I regret that because I was fired. It's the only time in my long and crazy career that I've ever been fired. That hurt a great deal. I always say, and even then I would usually say before accepting a role, "Who wrote it? Who is going to direct it? And who is the leading lady, if there is one?"

Interviewer: Those are the things theater people all remember—one bad review, that time we were fired. The rest of it somehow doesn't hold as large a place in our brains.

Grizzard: Oh yes, those reviews. When I was a kid I read them. When I was at the Arena, I did *Desire Under the Elms*. Ernie Shearer was writing for the *Washington Times-Herald* in those days. He said that Mr. Danilowicz was "starkly brilliant" as the old man and that Marian Reardon played Abby "with a cold brilliance," and Mr. Grizzard, "when he wasn't muttering unintelligibly, sounded something like the Lone Ranger." There's one that I remember word for word! You don't remember the good ones, but those bad ones are burned into your head.

Interviewer: Do you think there are theater performers who are "critic-proof"?

Grizzard: Julie Harris comes as close as anybody I know in the theater. She is our First Lady now. Helen Hayes once held the crown, and Julie Harris is now as close to a critics' darling and to an actors' darling as anybody I know in the theater. She is the last name star who will still tour. She will go to any place to play on the stage. They have given her five Tonys, and I'm sure she deserves every one of them. She's a wonderful actress. She seems to be the critics' darling.

Interviewer: Among playwrights, Neil Simon certainly isn't "critic-proof" anymore; but he doesn't need the money, does he?

Grizzard: No. When I did Neil's *California Suite*, in 1976, he had already made several million dollars just on the plays, not on the television or the movies—so he's all right. I don't worry about Neil. I worry about Edward Albee because he is a brilliant mind and a fascinating man. I wish he would get angry again, not at the critics but at something else. His new language is not as interesting as his old language.

Interviewer: Speaking of Edward Albee, could you tell us something about the rehearsal process you all went through in putting together *Virginia Woolf?*

Grizzard: Yes, it was interesting because my great mentor Alan Schneider directed it. Arthur Hill, who played George, wasn't there for about the first ten days because he was finishing a movie in England. I played Nick, and Melinda Dillon eventually played Honey, but another actress started out playing Honey. I really got angry with Alan because without saying anything to me the first girl was just gone and there was Melinda. I didn't know her at the time. I was to be the stud in the play, the jock. I looked around and there was Uta [Hagen] and Arthur and Melinda and I thought, "It's Mickey Mouse on parade here." I had my agent come for three days to watch rehearsals. I almost quit because everybody was bigger than I was and I had to have this feeling of bigness; I had to be this big jock. That was frightening. Edward would show up once a week. Alan would call him every night and tell him what had gone on. Terrence McNally, who was a protégé of Edward's at the time, sat through all of the rehearsals. There were very few changes. Edward wrote this play that looked like the Manhattan phone book. You carried it around act by act because each act was like a full-length play. Arthur kept saying, "When do you think he is going to cut it?" I said, "I don't think he is"— and he didn't. Everything on Broadway started at 8:30 then, but we went up at 8:00 so that we would get down before the stagehands went into golden time at 11:30; we came down at something like 11:25. Edward would come in once a week and see a run-through, a rehearsal of whatever we had done, and say, "You're all brilliant," and he would go back to the beach. We wouldn't see him. He was wonderfully trusting. At the end, he cut nine pages out of the beginning of the third act, and he cut one speech at the end of the play in which George summed up what the evening was about, which he felt wasn't needed. That's about what was done. He had a finished play when we started rehearsing.

One of the interesting sidebars to this is that Disney would not let us use the melody for "Who's Afraid of the Big Bad Wolf" in the play, so we had to use "Here We Go Round the Mulberry Bush." If we had used the other, we would have had to pay a royalty every night to the Disney dynasty. Another interesting thing is that every play up to then that I had been in—I had been in something like five Broadway plays—had always played in Philadelphia, in Boston, in New Haven. They had all gone out of town somewhere. With *Virginia Woolf* we didn't. They put the money in the set. They had the set built.

We stayed in New York and rehearsed there on the set and previewed there. The play was budgeted at seventy-five thousand dollars. It came in for sixty-nine. In six weeks it was paid off and it was all gravy. Philadelphia went down the drain. People stopped going on the road. They started staying in New York and previewing. I haven't been out of town since then. Of course, we did start *California Suite* in California, but the fact that the finances worked out so well for *Virginia Woolf* kind of killed the road.

Interviewer: Did you enjoy your role in the 1975 revival of *The Royal Family*?

Grizzard: I had a wonderful time because I decided instead of playing Barrymore I'd play Doug Fairbanks. I had my hair curled, and there was Rosemary Harris and Eva Le Gallienne and Sam Levene; it was an absolutely wonderful company. I loved doing it. I didn't do it very long because we weren't supposed to go to Broadway. It was just for the Kennedy Center, the Brooklyn Academy, and the McCarter Theatre in Princeton. Then in Brooklyn they came to me and said, "We're going to Broadway." I said, "Listen, I'm not going to Broadway." I was going to do *California Suite,* so I couldn't go. I went to Broadway just for two weeks so that they wouldn't have to rehearse during Christmas to replace me, because we opened, I think, on New Year's Eve. After I left, Ellis Rabb, who had directed the play, took over and played it much longer than I did. I had a wonderful time in that play. It was a real company play, and delicious people. It was great fun to do that. I did *Crown Matrimonial* about the same time, which was about the abdication of Edward VIII. People now get them confused because it's *The Royal Family* and *Crown Matrimonial,* and they are always talking about Queen Mary and *The Royal Family.* I say, "No, she's in the other one." I've played a lot of kings. I want to play a sharecropper; I want to do *Tobacco Road.*

Interviewer: What project is coming up for you?

Grizzard: Retirement. I think I'm totally retired. I think they just haven't told me yet, but I think that's it. I have nothing planned at all. I'm going to do *Love Letters* again, which I have been doing with Julie Harris; then I'm going to do it with Eva Marie Saint down at Chapel Hill for the two hundredth anniversary of the founding of the university. I don't know what I'm going to do after that. Have a good time, I suppose. I think you should never ask for things, because you get them. When I was in junior high school, the high school drama club came over and they did a scene from *Charley's Aunt.* I thought, "When I get to high school, I want to be in the drama club." I was in it the first year, I was vice president the second year, and I was president the third year. Then I thought, "Boy, I want to be an actor." I eventually got to do that. Then I wanted to go to Broadway—and I did eighteen plays on Broadway. Then I said, "I'm tired. I just want to live in the country and have them send money." Well, I retired in April; and, because you have to belong to three unions, now they are all sending money and I'm living in the country. It's taken any incentive I ever had right away! I'm just anybody's now. I don't have any desire. There's no part that I know that's been written that I haven't played that I want to play. Possibly there is a *Tempest* in me sometime; I don't know. Maybe I can do a Prospero. I can't do Lear; I don't have the stature or the voice to play Lear. Unless somebody writes something new and exciting, I can't think of any play that I would like to do that I haven't done. I have no goals in life. I'm just happy as a lark. I just couldn't care less anymore. I loved it when I was a kid, but it's too painful for me. You use yourself. *Virginia Woolf* was a very painful part because I played Nick as if I were Nick. When they started sticking knives in me and the audience started laughing, and the more knives the heartier the audience laughed, it was painful because I was Nick. It just hurt me to be destroyed. Edward wanted that boy destroyed and he got him destroyed. It's painful to play. But acting is also a great hiding place. If you're going through a bad time in your life, Doctor Theater is wonderful because you go there and your concentration in that part is such an escape from what your own life is about at that time. You give some of your best performances when you are in misery.

Interviewer: What about teaching or coaching acting, now that you're "retired"?

Grizzard: I think about that a lot. I really do, because I think I could help some young people with problems that I had. I could also help them be better, because if I can't do it, I can still see that they can do it and help them to do it. But then I would have to stay in the city a lot, and I don't enjoy that. I have a house in Connecticut, which I've had for twenty-five years.

Interviewer: How about setting up a workshop out there?

Grizzard: Yes, but I also want to work with talented people, and they seem to go to the big cities. In Connecticut, we have dairy farmers who are not terribly interested in theater. It would be hard to recruit up there, I think.

Interviewer: Do you have any particular actors that you especially admire?

Grizzard: As I said earlier, Jason Robards is the most exciting actor that I have been on the stage with. We play together wonderfully, give and take. Rosemary Harris. I think Zoe Caldwell is a wonderful actress. I think Liz Ashley is a wonderful actress. Most people I have worked with I think are—Uta, Melinda Dillon, all those people. I don't get to work with men much. I was so pleased to have worked with Jason three times, because usually you are the man and then there is the woman. I have worked with most of the wonderful actresses that we have, the older ones, I mean. I don't get to work with the kids much anymore. It has just been a great experience. I keep thinking I should write some of this down because I've got some of the funniest theater stories. You do two plays with Maureen Stapleton and you've got to have stories. She's the funniest woman I know. She just says some of the greatest things.

Interviewer: You've worked quite a bit on plays by A. R. Gurney. What was it like working with him?

Grizzard: It was a wonderful experience. Pete Gurney wrote *Love Letters* and *The Dining Room*. He's got a play now called *Later Life* that is playing. He wrote *The Perfect Party*, which I did at the Kennedy Center. He's a neighbor in Connecticut. When we did *Another Antigone*, we rehearsed in New York, opened it at the Old Globe Theatre in San Diego, and then brought it to New York, to off-Broadway, to Playwrights Horizons. It was a prelude to Mamet's *Oleanna*. It's about a professor and a female student, except in this the man was not accused of sexually abusing her. He was accused of being anti-Semitic, because she was a Jewish girl. It was the destruction of his life. He was a classics professor and teacher and loved teaching and loved students. She was out to get him and she got him. We may try to do that play again. John Tillinger, who directed it, is an associate artistic director at the Long Wharf Theatre in New Haven, Arvin Brown's theater. He is trying to talk Arvin into letting us do it there and recasting the girl. We had the most adorable, sweet girl, but she was a Hispanic girl because they were frightened that if we had a Jewish girl everybody would say it was anti-Semitic. The girl is brilliant, funny, pushy, and self-involved, and they were afraid, I think, to play that. They thought that would look anti-Semitic, and they were dead wrong. That's what killed the play. If we had had that, I think the play would have been a much more important play than it turned out to be. It was a great experience for me, and I keep saying to Pete, "What's that man doing ten years later? Write a play now about that man." But he is not. He has written a play about a dog [*Sylvia*]. He talked about it the other night at dinner. It's a bitch, and I kept saying, "Could a guy play it?" No, it has to be a woman. He was asking because Nancy Marchand and Maryann Plunkett were there at this dinner. He was saying, "Would a woman object to playing a dog?" We told him that they would jump at it because they get to play women all the time but don't get to play dogs very often. It's like the guy who plays the lion in *Androcles and the Lion*. He has a wonderful chance to be creative. This dog just sits on the floor a lot. But she is dressed very chicly. She is a very chic dog. It sounds like a wonderful part for some actress. Some actress is going to have a great time next season.

Interviewer: How did you develop your wonderful voice?

Grizzard: I'm very flattered, because I don't think I have a good voice. I have a gravelly voice. I studied with a man named Arthur Lessac, who has a method. He teaches cantors at the Jewish Theological Seminary. When I was in *Virginia Woolf*, I would go to him for one hour one afternoon a week because I was going to play Hamlet. He was a miracle man. He helped me make sounds that made me cry. I didn't think it would ever be possible for me to make sounds like that. I don't do it anymore. I did an uncut four-hour *Ham-

let, and it takes a great deal of vocal stamina to play that long. He was a great help. I do warm-ups now before I do a play. I do soliloquies from Shakespeare, things that I've worked on. I don't work on the voice anymore. I used to do voice-overs for television commercials. They won't hire me to do that anymore. I just feel like that whole career, which was very lucrative, is over, and that's a shame. It was a wonderful outlet for me to make some money. I never think of having a voice, because I am always kind of ashamed of it. It's not big. I don't have the chest sound that Jason has, for instance. He has a wonderful, wonderful voice. Guthrie was so interested in sound and the voice. He expected us to do six lines of iambic pentameter in one breath. It's tough to do it at stage level. He could always do it, but he wouldn't have full volume because if he used full volume it would take more air. I could do four, maybe five, but I couldn't do six. That's what fascinated him, the sound. I never had a musical sound, and I know I disappointed him in so many ways. The brilliance of his direction was if I couldn't do something he would find another way to do it that would be just as exciting. He wanted me to sing one time in *Hamlet* and I said, "I can't sing. I really can't sing. I'm going to sound like a country-western star if I try to sing this phrase." He said, "Don't worry. We'll whisper it." So I whispered the whole thing, and it was much more exciting, I think, than it would have been if I'd sung it. There was a time in *Henry V* when he wanted me to go and climb up the ladder in the "once more unto the breach" speech. I had on armor and a sword. I said, "Tony, how am I going to do this?" So he had two guys come and pick me up and I was on their shoulders. He would always find another way so that you weren't humiliated by your own shortcomings. He always made it so that it would be just as exciting to do it another way. He never picked on you for not being able to do it. That's a very good director.

Julie Harris

Julia Ann Harris was born in Grosse Pointe Park, Michigan, on December 2, 1925. She studied at the Perry-Mansfield School of the Dance and Theatre, the Yale School of Drama, and the Actors Studio. She made her Broadway debut as Atlanta in It's a Gift *in 1945. Other professional roles include Nelly,* Playboy of the Western World *(1946);* The White Rabbit, Alice in Wonderland *(1947); Third Witch,* Macbeth *(1948); Angel Tuttle,* Magnolia Alley *(1949); Frankie Addams,* The Member of the Wedding *(1950); Sally Bowles,* I Am a Camera *(1951; Tony Award); Joan,* The Lark *(1955; Tony Award); Margery,* The Country Wife *(1957); Ruth Arnold,* The Warm Peninsula *(1959); Brigid Mary,* Little Moon of Alban *(1960); Juliet,* Romeo and Juliet; *Blanche of Spain,* King John *(both at Stratford, Ontario, in 1960); Josefa Lantenay,* A Shot in the Dark *(1961); Ophelia,* Hamlet *(1964); Annie,* Ready When You Are, C.B.! *(1964); Georgina,* Skyscraper *(1965); Blanche DuBois,* A Streetcar Named Desire *(1967); Ann Stanley,* Forty Carats *(1968; Tony Award); Anna Reardon, And*

Miss Reardon Drinks a Little *(1971)*; *Claire,* Voices *(1972)*; *Mary Lincoln,* The Last of Mrs. Lincoln *(1972; Tony Award)*; *Mrs. Rogers,* The Au Pair Man *(1973)*; *Emily Dickinson,* The Belle of Amherst *(1976; Tony Award)*; *Ethel Thayer,* On Golden Pond *(1980)*; *Clarice,* Mixed Couples *(1980)*; *Melissa Gardner,* Love Letters *(1989)*; *Daisy Werthan,* Driving Miss Daisy *(1988)*; *Isak Dinesen,* Lucifer's Child *(1992)*; *Eunice,* The Fiery Furnace *(1993)*; *Amanda Wingfield,* The Glass Menagerie *(1994)*; *Fonsia Dorsey,* The Gin Game *(1997)*; *Mrs. Morant,* Scent of the Roses *(1999)*; *and Mag Folan,* The Beauty Queen of Leenane *(2000)*.

Her films include The Trouble with Women *(1947)*, The Member of the Wedding *(1952)*, I Am a Camera *(1955)*, East of Eden *(1955)*, The Truth About Women *(1958)*, Requiem for a Heavyweight *(1962)*, The Haunting *(1963)*, You're a Big Boy Now *(1966)*, Harper *(1966)*, Reflections in a Golden Eye *(1967)*, The People Next Door *(1970)*, The Hiding Place *(1975)*, Voyage of the Damned *(1976)*, The Bell Jar *(1979)*, Gorillas in the Mist *(1988)*, Housesitter *(1992)*, The Dark Half *(1993)*, Little Surprises *(1995)*, Carried Away *(1996)*, Ethan Frome *(1997)*, Bad Manners *(1998)*, The First of May *(2000)*, *and* Passage to Paradise *(2000)*.

On television, she has appeared in Little Moon of Alban *(1959; Emmy Award)*, Victoria Regina *(1961; Emmy Award)*, The Power and the Glory *(1961)*, The House on Greenapple Road *(1970)*, How Awful About Allan *(1970)*, Home for the Holidays *(1972)*, Thicker than Water *(1973)*, The Greatest Gift *(1974)*, The Family Holvak *(1975)*, The Gift *(1979)*, Backstairs at the White House *(1979)*, Annihilator *(1986)*, The Woman He Loved *(1988)*, Too Good to Be True *(1988)*, The Christmas Wife *(1988)*, Single Women, Married Men *(1989)*, They've Taken Our Children: The Chowchilla Kidnapping *(1993)*, When Love Kills: The Seduction of John Hearn *(1993)*, Scarlett *(1994)*, One Christmas *(1994)*, Secrets *(1995)*, The Christmas Tree *(1996)*, Ellen Foster *(1997)*, Love Is Strange *(1998)*, *and in guest appearances on* Inside the Actors Studio, Goodyear Television Playhouse, United States Steel Hour, The Virginian, Daniel Boone, Laredo, The Big Valley, Garrison's Gorillas, Hawkins, Columbo, Tales of the Unexpected, Knots Landing, *and* The Outer Limits.

She was elected to the Theater Hall of Fame in 1976.

This interview took place on October 2 and November 12, 1999.

•————————————————————————•

Interviewer: Let's start at the beginning. You grew up in Grosse Pointe, Michigan. Can you remember when you first became aware of theater as a child?

Harris: I can't actually remember the first experience. What I *can* re-member is going to see a Broadway show coming through Detroit at the Cass

Theatre, a play called *Brother Rat,* a comedy with Wayne Morris. Oh God, where does that come from! I thought it was so funny, and I thought, "This is really great!" But before that I must have seen things. I must have seen Maurice Evans. No, that was probably around the same time. I saw Maurice Evans's *Hamlet.* I saw many great performances. I saw Ethel Waters in *Mamba's Daughters,* directed by Guthrie McClintic, and I saw Ethel in *Cabin in the Sky.* I saw Helen Hayes and Ruth Gordon; I saw all those great theater stars.

Interviewer: They all came through Detroit?

Harris: They all came through Detroit in their Broadway successes. I also saw the Lunts.

Interviewer: Did you, at a fairly early stage, decide that that was something you might like to do—or was that later?

Harris: I think by that time—it was the early forties—I had thought I would try to be an actress, yes.

Interviewer: Was there anything that sparked it?

Harris: It came from a combination of movies and theater. I felt absolutely that it wasn't possible for me to be in movies because I wasn't Jean Arthur or Margaret Sullavan or my favorite, Lana Turner. I would have loved to have been Lana Turner! But I wasn't those perfectly photogenic women. So I thought, "Well, I could be on the stage and I could pretend I was nice to look at if I make myself up. The audience is far enough away, lights are nice, and no close-ups." So I gravitated toward the theater. Then, when I was in high school, we had a theater class and we put on plays. I was a good show-off, and so I got good parts in them. I did Lady Bracknell in *The Importance of Being Earnest,* and I did *Will o' the Wisp* by William Butler Yeats; I did some interesting plays in high school. By that time in the summertime I had been going to the Perry-Mansfield theater workshop in Steamboat Springs, Colorado. Charlotte Perry, who was the acting teacher there, gave me the nickname "Gopher" because I said, "I'm out west. Can I see a gopher?" She said, "Gopher, I think you could be in the theater." And I thought, "Wow! Now somebody's telling me I could be an actor, and I could go home and say to my mother and father, 'I want to study acting.'" Those three summers that I spent at Perry-Mansfield were very important to me because someone actually had said, "Yes, I think you could think about the theater for a career."

Then, by the time I finished high school, I convinced my family that I wanted to study acting. It was the end of the Second World War, and my father, who had gone to Yale University, got me into the Yale Drama School, I think. I have no idea how this happened, because I wasn't a college graduate when I entered the Yale Drama School. The Yale Drama School is and was at that time a graduate school. They let me in, but I shouldn't have been there. I survived one year and got a job in a play in New York during that year. It closed in six weeks, but it was a job. I said to Walter Pritchard Eaton, who was the head of the drama school, "Mr. Eaton, I have tried out for this play in New York, and they offered me the part. What should I do?" He was smoking his pipe; he took his pipe out of his mouth, looked at me across the desk, and said, "What did you come here for?" I said, "I came here to study acting." He said, "Well, don't you think you'd better take that part?" And I said, "Oh!" He said, "If it doesn't work out, you can always come back to school."

Interviewer: And you never did?

Harris: I did. It closed in six weeks, and I came back for the rest of the term.

Interviewer: Then you went back to New York after that?

Harris: I went back to New York. I worked with the Amateur Comedy Club and did *The Devil's Disciple*. I stayed, and I auditioned for things, and one thing came after another. I got understudies and walk-ons and that sort of thing.

Interviewer: Do you think that things have changed a great deal in the theater since then? There are a great many talented young people who come to New York now who don't get very far.

Harris: I think things *have* changed, and I think young people have changed. I think they are far ahead of where I was when I was eighteen and nineteen. By that I mean I think they're more sophisticated; they're better prepared for life than I was. I was a terrible innocent; I didn't know what was ahead of me. I wasn't very well prepared to take on this career. I didn't have much of a voice. I didn't know really how to work in forming a character. I was making it all up as I went along. Every day was a struggle.

Interviewer: Do you think you had on-the-job training?

Harris: I absolutely had on-the-job training.

Interviewer: Did you take acting classes?

Harris: I did take classes. The first year of the Actors Studio I was taken in as a member. That was before *The Member of the Wedding*.

Interviewer: That was after you'd done some work in New York already?

Harris: I'd done three or four years or so, and then I was taken into the Actors Studio. I studied with Mr. Kazan and with Lee Strasberg, and I was getting parts here and there.

Interviewer: Who was in that first group at the Actors Studio with you?

Harris: In our class there was Cloris Leachman, there was Eddie Binns. I think Rod Steiger was in that class.

Interviewer: Was that work at the Actors Studio helpful to you?

Harris: Well, I was terrified.

Interviewer: What was your experience of getting in? Some people tried again and again and again and they never got in.

Harris: I don't remember. I don't actually remember if I auditioned. I must have. I can't remember how I got in. I was invited in. I didn't know any actors really. I was married pretty early, so I was in my little cocoon and I didn't really go out and mingle with actors. But once I got into the Studio, then I met people in class and we did scenes together. I was always a wreck doing a scene for the class. After I had done the scene, I would run a fever. I would think, "I don't know if I can do this. I don't know if I'm ready for this." It was an effort and an emotional experience. I remember Joe Sullivan and I did the Gentleman Caller scene from *The Glass Menagerie*. We rehearsed it and then we presented it. When we did the scene, he took me up to dance with me and he swung my legs around and my foot caught one of the little glass animals. Whether it was just *the* unicorn or whether we had more, I don't really remember. But it was the unicorn's horn that broke. When I went to pick up the unicorn, I cut myself. But as I picked it up, I was crying. I had never done that in rehearsal. I picked it up and I started to sob inconsolably. Poor Joe was looking at me: "What the hell are you doing? This never happened." But I couldn't stop crying. I was trying to speak to him through the tears; I was sobbing and was trying to say, "It doesn't matter. It doesn't matter. Now he's lost his horn and he's just like all the other horses." I was trying to make him feel better, but I couldn't stop crying. After the scene was over, the class said, "Wow! What a choice you made!" And I said, "No. It was an accident. I couldn't do that again to save my life." I'd never done it before. That was an illustration that made me think, "If we had been rehearsing the scene in a production and that had happened to me, I would say, 'Well, that's right, isn't it? I'll try and do that again; I'll try and find that again.'" But I didn't know how to find it and I thought, "It's the emotional thing that I was looking for, searching for." I said to myself, "This is what acting is—to find the reality of this moment that I found by accident and to be able to reproduce it eight times a week. That's what it is. That's what I'm after. How do I do that?" My whole life has been geared to say, "How do I do that?"

Interviewer: And you're still trying to do it?

Harris: I'm still trying to do it!

Interviewer: How did you get into *The Member of the Wedding*? That was your first big break, wasn't it?

Harris: Harold Clurman had directed me in a play called *The Young and Fair,* so he knew my work. He had also seen me in the Actors Studio production of Bessie Breuer's play *Sundown Beach,* where I played a little southern white girl. He hired me without reading for the part. I never had to read for Frankie Addams. It was a dream for me to play that part, because I had read the book first. I had read *The Heart Is a Lonely Hunter* too and I thought, "I'm the only one who understands Carson McCullers." She was talking about me. Of course every girl in America was saying the same thing: "She's talking about me; I know that Frankie Addams."

Interviewer: It must have been a great thrill for you to be on the stage with Ethel Waters.

Harris: With my heroine, Ethel Waters, yes! When I saw her in *Mamba's Daughters* and *Cabin in the Sky,* I thought, "That's what I want to be. That's the greatest actress I've ever seen." It would remain so, except for Laurette Taylor. Ethel Waters was one of the greatest actors I ever saw in my life. I said, "That's what it's all about."

Interviewer: Did you learn a lot in that production from her, just from being with her?

Harris: Yes, I suppose by osmosis.

Interviewer: What made her such a great actress?

Harris: I've seen a lot of great actresses onstage—Laurette Taylor, Irene Worth, Ruth Gordon, Wendy Hiller, and now Janet McTeer. Ethel was a supreme actress because she had such power. I used to think she was a natural phenomenon like Niagara Falls. She was glorious and she was true and she was funny. When I heard her sing certain songs, I'd say, "Now I know what the meaning of cute is. Sometimes, Ethel, you are just so cute." It was her humor. It was her smile. It was the way she wrapped her humor around things. She was adorable. She was also shockingly tragic, like a face of Michelangelo. She was really much larger than life and just glorious—and always so true.

Interviewer: Was there kind of a presence there that she shared with everybody?

Harris: Oh yes, that's right. Everybody identified with that power.

Interviewer: Did she significantly change her performance each night?

Harris: It didn't seem to me it changed much. It was just so full.

Interviewer: Did she bring out the best in other actors?

Harris: Always, when you're working with someone that good, it tends to make you a little better.

Interviewer: What was it about Laurette Taylor's performance? You said you saw her once, I believe.

Harris: Yes, I saw a matinee of *The Glass Menagerie,* and it shocked me. By that I mean I was laughing and crying the whole afternoon. At the end of the play I didn't know where I was. It was too much. My whole life up to that time—I think I was about eighteen or nineteen—passed in front of my eyes. She evoked things that I felt with my brothers and my mother and father. Incredible! It was the essence of why I wanted to be in the theater. It evoked this passion and this humanity.

Interviewer: Do you remember any details that made it so memorable? Is there anything that stands out especially in your mind?

Harris: It was so funny and so true. You were laughing and then in the next second you were weeping. I remember the expression on her face when she and Tom had a fight and the next morning she wakes him up with "Rise and shine!" She brings him his coffee. Eddie Dowling played Tom. He was a little too old for the part but that was okay. She wanted to make up with him because they'd had this terrible row the night before, but she wasn't going to speak to him. She said, "I won't speak to you until you apologize," and she watched him getting ready to go to work and blowing on his coffee—and she very softly made the gesture to blow on the coffee. It was so adorable. It was the actress's choice of doing something that would show her sort of contempt for him but, at the same time, maybe allow him to take in her presence and say, "I'm sorry, Mother. I apologize." She was full of those things.

Interviewer: Was it that vivid memory that kept you from playing Amanda for so many years?

Harris: Well, it didn't keep me; nobody asked me. I just never thought of doing *The Glass Menagerie,* because I'd seen it done to perfection. For years I had no desire to play it because of that memory.

Interviewer: And then you were asked.

Harris: I wasn't asked. My old friend Leo Lerman, an editor at Condé Nast, had known Carson McCullers and Truman [Capote]. Leo had a literary salon, the only literary salon I've ever gone to, where you met people like Tennessee Williams and William Faulkner. Leo said to me a few years ago, "You should play Amanda." I think it was he who called Todd Haines at the Roundabout and said, "You should have Julie Harris play that part." That's how it happened.

Interviewer: You were involved in the casting of that production. Could you talk about that?

Harris: Yes. I said to Frank Galati, who was going to direct the play, "I've never asked this before of a director, but I'm asking you. I have to have the final say for this cast. It's only three other people, Tom, Laura, and the Gentleman Caller. I have to say which of the actors I want that we see." Frank looked at me sort of strangely, but he said, "Yes, all right." I sat in the casting director's office when we saw actors the first day. We saw Calista Flockhart and Kevin Kilner, who had almost memorized the Gentleman Caller scene. By the time the scene was over, we were all crying. After they left the room, I turned to Frank and Todd Haines and said, "Well, there they are. There's two; we only have one to go." They said, "Kevin's awfully tall." I said, "I don't care how tall he is, he's the Gentleman Caller!" Then the next day we saw Zeljko Ivanek. He did a scene with Cynthia Nixon, who read Laura; she's a lovely actress. They did the scene where Tom comes home after he's been drinking and loses his keys. Zeljko was the only actor I've ever seen who did Tom with a slight southern accent like Tennessee would have had. They all would have had slight southern accents, coming from Mississippi. He was a beautiful Tom.

Interviewer: With respect to roles you've created in new plays, to what extent were you a part of the creative team in shaping the script? With *The Belle of Amherst*, for example, what about the selection of poems?

Harris: Well, I had done my own solo performance of Emily Dickinson for high school children. Charles Nelson Reilly had seen that, so there were certain poems I had already selected that we kept in the play that Bill Luce came in to write. "A narrow fellow in the grass" and "I'm nobody! Who are you?" and certain of those favorite poems of mine we did keep in.

Interviewer: Were there any that you would like to have kept in but didn't quite fit?

Harris: There were so many. I think when we first started out the play was maybe two and a half or almost three hours long. We just had to cut it. "I measure every grief I meet"; I'd love to have put that in the play, but we couldn't.

Interviewer: Why?

Harris: There wasn't time. There were others—"Because I could not stop for Death," for example.

Interviewer: What has been your most challenging role, would you say?

Harris: I'd say they all have had challenges. I don't think one has been more so than others. I guess the first time I did a solo play was *The Belle of Amherst*, and that was a big challenge, to find myself on the stage with nobody else.

Interviewer: Is there any role that you've passed on and then later regretted having done so?

Harris: I was offered *Two for the Seesaw*, and I just felt that because she was so ethnic, such a New York girl, I wasn't really right for the part. Now I think, "Why didn't you try for it? Why didn't you say, 'I can be a New York girl and use the accent and everything'?" But I just didn't; I don't know why.

Interviewer: Is there a role that you *did* do that you later regretted doing?

Harris: No, I don't think so.

Interviewer: What is your notion of the ideal actor-director relationship? What kind of a director do you like to work with?

Harris: I don't think I have any conception of what that should be, because every individual is so different. Michael Langham, Harold Clurman, Elia Kazan, Charles Nelson Reilly—they all bring what they are to directing. I think the relationship is like father and child. I think you have to trust the director; whatever they say or do, it has to be something that is not only kindly but forces you to think and feel and shakes you out of your everyday world and makes you go somewhere else.

Interviewer: I think once, in speaking of directors, you used the analogy of a circus act in which dogs jumped off ladders with the owner catching them as they fell. Could you talk about that?

Harris: I love sports because they show the range of the human condition. They show how human beings can be molded into a place where they don't ordinarily go; through discipline and hard work, they do something really remarkable. I do love the circus and clowns and the whole devotion to what they're doing. Everybody in the circus is trying to make the circus work, even the animals. In the Ringling Brothers circus, they always had a dog act with little poodles. They'd put up this ladder, which would go up, up, almost to the top of the tent. The dogs would climb up the ladder, and then the owner would stand at the bottom and throw out his arms and say, "Jump!" The little dogs would jump and land in his arms, and he would kiss them and hug them. When we do a play, it is like we go up, up, up, up, every day at rehearsal; and for the performance, when the audience comes in, we jump and we do it. The director's there to catch us, we hope, and to tell us what we did right, what we did wrong, and to bring it all together. He or she has that power. It's very hard because you can't express your personal journey to anyone else. We had a kind of an interesting day yesterday in rehearsal. There is a scene in *Scent of the Roses* where I'm relating something that happened to my daughter, and I got very emotional about it. They said, "No, that's too heavy. That's too emotional." This is only the first day I've done it, and I had to go and think that through. When it's emotion, you're out there on that tightrope or that ladder, and you have to have absolute faith that you're going to make it. It's a perilous journey, and you have to have someone who really is strong and kind and is going to help you.

Interviewer: Someone who's going to catch you?

Harris: Yes, yes.

Interviewer: What about the actor-actor relationship? What kinds of actors do you like to have on the stage with you?

Harris: There are all kinds of actors. I love actors. I just spent over a year with a great actor, Charles Durning, touring in *The Gin Game,* and it didn't even feel like we were acting. We were just having a good time. We'd be caught up in this sad story that we were telling, but we were having a good time. He was always there one hundred percent with me.

Interviewer: Can you think of an experience (without naming names if you don't want to) where you haven't had a good experience with an actor and what it was based on?

Harris: Rex Harrison, who's no longer with us, was a brilliant actor but a very difficult man. He would say to me in rehearsal, "Are you going to do it that way?" I'd think, "Well, I don't know quite how I'm going to do it yet." "Why can't you get it?" he would say. He was difficult, but in the playing of it he was an angel. He was just heavenly to work with, but he was a difficult human being. When you were acting together, he was sublime.

Interviewer: Can you think of an occasion when you've been onstage with an actor or actress in a production where it was very difficult, perhaps because they weren't very much in the moment? Doesn't it occasionally happen that you find yourself onstage with someone who isn't giving back to you in the way you're giving to them?

Harris: I've gotten to the stage in my life where I use whatever the actor gives me. I don't care whether it's too much or too little. Whatever is there I use. I don't say, "Why aren't they doing more?" or "They should be doing less." I just take whatever's given to me and use that. I don't demand from a fellow actor.

Interviewer: But it's easier with someone who . . .

Harris: Gives, with a person who gives and gives. Oh yes.

Interviewer: Who are some of them?

Harris: Ethel Waters was always there. Charles Durning, Christopher Plummer, and Rex. I've worked with wonderful actors. Estelle Parsons was sometimes a difficult lady, but she's a great actress.

Interviewer: This is a question that some actors have difficulty answering. When you're working on a part, how do you work on it?

Harris: I learn the lines.

Interviewer: What we've found is that some actors work from the outside in and others work from the inside out.

Harris: I think I'm an "outsy."

Interviewer: You work from external things first?

Harris: I learn the lines, especially if it's a big part. I get what the part is about from the lines. When I did Josefa in *A Shot in the Dark,* I had an image of Brigitte Bardot, and that helped me. I had this image of a very wonderful-looking French girl, her style of hair, makeup, and whether she wore nail polish or red lipstick, and that sort of helped me.

Interviewer: Is that the exception rather than the rule, when you did it that way?

Harris: I've done a number of parts that are real people, so you can read about them. You can read what they wrote. You can look at pictures of them. You have a sense of what they looked like, what they were. You can read their words, what they were thinking, what they hoped.

Interviewer: In those cases where you did one-woman shows, you really did try to re-create the person as carefully and as exactly as you could?

Harris: Oh yes.

Interviewer: When you did Amanda in *The Glass Menagerie,* did you try to forget Laurette Taylor?

Harris: I didn't think of her.

Interviewer: Did you have to do that deliberately?

Harris: No, it was so long ago that I didn't have her voice in my mind. I'm entirely different than she is.

Interviewer: We do have to mention the horrible *c* word, critics. Do you read the critics when you're in a play?

Harris: I do. I read the critics, and sometimes it's very painful. In my time of life now, say we're doing *The Gin Game* and we come to Cleveland; the next day you run out and get the newspapers and read the critics because it means whether you're going to have two good weeks or not. If they liked you, then people are going to come and see it.

Interviewer: Did it vary a lot?

Harris: Not with *The Gin Game,* no.

Interviewer: But with some plays?

Harris: Some plays, yes. *The Belle of Amherst,* for instance. We opened in Seattle and we went to Denver, Chicago, Boston, and New York. Out of those, Seattle, Denver, Chicago, and Boston were all raves. When we came to New York, nobody liked the play or me particularly. We were ready to close. Walter Kerr came out the following Sunday and said, "If you see anything in New York, see *The Belle of Amherst.*" There was a line at the box office. Brooks Atkinson, writing about *The Member of the Wedding,* said, "It's not a play, but it's great art." We had no advance sales for that play at all; we had nothing. We didn't do good business in Philadelphia. I can't remember what the reviews were like in Philadelphia; I think they weren't bad. But the next day, after Brooks Atkinson's review, there was a line at the box office, and we lasted a year and a half.

Interviewer: Do you ever pay attention to anything that a critic has said about your performance?

Harris: If it's bad, yes.

Interviewer: You do care?

Harris: Oh yes. You say, "Why?" People used to say that I was strident, shrill; so you say, "There must be a reason for that. There has to be something I can do about it."

Interviewer: Have you altered a performance because of something a critic has said?

Harris: No, not that specific. But you say, "I've got to be careful not to do this, not to do that." Mannerisms.

Interviewer: This is a question that may not apply in your case, because you've played so many roles. Is there a role you haven't played yet that you'd like to play?

Harris: There are two plays and roles ahead of me that I'm thinking about. One is Alice B. Toklas in *Staying On Alone,* Bruce Kellner's play, and the other is a play I have commissioned a young Canadian playwright, Stacey Engels, to write for me about Emily Carr. Do you know Emily Carr? She is a Canadian painter from the city of Victoria on Vancouver Island. She's a great Canadian painter and a great writer. She wrote quite a few books. She's an amazing woman, and I would love to play her.

Interviewer: Would that take you back to Stratford, Ontario, possibly?

Harris: We don't know where it would be.

Interviewer: Did you like your repertory experience at Stratford?

Harris: Oh yes! I especially loved doing *King John.* I played the Lady Blanche, and I came in on Christopher Plummer's arm; Chris was playing the bastard. He was marvelous. I can still hear that last speech, his voice ringing. My first line was "Oh well did he become that lion's robe that did disrobe the lion of that robe." I thought, "If I forget that line, what am I going to do?" I always expected someone in the audience to say, "Say that again?"

Interviewer: What a tongue-twister! Shakespeare's revenge on every actor.

Harris: And I'd better get it right, because Douglas Seale was the director.

Interviewer: How did you feel about alternating the roles of Juliet and Blanche?

Harris: Fortunately, Blanche was a very small part and Juliet was a very big part. When I played the Lady Blanche, it was kind of a relief. Michael Langham is a great director and was wonderful to work with, but I was terrified of Juliet. I had never done a major Shakespearean part before. I had no really good vocal training. Iris Warren was our voice coach, and she came from Stratford-on-Avon. She had taught the Shakespearean actors in England, and she was a great vocal coach. I was hopeless; I was struggling; but I did get through the season, and I did play it. It's like when you ask an actor who plays Hamlet for the first time and he says, "I have to do it again. I hope I live long enough to play that part again." Of course I never played Juliet again, but I wish I had. It was just a daunting experience to play it for the first time.

Interviewer: Would you have preferred to have played it eight times a week?

Harris: I think I would almost, yes.

Interviewer: Is the idea of the repertory where you play a role three or four times a week attractive to you?

Harris: I love that. I would like to have spent my life doing that. But I got sidetracked into Broadway and didn't go with a repertory company.

Interviewer: This is the question I'm sure everybody asks you. You're almost the only major American actor or actress who still constantly tours—when you certainly don't have to. There must be a reason why you continue to go out on the road so much when you have a lovely house on Cape Cod. Why have you continued to do tours?

Harris: The last tour I did before *The Gin Game* was *Lettice and Lovage,* a wonderful play by Peter Shaffer. It was a great experience for me to work with Roberta Maxwell. With *The Gin Game,* it was exciting because Charlie Durning and I had made a success in New York with the play and we felt we wanted to do it on the road, have people see it, and see the two of us together playing this wonderful play.

Interviewer: Is it more physically exhausting to play on the road, going from city to city, than it is to be in New York?

Harris: It isn't anymore, because you're not doing one-night stands. If it were one-night stands, then it would be tiring. You do a week here, two weeks there, sometimes three weeks. You fly everyplace, and it's quite comfortable. For both *Lettice and Lovage* and *The Gin Game,* we had wonderful crews, really great people helping us all along the way.

Interviewer: Is it difficult to adjust to different stage spaces?

Harris: That's exciting. I love being in different theaters. I just love it. And across this country, you get to know the wonderful theaters and you get to experience them. It's really great.

Interviewer: Do the audiences vary tremendously too? Is that part of the excitement of it?

Harris: Not that much. Before *Lettice and Lovage,* I toured with Brock Peters and Stephen Root in *Driving Miss Daisy,* and that was a great experience. I loved Brock and Stephen, and we had a wonderful time together. In Seattle, we played the Fifth Avenue Playhouse, which is a sort of musical house. There were three of us onstage, and you know what *Driving Miss Daisy*'s like. It's an imaginary set with two little stools for the car. One of the critics said it was like watching hummingbirds in an elephant's house!

Interviewer: Was that exciting for you?

Harris: Absolutely! It was very exciting.

Interviewer: So, in a sense, if you do a Broadway show for a long run, there's a certain kind of, perhaps not boredom, but there's a certain kind of sameness; whereas if you do something on the road, it's different, isn't it?

Harris: It's different all the time. It keeps it very stimulating.

Interviewer: When you go to the theater as an audience member, do you think you see it very differently because you're an actor? Do you look for different things when you go to the theater?

Harris: I don't know. I have never grown up, so to speak, from being a member of the audience. When I go to a play I am expecting something miraculous, and lots of times I get something miraculous. When I saw Janet McTeer do *A Doll's House,* from the time the curtain went up, I sat forward on my seat. I saw Michael Crawford in *The Phantom of the Opera* six times. I saw Janet McTeer three times. I saw one of my favorite theater experiences, *Nicholas Nickleby,* seven times. I would live in that theater. I love to experience a play. I've never grown up from that. Ralph Richardson once said in an interview, "If I can see Ethel Merman, I can live on that for the next five years." That's what I feel about theater. Theater is food for me. It's nourishment; it's just mesmerizing.

Interviewer: What about making films? You've re-created two of your best stage roles in film: Frankie in *The Member of the Wedding* and Sally Bowles in *I Am a Camera.* What was it like as a stage actor being in a movie? It's a very different process, isn't it?

Harris: It's very different. When I did *The Member of the Wedding* and *I Am a Camera,* I wish I had known what I know now; it wouldn't have been so difficult. When I made *The Member of the Wedding,* I was still doing a stage performance for the camera—which wasn't right. Fred Zinnemann, who directed *The Member of the Wedding,* was constantly having to say to me, "No. Do less, do less. Bring it down." My system was geared to the second balcony in the Empire Theatre, and it was hard to shed that. Now I understand that the reality of filmmaking is very exciting for the actor because it's another dimension; but it has to be realer than real—like Judi Dench in *Mrs. Brown.* That performance is miraculous because you think, "There couldn't have been a camera there. There was no camera there. I don't know how that was captured on film. She was there, she's that woman." That's the magic of film to me, to capture that kind of reality. How did they do that? It was magic.

Interviewer: Some people feel that your performance in *East of Eden* is your best on film. How do you feel about it?

Harris: I can't judge myself.

Interviewer: Is that a strange situation, seeing yourself in a film? Obviously, onstage you don't see yourself.

Harris: Oh yes. There was a picture I made with Eileen Heckart, *The Hiding Place,* and I can look at myself in that and feel removed from it. But there aren't many movies like that. Sometimes there are flashes of me in *Voyage of the Damned,* some flashes when I say, "Is that me?"

Interviewer: Do you think that's maybe some of your best work, when you don't recognize yourself?

Harris: Yes.

Interviewer: Some actors say that they feel the most content with an individual performance when they feel they lose themselves in the part. Is that similar to what you're talking about in a movie—in the sense that when you completely get into a role, it's as if Julie Harris isn't there anymore?

Harris: I think so. You'd rather be very unconscious of what *you* are and just be in that place.

Interviewer: Can you tell when that's happening in the course of a run of a play, when you have an evening where you really feel you got it? Are you conscious of when you've given a good performance?

Harris: Sometimes it's wrong, though. Sometimes you say, "I felt really good tonight," and then somebody will tell you something you've done and you say, "I didn't know that." Sometimes you feel bad and actually somebody's gotten something from it, even though you felt awful. It's very hard to judge and better not to try, I think. It's best when you're not judging yourself, when you're not thinking of what you're doing, so to speak. You're doing it, you're in the moment. Charlie Durning would always say to me, "You're always in the moment. If I say something, you adjust to it." That's what it all is. It's that adjusting; you're shifting, you're adjusting, you're in it.

Interviewer: What about the differences between comedy and serious acting? Is it all just acting for you, or do you feel that there are differences when you do comedy?

Harris: It depends. The great comedians like Bert Lahr and Robin Williams are always so real. I love Robin Williams. He's always so moving. He's in the moment. Jonathan Winters and Robin Williams are sort of short-circuited. By that I mean they're on a different plane; but it's real, it's very real. Art Carney with Jackie Gleason, he was just superb. There wasn't a moment when he wasn't real, when it wasn't deeply felt, when it wasn't genuine. But it was comedy; people screamed with laughter. It's very interesting what comedy is.

Interviewer: How about some memories of the people you've worked with—Brando in *Reflections in a Golden Eye*? How was it working with him?

Harris: Oh, it was wonderful. He was just extraordinary. He was such a naughty boy. By that I mean he was always playing around and sort of devil-may-care. Then they would say, "All right, action!" You'd look up and it would be this other person.

Interviewer: Just like that?

Harris: Just like that. You would be mesmerized because it would be another person.

Interviewer: He could do it that quickly?

Harris: A genius, really a genius.

Interviewer: What about James Dean in that way?

Harris: Of course, *East of Eden* was Jimmy's second movie. *Rebel Without a Cause* was his first. He was captivating because he was so into the moment too and so extraordinary and so full of feeling and inventiveness. I loved working with him.

Interviewer: Brando and Dean have a quality Kazan talks about in his autobiography, the sense of danger that some actors have. You never know what they're going to say, or at least you think you don't know.

Harris: George C. Scott too.

Interviewer: With Dean and Brando and Scott, you feel they're making it up as they're going along and that they might do anything onstage. Montgomery Clift was another one.

Harris: I worked with him once. We recorded *The Glass Menagerie;* he played Tom. He was beautiful. When he said my name, "Laura," it went right through me. It was like, "That's my name. My brother's calling me." There was nothing Monty couldn't do, that wouldn't have that richness to it.

Interviewer: These people that we've just mentioned are actors who abandoned the stage and became movie actors pretty much permanently. Do you think they were great losses to the stage?

Harris: Oh yes. Monty Clift died young, or youngish. But they had tragic overtones, undertones. Monty had that dreadful accident. We can't say Marlon shouldn't have abandoned the stage, because who are we to say what he should have done? That he didn't play the great parts is a great loss to us.

Interviewer: Do you think James Dean would have been a great stage actor?

Harris: He certainly had a desire to go on with his stage work. He expressed to me an interest in playing Hamlet—and what a Hamlet he might have been!

Interviewer: What would you say the biggest influences have been on your career?

Harris: Certainly Laurence Olivier and his work in the theater.

Interviewer: Is there any specific work that comes to mind with Olivier?

Harris: Everything he ever did was an inspiration to me. He was almost the last of the great actor-managers. We don't have those now anymore, actors who direct their own companies.

Interviewer: Kenneth Branagh tries to do it.

Harris: Kenneth Branagh does, but he doesn't have a company of actors on the stage, in the theater. Olivier did—and Ralph Richardson, John Gielgud. We don't have those actor-managers.

Interviewer: Are there other influences?

Harris: Some directors like Harold Clurman and Elia Kazan. And film directors that I never worked with—Fellini, Kurosawa, Bergman.

Interviewer: They were influences because when you saw their movies, you took something from them?

Harris: Yes.

Interviewer: Have you ever directed?

Harris: No.

Interviewer: Would you ever want to?

Harris: I think it's really beyond me now, but there are certain stories I've read—by Flannery O'Connor, for instance—that I'd love to make into a movie, but I don't suppose I ever will.

Interviewer: At an earlier stage in your career, if someone had asked you to direct, would you have accepted?

Harris: Onstage?

Interviewer: Yes.

Harris: I don't think so. I don't know why, but I felt I could direct a film.

Interviewer: That's interesting.

Harris: I wonder why that is. I don't know.

Interviewer: What are some of the things that you have learned about the craft of acting over your career? In what ways are you a better actress than twenty-five or thirty years ago?

Harris: I don't know that I'm better, but I think I've learned not to push myself, not to make inordinate demands on myself, and to trust myself. If I feel something strongly about the part, it will come out; and I just have to do it step by step.

Interviewer: What do you think about the state of the theater today? Are you a pessimist or an optimist?

Harris: Oh, I'm an optimist.

Interviewer: I think I knew that!

Harris: I think the theater is going great guns at the moment—and all over the world, from what I can read about what's happening in different countries. It's flourishing. I know because I'm one of the play readers for the Beverly Hills Playwriting Contest. I'm one of the readers that read the five finalist plays each year. The first-prize winner, I think, gets five thousand dollars, and we usually get five plays to read for the final winner. I can't remember this year, but last year all five plays, I thought, were tens. That's very exciting because people are out there writing plays for the theater, not for movies, but for live audiences. I've done two plays this summer that were new plays—one in Chicago at the Victory Gardens Theater and one at the Pendragon Theatre in Saranac Lake, New York—so people are writing plays. I find that fascinating, that people are still going to the theater. I remember in Cleveland a woman came backstage—this was with *The Gin Game*—and she said, "This is the first time I've seen a play." I asked, "How old are you?" She said she was about thirty-five, and I said, "How did you escape the theater?" That's sad to me. I saw plays when I was fourteen. Because of my mother and father, I gravitated to the theater. But there are people out there who have never seen a live stage performance. But it's all around us. I think the theater is very full of blood, really pumping.

Interviewer: You have one great advantage. Being on the road, you see it all over the country. Some people think of American theater as New York, but

American theater is not just New York. It's Cleveland, Denver, Seattle, Chicago, and all the places you go to on the road. If you had one wish for the American theater, what would it be?

Harris: That theater could be as popular as sports. That we could have theater complexes as exciting as football stadiums. Especially in a city like New York, you see all the creative power that is in the dance companies, the opera companies, the theater companies, the comedy companies. You see so much talent here, it's just extraordinary. That is the excitement about creativity, that it never ends. It's constantly exciting us and reacquainting us with life and the past and future and the present. It's a never-ending chain.

Eileen Heckart

Anna Eileen Heckart was born in Columbus, Ohio, on March 29, 1919. She attended Ohio State University, studied acting at the American Theatre Wing, and made her Broadway debut as an understudy and assistant stage manager for The Voice of the Turtle *in 1943. She made her London debut as Mrs. Baker in* Butterflies Are Free *(1970). Her other Broadway roles include Eva McKeon,* The Traitor *(1949); Nell Bromley,* Hilda Crane *(1950); Valerie McGuire,* In Any Language *(1952); Rosemary Sidney,* Picnic *(1953); Mrs. Daigle,* The Bad Seed *(1954); Beatrice,* A View from the Bridge *(1955); Agnes,* A Memory of Two Mondays *(1955); Lottie Lacey,* The Dark at the Top of the Stairs *(1957); Deedee Grogan,* Invitation to a March *(1960); Melba Snyder,* Pal Joey *(1961); title role,* Everybody Loves Opal *(1961); Tilly Siegel,* A Family Affair *(1962); Nurse Sweetie,* Too True to Be Good *(1963); Ruby,* And Things That Go Bump in the Night *(1965); Mrs. Banks,* Barefoot in the Park *(1965); Harriet, Edith, Muriel,* You Know I Can't Hear You When the Water's Running *(1967);*

Mrs. Haber, The Mother Lover *(1969); Mrs. Baker,* Butterflies Are Free *(1969); The Woman,* Veronica's Room *(1973); title role,* Eleanor *(1976); title role,* Margaret Sanger: Unfinished Business *(1989); Dorothea,* Eleemosynary *(1989); Lucille,* The Cemetery Club *(1990); Mair,* Northeast Local *(1995); and Gladys Green,* The Waverly Gallery *(1999 and 2000).*

She made her movie debut in Miracle in the Rain *(1956). Among her many films are* Somebody Up There Likes Me *(1956),* Bus Stop *(1956),* The Bad Seed *(1956),* Heller in Pink Tights *(1960),* My Six Loves *(1963),* Up the Down Staircase *(1967),* No Way to Treat a Lady *(1968),* Butterflies Are Free *(1972; Academy Award),* Zandy's Bride *(1974),* The Hiding Place *(1975),* Burnt Offerings *(1976),* Seize the Day *(1986),* Heartbreak Ridge *(1986), and* The First Wives Club *(1996).*

She has made guest television appearances on Home Improvement, Ellen, Cybill, Buffalo Gals, Murder One, Love and War, Highway to Heaven, An Investment in Caring, Little House on the Prairie, Trapper John, M.D., Backstairs at the White House, Lou Grant, The Mary Tyler Moore Show, Trauma Center, Love Story, The Streets of San Francisco, The FBI, Gunsmoke, The Fugitive, Out of the Blue, Naked City, Alfred Hitchcock Presents, Alcoa Hour, Goodyear Television Playhouse, The Five Mrs. Buchanans, *and* Philco Television Playhouse. *Other television shows include* Save Me a Place at Forest Lawn *(1966; Emmy Award),* The Victim *(1972),* FBI Story: The FBI versus Alvin Karpis, Public Enemy Number One *(1974),* Sunshine Christmas *(1977),* Love Suddenly *(1978),* The Sorrows of Gin *(1979),* F.D.R.: The Last Year *(1980),* White Mama *(1980),* The Big Black Pill *(1981),* Games Mother Never Taught You *(1981),* Partners in Crime *(1984),* The Recovery Room *(1985),* Annie McGuire *(1988),* Stuck with Each Other *(1989),* Triumph over Disaster: The Hurricane Andrew Story *(1993),* Love and War *(1993; Emmy Award),* Breathing Lessons *(1994), and* Ultimate Betrayal *(1994).*

She was elected to the Theater Hall of Fame in 1994 and received a Tony Award for Lifetime Achievement in 2000.

This interview took place on October 25, 1993.

Interviewer: The first memory I have of you—it's a terrible thing to say to anybody—but you were drunk. It was Maxwell Anderson's *The Bad Seed*; and it was a heart-wrenching scene.

Heckart: That was just my second time on Broadway, and I did have a very showy part, even though it was only a total of eight minutes—four minutes in one scene, four in another. The trick to a part like that is that you're talked about when you're not onstage. You can come on and do a wonderful turn for four minutes and it's not remembered; but if they keep referring to your character, it seems like a larger part. Anyway, I read Dick Coe's opening-night review in the *Washington Post*, and it was glowing, but my name wasn't mentioned. I was so hurt, and I said something to Nancy Kelly, who played the lead in the show. Nancy's a great friend of Dick's, and two days later in the mail comes his last paragraph, which, because of time and space, they had cut. And his last paragraph was all devoted to me, and it was a wonderful notice. I thought, "Oh, that's a sweet man, who would know how much I cared, and the fact that it was good, and I didn't even know it."

Interviewer: You wanted to tell a story about *The Dark at the Top of the Stairs,* the William Inge play you starred in in the 1950s.

Heckart: We had been playing about six months on Broadway, and at the entrance of the set was a small alcove, which had a couple of little spindly chairs; you saw it through these little windows, and people came through that main entrance. It was sort of screened from the audience, but they had an awareness of it. One night I walk onstage to play my opening scene, and there's a man standing on our stage in the alcove. I didn't recognize him, but it wouldn't have mattered, he was on our stage. I was so livid, I could hardly play the scene. I ran upstairs, and I called the stage manager. I said, "Who is that creature?" and he said, "That's Archibald MacLeish, the poet laureate of America." I said, "I don't care who he is, get him out of there!" I went down, and he was still there for the next scene. I was apoplectic. Anyway, he eventually got off, but everybody knew how I felt about somebody being on our stage. At this point, I hear these people at the end of the first act climbing the stairs—Elia Kazan, who was the director of the play, and MacLeish. And he keeps saying, "How angry is she?" "I don't know, we'll find out." So they knock on the door, and Kazan said, "You know, Archie has never been backstage in the theater before." I said—he was about to do his own play, *J.B.*, and Kazan was going to direct it—I said, "Mr. MacLeish, you go and you sit on your stage when you do *J.B.* You do not come into our house and sit on our stage." The next night, the whole dressing room was just filled with flowers from Archibald MacLeish.

Interviewer: What makes a play? When you read a script, what happens to you?

Heckart: In the first place, I think, for me, in any good play, there is a choice someplace in the play. A person can choose the wrong road to go, and it can become very tragic. Something has to happen to the characters; they have to grow. So many plays I see today, it's all static. Things happen to the people, but they're not changed at all. They didn't learn anything. That's what a play means to me.

Interviewer: Then how do you find a play that you really truly want to do? What makes you get excited about it? How do you see what you can do with it?

Heckart: The first play I ever did on Broadway was Inge's *Picnic*, and I was the schoolteacher. The second play was *The Bad Seed*. After *The Bad Seed* I had a very difficult time getting roles, because everything sent me was to play an alcoholic. And I knew that I could get in that trap; I could make a living playing alcoholics whenever they came up. I sat out. I went on unemployment insurance instead, because I just turned down all the alcoholic scripts until something came that I wanted to do. You look at each script; each one is so personal. Does it stretch you as an actress? Are you able to learn something from it? Does it have facets that you have not shown of your personality, or facets of someone else that you would never attempt doing? Different parts mean different things at different moments in your life. That's what your choices are.

Interviewer: Sometimes you'll read a play, or someone will tell you, "This is a part we want you to do very badly." What happens then?

Heckart: Well, it depends. Katharine Cornell's husband was Guthrie McClintic. I was very young in the theater, and he had obviously seen something I'd done. It was Maxwell Anderson's last play—Max had died—and McClintic said, "There's a wonderful part in there for Eileen Heckart." So I went into McClintic's office, and my heart was in my mouth. That this important man would even deign to call me! He said, "I want you to read this script, and Max would've liked you to play this part." I couldn't wait to get on the train to go back to Connecticut. I had read the play by the time I got home. It was just terrible, and I was due back in four days' time to tell Mr. McClintic that I would play this part. I had to walk in and say, "Mr. McClintic, I have to tell you, I do not like this play very much." I could tell he was just so angry, he was raging. I think his thought was "Here I am as a director, Guthrie McClintic, and here's a play by Maxwell Anderson, and here's this know-nothing who has the nerve to tell us that it's not any good?" He said, "Well, thank you very much, just leave the script right on the desk. Thank you for coming in." I got to the door, and he said, "Just a moment." I turned around, and he said, "Kit [Katharine Cornell] said the same damn thing." So that was kind of nice.

Interviewer: You've acted not just in comedy but also in plays like Inge's *The Dark at the Top of the Stairs*. You played Lottie, a very touching figure. She is somebody quite different from what you'd been doing.

Heckart: Well, in the first place, everything I've ever done, as I see my own life, has a touch of humor to it. I think to get through life we have to have humor. I mean, just look at the things that happen to us in the course of a lifetime. I think the worst notice I ever received was from somebody in Boston on *The Bad Seed*, and he said there were too many laughs in the part. Well, I deliberately chose where I wanted to release the pressure for the audience so they would accept the pathos. You can't go on and just play misery, or just play self-pity; that's the most boring thing in the world. A person with real guts has to be able to look at the situation and say, "There's something kind of funny about it too," in the midst of things so tortured.

Interviewer: You began in Ohio. Do you remember the first play you ever saw?

Heckart: Yes, it was a musical, with Ethel Waters and Clifton Webb.

Interviewer: *As Thousands Cheer?*

Heckart: Yes, *As Thousands Cheer.* All I know is she came on and sang, "We're havin' a heat wave, a tropical heat wave," right? I came from a poor family; we couldn't afford tickets to the theater. That was all too ritzy, and there wasn't money for it. I saved my money and got a balcony ticket for *The Philadelphia Story;* it was with Katharine Hepburn on tour with Joe Cotton and Van Heflin. When I later did *A View from the Bridge* on Broadway and Van Heflin walked in playing the lead and I was playing his wife, I was going to say, "You were in the second play I ever saw." But I thought, "No, that's rather aging. I'm not going to say that to him and ruin this whole relationship." But that was the second one I ever saw.

Interviewer: If you were starting out today, what would you do?

Heckart: There isn't any other way to do it in the first place. When young actors ask me for advice, which they do—you have to learn about yourself. And you do not learn about yourself in a television studio. By the time you hit television, you better know what you are doing, because there are a lot of bad directors. Not that there aren't bad directors in the theater, there are, but you better know what of you sells with an audience and how far to go as far as film is concerned. One of the things that was really wrong with my work in the film *The Bad Seed,* when I look back on it now, is that I played a stage performance. I shouldn't have; it should have been smaller.

Interviewer: What about technique?

Heckart: You have to know yourself. Audiences respond, and so much of it is a certain technique. Technique can't be laughed at. I mean, for instance, it's a small matter of a laugh. A laugh builds, and it hits its peak, and you come in with your next line as it starts its curve down. You hear them, every night; every audience is just that much different, but they have their own rhythm and it builds and you hear that thing and you say, "Pow, I plow right into that one!" In other words, you don't let the laughter die and sit there with egg on your face. You move. But those are things you only learn on a stage. You don't learn that in movies, and you don't learn that in television. I sometimes take a cab down Broadway and there's somebody's name sixty feet tall I've never heard of in my whole life, and I say, "Who is that?" And it turns out he's got a hot new television show. Well, if they're not prepared and they're going on personality alone—and goodness knows, there's a big market for that too—so often they don't know their craft. When that particular show is over, if they haven't saved their money, which most of them don't, it's hard to build a career. You don't build a career from that.

Interviewer: When you saw *The Philadelphia Story* with those three fine actors, what did you think to yourself: "I could do that" or "I'd like to be a part of that"?

Heckart: "I want to do that! I want to do that!" I always wanted to do that. Mama loved movies, so on weekends, we would go downtown in Columbus, Ohio, and we would hit eight movies on Saturday and Sunday. They were double features, and we would do four a day. For the ones that Mama couldn't see, I'd come home and act all the parts for her. Of course, my big dream was to swing a mink stole like Joan Crawford. I thought that was the end. I never got those parts; I was always in the kitchen someplace. I think every child goes through a thing where they think, "Oh, that would be very glamorous and wonderful," but there's a stick-to-it-ivity. If you know that that's what you want to do—it doesn't have to be an actor, whatever the endeavor is—no one can rid you of it. I knew what I wanted to do, and there wasn't anybody who could say, "You're just awful and you're not going to make it," because they were so wrong. My heart said, "You just do what you have to do."

Interviewer: You got your first job with the Blackfriars' Guild. What was the Blackfriars' Guild?

Heckart: In those days, there were only two off-Broadway theaters. Now we have hundreds of them. There was the Cherry Lane Theatre and the Blackfriars' Guild, which was a Catholic organization. I'm Catholic, so I went trotting down to those little priests. I tried out and got the part of a cow who sat on a piano and sang "My Bill" à la Helen Morgan. She was a wonderful cow. Elliot Nugent and Raymond Massey came in to a matinee, and the next day I got a call to be understudy to Audrey Christie in *The Voice of the Turtle*.

Interviewer: No kidding! What an experience. That was only a three-character play. Did you go on sometimes?

Heckart: No, and it's kind of wonderful, because I learned a great lesson in that show. I stayed for six months. I was assistant stage manager too, so I read every script that came into producer Alfred de Liagre's office. You think all your friends are talented and there are millions of good plays around. I read so many rotten plays, and these were going to a Broadway producer. They were really terrible. I only read one good one in the whole six months. But I wanted to go on before I left. I had gone out with my meager salary and covered myself with costumes from Macy's that kind of worked like Audrey Christie's, so they couldn't say to me, "Oh no, you don't have a wardrobe, you can't go on." I got a job in summer stock in Milwaukee as leading lady for Morton Da

Costa, and I went to de Liagre's office and I said, "I would like to play before I leave." I thought understudies got to play. He just looked at me and said, "Well, I'll discuss it with John Van Druten," who had written the play. Audrey Christie knew that I wanted to play. They said all right, on a certain weekend; in the meantime I went out and I bought thirty-six tickets out of my pocket for agents, so people would see me, and then they found an excuse for me not to play. They did give me my money back for the tickets, but I was still going out to do stock, and they said, "How can you leave a Broadway play as an understudy to go out and do summer stock?" I said, "Because out there in Milwaukee, I'll be on a stage. I'll be playing a lead every single week. I'm the leading woman in the company." They thought that was wrong thinking. Anyway, the last weekend, Audrey Christie went to Alfred de Liagre and said, "Heckart will have to go on for the Saturday matinee," which was my last show, "because I have a toothache." And he said, "I beg your pardon?" She said, "Take me to Equity on charges; I have a toothache on Saturday." So I played, and they offered me a third company—on the road—because of it. But I was too anxious to get out to Milwaukee to make my name, right? What it did for me was from the time I was important enough or had enough good parts under my belt, I have had it in my contract that my understudy gets to go on at a certain performance someplace, because that's the most wonderful thing Audrey could have done for me.

Interviewer: You have that in your contract?

Heckart: I do now, yes.

Interviewer: That's terrific, really.

Heckart: Audrey taught me that. It wouldn't have occurred to me, because you see, in the first place, I'm a character woman. If I don't go on, it's not going to mean anything at the box office. Now, if Carol Channing doesn't go on, if Ethel Merman doesn't go on—that makes a difference. But these people, they have a right to be seen.

Interviewer: That's marvelous. That illustrates to me another thing I love about theater people. I don't find all the backbiting and jealousy that's supposed to go on in the theater.

Heckart: Oh, you are so naive!

Interviewer: I *am* an innocent. I only hear good things about other actors from the best actors. It really has astonished me. They're excited that so-and-so has a hit, because as one of them once explained to me, "If she's got a hit, and they sell out, they're bound to come to us next door." Of course, that's true.

Heckart: Actors, if anybody's in trouble—and this is true for playwrights too, or directors—if somebody calls for you on the road, if Sinatra cancels out, boy, Tony Bennett is in there to sub for him for the evening. They're the most generous people in the world. What always tickles me, though, is the night of the Actors' Fund Benefit, you've had hit notices, and all these actors are sitting there, just waiting. And they come storming back to your dressing room, saying it was marvelous, it was marvelous, and they walk out and say, "Was that a piece of shit! How did it win the Pulitzer?"

Interviewer: It really is true that the people who survive in the theater are great admirers of one another, because they know what it's taken to get there. You see, you were very fortunate to get that job down in the Village, at the Blackfriars'.

Heckart: If you've been in the theater for a while and you have a choice of eleven scripts, that's wonderful. But when you're young, don't wait for another job that might be coming up; you take what's there at the moment. That's the only thing to do, so it doesn't matter. You go by your choices, what you have.

Interviewer: Does surviving as an actor also mean a particular longing on the part of the actor? I've known actors who come from acting families who somehow just don't pursue it the way they might. And their parents kind of look at them: "What's wrong with you, you're not really trying." Then they get out of it completely, they avoid it. But you were lucky with your children.

Heckart: Luke started as an actor, and finally he said to me one day, "I don't know how you take the rejection." If you're not careful, you're too tall for radio. There's always a reason why you don't get the part. He said, "I really want to direct." He had gone to Juilliard, and he graduated from NYU in their arts department on their exchange, and it's been wonderful. He's doing *Oleanna* now at Coconut Grove. Last week he was observing all week long on *Murphy Brown* because he wants to know something about television, because he wants to make a living too and you don't always do that in the theater. I don't worry about him. He makes the most of his opportunities; he's a mover, he's a goer, and he's talented. He directed me in *Driving Miss Daisy.* His brother said to him, "Oh God, you want to direct her? Is that going to be normal?" And he said, "I don't even know how to address you. I'm not going to say 'Mama.'" I said, "I think 'Ms. Heckart' is a little too formal. Why don't you try 'Eileen'?" He said, "All right." He was very good. He had good suggestions. When I thought he was wrong, we discussed it privately. We got along just fine.

Interviewer: In today's world, so many working mothers are away at the same time the fathers are away. In your world, with your offbeat hours, you're working while we're being entertained by you. But you spent a lot of time with your kids while they were growing up, didn't you?

Heckart: Yes. I never had an apartment in New York. I went home to Connecticut every night. Even on matinee days, it didn't matter to me, because that's where it is. That's my life pulse, right there. Jack and I have been married for fifty years, and he knew getting out of college what I wanted to do, so there was never a big thing about the choice: "Oh boy, I don't want to be married to an actress." I was also very fortunate in that about thirty-six years ago—now about forty years ago—a wonderful Scotswoman came to us. And she stayed for thirty-six years; we now have her in a nursing home very close to us. We go every day. She was the children's nurse. She wasn't just a nine-to-five person. She had her own guest house, her own garage, and her own little garden. If I was out making a film, I came home every weekend, but when I finished the stint I'd say, "Where do you want to go?" She'd want to go back to Scotland to visit her family, or she'd want to go to St. Croix or something. I'd say, "Go." But I know a lot of people who treat people as nine to five, and when you do that, then they are looking for their Thursday afternoon off, they can't wait until Saturday comes. She was a member of the family.

Interviewer: That was really very lucky, wasn't it?

Heckart: It certainly was. Then another lucky thing for me was that Jack was really women's lib before women's lib, so he wanted me to do my thing. I couldn't have done it without an understanding husband. I couldn't have done it.

Interviewer: And you worked so regularly! My golly, you've always worked.

Heckart: I've been very lucky, yes.

Interviewer: Films would come along, and if it was worth doing, you'd go to the Coast but come home on the weekend?

Heckart: Well, you do films for money. So you can survive and do more in the theater. I think I have a total of seventeen films. That is really nothing. It's so seldom you see a good movie script. I read one written by Robert Benton called *Nobody's Fool.* Paul Newman was playing the lead, and it was the part of his housekeeper. I wanted that part. I went in to meet the director; I wasn't reading or anything, I just went to meet him. He had my picture and my bio and everything and he said, "Really this woman should be old enough to be Paul's mother." I said, "I played Paul's mother." He said, "When?" I said, "*Somebody Up There Likes Me.* Forty years ago, I played Paul's mother." And he said, "Well, you can't play his mother today." I said, "I'm seventy-four years old, what do you want from me?" He said, "You're not the right kind of seventy-four." And I said, "How can you have so little imagination? You take off my makeup, you take my bangs away, you put me in a Peter Pan collar and shoes, I slump my shoulders, and I can be any age you want. I won an Emmy for playing eighty-six!" He would not give me that job.

Interviewer: You've done musicals, too, haven't you? You did *Pal Joey* somewhere along the line, didn't you?

Heckart: At the City Center. I had a marvelous experience. This is very heady for an actress. Bob Fosse was playing the lead, with Carol Bruce, and I was miserable. If you do a play and the play is in trouble, and it's one act that's not right, you work on that act during the daytime. After about a week, maybe, of rehearsing it and making the changes, you're ready to put it in and try, and then it takes another couple of weeks to get it up to match the rest of the play if that's what you want. A musical, you do a number one night and they say, "Oh, cut that number, that's terrible. We'll do another number tomorrow." If you're not a musical person, that's the most frightening thing in the whole world. When I did *Joey,* Gus Schirmer Jr. was directing, and I had an agreement with him—it was just a handshake. I said, "Listen, if I'm unhappy"—I had never done a musical—"if I'm unhappy, you have a small boy come on and play this part, because I'll be right out that door." I did the choreography and I worked and everything. Bobby Fosse kept saying, "But wait until the musicians get here." Well, the musicians got there, thirty-seven of them were sitting in that pit, and I just sat with my mouth open and Bobby said, "What do you think?" And I said, "Well, thirty-seven men and I are a million miles apart." And he said, "Well, I have to tell you, it's the worst rendition of 'Zip' I've ever heard in my life." He said, "Would you take some help from me?" Bobby Fosse! He said, "Come to dinner," and I did. Of course, he was married to Gwen Verdon, so Gwen cooked. Bobby had rented a studio, rented a pianist, and for two hours Gwen Verdon danced beside me, Bob Fosse danced in front of me, and I opened and boy, it was wonderful. Yes, it was quite magnificent. For a nonmusical person to have them be as giving as they both were to me was wonderful.

Interviewer: It must have been great fun, though, to start out with that.

Heckart: The hardest workers in all that business for me are the dancers. And their life is short—thirty, thirty-five and they've had it. Every once in a while you'll have a gypsy that hits forty, but not often. Every night I was in the wings watching Fosse's four numbers. I was the only one. There wasn't a single dancer who wasn't onstage, but none of the other actors was there. I came on to do my one "Zip" number, and because I had an acting scene in front of it, every dancer in the entire house was down there every night to watch that show.

A sweet thing happened, though, really dear. I learned very early that you do not trust musical people on matinees. Being at the City Center, you took an elevator up to the fifth floor and there was a greenroom, and they said, "Will you come and have a drink with us?" In the first place, that's dangerous, that drinking between shows. They brought in martinis in milk cartons. Gin is there all through the matinee, and then these kids drank these warm martinis and played that night. I had a swallow, and I went off to have dinner and everything. Well, we were about to close and they said, "Will you come join us?" And I thought, "Oh God, another hot martini!" All week long, they would knock at the door and would say, "Are we going to see you on Saturday?" And I said, "I'll be there, I'll be there." So I got up there, and there's a ritual in the music theater, it's called a gypsy robe, and it goes to the most popular member of the chorus of each musical. They had made a throne for me; it was a big wicker chair. They had rolled toilet paper all the way to the ceiling. And they had made me my own gypsy robe, with a scroll saying here's this legitimate type whom we're making an honorary gypsy. The robe was absolutely obscene. It was in purple taffeta, it was trimmed with pink marabou, it had GYPSY in silver across the back, and it had Bobby Fosse's white gloves right over here—it said a lot of rotten things on it. I started to cry and they said, "Isn't that a legit type for you? She's crying." I was so proud of that robe, and that night we were going down in the elevator and somebody said to Carol Bruce, "Did you hear about Heckart's gypsy robe?" And Carol was like, "A gypsy robe? You gave it to Heckart, on her first musical?" There was a kind of silence in the elevator, with about five of these dancers standing there, and she said, "I never got a gypsy robe," and one of them said, "Oh, Carol, you were *born* a gypsy." Very sweet.

Interviewer: Musicals have all these people around; but you've also done one-person plays. How about those? You did Eleanor Roosevelt.

Heckart: And Margaret Sanger. I must say, rehearsing any one-person show is just terrible. There's nobody to play off. You have a director; that's it. And it is such hard work. When I opened *Eleanor* at Ford's Theatre, in Washington, on about my fifth night—it hadn't affected me before—I looked up at Lincoln's box and I didn't know where I was. All I could think of was "That's where he sat!" So I walked off the stage. Now, in a one-person show, when you leave a stage, the audience has to think, "She's going to the loo; there couldn't be any other reason." And I said to the stage manager, "Where am I?" and he said, "The Russians," and I said, "Thank you," and went back on and picked it up. As you play it, you try things and you get more and more comfortable. You certainly know the material, and then there's a terrible sense of power that comes over you. Nobody can tell you what to do. That curtain goes up and it's your baby. I must have done *Eleanor* off and on for about a year and a half, and somebody sent me a two-character play. I usually don't like two-character plays; you have to have a dog or a telephone to create the feeling of other people. I read it, and Jack said, "What do you think?" and I said, "Well, there's nothing for me to do!" It spoils you in that way. It's a strange format, because there are a lot of audiences who don't like single-person plays. Certainly there's Hal Holbrook, who's so marvelous in his Mark Twain; and Jimmy Whitmore's Truman was wonderful. But it's a very hard format. There are many people who don't want to sit and just watch one person; they think they're boring. A lot of times I agree with them. Once Tad Mosel came to me and said he would write me a one-woman show on Dorothy Thompson. She's a wonderful character, but she doesn't mean anything to the audience today.

Even with Eleanor Roosevelt this was partially true; I was giving a history lesson. People came up to me afterwards and said, "Oh boy, I don't know much about this lady," especially the young people, "but I want to learn about her now." Well, that's marvelous in its way, but I was there as an actress, not to give a history lesson. Let somebody else do that. My Margaret Sanger was a better vehicle than my Eleanor Roosevelt.

Interviewer: The loneliness must be very appalling.

Heckart: It's terrible. You've got your company manager, on the road, and your dresser who does your wigs, and who else did I have? A stage manager. Whoop-de-doo! Boring.

Interviewer: Would you do the Eleanor Roosevelt play again?

Heckart: No, it was an episodic script, so much so that—she has such a rich life—instead of taking five marvelous moments and really working those, I played from seventeen to eighty-six and aged onstage. There'd be a blip and then it was over, that moment in my life, and then I was someplace else. I have found that I'm not good at going back and repeating something that I did before. It served its purpose then, but no, I wouldn't like to do it again.

Interviewer: I'm sure that this is a dreadful question, which one should never ask, but nonetheless—how do you learn all those lines?

Heckart: I have learned that people learn lines in two ways. Very quickly, which is my way of doing it, and when the play's over, two days later I couldn't repeat a line. If I have to do the performance again in three or four years, I have to learn it all over again. The people who memorize very slowly, they'll stop you on the street and quote passages of Shakespeare to you, but they have a retentive memory. I don't have one. But now it's not as speedy as it was when I was twenty. That's so much your stock-in-trade, your technique, that you don't even think about it. Obviously, the lines are there, and you have to say what the playwright wrote. You are there to interpret him. What so many people want to do today, especially the young people who don't know their craft, is impose themselves and play themselves and phrase it the way they would.

Interviewer: But there's another funny thing about some of this memory work. When you, as a nonmusician, came to your song, you were well trained by a master on how to do that particular number.

Heckart: Well, in the first place, with someone like Elaine Stritch, like [Carol] Channing, like Bobby Morse, it's selling a song. You are acting, performing, a number. That's what it comes down to. And you are selling the number. That's a lot different than being the soprano.

Interviewer: The last time you played in Washington, if I remember correctly, was *The Cemetery Club*. It was on a low level, but on the other hand it worked with the audience, and I would have thought that in New York particularly it would have had a chance.

Heckart: The playwright was very young. His father had been on the borscht circuit, so he had heard these jokes over and over again from his father. It was one of the few times in my life I went and I said to him, "There are too many jokes. Can't you cut some of the jokes? Because these three ladies have serious lives, for them." It wasn't very satisfying. If they thought they were going to get all the Jewish ladies from Brooklyn, they didn't. It didn't happen.

Interviewer: And it didn't seem to work as a movie either. It just seemed like a long sitcom, really; that was the problem.

Heckart: I must say, there's another thing about movies that's so wonderful. I was one of the three leads in the play, and they cast Diane Ladd in my part in the film. They asked me if I'd want to come in and read for a bit part. Is it any wonder we have no ego? Rejection, rejection!

Interviewer: Well, how do you cope with agents? Everybody hears about this agent problem, and frequently actors change agents: "So-and-so isn't doing much of a job," and then, "Oh, I've got a new agent; the world is going to change overnight." Sometimes it does, and then sometimes it doesn't. Are you friendly with your agent?

Heckart: Yes, but you see, I've had very few agents in my life. Many people misunderstand what an agent does. An agent does not get you a job. Other people call for you; he can submit you, but he doesn't get you the job. He's there to negotiate your contract, to get you the most money and the things that you care about—if you want air conditioning in your trailer or whatever it is. But a lot of people think that agents get you jobs, and if you have that feeling, then you're not going to be happy with your agent. But if you've known someone a long time: Maynard Morris was my agent until he died. I was with Milton Goldman for twenty-three years; then I went with William Morris a while—and it's just fine.

Interviewer: But now people will come to you and say, "Would you be interested in this?"

Heckart: Absolutely. At this point mostly a playwright will just call me from the Coast or call me directly, and if I say, "Yes, I'll do it; call my agent," then I do it.

Interviewer: Young people whose work is not known, they feel they have to have an agent.

Heckart: Well, they do to get submitted. You can't get a good agent unless they see you do something off-off-Broadway. You have to go out and get that part, and they don't want to come to those things off-off-Broadway. It's very hard; it's a catch-22.

Interviewer: These days, on Broadway and off Broadway in New York, serious plays have a tough time surviving. What about around the rest of the country? How do we go about trying to get new plays and new playwrights going?

Heckart: I think that television has ruined a great deal. I find audiences don't even want to sit for a serious play. I mean, fifteen minutes and they're, "Where's the popcorn?" It's a mind-set. This has gradually crept in, and it goes with those commercials that come on those sitcoms. They're used to getting up and moving around. They're also much more vocal, because you can sit in front of your television set and say, "Look at her hair tonight. Oh, why did she change her hair?" You hear that in the theater now too: "Oh my God, what a terrible dress!" People didn't use to be vocal in the theater; if they didn't like it they said it at the intermission. You hear murmurings now.

Interviewer: They think they're in their living rooms, and they're just talking out loud.

Heckart: It is true that musicals fill the place. Serious drama is very difficult. And it usually has a limited run.

Interviewer: Were you pleased with the path you chose in raising your family on the East Coast? How that has impacted your career as opposed to being in Hollywood?

Heckart: I'm a theater person. Everybody has always known that I'll go and do a job but I come home; I live here.

Interviewer: Different actors and actresses approach roles differently. Some approach a role from the outside and work inward; others work from the inside to the outside. How do you do it?

Heckart: I think I'm more "insy" than "outsy." They say that about belly buttons, don't they? I have to know what she's about and how close she is to me, what I can draw on from me, and then find out the parts of her that I don't understand at all.

Interviewer: When I hear your name, the first thing that comes to my mind is your marvelous voice. How has it benefited you and how has it hurt you?

Heckart: I don't know how it's hurt me. I'm sure that it has. I'm sure that it's been limiting in certain ways. I was a smoker in college. I walked around with whooping cough, and I thought it was a smoking cough for six weeks. This was my junior year. I went to Erie, Pennsylvania, to play summer stock, and the doctor, when I got over the whooping cough, said to me—my voice dropped almost an octave, I mean five notes or something—and he said, "You get out in the sun and you rest your voice all summer." I was a leading woman in summer stock; so how was I going to rest my voice? It just dropped then. Remember Margaret Sullavan? She got laryngitis for opening night on Broadway and everybody said, "That's the greatest voice I've ever heard in my life," and she went to her doctor and said, "How do I get laryngitis permanently?"

Interviewer: What happens if you find a marvelous part in a play, but you don't like other parts of the play? Do you just tell the person, "No, I'm not going to do it," or do you say, "Yes, but it needs work," or what?

Heckart: Yes, I will certainly say what my reservations are about it and what I don't like. But usually, no matter how much I like it and want it, if the play doesn't work there's no point. Unless I need the exercise as an actress, that's just a waste. It's hard enough to get a hit per se and have everything work well. But to have fighting and all these disparate personalities pulling at it, you're never going to get a cohesive piece.

Interviewer: Speaking of highs and lows in your career, can you point out your highest point in your experience and your lowest?

Heckart: The best thing I ever played, in my mind, was *Mother Courage* for Michael Kahn at Princeton. I had played it in California, on a limited engagement, many years before, but I was too young for it. I wasn't ripe enough. Then Michael and I did it in Princeton, and that was the most satisfying moment. How many people saw it in Princeton? It doesn't matter. That's what it meant to me. The lowest: oh, there've been a lot of lows. I really can't think of anything that was just so bottom that I thought, "I'll never drag myself up again." But there've been a lot of low ones. I wish I could be more specific.

Interviewer: You've been on the Tony nominating committee, haven't you? What is that like?

Heckart: Yes, I have been. While that sounds wonderful, because I had to see every single play, how many times can you see *Three Men on a Horse*? How many revivals are there? I had to see everything, and that means the good and the bad. And then everybody wants to open in March so it's fresh in the voters' minds. I was out doing a show, and I came back and found out I had to see eight plays in seven days. I was a wreck. I got them in somehow. *Tommy* I thought was quite marvelous, because growing up with kids and that music of the sixties and the seventies, I thought, "Oh, I cannot stand that sound"—but it was wonderful. Then to start the new season at the Roundabout, which is a small theater but on Broadway, we went to see a revival of *She Loves Me.* Jack and I beamed all the way home. It was so marvelous to see a show which was romantic and easy and well done and charming—and it wasn't hitting you with all this gloss and all this fancy magnified music and everything. There's hope. It's a little hope, but there's hope.

Interviewer: What about the critics? One of the things I feel bad about in the theater is—because now we're limited to the *New York Times*—the people who read the *Times* are the only ones who can afford to buy theater tickets. The blue-collar worker simply can't do it.

Heckart: We have nothing but the *Times;* it doesn't matter what the other publications say. That paper makes you or breaks you. It isn't like London was twenty years ago where you paid six dollars for a ticket and you went and you made up your own mind. At seventy-five, eighty-five, a hundred and a quarter, who can make up their mind? You want to know "Is it good?" before you invest that much.

Interviewer: Talk a little bit about directors you've worked with. What are the different ways in which directors work with actors and actresses? What kind of director have you worked best with—or is it a constant adjusting to different styles?

Heckart: The most exciting director I ever worked with was Elia Kazan. It was the only time in my life that I couldn't wait to get to rehearsal. There are many people who love the rehearsal process. I don't; it's quite agonizing for me. I want the curtain to go up, and the audience and I will decide whether a moment works. He called you in for a private appointment once a week before rehearsal started in the morning, say, at nine o'clock. And for an hour you sat with him alone, and he had ideas that he'd written down in red just on your character for that appointment that morning. It was so exciting—to try them, to discard them, or keep them—it was wonderful! Then you have a director like Josh Logan, who was so enthusiastic. With Josh, it didn't matter that you'd read fifteen times for the part before you finally got it; he was, "You got it, and that makes you the most important person in the entire world." Of course, after you open, they all walk away from you—but during that period you are so coddled and taken care of. Josh, for instance, had been an actor himself. He said the reason he stopped acting was if the audience laughed, he did it for them four more times; he didn't know when to stop. I was playing Rosemary, the schoolteacher, in *Picnic,* and once he got up and did a bit of business that was so good I couldn't copy it. I wanted to say, "I wish he hadn't done that." In his mind, he knew what he wanted. When you get a director who is not good and has a limited imagination, you're on your own. Most of the directors I have worked with in my life have asked me back to work with them again, but I have a little blacklist of a few that I'll not go near; whether it's personality or whatever it is, there are too many things involved. That's what I was saying before about the process. We should all be working toward the same end, to have the best possible play, to bring alive whatever the playwright was saying.

Interviewer: You have a story about Karl Malden.

Heckart: Karl Malden was doing *Desperate Hours* on Broadway. I sat in his dressing room and I said, "Karl, I'm going out to make my first movie. What do you do?" He said, "Well, I'll tell you what Spencer Tracy told me: 'Find out where the camera is. Now, if the camera is a long shot, you behave as you do on a stage. If they say it's a medium shot, you behave conversationally, as we are right now. If they say close-up, you move your eyes right, and you move them left.'" Of course, when I did *Bus Stop,* no one told me it was Cinemascope. I just wished I didn't have any eyebrows. I thought, "Who is that woman working those eyebrows all the time?" You see, that's the thing: if you don't go and look for yourself, you don't know, because obviously the eyebrows didn't bother Josh, who directed that movie. Oh, it was a terrible moment for me. That's why one must go to the rushes; there's nobody else who's going to monitor it who sees what you see and what you're trying to convey. If you think you're doing that and you're not, there's a problem. You have to find out for yourself.

Interviewer: Which do you find easier to do, comedy or serious drama?

Heckart: It doesn't matter. I don't prefer one to the other, and I don't do one better than the other.

Cherry Jones

Cherry Jones was born in Paris, Tennessee, on November 21, 1956. She studied for the stage at Carnegie-Mellon University. She made her stage debut as Rosalind in As You Like It *at the American Repertory Theatre in 1980 and her Broadway debut as Lynn in* Stepping Out *in 1987. For American Repertory her plays have included* A Midsummer Night's Dream *(1981),* The Boys from Syracuse *(1983), and* The Three Sisters *(1983). Her other roles in New York are Liz,* The Philanthropist *(1983); Kitty Chase,* The Ballad of Soapy Smith *(1984); Sally Bowles,* I Am a Camera *(1984); Cecily Cardew,* The Importance of Being Earnest *(1985); Sara Littlefield,* Claptrap *(1987); Fran,* Big Time: Scenes from a Service Economy *(1988); Lady Macduff,* Macbeth *(1988); Liz,* Our Country's Good *(1991); Anna,* The Baltimore Waltz *(1992); Catherine Sloper,* The Heiress *(1995; Tony Award); Hannah Jelkes,* The Night of the Iguana *(1996); Mabel Tidings Bigelow,* Pride's Crossing *(1998); Maxine,* Tongue of the Bird *(1999); and Josie Hogan,* A Moon for the Misbegotten *(2000).*

Among her film credits are Alex: The Life of a Child *(1986),* The Big Town *(1987),* Housesitter *(1992),* The Tears of Julian Po *(1997),* Out of the Past *(1998),* The Horse Whisperer *(1998),* Cradle Will Rock *(1999),* Erin Brockovich *(2000), and* The Perfect Storm *(2000).*

She has appeared on the television shows Spenser: For Hire *and* Murder in a Small Town.

This interview took place on May 24, 1996.

• ————————————————————————————— •

Interviewer: Why don't we go back to the beginning? You were born in Tennessee?

Jones: I was born in Paris, Tennessee.

Interviewer: Were you interested in theater as a kid?

Jones: I was always interested in theater. My mother was an English lit teacher, so I was introduced to Shakespeare at an early age. And my grandmother Thelma Cherry was a great lover not so much of theater (I don't think she saw more than two live productions in her life, having been born at the turn of the century in middle Tennessee), but she loved acting and she loved films. I was going to be her actress, so I had encouragement from my grandmother, who we lived with until I was four. Then she lived with us until she died when I was seventeen, right about the time I found out I'd gotten accepted to Carnegie-Mellon. I participated in the high school drama program and, as a child, was very fortunate to have been taught by the Pied Piper of creative dramatics, Miss Ruby Krider. I took a little creative dramatics class with her once a week and exercised my imagination theatrically. I was in the woods exercising my imagination every other afternoon of the week. I was a tomboy and would go into the woods and create amazing, elaborate fantasy situations. I was always in the top of a tree, very athletic, which I had no idea was going to become such an important tool in my later life as an actor.

Interviewer: Isn't acting very much like athletics? It requires the same kind of stamina.

Jones: It is, it is! In fact, Billy Petersen, when we were doing *Night of the Iguana*, said, "I think what we do is harder than what professional athletes do." He said, "Those basketball players only play three games a week. We play eight, back to back."

Interviewer: What's the first play you remember seeing, and what's the first play you were in in high school?

Jones: The first play I ever saw was *The Country Girl* at the Barter Theatre.

Interviewer: In Virginia?

Jones: Yes. I was maybe ten. I took a trip to the Smokies and up into the Blue Ridge Mountains with my parents, and we went to see *The Country Girl.* I'll never forget, we were sitting in the front row, and this marvelous actress, I wish I knew her name (I probably *know* her now), came to the lip of the stage and delivered the final lines of the play. I remember them being very poignant, and the lights slowly coming down, dimming on her, and as they went out, ghosting, there was sort of a final burst of dim light—and I didn't understand that that was a technical thing. I thought it was her spirit surging one last time, that it came from her—and that sort of did it. I knew I wanted to do that. In high school, I got to play Annie Sullivan in *The Miracle Worker,* the doctor in *Flowers for Algernon,* and Mame in *Mame.* I participated in the National Forensic League and did dramatic interpretation at speech contests and was very good at it. I went to nationals my three years in high school, representing Tennessee. Many of my girlfriends would scream as they saw their names listed for the finals and I would think, "How silly." For me, it wasn't about winning, it was about getting the chance to do it *one more time,* and for a larger audience. I needed to pass on to the next stage in those competitions because I loved it so much. I just had to keep doing it. And then I got into Carnegie-Mellon.

Interviewer: Did you apply there because you knew it had a great drama program?

Jones: Yes. Actually, I'd spent my sixteenth summer at Northwestern, at the High School Institute of Speech and Drama. That was my first opportunity to meet my peers who were as interested in and as serious about theater as I. A woman there, Libbie Appel, who's now the artistic director of the Indiana Rep, told me about Carnegie-Mellon. I had very low scholastic scores, and when I sent them to Carnegie-Mellon, they were the only university who wrote back and said, "Oh, congratulations on your scores; we would love to have you audition for our program," and I thought, "Boy, this is the place for me!" Then I auditioned and got in. I remember Jewel Walker very clearly at that audition. He gave us a very simple exercise; we had to walk across the room just like he had, and I remember thinking it seemed the simplest thing in the world. But of course it's not, observing exactly what someone has done and then repeating it.

Interviewer: What piece did you use for your audition?

Jones: *This Property Is Condemned,* the only other Tennessee Williams I ever performed before *Iguana.* Those four years at Carnegie were very interesting, because we had four different acting heads. Each new head brought in a new regime. They each basically told us they were the one way, the true way, and the only way, and we were to forget anything else we'd ever known before them! Of course, what it did was to give us a very realistic look at what it was going to be like working in the real, professional world. American actors come from so many different schools, and often you watch directors struggling with trying to get a cast from all these different schools to come together in the same world. With a resident company, it's much easier for directors to get a group of actors into one cohesive world; when you've worked together before, you start to speak the same language. I'm very grateful that Carnegie was as turbulent in those years as it was, because it gave me a lot of different techniques and schools to draw from.

Interviewer: Did you play a lot of roles at Carnegie-Mellon?

Jones: I did. Being a big girl, I played a lot of the more mature roles for the most part. One of my big hits was a kitchen drama by Jason Miller called *The Circus Lady,* where I played an extremely obese woman, which was fantastic to attempt as a nineteen-year-old. I was in Oden von Horvath's *Faith, Hope, and Charity,* where I played the only ingenue I thought I'd ever get to play, not being your typical ingenue.

Interviewer: What did you do in the summers when you were at Carnegie?

Jones: I was very fortunate, because the head of the drama department my last two years was Walter Eysselinck. Walter became a great supporter and included me in the summer Equity company my junior and senior years, which was my first experience with professionals. Between high school and college I had done summer stock at Theatre-by-the-Sea in Rhode Island. After my freshman year I'd gotten into a dinner theater company down in Tennessee, and we toured dinner theaters doing *The Good Doctor,* and that was a wonderful experience. But the Equity summer program at Carnegie was my first experience with New York professional actors and directors.

Interviewer: He would import New York actors, and he would use some of his own students?

Jones: Very few of us. There were only a couple of us hired, because there are few juvenile parts in most plays. I did a production of a play called *Quail Southwest* by Larry Ketron, and one of the New York actors' agents who'd come to see his client's work also saw me, so I actually came to New York with an agent, which was the greatest gift that Carnegie-Mellon gave me. That's always the catch-22: how do you get an agent? When young people ask me that question I'm always at a loss.

Interviewer: Then you came to New York?

Jones: Yes. I got a job at a health food deli on Columbus and 72nd Street. It was a great place for a kid just coming to New York to work, because many of my idols drifted in off the street to be waited on. A few days after I'd seen one of Maureen Stapleton's earliest performances in *The Gin Game* (she and E. G. Marshall had taken over for Jessica Tandy and Hume Cronyn), in walked Maureen Stapleton. I was a huge fan. I remember seeing her in

Airport and recognizing for the first time that I was watching great acting. When Van Heflin pulls away in the airplane, she knows he's going to do something dreadful, and she's left standing there looking at the runway, just completely despondent. I'll never forget that performance as long as I live. And a few days after *Gin Game,* in walked Ms. Stapleton. I said, "Ms. Stapleton, I saw your performance the other night, I think it was your second performance, and you were just miraculous." Her eyes literally rolled back in her head and she said, "Oh, it was a nightmare!" and she sort of went running out of the store. So that was my one moment with Maureen Stapleton! I have since come to understand exactly what she meant by that, and what those nights can be like!

Interviewer: Did you also get jobs in the theater right away?

Jones: I came to New York and for about a year and a half, nothing came my way. My agent was sending me out a great deal, and I came close to things, but I never got the work. I was very overweight, five feet eight and a half inches with this little-girl face, and no one knew what to do with me. I was convinced that I wasn't going to work until I was thirty-five years old, because those were the parts I'd played in college. I became very serious about my career and lost some weight and took a course on how to audition. It wasn't so much that I needed to know how to audition, I just needed to perform for somebody again. So I took the class so that I could get up in front of a handful of people and do it, because my muscles were beginning to atrophy and I was most unhappy. I think because of that class I regained some confidence and got a role (that I was not particularly well suited for) at the Brooklyn Academy of Music Theatre Company, in *He and She* by Rachel Crothers, a 1911 early feminist play that Emily Mann directed. BAM was my first company experience. It was thrilling to witness a theatrical family and institution in its first year. There were a lot of mistakes made that first year. There was also a subway strike, which just about finished the company. I was not asked back for the second year and was crushed. I didn't have the experience; I was only twenty-two or twenty-three, and it had been my first job. They were struggling, and ultimately the company only lasted the second year and then folded. But a crazy Romanian director named André Belgrader, and I say crazy with a great deal of affection—I think most Romanians are crazy—saw something in me, miscast as I was in this production, and brought me in to audition for Rosalind in *As You Like It* for the American Repertory Theatre and subsequently brought me to Cambridge to play the role. I felt overwhelmed. I remember an old salty dog in my agency at the time saying, "Well, in what language did Shakespeare write?" And I said, "English." He said, "What language do you speak?" I said, "English." He said, "There you are. You'll have no problem." So that's how I began at ART.

Interviewer: ART was—and is—a regional repertory theater. What are the differences between regional theater and acting in New York? Are audiences different in regional theaters? Are the expectations different?

Jones: In New York, especially if you're in something that is successful, at times a certain amount of hype is attached to the experience. In regional theater, it really is all about the work, and, because of that, there's a great sense of freedom in being able to focus almost exclusively on the work. The greatest extent of my regional experience has been at ART, which is a resident repertory company; so we'd be rehearsing *Major Barbara* by day and playing *Twelfth Night* by night. These were twelve-, thirteen-, and fourteen-hour days, so we were all in this euphoric, constantly delirious state of overwork, but it fueled us because we were exercising everything all the time. We were sort of in top form, both physically and emotionally.

Interviewer: Also, it's not about whether it's a hit either, because it's a subscription audience and they're going to come or not come.

Jones: Yes. In fact, there were a couple of regional theater shows that were complete bombs, and we still had to play them for seven weeks. That's when you miss capitalism and commercialism, because you'd be out of your misery in a couple of nights! But the joy of getting to do something for four or five or six weeks and then move on to the next piece is also a real adrenaline high because you can fall so in love with a character, and you never have the time to fall out of love with it or become sort of downtrodden by the routine of it. You have to kiss it good-bye in the middle of the affair and move on to the next one. So that's a real high of regional and repertory work—if it's a resident company. Most regional theaters just job in people for individual shows, but I would hope that more and more resident and repertory companies would spring up around the country in the next few decades, because it's the greatest training for a young actor.

Interviewer: What are the advantages and disadvantages—if it is a resident company—of acting with the same actors and actresses over and over again? Is that basically a positive experience?

Jones: It is. There are always going to be new actors coming into that pool because, especially in this country, people are always looking for the better job, the better experience; so there's always a fair amount of turnover. But for several years at the ART there was a group of young actors who committed to three or four seasons together, and there came a point—and I don't think it was arrogance; I think it had more to do with enthusiasm and youthful exuberance—when we felt you could throw us any play and we could do it justice. We were a well-oiled machine, a seasoned team. We knew each other's strengths, we knew each other's weaknesses, and we knew how to pass the ball. And audiences love coming to know companies of actors. They love seeing actors switch and change and grow. It's a very exciting process, that alchemy that happens before their eyes.

Interviewer: Because that was one of your earliest professional theater experiences, do you think that it was an advantage in giving you confidence to go on?

Jones: I think I did twenty-five productions with the ART, and it gave me a tremendous amount of confidence. I don't know that I would still be an actress if I hadn't had that training and support within a community.

Interviewer: Can you talk a little about your process with a character, what you do when you get a script? What is your process when you decide to do a role?

Jones: Well, the first time I read a script, more often than not, because I'm not an intellect and I'm not a scholar and I'm not a lot of the things that would aid me in analyzing a text, I almost feel—this sounds strange—a muscular connection to the character. Before anything else, I start to feel how they slump in a chair or sit erectly in a chair, how they breathe quickly or how they breathe very slowly. Through the text I feel a muscular connection to them, and it's almost from that that I then start to understand their emotional life. I don't ever really think about it; it just sort of comes. There are specifics that I then have to work on, but that initial contact is very physical. I usually only read a play once or twice before I go into a rehearsal process, because I want it to be fresh and new. I might actually work a little bit on lines just to start getting them in my memory bank, but in a completely neutral way. At the first read-through, I want to hear what the other actors are finding and what the director's vision of the world is going to be so I can start to zero in on the same world. Then before we begin blocking I always have to have my lines memorized because I can't do two things at once; I can't hold a book and read and feel any sense of freedom in discovering the greater temple of the character. So I always have my lines learned as neutrally as possible so that I can then be free to connect with my fellow actors and take from them, because it's all about listening in the moment to what is being given by the other actor. Through that I start to understand in a more, perhaps, intellectual way what's going on and what's needed to deepen it.

Interviewer: What about the actor-director relationship? What is the ideal actor-director relationship, and what are the differences that happen to you as an actor depending on the kind of director it is?

Jones: Well, ideally I love brilliant, strong, almost dictatorial directors. That's my preference. Because I'm a very malleable actor, I love direction, direction toward a vision and cohesive storytelling. That's all we're doing, telling a story. I have a great deal of difficulty with directors who are lazy and undisciplined and prefer that the actors do their work for them.

Interviewer: Do you have a favorite director?

Jones: I need a strong hand. I'm a bit of a child; I prefer an authority figure. André Serban and Gerry Gutierrez are both dictators in the rehearsal room, and yet collaboration within their vision is what they treasure. They give you the ground rules, make clear the world, and once we understand each other, the love affair of how we get there begins, because it's a complete collaboration. When there's freedom within the structure and clarity in how the story is being told, you can bring an exciting, cohesive work to the stage. If that's not the case, it's often sloppy and less than satisfying for both the player and the audience. Discipline creates better work, always.

Interviewer: Do you think you did your best work with these two?

Jones: Yes, I do.

Interviewer: Which roles?

Jones: I did a Viola in *Twelfth Night* with Serban that was a turning point. I don't know that it's my best work, but it was a moment when I realized I'd taken a huge step as an actor and had matured to a new level. It was the production where I felt I could hang out my shingle as a professional actor. Anything before that had been an apprenticeship.

Interviewer: When was that?

Jones: That was in 1989. It was a tremendously exciting time to be working with André. It was the Christmas the Ceaucescus were overthrown. We began rehearsals in the fall when Hungary opened her borders to waves of East Germans, and then came the dismantling of the Berlin Wall. With each stunning event, André and his expatriate friend Dan said, "It will never happen in Romania." But within a few weeks of that statement, they were watching on television as they saw their high school friends leading the marches into the squares.

Interviewer: Do you think that had an effect on him as a director, the exhilaration of that time?

Jones: Yes, I do think it had a huge effect on him. It was a miracle.

Interviewer: In what ways was that a turning point for you, though, in your career, if you can articulate it in terms of what that production gave you?

Jones: I had finally brought together a mature emotional, physical instrument that was now capable of utter concentration.

Interviewer: And the other moment? With your other favorite director?

Jones: Gerry Gutierrez. His rehearsals are actually terribly undisciplined in that he loves to entertain and is wildly entertaining. I would find myself acting like an elderly Russian ballet master, clapping my hands three times sharply to encourage him to move on. It became a joke in the rehearsal room. But once we got into previews, he was like a laser. He knew exactly what it had to be, when it had to be there, how it had to move, how it had to pick up speed here; the focus could be softer here so it could then become completely brilliant a moment later. I had never seen that kind of mature sculpting.

Interviewer: Can you give a specific example of a scene?

Jones: Never when I'm asked to! I should think about it and write it down. This is not a good example, but I remember during rehearsals for *The Heiress,* the moment that Catherine realizes that her lover has abandoned her and is not going to come for her. In that moment her world is destroyed, and it's the beginning of the turning of the tide for this character. In trying to make it clear to me what Gerry needed in that moment from me—I remember I was riding my bicycle home, and I ran into him right in front of Lincoln Center at Broadway, and we were literally in the median of Broadway, and he said, "It's gotta be Jackie Kennedy." I said, "What?" He said, "You may be too young to remember Kennedy's funeral." I said, "It was the day after my seventh birthday and I remember it completely." I said, "I campaigned for Kennedy when I was four, so it's very vivid in my memory." He said, "It has to be what we feared for Jackie Kennedy." I'm not expressing this well, because he said it so concisely: that our worst fear, our fantasy of what might happen, is always, more often than not, so much worse than what actually does occur. He needed me to bring to life that *worst* fantasy—of a woman that we'd all come to love and respect and admire so tremendously, completely crumbling and losing all dignity, becoming hideous in grief. That's what he wanted, and that was the example he used.

Interviewer: And you understood?

Jones: I understood. I understood exactly.

Interviewer: Did you use that then?

Jones: I didn't use that, but I knew what he meant and was able to then try to make it my own. I never achieved what I wanted to achieve in that moment, partially because I knew I had to do it eight times a week and I was afraid I didn't have the complete vocal skill to do what was really required. I had to protect my voice and as a professional do the next best thing so that I could repeat it eight times a week. If it had been on film, and I'd only had two or three takes, it would have been much more terrifying and hideous.

Interviewer: What was the difference? What would have been the difference between that and what you had to do eight times? Volume? Intensity?

Jones: Yes. It would have been real. I mean, it would have been horrific. It would have been completely exhausting.

Interviewer: It would have been much less controlled?

Jones: It would have been much less controlled.

Interviewer: You would have let it all go?

Jones: I remember someone doing a cry that was so bloodcurdling, and not because it was loud, that's not what I'm talking about. Technically I should have found something that was closer to that, that I could replicate eight times a week. And I never really got there with it.

Interviewer: *The Heiress,* as you say, was a show you did for eight performances a week on Broadway. Surely some nights were better than others. What are some of the factors that made those nights better?

Jones: It usually—for me—involves ease. *E-a-s-e.* That's the frustrating thing for an actor, because you have no control over when ease is going to enter your life and when it's going to be snatched away. It's your job to be as calm and as focused and as prepared for the evening as possible; all good professionals do that. But then there are just going to be those nights that it's going to be hard drudgery and other nights when, for whatever reason, the Muse is with you and the words come with a simplicity and a grace and an ease and you don't have to work, you're just there. You're riding the wave. Other times, you're utilizing all of that technique that you've developed through the years, and depending on one's years of experience and knowing how to create the illusion that one is at ease as opposed to literally being one with the text, with the audience, and with your fellow actors. That's what we all live for, those nights, and sometimes in a short regional theater run you can count those nights on one finger, when it all comes together for the entire production. Those nights are absolute, pure bliss. The difficult nights you can still enjoy, but it's work.

Interviewer: Can you relate those in any way to other factors, to something going on in your own life where you had a bad day, or is it totally unpredictable?

Jones: I find that it is totally unpredictable. You can be going through a tremendously difficult time, and you walk onstage, and it becomes this haven, and you're able to connect in a way that you've never been able to connect. Other times you can be in the greatest mood you've ever been in, and you're about to go out and play a tragedy, and somehow that effervescent quality is transmuted (is that the word?) into the tragedy of the text, and you're able to do things you never dreamt you could do with it. It's so unpredictable.

Interviewer: Do the changes in the cast of a long run have any significant effect on your performance?

Jones: I had three fathers in *The Heiress,* and it changed tremendously because, of course, for Catherine Sloper, the key to that character was the loins from which she sprang, the soul and the spirit and the mind of that father. I had to make subtle shifts with each new father, because the three actors were tremendously different.

Interviewer: Can you give any specifics of how you had to change and what you did?

Jones: Well, Philip Bosco, my first father, for example, is a big theatrical force of nature. He's a meat-eater. He comes on that stage and it's an event. He moves like a freight train, and you have to keep up, and you have to keep sharp, and you have to play the theatricality of it. Donald Moffatt took over from Philip. Donald is much more psychological and more naturalistic, and he has such dignity that he forces everyone around him to be as truthful as possible. I could not do with Donald what I was doing a few nights before with Philip. I had to bring everything down; I had to become more psychological and slightly more naturalistic. Donald's dignity and integrity made it very heartbreaking that he had such a blind spot about his child. Remak Ramsay, my third dad, on the other hand, had the arrogance of a blueblood. I found that, depending on who was playing my father, the audience's take on what was going to happen to my character after the curtain was completely different. When I was Donald Moffatt's child, they thought there was a real chance I would become a philanthropist, making huge endowments to worthy institutions throughout the city of New York in the latter part of the nineteenth century. With Remak, because of his arrogance and—I'm trying to think of a better word—because he was not an egalitarian, the audience was less optimistic that Catherine would evolve into a benificent matriarch.

Interviewer: You didn't have much time in between fathers either, did you?

Jones: No, no time. One actor took his final bow on a Sunday night, and the new actor would come in on the next Tuesday night. We would have a couple of weeks' rehearsal during the day while playing the evening performance at night with the old father.

Interviewer: You must have felt slightly paranoid!

Jones: Those first three weeks in performance with the new father were always very difficult because I'm a very loyal person and I was always sort of mourning the daddy I'd lost. And that was just the fathers! Then I had to deal with the three lovers! I had three lovers in the course of the experience, which also changed things but was not as marked a difference as the fathers.

Interviewer: Was that the first time you'd ever had that kind of extended, long run, where you had that experience?

Jones: Yes. I'd mostly worked in regional theater, and the Broadway shows I'd done always closed within seven weeks of my joining the company or of our coming into town, so this was the first long run.

Interviewer: What about the actor-actor relationship? What are you looking for in another actor that is an ideal for you when you're acting onstage?

Jones: Utter concentration, openness, and knowing that when I'm speaking they're listening and that when I'm listening they're speaking to me. I keep going back to the expression "love affair," but that's what it has to be; it has to be that concentrated and focused that it becomes like a love affair. It's absolute, complete, and a high each time. You can have a love affair with your Aunt Penniman onstage, in that you're completely copasetic and you're completely there together and you understand what the task at hand is and you're approaching it in a similar way, not the same way, but in a similar way that is of the same world. Because, again, there's this problem of American actors coming from so many different schools: you can have two perfectly marvelous actors onstage together, but if they're not copasetic, it misses. They miss each other, and therefore we miss them, and we miss the words and the story that they're telling us.

Interviewer: Any favorite moments that can demonstrate this?

Jones: With a fellow actor onstage?

Interviewer: Yes, where it really clicked?

Jones: Diane Lane and I actually had an incredible time together in *Twelfth Night* because the whole experience was so heightened. As I said before, André Serban is one of my favorite directors. It was a role I was absolutely the right age for and in prime shape for physically and emotionally, and the focus was there. Diane had not worked with André since she was seven or eight, in his trilogy, his Greek trilogy at La MaMa. She was the child in his *Cherry Orchard* at Lincoln Center; she was the sprite who brought on the cherry bough and placed it in Firs's lap at the end of *The Cherry Orchard*. She was in between movies, we'd lost our Olivia, he gave her a call, and she came. She hadn't been onstage since she was a child, she'd never done Shakespeare, but she's so smart and has so many wonderful instincts that she came alive within that text and understood Olivia so beautifully, so that she was completely in a heightened place. We *all* were in that production; that's what made it so exciting. Everyone in that production was absolutely right for their roles and at some sort of peak in their life for that role. There was a kind of sexiness that everyone brought onstage; André in that production allowed everyone to feel sexually alive. Jewel Walker used to say that it's all about sex, and I used to think, "What a dirty old man! That's just ridiculous, it's about higher ideals and blah blah blah." But in dramatic literature, that is a very important thread that runs through everything. It *is* the basis.

Interviewer: It's all about chemistry, and sex is all about chemistry.

Jones: Exactly. It's all about chemistry, and sex is all about chemistry. So there was this wonderful heightened thing going on with everyone in this production. I remember that there was an especially creative bond that Diane and I both had at that moment with those two women that was very exciting and rewarding. We developed a wonderful friendship out of it because it was such a high point for each of us in our learning and in our process. But I have so many experiences like that with so many wonderful actors. That was just the first one that comes to mind because of having talked about *Twelfth Night* before.

Interviewer: Let's talk about things that haven't happened. What's a role you've never played that you'd want to play?

Jones: Well, there's always the Saint Joan thing.

Interviewer: You'd be a great Saint Joan.

Jones: I *would* be a great Saint Joan, and I've walked around for years with a Saint Joan haircut like a sandwich board on my head advertising to play it, and the only time I even got asked to audition for it was right after I had major reconstructive knee surgery, and I couldn't have done it unless I was allowed to drag a pew along behind me so I could kneel on a nice soft velvet cushion. I'll be forty in November, and I know I still have a couple more years in a big house to play Joan, but I almost feel like at this point, having played one heroine after another, I kind of feel like I've played her.

Interviewer: What about the role really appeals to you?

Jones: Well, the spiritual strength, the power; that it's a power that comes from a spirituality; that she's incredibly pragmatic; her love of camaraderie with men; to be in a cast surrounded by thirty great men with amazing voices. For those of us who are reasonably strong-spirited actresses, we don't get to play the kings and the princes, and Joan is the closest we'll get to it. That's the problem with so many of Shakespeare's heroines; they're always attached to these sort of pathetic examples of men. It's never about the greater good of the nation, it's always about how they're going to get the guy; it's always diminished to a sort of domestic love squabble. It's universal in that it's about love, but it doesn't have the power and the sweep of the guys' parts.

Interviewer: What about Cleopatra?

Jones: Well now, I've got to look at that role. I have to look at that role because I've done several Shakespeares but they've been years ago now. Very few American actors, unless they're really brilliant, feel that they have the education to attempt the most difficult roles in Shakespeare; so I'm a little timid about it. I'd almost rather pay the airfare and go to Britain to see one of the great English actresses do it than attempt it myself, because it seems so daunting.

Interviewer: Hedda?

Jones: Now that's another thing. I've got to start turning my sights toward those Scandinavian fellows, and the Greeks. I'm afraid temperamentally I was born a heroine and I'm going to die a heroine, and those parts that I'm now growing into I'll have to learn to love. They're not as much fun to me, I guess, because they're so deeply troubled, and I don't have the intellect of an Eileen Atkins or a Fiona Shaw who have a field day with the psychology of these women. I've got to start to look at that and realize that I am capable of that.

Interviewer: That's not the only way to approach them, is it?

Jones: Beats me. I'm going to put them off as long as I can. Play the heroines until they start laughing at me and then move on to the other gals. I have to admit, I've seen the Greeks done well only a handful of times. I'm not a fan of the Greeks. They're just too much. They begin at the end and get worse. I can never take them seriously; to me they're big gory soap operas. I don't care about the people. It's terrible, but I'm so rarely made to care. So when and if I do them, I've got to work with directors who will make me care about these people and make clear why we keep telling these, to me, ridiculous stories of familial betrayal.

Interviewer: What's the most challenging role you've done?

Jones: Well, having just completed *Night of the Iguana*—I don't think it's because it's the most recent one—I would have to say Hannah Jelkes, because of the rigors of the style that Tennessee gives you in those magnificent and daunting stage directions. The first stage direction for Hannah is that she is ethereal, almost ghostly, looking like a medieval Gothic cathedral saint, completely, totally feminine and yet androgynous-looking, and timeless. I may have left out a few other things, but that's the gist. In fact, I think it's very close to verbatim. Hand in hand with that incredibly stylized description comes the responsibility of making her utterly real and alive and grounded and deeply spiritual, with tremendous maturity and understanding and compassion. She is the most brilliant woman I've tried to bring to the stage; there's a reason why most of the actresses who've played Hannah Jelkes have been either well into their forties or even well into their fifties. The only thing I left out of that description is that she's somewhere between thirty and forty and you don't know where. There's a gravity that age gives you as an actress. You can cheat down, but you cannot cheat up. You can't fake experience. You can approximate your imagined idea, but you're always going to be putting one over on the audience. She's something else, Hannah Jelkes. And also, I had almost too much respect for her, which is a danger. When you put a character on a pedestal, it's very difficult to climb. So I began in the most overt and physical way I think I've ever begun with a character, because I felt I had to build her a home first, and then maybe slowly but surely she would begin to inhabit it and take me by the hand and lead me closer to her. She really feels to me as though she exists. I wish I could have gotten closer, but I haven't put a lot of pressure on myself. Actresses are always our own worst critics, and we can torment ourselves for our shortcomings, but I'm becoming much more philosophical about that. I realize my failings and shortcomings with Hannah have more to do with life experience than anything else. And that's what I lacked for Hannah.

Interviewer: Did you at any time see the film, with Deborah Kerr?

Jones: Yes. I saw it as a child; I haven't seen it since.

Interviewer: Do you deliberately avoid film versions of a role you're doing?

Jones: No. I did see Olivia de Havilland in *The Heiress,* but I hardly remember a thing about it because I think I was subconsciously or even maybe consciously shredding as I watched. I watched that film mainly to see if there were any technical things I could steal from Miss de Havilland. I wanted to see when William Wyler and Olivia de Havilland thought it appropriate to curtsy, and exactly what kind of curtsy they thought was appropriate to 1851. Gerry and I had a different take on most of the play, which is very different from the film for starters in that you never leave that powder keg of a parlor. I thought Olivia de Havilland made her very human and very real. I remember the earliest scenes took away some of the rigidity of the period I saw, some of the formality that keeps a character from fully being alive and real for an audience. She sort of broke that barrier for me. There's a scene where her Aunt Penniman's helping her change clothes and she was just a lovely girl, a dear sweet lovely person changing clothes in a room, and I enjoyed seeing that.

Interviewer: Did you know *The Heiress* as a play at all before you did it?

Jones: Not only did I not know it, I thought I was auditioning for the part of Aunt Penniman! My agency told me "Lavinia." I read the script, and of course I wasn't but a few pages in when I realized how ridiculous it was. I was thirty-eight years old, and this was clearly a part written for a woman at least in her fifties, and there were so many brilliant actresses in New York in their fifties who have difficulty working because of that damn age range in dramatic literature for women, that I knew I wouldn't even audition for it. But I couldn't put it down, and I'm a slow, distracted reader. Something really has to grab me to keep me turning those pages, and of course that story is like a spiderweb. It's ironclad; you cannot put it down. I remember just flying through it and thinking, "Oh, whatever young girl gets to play Catherine is so lucky." So when they called and said, "Not Lavinia, Catherine," I said, "Oh, well, that's different." I just couldn't believe it, and in fact it was an offer. I didn't even have to audition for it, so it was just a blessed experience from the beginning.

That's another wonderful trait of Gerry Gutierrez's. He makes sure he sees a lot of work; he knows who's in the acting pool, so that he builds an amazing family of actors. I think maybe one or two people in our cast had to audition; the rest were out-and-out offers. So you know from the get-go he wanted you, and that's a tremendous vote of confidence. He's not a director who's sitting in auditions going, "Well, we could go this direction, or we could go that direction." Gerry knows where he's headed.

Interviewer: You haven't done very many new plays, have you? Most of the roles you've done have been classical roles. Is that by choice or just the way things have happened?

Jones: No, it's just the way things have happened. At ART I did a handful of new plays on the Hasty Pudding Stage. For the spring part of the season there would always be a new play series that Robert Brustein produced. I got to do a new Chris Durang play, a Bill Hauptman play called *Gillette,* a play about J. M. Barrie and the Darling boys, and in New York for Circle Repertory Company I worked closely with Paula Vogel on three of her new plays, including *The Baltimore Waltz.* I did a play of Keith Reddin's. I've done a fair share, but out of fifty-three productions probably only ten have been contemporary.

Interviewer: Do you get sent new plays now?

Jones: Yes, I do, and I have to open my heart and my mind to new plays because I've been so spoiled by the language of classical works, by the wings that they give you, and by the universality of the classics that new plays more often than not do not have. I think that's also my problem with branching out into film. I pick up scripts in which the language is so pedestrian that I always find it a little disheartening. We seem to be producing very few poets. With a new play, you feel very protective of the playwright. You feel every time you suit up that you're going out to make the playwright as proud as you possibly can and somehow put forth to the public what the playwright had in mind. You know when you're getting close to that, and you know when you're sailing as a production. And so that's very frustrating.

Interviewer: What about the difference of the playwright being around? Obviously, Shakespeare wasn't around when you did *Twelfth Night,* but Paula Vogel was there when you did her plays. Is that a positive or a negative?

Jones: It's always a positive, because the playwrights I've been blessed to work with have been very supportive. They are the ones who are most vulnerable; yet they become superheroes to me, because they subordinate their own egos to the production and support those who have to go onstage every night. They're out there sitting elbow to elbow with audience members who are either truly getting what they've written or completely dismissing it, sometimes in the most horrible ways. I don't know how they put one foot in front of the other. They'll come back after the most dreadful performances, when we've just been all over the place, and be so generous and kind. I don't know why they don't just all have nervous breakdowns during the preview process, because we stumble so with their work. I have yet to see a playwright who wasn't the most supergenerous artist at that point.

Interviewer: As an actor, when you go to the theater, do you think you view it differently from the way a nonprofessional would view it?

Jones: I'm sure that I do. If it's good, I think I'm the biggest child in the audience. All theater to me, if it's good, becomes a fairy tale I become completely lost in. If it's not so good, I'm sitting there thinking exactly why it's not so good and—

Interviewer: Starting to take it apart?

Jones: I do. I can't help it. Sometimes even mediocre plays can carry me away, or mediocre productions can carry me away, but if there are too many things working against it you can't help but sit there and think, "Oh, if only this, if only that."

Interviewer: Have you ever wanted to direct, or have you directed?

Jones: Never.

Interviewer: Why not?

Jones: I just don't have that kind of mind. My mind has not ever worked with a beginning, a middle, or an end. Maybe that's why I'm a decent actor, because I'm completely in the moment. I do not have an organized mind.

Interviewer: Like a strong director?

Jones: Exactly. I need someone to give that kind of focus to the storytelling. I literally cannot quote my lines out of context. When I was doing *The Heiress* for a year, if someone had said, "Oh, what's that line you have with Morris in Act Three?" I would think and think and think and not be able to tell you, because it only exists in sequence and in that world. I truly don't know what the actor opposite me is going to say next until they say it, from night to night. I don't know if it's early Alzheimer's or what, but it's just the way my mind works. It's a blessing and a curse.

Interviewer: What are some performances you've seen that you've really admired over the years?

Jones: Judith Ivey in a Lanford Wilson piece at the Circle Repertory Company called *The Moonshot Tape*.

Interviewer: What was it about her?

Jones: Ease. Ease, and tremendous wit, and intelligence, and her ability to just bring you into her with such humor, and a poignancy. There's a vulnerability that she allows through the bravura of her charm and humor and technique that always just sucks you right into Judith; and at the same time, while she's sucking you in, she's entertaining the pants off you. Eileen Atkins in both *Vita and Virginia* and in *Indiscretions* brings together a facility for language, a brilliance, a wit, a soul, and an ease—utter, utter ease. I never dreamt that I would go to a small theater where Vanessa Redgrave was onstage and not be able to take my eyes off the other actress. She was just mouthwatering, and Eileen in those two performances literally orchestrated one's breathing. You know she's never going to do headstands, but she still absolutely keeps you on the edge of your seat each moment, because within that complete control and measuredness of her performance, whole worlds are going to erupt before you—emotional states and visual images. That comes from her facility with language. Maggie Smith also. That facility with language. Colleen Dewhurst in *A Moon for the Misbegotten* made the earth stop spinning.

Interviewer: Is there any difference between acting comedy and acting serious drama, or is it all just acting? Is it all about being honest?

Jones: I've actually done very little comedy.

Interviewer: *Twelfth Night* is a comedy.

Jones: It is, but it's so character-based, and Viola is not as much a part of the comedy as the clowns, and our production was a rather dark production. So if there is a difference, I don't know what it is. I'm terrible at the obvious punch line, because I've done so little comedy and no commercial comedy where there's the setup, the setup, the setup, and then the land. I'm like a horse about to be bridled; when I see an obvious setup and a land coming, I rear away from it because it puts a technical demand on you that often is not character-driven.

Interviewer: I know you haven't done many films, but how would you compare film acting and stage acting?

Jones: I haven't done enough of it to even be able to approach that question. All I know is that in a smaller part in film you have to hit your mark, which I find completely impossible, because it's nothing you ever have to think of in theater. And you have to be able to repeat a series of movements on the same syllables in the same way as you did it the take before, so they can match the shot. If you're the star I don't think it matters, but if you're one of the secondary characters or less, there're all sorts of rigid technical strictures because of the camera and matching shots that I just can't deal with yet. I like the freedom of the human eye, the audience being allowed to edit for themselves, not having to depend on a camera for the editing. In theater everything is heightened. I love that, though I'm beginning to appreciate how much is accomplished with just the eyes and mind of the actor on film.

Interviewer: The first play I ever saw you in was *Macbeth* with Christopher Plummer and Glenda Jackson. Can you remember any significant moments from that production?

Jones: Oh, lots of moments from that! We went through a series of directors, we went through five Macduffs; it was your typically fraught production of that play—and on the road to boot during most of these turnovers. At one point, our new director was rehearsing us by day while we were still performing the former director's production by night. We were in Baltimore and they didn't have a proper rehearsal space for us, so our producers finally found a proscenium stage at the municipal hockey rink in Baltimore! There was just a blood-red curtain separating us from the ice, and so we were literally bundled up within an inch of our lives, with mufflers and mittens, and at this point Chris had had a series of back or neck problems—which he later overcame, and was an unbelievably athletic and virile Macbeth. But at that moment he was suffering from a neck ailment that had him in a wheelchair and a neck brace on the proscenium of this icy, icy hockey rink, with Glenda wheeling him around as they played their scenes, and it was amazing! Anyone who loves to talk about the curse of that play, we were definitely the poster child production at that point. But I enjoyed Glenda and Chris so much and learned a great deal from both of them. I loved, in particular, Glenda's mad scene, which I thought was just terrific.

Interviewer: You're in the position where, I'm sure, roles are offered to you a lot. What makes you decide to do something?

Jones: The story, the use of language, that muscularity that I feel or don't feel, the director, the fellow actors, the . . .

Interviewer: Challenge?

Jones: Oh, every part's a challenge.

Interviewer: Really?

Jones: Every single part's a challenge.

Interviewer: You don't ever come up against a role and say, "Well, I've done that"?

Jones: I haven't so far. Everything I've come across has been a challenge.

James Earl Jones

Photo © Tania Mara

James Earl Jones was born in Arkabutla, Mississippi, on January 17, 1931. He studied acting at the American Theatre Wing with Lee Strasberg and Ted Danielewski. He made his New York debut as Gregory in Romeo and Juliet *in 1955 and his Broadway debut in 1958 as Edward in* Sunrise at Campobello. *Other professional roles include Williams,* Henry V *(1960); Deodatus Village,* The Blacks: A Clown Play *(1961); Oberon,* A Midsummer Night's Dream *(1961); Caliban,* The Tempest *(1962); Macduff,* Macbeth *(1962); title role,* Othello *(1963, 1964, 1966, 1968, 1971, 1981, and 1982); Zachariah Pieterson,* The Blood Knot *(1964 and 1968); title role,* The Emperor Jones *(1964); Ekart,* Baal *(1965); title role,* Macbeth *(1966); Jack Jefferson,* The Great White Hope *(1968; Tony Award); Boesman,* Boesman and Lena *(1970); Claudius,* Hamlet *(1972); Lopakin,* The Cherry Orchard *(1973); title role,* King Lear *(1973); Theodore "Hickey" Hickman,* The Iceman Cometh *(1973); Lennie,* Of Mice and Men *(1974); title role,* Paul Robeson *(1977);*

Judge Brack, Hedda Gabler *(1980); Troy Maxon,* Fences *(1987; Tony Award).*

His films include Dr. Strangelove, or How I Learned to Stop Worrying and Love the Bomb *(1963),* The End of the Road *(1970),* The Great White Hope *(1970),* The Man *(1972),* The Bingo Long Traveling All-Stars and Motor Kings *(1976),* The Greatest *(1977),* Star Wars *(1977),* The Empire Strikes Back *(1980),* Return of the Jedi *(1983),* Soul Man *(1986),* Matewan *(1987),* Coming to America *(1988),* Field of Dreams *(1989),* The Hunt for Red October *(1990),* The Meteor Man *(1993),* Sommersby *(1993),* The Lion King *(1994),* Clear and Present Danger *(1994),* Cry, the Beloved Country *(1995),* Jefferson in Paris *(1995), and* Star Wars: Special Edition *(1997).*

His television shows include As the World Turns *(1965),* Guiding Light *(1967),* King Lear *(1973),* The Cay *(1974),* The Greatest Thing That Almost Happened *(1977),* Jesus of Nazareth *(1977),* Roots II: The Next Generation *(1979),* Paul Robeson *(1979),* Paris *(1979–80),* Guyana Tragedy: The Jim Jones Story *(1980),* The Atlanta Child Murders *(1984),* The Golden Moment: An Olympic Love Story *(1980),* Long Ago and Far Away *(1989–91),* The Last Flight Out *(1990),* Gabriel's Fire *(1990–91; Emmy Award),* Portrait of Cuba and the Caribbean *(1991),* Visitors from the Unknown *(1991),* When It Was a Game *(1991),* Pros and Cons *(1991–92),* Michael Jackson . . . the Legend Continues *(1992),* Alone *(1997),* What the Deaf Man Heard *(1997),* Merlin *(1998),* Finder's Fee *(2000), and* When Willows Touch *(2000). He has also appeared on episodes of* The Defenders, East Side/West Side, Channing, Dr. Kildare, Tarzan, N.Y.P.D., Law and Order, Picket Fences, Touched by an Angel, Frasier, Homicide, *and* The Simpsons.

He was inducted into the Theater Hall of Fame in 1985 and received the National Medal of the Arts in 1992.

This interview took place on June 14, 1999.

● ———————————————————————— ●

Interviewer: Reflect, if you will, on the fundamental differences in the American theater today and at the time when you first began acting.

Jones: I don't know. When I first started in 1957, I came to New York looking for a career in the traditional theater. I looked around me, and there was all this other remarkable energy, all this unorthodox work going on off-Broadway and off-off-Broadway. The avant-garde theater was breaking form then—in its use of more intimate spaces, in its violation of the three-act structure, and its other lively innovations. As I've said before, many wonderful renegades have worked hard in the ferment of the avant-garde theater, and that influence eventually filters into the Broadway theater. I don't know if anything has changed profoundly, except that we have gotten back to more reliable forms and more commercially acceptable forms.

Interviewer: What about the differences, if any, between acting in regional theater and in New York—on Broadway or off Broadway?

Jones: I've always felt that the difference is that every town has its own doctor and dentist, and I think regional actors are like the town doctor and the town dentist. They work hard locally and then they go to New York for a convention, as it were, to the greater showcase that New York offers the English-language theater. There is always less pressure in regional theater. That's why sometimes our best products come from the outlying theaters, because they are away from the pressure cooker of New York. Plays are developed more slowly, often with the author present.

When Lloyd Richards was the head of the drama department at Yale, he gave playwrights such as Athol Fugard and August Wilson a great place to work, and not too far from New York. But they might as well have been in Kansas. Until they opened in New York, they were free from all that pressure—the career pressure—your agent, your family, everyone hovering and saying, "Is it going to be a success or not?" That can keep the artist from really being free. It can make the artist afraid to experiment, to try things, from fear of failure. The greatest asset of the regional theater is that it is free from the career pressures of Broadway. Often Broadway depends on those places to produce the best theater. This has been true in my career; *Fences* and some of my key experiences had their origins in regional theater.

Interviewer: What would you change about the American theater?

Jones: I love it so much I wouldn't change a thing! It's like a good organism; it's always changing anyway. I think the old phoenix legend applies to the theater. It never dies completely. It may go dormant, like any hibernating creature, but it comes back to life again. I never know from one season to the next whether it is dead or dormant, you know. George C. Scott once said he wanted to build a theater right in the middle of Manhattan. The whole theater would be made out of glass. From day one of rehearsals, the audience could just walk by on the street and look in just as you look through those cutouts on construction sites. He wanted to open up the theater by exposing what we do to the public and taking the pressure off. I don't know whether he thought of having the voices piped out to the audience in the street or not; probably so. This was just a fantasy of his—but a great one. I don't have any fantasies or ideas like that. I don't want to change the theater at all. It is not that it has always served me well, or served the audience well. It's just that it has a mind of its own, a heart of its own, and certainly a spirit of its own. The theater is always changing. To try to keep its head above water, it is changing.

I can remember when big theater was very possible, and you don't see the spacious stage and immense casts very much anymore. I was in a production called *The Great White Hope,* and in the same decade there occurred *Equus,* and a decade before that there was the musical *Jesus Christ Superstar.* Melvin

Van Peebles was making big theater, with *Ain't Supposed to Die a Natural Death* and *Don't Play Us Cheap. Cats* would be a more recent attempt at big theater. People don't do that much anymore. It is so expensive to make big theater—sets and costumes alone. But there was a time that there was a place on Broadway for people with that kind of ambitious vision. I suppose it is just too costly now.

Interviewer: Who were the strongest influences on your career?

Jones: None! I don't think people should be influenced by other people. I think you start losing originality that way. Of course, there were directors I worked with, especially off-Broadway, who had a great effect on me, as I hope I had on them, but they didn't shape me. They were part of whatever was shaping us all. Tom Gruenwald and Gladys Vaughan are two of my favorites. Ed Sherin, my director for *The Great White Hope,* came from that world off-Broadway and became very important in the larger theater too. I worked with Tom in an Equity Library Theatre production. Our union permitted a program where actors could work without pay to do workshop materials and to do full productions off-Broadway. It was free theater. I don't think we were allowed to charge admission. But Tom and I and a bunch of actors got together and did Norman Rosten's *Mister Johnson* for the stage. I felt liberated. Often actors don't feel liberated in terms of "You go do what you can with this role, and fly with it." Tom was that kind of director. He didn't direct us, he liberated everybody. He showed us the open skylight.

Interviewer: How has your acting process evolved? How do you get inside a character?

Jones: I don't know if I do. I recently played Lennie in a scene from *Of Mice and Men* for my son's school benefit. It's a play that I've done before, first in workshop early on with Tad Danielewski, my acting teacher in some workshops that had grown out of the American Theatre Wing. I did research into what it means to be retarded, as they termed it in those days, and into what it meant to be a bindle bum on the road in the days when you could get arrested for not having a job. Lennie was a gentle brute with a hulking physical presence. I decided to let my shoulders slump, to help convey his character. I spent some time at a center for the mentally disabled to try for a better understanding of how Lennie would look at the world. I wanted to believe that Lennie meant it, and realized he could, as he put it, "Go off and live by myself," but I soon learned from the real retardates that this would not have been possible. I once actually took certain psychological tests dressed as Lennie and responding as I thought Lennie would. The psychology graduate student administering the tests had no idea that I was an actor playing a role. In fact, when he saw the results, he told his professor that they should have me committed before I did something violent! All I could think of when I played Lennie was that this is life at its most basic, and I realized how valuable it is for an actor to return to those kinds of elemental roles.

Athol Fugard wrote a play called *Boesman and Lena* about bums in South Africa, about people with nothing to lose because they had never gained anything. When you play those roles, you end up as an actor just getting in touch with the basic fact of survival. The idea of heroism never occurs to you because there is no damsel to rescue from the dragon. Shakespeare explored this with King Lear when he had Lear out on the heath confronting another shivering soul whose ass was literally hanging out in the air. He said, "Ah, this is the elemental man." This was man at his most basic. And Lear said to Edgar, "Ha! Here's three on's are sophisticated!—Thou art the thing itself: unaccommodated man is no more but such a poor, bare, forked animal as thou art." I just always felt that whenever we had elemental roles like that to do, we were fortunate, and then we could go back and play the sophisticated people more effectively—people with something to lose and something to gain.

I am straying a bit here, but there is a point I want to get to, something I have learned. I think that is all we owe the audience: to try to enact the basic experience of a character. We are often confronted with roles such as Iago, very distasteful people, and we sometimes make the mistake my co-actors in productions of *Othello* do: they make it a farce, and play it for the jokes because they are afraid to see it as anything but a "bloody farce." Rymer, one of the early British critics of the play, claimed it was just that—a "bloody farce." Rymer was a racist, too, and he couldn't believe Shakespeare could be serious about the idea of a black man being the hero. (He is not alone there.) But that is often the temptation—to avoid the character. I think, in a way, Anthony Hopkins does it with Hannibal Lecter. He makes him kind of delicious, you know, when Hannibal should make our skins crawl.

I, like other actors, have been accused of wanting to make the audience like my characters, and we rationalize it by saying, "Well, I want to keep in touch with the humanity of the character. Even the most evil person starts out as somebody's son or daughter or beloved." But sometimes I think I have worked too hard to make the character palatable. Sometimes our job is just the opposite—to strip ourselves of all sentimentality about what a human being is and to play that character as conceived by the author. I think I am ready at this late date to try that sometime. I don't know what role it will be, but to strip the character down naked to what he really is, with no apologies. I think we have to try to find a parallel track in our own lives that runs with the character's track, and that can be scary.

Interviewer: How did that work with *The Great White Hope*?

Jones: I probably gave the closest to a nonapologetic performance with that role, because the proof is that I got tired of it real quick! The truth is it took a lot of energy. I remember in Jean Genet's *The Blacks,* even though they were not the fully realized characters that you would find in a conventional drama, the characters had some distasteful qualities about them, you know, and if you weren't apologizing for them, they became a burden for the actors who played them.

Back to the Iago problem: if an actor does not have a director who understands the character and his relationship with all the other people in the drama, the actor is loath to go to the root of what Iago is really about. Most actors avoid going there, without any help. With help from the director, the fulfillment of all the negatives can be satisfying. After all, in every play, for every villain, there is also usually a hero, so that the heroes bask in the audience's adoration and sympathy.

Interviewer: Is there such a thing, then, as the ideal actor-director relationship?

Jones: I can define it in film better than in theater because I've had, I think, purer relationships in film. I have had directors such as John Sayles who casts the film and then just rolls the camera. He will not give you a single direction unless you are in trouble, unless you are misdirecting yourself, or unless you need help. I've had directors such as Richard Pearce, the director of *A Family Thing,* who was a teacher. It would be a wonderful experience for any young actor in film to have a director like that, for he was very gently teaching you as you proceeded, and the rehearsal process was most interesting because he was obviously teaching, and teaching himself, too, about your character and about the story. I think the simplest films I've been involved with have probably been the clearest in terms of a positive relationship with a director. There was no great dynamic, there was no tyranny on the set, there was no "I will have my will, I will have my way, I will have *my* interpretation."

John Berry is a director I admired and loved. He directed the first Athol Fugard play I was involved in. J. D. Cannon and I were playing brothers in *The Blood Knot.* One day, John just blew up and said, "You guys are destroying my play." And we hadn't thought of it as *his* play, we had thought of it as *our* play. We were on the wrong track, obviously, but the way he put it was odd, I thought, and proprietary. Perhaps most directors have to be like that; they wield control the easiest and quickest way, through tyranny. They have a lot riding on the play, of course, and serious economic considerations hinging on the success or failure of the production. I guess I understand that is why, when he won the Academy Award for *Titanic,* James Cameron said, "I am the king of the world." Probably my most interesting relationship with a director, because it involved several productions, several agendas, and both highs and lows, was with John Berry. But the relationship I admire most is the John Sayles relationship, when you end up being cast in a project and you are released to go with why you were cast.

Interviewer: It occurs to me that you have had the opportunity with *Othello* to do the same role with different directors. Has that altered your conception or performance of the role?

Jones: That's really curious. That's a study unto itself, I guess. The most important production of *Othello* was the one Gladys Vaughan directed, and because of her I am convinced that that play, and probably others of Shakespeare's, are probably best directed by women. The last two productions of *Othello* I tried both were failures. One was directed by the great John Berry, but again we fell into a dark hole where we weren't communicating, and he thought that Tony Zerbe and I were insisting on playing the roles as we had done in other productions for other directors. In the last case, the director was Peter Coe, and he never quite came to terms with the female character—with who Desdemona was, even in the casting. Indicative of that is the fact that we ended up with four Desdemonas, and my wife, Ceci, was the fourth. Without the love center of that play, *Othello* couldn't work except as a farce, except as some strange duel between these two males. It was curious that when Dianne Wiest took over as the third Desdemona, she lamented one day, "I came too late. All the love has been used up in this play. All the love has been burnt between Othello and Iago, and there is none for me." It was a poetic way of putting it, but that is exactly what had happened, so it was a really misguided production. Yet in the cynicism of the times, when that play opened, the year of my son's birth, it was a great hit.

Interviewer: Elaborate on the sensibility that Gladys Vaughan brought to the earlier production of *Othello*. I am intrigued by that.

Jones: I can only compare her to the great director Margaret Webster. I didn't know Margaret Webster, but I do know a little about the production she directed with Paul Robeson as Othello, José Ferrer as Iago, and Uta Hagen as Desdemona. The fact that the play worked indicated to me that the third character, Desdemona, was fully realized. Shakespeare couldn't tax his female characters too much because they were always played by young boys, so the roles are always underwritten, whether it is Desdemona or the Scotsman's lady. All of Shakespeare's women are underwritten, and if the play works at all, it means that the role has been realized both by the actress and by the director. I didn't make that connection until the production was over.

There was another interesting difficulty in the 1964 production of *Othello,* produced by Joe Papp for the New York Shakespeare Festival. In those explosive times, Joe wanted me to play Othello as a tough and militant "Western" black man, meeting hostility with hostility. Gladys said no to this conception. Othello was not a Western black man. She did not want me to imbue Othello with the racial anger of the times. She envisioned him as the cultured, gentle, graceful leader that historically he would have been. She told me that Othello would have had no concept of what it was to be a second-class citizen. He would have had no concept of inferiority or racial animosity. Why would he fall victim to so much evil if he had been defensive?

Indeed, I did see the Trinidadian actor-playwright Errol John play Othello in London with Leo Kern, and Errol was insisting on being so hip that the play couldn't work. I don't mean that Othello has to be a dope or an innocent, but that he has no concept of inferiority and racial animosity. No clue. You play the character with racial animosity and the play doesn't work. Gladys was aware of that, even though Joe kept saying, "You are giving me an Eisenhower. I want a Patton." She knew that what Joe meant was that he wanted an Othello with a chip on his shoulder. John Berry and I explored what I would call the Othello Cynicism, and certainly for Othello, as a Muslim in that impressive culture that he came from, there was a place for cynicism. But I am not sure whether that is what Shakespeare wrote or not.

Interviewer: Speaking of writers, to what extent have you wanted to participate or been able to participate as a member of a creative team shaping the final script of a play?

Jones: We had that with *The Great White Hope,* and to some extent with *Fences.* It was a totally harmonious experience with *The Great White Hope,* and an often disharmonious experience with *Fences,* in that I never really talked to the playwright. All my communication throughout *Fences* was conducted through the director. I felt strongly that *Fences* had no resolution. Ultimately, a conclusion was achieved through the director. Lloyd Richards created some symbolic behavior on the stage, without rewriting the script. In that moment, the play reached a resolution which it did not have before. August Wilson, the playwright, really felt incapable of rewriting. He is that pure: "The baby came out like it is. You want to give it a third arm?" He didn't want to do that.

With the script for *The Great White Hope,* my agent Lucy Kroll read the play and said, "Jimmy, I am giving you a play that is really an old-fashioned piece of work. I just want you to know my feeling about it, but the character is interesting." I read it and I said, "I don't care how old-fashioned the play is, I want to do this role." I don't know whether Lucy was right or wrong. The play probably could have been classified as quite avant-garde. Walter Kerr called it "Theater of Inundation." The play so inundated the audience that the film was almost impossible to do. The play used up all the cinematic energies, so there was no room for the movie after that. The play also started out as a four-hour piece. The first previews in Washington were running about four hours with only two intermissions, and then they made some cuts. And cuts. And losses. And then the final cut and loss was, of course, the movie.

Interviewer: Do you have to live with a script for a while before you see changes that you deeply feel are necessary?

Jones: With *Fences,* I didn't realize it right away. I just kept coming home from rehearsals depressed. By then, I had a son of my own, and I couldn't understand why the relationship between the father and the son in the play was so unfulfilling for me, and then I realized it was *unfulfilled,* it was unrealized. The mother came in at the moment when the father and son could have come to grips with each other. The play lacked a climax—that moment when the play hits the tuning fork and you go, "Aha! This is what it's all about." And you know you can start zipping up your pants and your pocketbook and getting ready to go home. Not that there is nothing left to watch, but you've got it. And, as written, *Fences* never had that moment when you got it. I said to Lloyd, "Does every father look forward to a relationship with a son in which he wants to *kill* his son?" How Freudian, perhaps, but it didn't make any sense to me. I started fighting for a conclusion to that relationship, and the author couldn't give it to us, so the director simply said, "Let's try this scene without the mother coming in to save the day. Let's see what happens symbolically between the two men without the mother." And the mother never came into the scene again. The two men resolved their conflict on their own. The mother arrives later, just at the moment when the father realizes he can't really kill his son. After that change, I did not go home depressed anymore.

Interviewer: It sounds as if a deep emotional instinct or reflex is at work when you confront a script.

Jones: Well, it's an area I really hate to get into because I am not a writer. I think it's the actor's job, even if a line doesn't quite make sense, to keep trying to understand it. You might find something quite unusual that you would have missed otherwise. That's in terms of why characters say what they do. The only thing I've learned, though, is that whatever they are saying, I have a lot to do with the *way* they say it, the words they use. I have a lot to do with that because I am a stutterer, and there are certain phrases I can't even memorize if the track of it is badly scanned or badly metered. I don't mean poetic meter, but something akin to that. All good writing has a flow, a rhythm and cadence, a kind of free form of poetry like Walt Whitman wrote. I think all good communication has that. I have an instinct for that flow, and eventually I might get around to saying to the author, "Can I find a different beat, a different rhythm, by adding or subtracting a word?" But it is never to interfere with what is being said, because the playwright is a temporary god, creating a universe from scratch, and I think it is wrong for anyone to upend "God."

Interviewer: Is there a role that you have never done that you would like to do?

Jones: No. To misuse that great phrase "fire in the belly," I no longer have burning desires to act. I love acting. I had a chance to do a movie that my wife, Ceci, thinks comes closer to the role of Troy Maxson in *Fences* than anything I've done since, but in order to have knee surgery, I had to pass. I feel no great loss. I have no problem now with having to make choices like that, whereas as a hungry, up-and-coming young actor, that would have been a real problem. It would have been a matter of trying to move heaven and earth to do certain things. I don't feel that way anymore. It's not about misgivings at all. It's about if the story is good enough, there will be somebody around who will be able to do it.

Interviewer: Is there a role that you've passed on that you've later regretted?

Jones: No, not really. I think career-wise, it would have been fun to do *Shaft,* though I passed on it before it was even a screenplay. I read it in galleys and said, "I am a farm boy. I don't think I could play an urban jungle character." I still don't think so. So I passed on that.

Interviewer: Is there a role you did and later regretted doing?

Jones: Not really. I joke about a little film called *Deadly Hero,* where I played a bad guy. It was not unlike *Conan the Barbarian;* I was really there as a foil to set up the hero's vengeance theme, but I in no way regret those roles.

Interviewer: What do you consider your most challenging role?

Jones: "Challenge" is a puzzling word—I don't see what the point is. "Challenge" and "struggle." I think there is a tendency for us, in the Western world, to think we are not really living unless we are engaged in struggle. I think life is a lot simpler and a lot easier than that, and I have a hard time applying the idea of challenge to my work. I enjoy it too much.

Interviewer: You have tried your hand at directing. How do you reconcile the actor's point of view and the director's point of view when you are directing?

Jones: I don't know if there should be two points of view. Take a wonderful actor like Billy Bob Thornton who often writes or directs others in a story. I don't think a line is drawn. The only thing I know, having tried directing myself, is that you are in charge of the whole story. As an actor, you are in charge of one character and how he harmonizes with the whole story. You have only to fully understand one character, and it probably isn't wise to try to understand all the other characters in the same way. As a director, you have to understand them all and care about each character. When you think of an actor's mission, it is quite a profound one. In spite of the fact that this is just an imaginary character, this is a creation, like any human being is a creation. This imaginary character doesn't have a prayer in hell without you. There is no way this character can be illuminated without you, the actor. The director has that charge with all the characters. There is no way they can be illuminated without him or her. Otherwise, I don't think there is anything different about the mission of the director and the mission of the actor.

It's all about trying to illuminate, about trying to realize something imaginary—to make it real. Billy Bob Thornton is a clear example of this process. I don't think there is any line between writing it, acting it, and directing it for him. It's all realizing it. I can't think of many examples like Billy Bob, for these are three complex processes. The interaction between actors and directors is an interesting kind of collaboration, but I think the actor's work is ultimately done in solitude, and so is the director's work. We pretend we are having a cooperative experience, but I think much of the work is done in private. If you watch Ceci prepare for a role, she spends a lot of her private time working on that role. Most of us do. We just have moments when we meet and bring our energies together, which makes our work seem less solitary than it actually is. The real encounter is not between you and the director, or you and your fellow actors, but between you and the character.

Interviewer: Are there roles written with you in mind?

Jones: I hear that all the time, but what people mean is that they've written a role with me in mind, based on some other role. But they don't really know who I am. They can't have written a role with *me* in mind.

Interviewer: How do you make a decision about accepting a role? Is it a visceral reaction or a rational decision?

Jones: Most of the things I've done have been the consequence of acknowledging a happy accident. The writer came along, the role came along, the director came along, and I came along. We met where Oedipus says three roads meet. It is the happy accident of the meeting of three roads. I think I have been chosen as much as I have chosen—I'll say by fate, certainly not luck, but by some confluence of energies.

Interviewer: In that process there is the encounter of the individual actor and his individual character. There are also those catalytic encounters between actor and actor. What is the ideal encounter or chemistry between actors? How has this worked for you?

Jones: I've never thought there was an ideal one. It's an act of futility to look for an ideal relationship. You just make the best of what you get. Often you have actors who are totally harmonious, and you harmonize whether you are on the set or backstage. You know that there is a basic trust and respect that goes on, and that there is a friendship. Other times you don't get to know the person at all, and yet it works. Some actors are very private. Some actors go to a dark place when they work, in terms of their persona and their psyche. They are frightened. They go to a place where they are utterly inaccessible. I don't know. Again, it's just the place where three roads meet. You get what you get on the road.

Interviewer: Are there roles you have taken so that you could work with certain actors?

Jones: I used to choose roles that way. I think all of us took roles in *Swashbuckler* just to work with Robert Shaw. I've done several roles just to work with Robert Duvall. Those happy accidents were available to me, and I knew why I was doing it—not because of the role, but because of the association.

Interviewer: Let me ask your opinion about theater critics.

Jones: I leave them alone and hope to God they leave me alone! I was shocked the first time I realized that as an actor, when I was in *The Great White Hope* in Washington, I was attending a party where a drama critic was also a guest. I didn't think we were supposed to be in the same room! I didn't think we were ever supposed to say hello to a critic.

The critic John Simon once laid me to waste over something I didn't even do. I had a part in *Coriolanus,* and he attacked me as "the actor with the Jamaican accent." He had mistaken me for another actor in the show, but the important thing was that he laid me to waste. He also expected me to counter-punch, through writing or some other abusive manner. This apparently was a habit of his—to attack, wait for the counterpunch, and then make up with the actor and so make a friend. It's kind of a sick way to make a friend. I've seen him do it with other people. But I didn't counterpunch.

Interviewer: When you go to the theater, do you watch a play as the professional actor or as the private person?

Jones: I watch the play as myself. I enter the experience of the play, and I hope to be transported. I don't become the critic. One of the best critics I know, Professor Richard Brown, says that when he has functioned as a film critic, he sees the movie twice—once for himself, and the second time for the journal. He is convinced that when the critic sits there and does not really respond, but takes it all in, allegedly objectively, he is fooling himself. You can't be objective. And if something about the film or the play annoys you *personally,* you give it a bad review. That's how objective you are.

Interviewer: Comment on the differences between an actor playing comedy and an actor playing "serious theater."

Jones: The best comedy *is* "serious theater." With *Born Yesterday,* for example, and even *Of Mice and Men,* the audience doesn't know whether to laugh or cry. That's the best kind of comedy. You are taken in, you are really transported, you are vulnerable to the experience as an audience. But I don't have a clue about what makes comedy work because I have not much of a sense of humor, and I don't know how to make a joke work, and I don't think I have ever played comedy. I have heard audiences laugh at something I said, but I wasn't trying to be funny. If I'm lucky, it is appropriate laughter, and for the most part it was, but on occasions it was inappropriate laughter, nervous laughter. Then my job is to hold the audience in focus like a skittish race-horse. I don't know what comedy is. It has something to do with timing. Severn Darden said, "Comedy is very easy. You simply make a statement, and one word in that statement you make *real* big." It's that chemistry of timing and emphasis. Of course, Severn was crazy, so who knows! But I think there is something to that. Maybe the one real big word was just shocking or silly or scary or nerve-touching enough to evoke laughter.

Interviewer: Is there a question I've not asked that you would like to address?

Jones: No. I usually start out an interview by confessing that the longer I live and the more I work, the less I know what to say. I guess it's that I accept that I am really involved in a learning process and the learning gets not less but more as I go along. I have no fewer opinions, I just have less room for opinions, and less need for opinions because they don't always serve me well. I have fewer conclusions. I hope to have more questions. I'm not sure I do yet, but that is my goal. My love for my work hasn't changed over the years. I don't know when I first acknowledged my love for acting. I guess you acknowledge it the first time you do something that works, or is halfway successful, and then you realize you can achieve it, and then it is always a pleasure when you are given a chance to try.

Interviewer: Any predictions for the future of American theater?

Jones: Of course, you have to realize that with television and the Internet, the theater has become an elite form, like the museum, the opera, and the ballet, but there will always be room for it. There are some societies that have made the ballet and the opera accessible to those who can't afford tickets or to those who are not so-called cultured. The fact that the theater is elite does not mean it is experienced only by the aristocrats. It is about rare form, and I think theater has become a rare form in our time. But there is always room for a young generation of actors, writers, directors, and audiences in the theater to enjoy rare form. The theater never dies. It just simply goes to ashes and comes back to life.

Stacy Keach

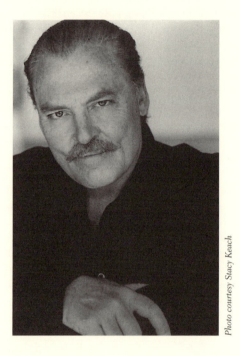

Photo courtesy Stacy Keach

Stacy Keach was born in Savannah, Georgia, on June 2, 1941. He studied at the University of California at Berkeley, the Yale School of Drama, and as a Fulbright scholar at the London Academy of Music and Dramatic Arts. He made his Broadway debut as Buffalo Bill in Arthur Kopit's Indians *in 1969. He received Obie Awards for his portrayals of the title role in* MacBird!, *Jamie in* Long Day's Journey into Night, *and the title role in* Hamlet *at the New York Shakespeare Festival. Other stage roles include Mercutio,* Romeo and Juliet; *Berowne,* Love's Labours Lost; *title role,* Henry V *(all at the Oregon Shakespeare Festival in 1963); Cutler and Turnkey,* Danton's Death *(1965); Mr. Horner,* The Country Wife *(1965);* The Caucasian Chalk Circle *(1966); August, "The Demonstration," and The Man, "Man and Dog,"* The Niggerlovers *(1967); Sir John Falstaff,* Henry IV, Part 1 *and Part 2 (1968); Edmund,* King Lear *(1968); title role,* Peer Gynt *(1969); Sydney Bruhl,* Deathtrap *(1979); title role,* Richard III *(1990); Richard Jannings,* Solitary Confinement *(1991); Michael Rowen,* Star

Rowen, Ezekiel Rowen, Jed Rowan, and Joshua Rowen, The Kentucky Cycle *(1994); title role,* Macbeth *(1995); Marc,* Art *(1998).*

His films are The Heart Is a Lonely Hunter *(1968),* The End of the Road *(1970),* Brewster McCloud *(1970),* Doc Holiday *(1971),* The Life and Times of Judge Roy Bean *(1971),* The New Centurions *(1972),* Fat City *(1972),* The Gravy Train *(1974),* The Ninth Configuration *(1979),* The Long Riders *(1980),* Butterfly *(1982),* That Championship Season *(1982),* False Identity *(1990),* Class of 1999 *(1990),* Sunset Grill *(1993),* The Sea Wolf *(1997),* Escape from L.A. *(1997),* Birds of Passage *(1998),* American History X *(1998),* Icebreaker *(1999), and* Mercy Streets *(2000).*

On television, he played the title role in Mickey Spillane's Mike Hammer *(1984–85) and* The New Mike Hammer *(1986–87) and has appeared in* Twelfth Night, Macbeth, Playhouse in New York, Dynasty, Jesus of Nazareth, Wait Until Dark, The Forgotten, Mission of the Shark, Revenge on the Highway, Rio Diablo, Against Their Will: Women in Prison, Nova, World's Most Amazing Videos, Caribe, The Blue and the Gray, Mistral's Daughter, Hemingway *(Golden Globe Award),* Titus, and The Courage to Love.

This interview took place on November 8, 1993.

• ─────────────────────────────────────── •

Interviewer: You represent what is best about American acting: onstage you have enormous power, range, and technique, and you are an actor who did both classical and modern theater at a time when most actors divided themselves into either classical or modern actors. How did this happen? Where are you from?

Keach: I grew up in a family with a theatrical background. My father, who still is an actor as a matter of fact, acted in college and then went on to become a teacher and acted at the Pasadena Playhouse in the forties. When I was born in Savannah, Georgia, he was teaching at a small college, and then he was called to the Pasadena Playhouse when I was six months old. He went to work there in their heyday—with Raymond Burr and Victor Jory and Dana Andrews—both as an actor and a director. As I was growing up in southern California, I was never encouraged really to do anything even remotely to do with the theater until I got into junior high school, and then I began to take a serious interest because I saw that my dad was very interested in the theater. I remember being cast in the ninth grade in the role of the Stage Manager in *Our Town;* and I remember coming home and asking my dad about how to play this part. He took such great pains to show me how the Stage Manager would reach his hand down into the ice cream trough and pull out the ice cream and how he would describe a butternut tree standing there. I was enthralled because I had never seen my father really so excited, so sort of alive, as he was during those times. The only other time was at Halloween. He would love to get me dressed up in incredible costumes. He would take great pains to put elaborate makeup on me. So I think that's really where my first love of the theater was generated.

As time went on and I went away to school, I became interested in classical theater. I remember going to the University of California at Berkeley and seeing Laurence Olivier play Richard III. I remember sitting there and watching the movie three times without leaving the theater. You didn't have to get up and leave the way you do today; you could stay there if you wanted to. I came home and I said that this was something I wanted to pursue, and my dad said, "No, you can't possibly entertain the notion of becoming a classical actor, and make a living, and be a responsible human being. There's no possible way for you to do that." I was very despondent about it. I talked to a teacher of mine at the University of California about it and he said, "No, you have to do what you want to do." So I began to rent films and go to films that had to do with classical performances. My heroes were Olivier and Gielgud, mostly English actors, because there were very few American actors who were doing classical theater and also contemporary theater. When Marlon Brando played Mark Antony in *Julius Caesar,* that was a major milestone because suddenly another one of my heroes was doing something classical. That was a great moment for me and gave me a lot of inspiration. So I began to pursue the idea of classical theater, primarily at the Oregon Shakespeare Festival during the summers of my college career at the University of California at Berkeley. I went there and started playing Shakespeare at the Oregon Shakespeare Festival, which is probably even today one of the best training grounds for young actors in the United States. In those days, it was a nonprofessional company; it was just for young actors. I guess that's a long way of answering your question about how I became interested in the classics!

Interviewer: Did you go directly from California to New York? What did you do after college? Did you study in England at all?

Keach: Yes, I did. I was overtrained! I went four years to the University of California at Berkeley, and then I got a scholarship to the Yale Drama School. I was not popular there, and I hated it!

Interviewer: How come?

Keach: Well, by this time I had done two summers of acting, so I had really had much more experience acting than most of my contemporaries who were students there. I think it also had something to do with my father telling me that it was very difficult to make a living; unless you wanted to "starve"—with quotes around that—you might as well forget it because you'll never make it on your own. I was determined to make it, so I had a lot of enthusiasm. On the first day of class, the acting instructor said, "I want everybody to come up onstage and perform a soliloquy," and she said, "Does anybody have one ready right now?" I had just played Mercutio in *Romeo and Juliet,* and I went right into the Queen Mab speech. I think I intimidated everybody. I certainly didn't gain any points with the instructor. Even though she acknowledged that I had some talent as an actor, she couldn't have her way with me in terms of how to do this or that. To make a long story short, I flunked both my acting courses. But I won the acting award that year!

Interviewer: Did you leave then?

Keach: No, I stayed there for one year. One of my best friends at that time was Arvin Brown, who was a year ahead of me. I did a one-man show for a junior college in southern California that Arvin directed. This happened to be the four hundredth anniversary of Shakespeare's birth; and Arvin said, "Why don't you apply for a Fulbright grant and go to England for a year, if you love English actors and you want to be a classically trained actor? What are you doing here? Why don't you go ahead and do it and get out of here?" So I applied. I had to wait quite a while to get the results. In the interim period, I had done a performance of *Henry V* at the Oregon Shakespeare Festival the summer just preceding my time at Yale; and Henry Hewes, then critic of the *Saturday Review,* said very nice things about it, and he said, "I'm going to get in touch with Joseph Papp and you should see him."

So during that first year at Yale, I took the train down to New York on a cold winter day. I remember going into this smoke-filled room, seeing Joe Papp there, and he said, "Hello, kid, what do you want?" I said, "Well, I've come to see you about an audition." He said, "Sit down. What are you going to do for an audition?" I did the "Upon the king" speech from *Henry V.* After I auditioned, he looked up and said, "Are you a member of Equity?" and I said, "No." He said, "Well, you're going to be. You're going to be in my production of *Hamlet.*" I was cast as Marcellus, and I was thrilled. Five months later, I got this note in the mail which said, "You have been accepted on the first level of your Fulbright application, and we want you to come in to audition in New York." Who was sitting there but Joseph Papp! He said, "What do you want to go to England for? Why don't you stay here?" Joe always felt very strongly about the fact that Americans can do Shakespeare better than the English, that we didn't necessarily have to go there to be trained in order to do well. He said, "Well, I don't think you should do this, but you don't have to audition for me because I've already seen you audition—go home." So I never auditioned. I got a notice in the mail about six or eight weeks later saying that I had been selected as an alternate to go to England on a Fulbright, and I was very depressed. Time went along, and I was playing Marcellus in *Hamlet,* and the actor who was playing the Player King passed away—a wonderful old character actor; I enjoyed him immensely. Joe said, "I want you to do a double. You're going to be Marcellus and the Player King." I was very happy about that. Two days later, I got a letter saying that the person who had taken the Fulbright grant had dropped out—so you're going to go.

Interviewer: When you went to England, what did you find was different? What did you get out of it?

Keach: It's interesting. I had heard that most of the training in England was very technical, that it concentrated on vocal technique [and] on physical technique and not much on the emotional life of the character. When I got to the London Academy of Music and Dramatic Art—we called it LAMDA—I was amazed by what I discovered there. First of all, the training was divided into two different categories: one was the emotional life of the actor and the other was the physical life of the actor. With the emotional life of the actor, there was a center given to each individual, which was somewhere in the base of the stomach, in your gut. That was your emotional center. The physical center was at the base of the spine. The entire year was devoted to developing those centers in many different ways. Physically, we spent a lot of time doing mime and pantomime and a lot of time with masks—which was also a way of working on the emotional center. We spent a lot of time lying on the floor and breathing. It was a way to get in touch with yourself, to get in touch with the self, the actor himself.

I remember that the head of LAMDA at that time always used to quote from Granville-Barker saying, "The success of an actor rests for a short time on his appearance and perhaps for a longer time on the sound of his voice and perhaps for a longer time on the characters he's playing; but ultimately the success of an actor is totally dependent on who the actor is." That was the philosophy of LAMDA in those days; so we would do a lot of things to try to develop not only your self but your ability, your aptitude for expanding your horizons, to visualize all the potential things you could do. Of course, much of that had to do with Shakespeare, because the Shakespearean roles, the big ones, are always the greatest challenges for any actor. Those would have been the roles that most of us who were there aspired to play, and we were encouraged to work with those parts. That was probably the most important year in my early training. The other thing we were exposed to was the theater. The theater in London that year, 1965–66, was extraordinary. Laurence Olivier was doing *The Master Builder* and *Othello.* Robert Stephens was doing *Royal Hunt of the Sun,* and Albert Finney was in *Black Comedy.* The Old Vic had the Berliner Ensemble doing *The Threepenny Opera.* It was the year of *The Homecoming* and *Marat/Sade.* It was an amazing year of theater and, as Fulbright students, they gave us fifteen pounds a week to go to the theater or buy books. If you didn't use that fifteen pounds a week, you had to give it back.

Interviewer: Did you have some sense when you came back that the theater was considerably different here in America?

Keach: When I first came back, I went to Lincoln Center. It was their very first season.

Interviewer: Lincoln Center was the first institutional theater in New York.

Keach: That's right. It had Herbert Blau and Jules Irving from the Actors Workshop in San Francisco. When I had been a student at Berkeley, I had seen much of the Actors Workshop work. This was during the late fifties and early sixties, when it was one of the most exciting theaters in America. They were an extraordinary group; it was a wonderful company. When they came to New York, however, they made a mistake. They came to New York saying, "We're going to show them," and the critics just were not going to be shown. Also, the selection of the season was very difficult.

Interviewer: *Danton's Death*. It was very brave.

Keach: I was in that. I played the third butcher on the left! They had good intentions; they really did. They wanted to bring serious theater to the American theater. There wasn't much serious drama on Broadway. They were going to do *Danton's Death* and Bertolt Brecht's *The Caucasian Chalk Circle;* the second show was William Wycherly's *The Country Wife,* and that was the play they asked me to play the lead in. I was on my way to Stanford, as a matter of fact, to join a new resident professional company out there. On my way through New York, I auditioned, and they said, "That's fine. We want you to play Harry Horner in *The Country Wife.*" So I moved bag and baggage to New York, and I was thrilled because this was the first year of the Vivian Beaumont. Well, all the excitement suddenly waned when those first reviews came out on *Danton's Death*. I was in rehearsal for *The Country Wife* when *Danton's Death* opened, and they were the worst reviews I've ever been involved with. To give you an idea, when *Country Wife* opened, they said that I was mediocre, and that was great compared to the reviews of *Danton's Death*. That was a very disillusioning experience, because coming from England, I wanted to be part of a company of actors and wanted to be rejuvenated in the sense of being a member of a group that was classically trained. It all fell apart.

That summer I went off to Williamstown to see Nikos Psacharopolous, who had been one of my teachers when I'd been at Yale two years before. I went up there and had a glorious summer, doing lots of different things: *Marat/Sade* (I played Jean-Paul Marat), *The Lion in Winter, Incident at Vichy,* and *Annie Get Your Gun*. While I was there, I was asked to go to the Long Wharf Theatre in New Haven for their season and do *Three Sisters* and *Oh! What a Lovely War*. I was at the Long Wharf and this guy came up to me, this friend of mine from Yale. He was a very talented designer, but now he was going to be a director. He said, "There's a girl I know who's written this play that I think we can get on in New York. It's a political satire." It was a play called *MacBird!* which suggested that Lyndon Johnson was responsible for the assassination of John F. Kennedy. It was a parody of the Scottish play. We did it down at the Village Gate, and it was a big hit, and that was really the beginning of my career as an actor in the New York theater. From that, my movie career began to open up a little bit.

Interviewer: Did you go to California right after *MacBird!*?

Keach: Joseph Strick, the film director, came to see me in *MacBird!* He asked me if I'd be interested in the film of *The Heart Is a Lonely Hunter* by Carson McCullers. I said, "Are you kidding?" A few weeks later, I got a call from my agent, and he said that Joseph Strick had been fired. I said, "Well, there it goes." But Robert Ellis Miller was hired in his place, and he came to see *MacBird!* He wanted me to play the part of the drifter in the film—it was a middle-aged character. I had already received the mantle of being an actor able to play characters many years older than I. I was in my twenties, and I think that that probably went back to *The Country Wife* because, when I did *The Country Wife,* I shaved my head thinking that all the men in the Restoration shaved their heads and wore wigs. I looked forty-five years old. And when I did *MacBird!,* of course, I was Lyndon Johnson. I wore glasses and was in my forties, even though I was in my twenties. So Robert Ellis Miller saw me and he said, after I read, "Okay, you've got the part," and that was my first movie. Even though movie roles began to follow, I didn't move back to California. I liked living in New York. After that, Robert Brustein asked if I would come up to Yale.

Interviewer: You had been doing these really large parts. I mean not just older characters, but in terms of scope. Did you find it was hard to adjust to films because you were a "big" actor?

Keach: Absolutely, yes. In fact, the very first movie I was involved in we shot in Selma, Alabama. Alan Arkin was the star, and James Wong Howe was the director of photography. I remember after the second day's shooting, Howe said, "Do you want to see the dailies?" I said, "I'd love to. Where?" He said, "They've rented a movie theater"—and it was a pretty good-sized theater. I'll never forget the experience of seeing myself on the screen for the first time. I just thought that I was the worst actor I'd ever seen. It was so big and exaggerated and grotesque. This was my own personal reaction to my own work; nobody else had that reaction. The director said, "Just keep doing what you're doing." With subsequent films, I would go to the dailies and I would tone down my performance and get rid of anything that wasn't just absolutely almost nothing. I think it's one of the worst techniques for actors to go and see their own dailies. Whenever I'm directing a film, I won't allow it, because actors can be the worst judges of their own performances. Because what happened after that was that I became totally antiseptic; my performances got sterile. I wasn't overacting, but there was nothing going on, absolutely nothing.

Interviewer: When did you do those great parts for Joe Papp after that?

Keach: After my first big film, I went back to Yale. Joseph Heller had written a play called *We Bombed in New Haven.* It had something to do with the armed services; it was one of those wacky *Catch-22*-type social commentary plays. It was a comedy basically, but a military satire, and this was the new show at Yale that particular season. We didn't bomb in New Haven. It was a big hit. Ron Liebman played Henderson, and Estelle Parsons was in it too. Four weeks after we closed, I got a call from my agent and he said, "The show is going to New York, but you're not going. They don't think you're a big enough name. Jason Robards is going to play it." And it was a big hit—well, it was a moderate hit—in New York.

Inteviewer: How did you come to do Hamlet for Joe Papp?

Keach: Well, *MacBird!* was the turning point, and he then acknowledged that I was on my way in terms of my career. He came up to see *Coriolanus* at Yale and asked me if I would come that summer to do Falstaff in both parts of *Henry IV.* The year I was at Yale I was also there as a teacher teaching students Shakespeare, recycling what I'd learned in England. Among my students were my brother, James, Henry Winkler, and James Naughton. I decided we were going to work on *Henry IV, Part 1* and *Part 2,* strictly because it was a way of doing my own research on Falstaff, and that's what we did. And that summer I did Falstaff, and then appeared in *Hamlet* the year after that. *Hamlet* was the last thing I did.

Interviewer: It's very rare that someone would ask an actor of twenty-four to play Falstaff. What did you do to play the role? As a twenty-four-year-old, you had to imagine yourself very different, didn't you?

Keach: I went to see *Chimes at Midnight,* where Orson Welles played Falstaff. At the time, it was sort of a revolutionary film. The thing about it that was so remarkable was that I felt Orson was playing that character so closely to himself. Granted, he was then in his late fifties or early sixties; it was different from a young actor in his twenties doing it. I don't know. Again, I keep going back to when I was the Stage Manager in *Our Town.* I was always the guy who played the father figure and the grandfather. I still am.

Interviewer: How did you start working on Falstaff?

Keach: I started working on that character definitely from the outside in. I put on the body-suit. I had to know what I looked like as Falstaff to know what I felt like. I had no idea what it was to be that heavy, although in that period one of my friends was a very heavyset guy, almost three hundred and ten pounds. The corpulence of Falstaff was one thing. The other thing was I understood the character emotionally (at least I thought I did), in terms of a man who desperately wanted the love and attention of this young prince. That's one of the things I really concentrated on. The showmanship aspect of Falstaff, his desire to be a "cut-up," was very easy for me. It wasn't until *Part 2* that I ran into trouble. It was much more difficult to play, in terms of where I was as a human being in those days. The "honor" speech was something that I tried many different ways. I finally did it very simply and it worked. Sam

Waterston—a wonderful actor—played Hal, and we had a relationship that worked.

As you ask the question, I'm thinking of what specifics I can remember about working on the role, and I've got to tell this story. I was doing a movie in Great Barrington, Massachusetts, called *The End of the Road,* a film that came and went very quickly. I would get up at five o'clock in the morning, get into makeup, shoot the film, and at four in the afternoon I would get in the car and drive down the Taconic Parkway for two and a half hours. About an hour outside of New York, I would get into the front seat and begin to put on my makeup for Falstaff. So I was making up in the car as Falstaff. I would arrive at the theater and I would drive right to the back of the building and get into my costume and go right onstage. After the performance, I would get back in the car and go straight back up the Taconic Parkway to Great Barrington, Massachusetts, and I'd get up the next morning at five and start shooting.

Interviewer: Your next great parts were Peer Gynt and Hamlet. What was it like to do Hamlet?

Keach: I did it three times. The first time I did it was with Arvin Brown at the Long Wharf Theatre. I was doing a film in Los Angeles at the time. I was just thirty years old. I felt this was the time to do it because Hamlet is thirty years old, so Arvin and I got together and discussed how we wanted to go about doing it. We decided we wanted to do it very simply, with as much elegance and clarity as we possibly could. So we did it at the Long Wharf Theatre, and it was very successful. Clive Barnes, who was then the theater critic of the *New York Times,* came to see it, and he was impressed with the clarity of the performance. Then Joe Papp contacted me and said, "I'd like to do it this summer in the park, but I don't want to do it with Arvin Brown and I don't want to do it with that company. I'll get the best possible company I can for you—and for us." And of course he did. It was one of the most illustrious companies I've ever worked with: James Earl Jones did Claudius, and Colleen Dewhurst was Gertrude; Barnard Hughes was Polonius; Sam Waterston did Laertes; Raul Julia played Osric; Charles Durning was the Gravedigger.

Interviewer: At this time, then, you were moving back and forth between New York and Los Angeles?

Keach: Yes, that was the last year in New York, and then I moved out to California.

Interviewer: What made you leave New York?

Keach: I think it was an unhappy personal relationship; I just wanted to get away from New York. The other thing was I really thought that, because I had made it as Hamlet, then the whole world would open up for me; Hamlet to me was the mountain that would allow me to do anything. I remember getting a call from an agent from a very high-powered agency who said, "Stacy, nobody's casting King Lear in Hollywood this week. Get out of your ivory tower; get your nose dirty. Nobody in the business cares about how good you are as a Shakespearean actor. You may care, and other select people may care, but the business doesn't care. So if you really want to be a star, you've got to get your nose dirty. You've got to get out here and start your career in either television or motion pictures." When I was at LAMDA, we were very proud of the fact that we were actors. RADA, the Royal Academy of Dramatic Arts, created stars. "Star" was a dirty word, a word that represented a sellout and a prostitute. It wasn't until many, many years later that I discovered why I wasn't getting the handsome offers that I wanted to get. Where were the scripts? Why was so-and-so getting parts that I wasn't getting? The answer was that he was a star and I wasn't. I began to think that wasn't such a dirty word after all. I began to pursue that so I would have the freedom to choose the type of roles that I would like to play.

Interviewer: Was that a hard decision?

Keach: Yes, very hard.

Interviewer: I think you're from the last generation of actors who were allowed to feel these differences. You either worked in theater or you worked in film. The theater was a serious art; films were a sort of a prostitution. Of course, things were also financially not like they are now. You could make a living as an Equity actor. Now it's different. It changed pretty much around the seventies, didn't it?

Keach: That's exactly right. The theater began to change, and the whole concept of television began to change. The idea of serious actors like George C. Scott doing a series on television was a big moment for young actors. Or when Laurence Olivier did a Polaroid commercial—these were major moments for actors. They shocked us out of our sensibilities. We began to see that there was no reason why you couldn't have a popular series, or be on a soap opera, for that matter, and still be a serious actor.

Interviewer: Did you have to have a personality change? It must have been difficult at the beginning of the seventies after playing those big stage roles to make that decision. I've always wondered what that was like.

Keach: I grew up in California, so it was like I was going home in a way. That was my justification: I was going to suddenly become the person my father had really wanted me to be, a successful "commercial" actor, not a classical actor. In fact, when I was in California in *The Kentucky Cycle* last spring, my father said, "Why do you want to do that? Why don't you sit out here and be available for some good movie or television show?" He still believes that. I think that for most actors the seesaw between doing something for love of the art and doing something to pay the bills is a constant battle. It's not something that anybody is immune to; every actor has that war.

Interviewer: But you're a model for young actors, because you have continued to do both. You and Dustin Hoffman and Al Pacino do films, do television, and then come back and do really important work in the theater.

Keach: Well, I have to. It's my lifeblood. When I did Richard III at the Shakespeare Theatre in Washington, it was the realization of a dream that I had had for almost twenty years. I had really wanted to do it ever since I saw Laurence Olivier in the movie. It rejuvenated my faith in the power of theater, because I hadn't done any theater. I'd done some commercial things, but I hadn't done any serious theater for a long time. In many ways, it put me back in touch with the things inside me that are important. That is not to say that I don't need to support myself and pay the rent. But by the same token, I've found ways of doing that and also realizing that my priorities have to do with the theater. It's not an easy task for me to face the reality of the fact that I have a five-year-old son, a three-year-old daughter, and that, as time goes on, I will have to put them through college. I'm a middle-aged daddy, and I realize that I've got to find that balance.

Interviewer: When you were working on Richard III, as with Falstaff, surely the physical aspect of the character must have been important to you.

Keach: Well, we talked a lot about Antony Sher, who was a wonderful Richard. He was completely encased; he had braces on both legs and braces on his arms. I think whenever you play a Shakespearean role, you have some obligation to the past. You have some obligation to the traditions preceding you. I think I learned that when I played Hamlet. Certainly when you play Hamlet, you are completely at the mercy of everybody who has ever seen another Hamlet. You are compared to every actor who has ever played it. That's why I played him three times; I kept trying to find out who *my* Hamlet was. Ultimately, you realize you don't really play Hamlet, Hamlet plays you. That's what really happens, and you just have to give yourself that experience. I used to sit down for hours and write journals and notes before I would go on in New York, trying to rid myself of any preoccupations I had about what I was going to be doing that particular evening. I was just trying to be totally open to that experience on that particular night instead of trying to premeditate. I think with Richard it was a different situation, because I felt I wanted to acknowledge the Richards of the past and yet make it my own Richard as well. I'm very proud of that performance, as proud of that as anything I've ever done.

Interviewer: As a good actor working through the process, you also found humor in Richard. You seem to relate to characters who are showmen, who in a way like the audience.

Keach: I've always been very comfortable playing characters who were very clearly schizophrenic in some way. You see the public side of the person and then you see the private side. I love characters that have that dichotomy. I think Buffalo Bill in Arthur Kopit's *Indians* was the first character I played that really examined that. He was a showman, but you saw what's behind the mask. That's always interesting in the theater. I remember seeing Paul Scofield do *Timon of Athens* when I was a student at LAMDA, thinking this is the greatest play Shakespeare ever wrote, because he managed to convey the sense of a man whose mask totally revealed the man underneath as time went on. It was an astounding performance.

Interviewer: Do you try to convey that whenever you can?

Keach: Yes, I do, because to me that's the clearest way of being able to be specific about the range of your character. You have at least what's public and private, what seems to be and what really is. That's something that you as an actor can really sink your teeth into, generally speaking. Mentioning Kopit reminds me that one of my laments as an actor is that I have never been given much opportunity to play anything comedic in film or television. Mike Hammer had a sort of joggy sense of humor, but it wasn't romantic comedy. I would love to be able to do more comedy, because I love comedy.

Interviewer: I thought you were wonderful in *The Kentucky Cycle*. You came to that play after it already had been done in Seattle. When you read the script, what attracted you to it?

Keach: I think the variety of roles certainly. Let's face it, it won the Pulitzer Prize. It was a serious piece of work, and I knew it was going to get a lot of attention. Also, I was so disappointed with *Solitary Confinement* when I played it in New York. I really had a great time doing it, but it was a slight piece of writing. In a sense it was what it was—a piece of entertainment. Nevertheless, it got clobbered in New York; it just got killed. I was very disappointed, and I really wanted to get back to New York as quickly as possible so I could redeem myself, at least in my eyes and the eyes of the audiences and critics.

Interviewer: It was interesting to see you in *The Kentucky Cycle* because in a way it was a retrospective of your work—from O'Neillian family tragedy to a sort of Aeschylean classical tragedy. It certainly permitted us to see the range of your acting talents.

Keach: One of the interesting things about that was to be able to play your own grandson. He was the patriarch; and playing your own progeny—I had never done that before.

Interviewer: That seems like a lot of work. All the members of the cast had to think, "Well, what would I be like if I were my own child?"

Keach: When I first got the script, which was like a telephone book, I was doing a movie in Australia, and I came to rehearsals late, ten days after they began. The rest of the cast had all done the play, both in Seattle and in Los Angeles, so I did something that I rarely do. I memorized the text as best as I possibly could before coming to rehearsal, which is a very dangerous thing for an actor to do because you can get caught in different kinds of line readings and different adjustments. I spent a lot of time on the phone talking with Warner Shook, the director, and Robert Schenkkan, the playwright, about the characters because I wasn't sure about them. Let me give you an example: Michael Rowen, who was the patriarch of the family, was an indentured servant from Ireland. He had a very thick Irish accent, and I wondered if his progeny Ezekiel would have an Irish accent as well. I didn't really know, so they had to take me from square one—this is on the telephone—telling me what the accents were, "This one has a heavy Kentucky accent," for all the other characters. I was working a lot from externals initially, at least for the first three characters: What did they sound like? What did they look like? And then what did they feel like? I think more often than not I work that way. Sometimes I work from the inside out, but most of the time I work that way.

Interviewer: What did you learn about *The Kentucky Cycle* by playing out of town before going into New York?

Keach: I think we learned a lot in Washington. We refined a lot of the performances. During the marathons, the days when we did both parts, with the two-hour break between Parts 1 and 2, I think there was more momentum. You got out earlier. Part 1 ran from two to five, then there was a break until seven, and then we went seven to ten; so people weren't in the theater at eleven-thirty at night, and I think it made a big difference. It was just too hard for people to stay that late and still get home at a reasonable hour.

Interviewer: What was the rehearsal process for such a marathon of a play?

Keach: It was *very* complicated. In the course of a normal day in the beginning stages, we rehearsed one or two plays, two plays at the most. It was a little bit like the juggler with the plates who starts with a plate over here and then gets another one going and then goes back to that first one and goes all the way down the line. That's the way we did it. We'd start with one play and then we'd do two more the next day and then we'd come back and pick up the first one and then do the next three plays and then come back. It was a constant moving back and forth. It was very difficult; it was one of the most agonizing rehearsals I've ever been through in my life. I was glad when it was over, I really was, because these were not rehearsals for fun; it was sheer hard work.

Interviewer: Were there changes during the rehearsal process?

Keach: Yes, there were. We were rewriting the last two plays right up until the last performance in Washington. Once you get it up onstage and you have a certain basic format, it's not so difficult to make those small changes, even though there were still a couple of lines where I didn't know the changes and I messed up quite badly.

Interviewer: Did you ever play a role where you felt you couldn't possibly have done it any better and, because of the nature of the character, the audience didn't respond?

Keach: I really can't think of one. But I will say this, though, in terms of that phenomenon of an actor not feeling responded to: that happens in the course of a run. There are certainly days when you're not giving as good a performance as you would on other days. That's part of the excitement of the theater; it's also part of the humanity of the theater, the shared experience of the theater. Actors are notorious for saying, "What a terrible audience tonight!" They never think it's them!

Interviewer: What do you look for in terms of a director? What do you want to get out of him or her to help your performance?

Keach: I think first of all a director has to love actors. There are directors who don't who are very good directors. None of them would I particularly want to work with. I've heard that John Dexter was a director who really didn't love actors very much, and I wouldn't want to work with a director like that. I've heard Antonioni was also a director who didn't love actors particularly. A director should understand the process the actor has to go through, the vulnerability an actor has, the childishness of actors: all of these things are very important things for a director to understand. Then of course there's the director's ability to deal with the text—how to make that text live, and how to encourage the actor to have the confidence to do whatever, and also to do what the director wants. It's a collaboration; it's also a vision that the director basically has to have that an actor has to be able to fall into. I also think it's important for the director to be able to work with not just the actors and the text but also the costumes, the sets, the lights, and to deal with all the political machinations that go on. Those are the things that I believe—and there are very few good directors!

Interviewer: Have you ever thought of directing yourself?

Keach: Well, I have, but never in the theater—except in college. I've done television. I directed one film, and my brother, James, and I co-wrote and co-produced a film called *The Long Riders,* which was about Frank and Jesse James. But I prefer acting.

Interviewer: Is there a role you've played that has had a significant impact on you spiritually and emotionally?

Keach: There are a couple of roles. One of them I mentioned earlier, Richard III, the culmination of a twenty-year dream of mine that allowed me to get back to my roots as an actor. Also, whatever role I'm working on at the moment; I know that sounds like a cop-out, but it isn't. I'm involved with these characters when I'm playing them at the moment. They mean a lot to me in terms of growth and development. It's always easier to relate to what you're doing right now, as opposed to what you did or what you would like to do.

Interviewer: What actor or actress you've worked with has brought out the best in you as an actor?

Keach: That's a tough one, because I've worked with so many wonderful actors. Working with Orson Welles was really a great thrill for me. I only had a brief moment; I worked with him on a terrible movie called *Butterfly* years ago. I loved working with him. I was able to share in his career; it was one of the great highlights of my life. We were in Las Vegas shooting this movie. We were eating dinner together. He was quite large in those days. I remember him sitting down and ordering two sides of roast beef, but no potatoes! This little old lady came over and asked for his autograph and he said, "No, I'm eating dinner." He was very gracious afterwards; he got up and went and said to the maître d', "There's a little old lady over there. Please give her this sheet with my autograph on it." He was wonderful. I just adored him. The thing was he didn't want to talk about his career. I wanted to ask him all these questions because he was one of my gods, but he said he didn't want to talk about it. He said, "I want to talk about you." He knew things that I had done, both as an actor and as a director. I was astounded he knew my work as well as he did. I'd like to think that since he knew he'd be working with me he asked somebody to get him my résumé.

Interviewer: Is there any major classical role that you have not yet played that you'd like to play?

Keach: There are a number actually. I'd like to do Lear one of these days. The thing about Lear is—although I'm not really ready for it—you can't wait too long. You can't actually wait until you're the age Lear is. In the meantime, I'd also love to do Prospero, Othello, Laertes, Shylock, and Timon of Athens—then do Lear again.

Interviewer: Do projects come your way, or do you have to go out and get them?

Keach: It depends. What I've learned in twenty-five or thirty years of this business is that you can never wait for projects to come your way. You constantly have to create work for yourself as much as you possibly can. If there's something you want to do, you have to pursue it. You have to do it yourself. In the course of doing that, a lot of other projects will come your way, but for the most part you've got to be your own burgomeister.

Interviewer: Do you have any wishes for the theater?

Keach: I would more and more like to find a way to make theater more accessible to young people. That's a difficult thing. It's not the same as a two-hour television production of a stage production. Television is not the same as live theater. For young people to come to the theater is not easy, given the prices today. One of the reasons I keep going back to Washington is because, believe it or not, there seems to be more of an opportunity to see cultural works there than there is probably in any other city in this country. I would like to see more of that happen in other places, but as long as the Shakespeare Theatre is there I'm grateful for it.

Shirley Knight

Shirley Enola Knight was born July 5, 1936, in Goessel, Kansas. She trained for the stage with Erwin Piscator and Lee Strasberg and studied with Jeff Corey. She made her stage debut as Alison in Look Back in Anger *in Pasadena, California; her New York debut as Katherine in* Journey to the Day *in 1963; and her Broadway debut as Trina in* The Three Sisters *in 1964. Her other stage roles include Constance,* We Have Always Lived in the Castle *(1966); Janet,* The Watering Place *(1969); Carla,* Kennedy's Children *(1975; Tony Award); Blanche DuBois,* A Streetcar Named Desire *(1976); Lieutenant Lillian Holiday,* Happy End *(1977); Betty,* Landscape of the Body *(1979); Ruth,* Losing Time *(1979); Lola,* Come Back, Little Sheba *(1984); Amanda,* The Glass Menagerie *(1990); Gillian,* The Marriage Play, *(1991); Lily Dale,* The Young Man from Atlanta *(1997); and Lady Bracknell,* The Importance of Being Earnest *(1999).*

Her films include Five Gates to Hell *(1959),* Ice Palace *(1960),* The Dark at the Top of the Stairs *(1960),* House of Women *(1962),* Sweet Bird of Youth

(1962), The Couch *(1962)*, Flight from Ashiya *(1964)*, The Group *(1966)*, Dutchman *(1966)*, Petulia *(1968)*, The Rain People *(1969)*, Secrets *(1971)*, Juggernaut *(1974)*, I Cannibali *(1979)*, Beyond the Poseidon Adventure *(1979)*, Prisoners *(1981)*, Endless Love *(1981)*, The Sender *(1982)*, Color of Night *(1994)*, Death in Venice *(1995)*, Stuart Saves His Family *(1995)*, Diabolique *(1996)*, As Good as It Gets *(1997)*, Little Boy Blue *(1998)*, 75 Degrees in July *(2000)*, Angel Eyes *(2000)*, *and* Till the End of Time *(2000)*.

On television, she has been in Buckskin *(1958)*, The Outsider *(1967)*, Shadow over Elveron *(1968)*, The Counterfeit Killer *(1968)*, Medical Story *(1975)*, Return to Earth *(1976)*, 21 Hours at Munich *(1976)*, The Defection of Simas Kudirka *(1978)*, Champions: A Love Story *(1979)*, Playing for Time *(1980)*, With Intent to Kill *(1984)*, Billionaire Boys Club *(1987)*, Hoggs' Heaven *(1991)*, Bump in the Night *(1991)*, Shadow of a Doubt *(1991)*, To Save a Child *(1991)*, A Part of the Family *(1993)*, When Love Kills: The Seduction of John Hearn *(1993)*, Angel Falls *(1993)*, A Mother's Revenge *(1993)*, The Secret Life of Houses *(1994)*, The Baby Brokers *(1994)*, The Yarn Princess *(1994)*, Stolen Memories: Secrets from the Rose Garden *(1995)*, A Good Day to Die *(1995)*, Fudge-a-Mania *(1995)*, Dad, the Angel, & Me *(1995)*, Indictment: The McMartin Trial *(1995; Emmy Award)*, The Uninvited *(1996)*, Mary & Tim *(1996)*, If These Walls Could Talk *(1996)*, A Promise to Carolyn *(1996)*, Dying to Be Perfect: The Ellen Hart Pena Story *(1997)*, The Wedding *(1998)*, A Father for Brittany *(1998)*, Maggie Winters *(1998)*, A Marriage of Convenience *(1998)*, *and episodes of* thirtysomething *(1987; Emmy Award)*, NYPD Blue *(1995; Emmy Award)*, Law and Order, Matlock, The Equalizer, Spenser: For Hire, Alias Smith and Jones, The Virginian, The Fugitive, The Outer Limits, Naked City, United States Steel Hour, Maverick, Rawhide, Buckskin, *and* Bronco.

This interview took place on November 29, 1993.

•———————————————————————————•

Interviewer: Can we start by talking about the writing and directing you've been doing recently?

Knight: Well, I'm fifty-seven years old, so obviously fifty-seven years is a lot of time to accumulate many things. I always say—and Jason Robards once made a joke about this when I talked about it—that I feel the act of creating artistic things is as necessary as the air we breathe and the food we eat. If we go back to when it all began, there must have been a man or a woman in a cave who went outside and saw a bird and saw the beauty of that bird and wanted that in his life and went back inside his cave and began to sketch that bird. He took a rock and carved the bird into the sides of his cave, discovering as he did that he couldn't match at all the beauty of the bird that he'd seen. So he sees the bird again another day and he continues and he continues.

The reason he does this is because he wants that beauty in his life and he wants that sense of achievement; it's very important to him. It gives him food. It gives him joy. It gives him a sense of accomplishment. After he has done this for many, many months probably, the man in the cave next door comes in, looks at what he's done, and says, "I really don't think this is terribly good." He's probably the first critic! But to come to what I've been doing: for the past several years, I've been working with the homeless. When I was accepted into the American Film Institute's Directing Workshop for Women, they said to me, "You can do anything you want. You can make a half-hour film. Here's the money, here's the equipment. It can be about anything you want it to be about." Because I was working with the homeless and because the things that were happening to them were such a part of my life, it had to be about them, and I created five characters for the film, which is called *Far from Home*. I put my daughter Kaitlin Hopkins, who is a lovely singer, in it.

Interviewer: How does one go about applying to the American Film Institute to create your own film?

Knight: As I mentioned, they have this program called the Directing Workshop for Women. It's to encourage more women directors, obviously. They choose twelve women every eighteen months, I think it is. They give you ten thousand dollars and a bit of equipment and you can make whatever film you want. The group that I was a part of had, I think, 412 applications and they chose twelve people; so it's very competitive. In my group, there were wonderful people like Rita Mae Brown, Joyce Van Patten, and Carol Armitage from the Armitage Ballet. I'm very interested to see the films that the other women make.

Interviewer: Do the women come to the program with an idea already in mind, or do they develop one once they are with a director? Is this a collaboration?

Knight: I chose to write mine myself because I wanted to do a musical. Some of the women have other writers they write with. You, of course, choose all of your technical people.

Interviewer: What made you decide to make it a musical?

Knight: I started out as an opera singer, and so music has been part of my whole life. I don't know why, but about five or six years ago, I was suddenly writing songs. I can't explain it. It began because of a friend of mine in Kansas that I've known since I was eight years old. When she married right out of high school, she married a Catholic farmer, a wheat farmer. She couldn't have children, so they adopted a boy. Then she proceeded to have three children of her own. One of them, when he grew up, was gay. This was very difficult for a family in the middle of Kansas, as you can imagine. Then he went to Kansas City, contracted AIDS, and came home to die. His brother said, "Well, we're not coming home, because we stood up for him in high school when he was called a sissy and everything." His sister came home from the University of Kansas and nursed him until he died. I'm telling you this story because my daughter Kaitlin and I were supposed to sing at an AIDS benefit in Los Angeles. She couldn't because she was doing a show in New York, so suddenly I had to sing something on my own, and I didn't know what to sing. I was driving my car on Wilshire Boulevard, and I don't know why, and I don't know how, but suddenly a song came through the air or nature or God or whatever and through me, and it became a song that I had to sing. It's called "The Quilt Song."

Interviewer: You are certainly a diversely talented woman. You've written and directed a film that's going to be done at the American Film Institute; you've written songs; you sing and you act. You also teach Shakespeare and classics classes. It just goes on and on.

Knight: I have a lot of energy.

Interviewer: One of the most fascinating things to me about your long list of accomplishments is how many roles have been written specifically for you. Tennessee Williams saw you in *A Streetcar Named Desire* and wrote *A Lovely Sunday for Crève Coeur.* How did that come about?

Knight: Well, first of all, he was very kind to me. He said that he wished that I had been around when he had first written *Streetcar.* I think Blanche was my part. I'm sure that other actors have said this as well, but sometimes you really connect to a part. I felt that way about *Dutchman,* the LeRoi Jones (or Amiri Baraka, as he now calls himself) play, that that part was mine. I felt very much that way about Blanche, even though it nearly killed me. It nearly kills every actress who does the role. It's like playing Hamlet. It's so long and difficult, and you have to do it quickly. When Tennessee says that she's a moth, you have to be a moth. Holly Hunter never thinks about what she's going to say; it just comes out, and that's why she speaks so quickly that you can't quite understand her half the time. Blanche is like that; I think it's a particular southern thing. If it isn't fast, the play is four and a half hours long; but if Blanche is fast, it's three and a half hours long. It's that big a difference. You know that when you first start working on it. I felt very close to that character. I felt the same way about *The Cherry Orchard* too, when I did that, with that genius Romanian director Lucien Pintele. I've had a fortunate career in many ways because I've worked with about four or five people that I consider great theater artists—Tennessee, of course, and Pintele. He lived in exile for many years in Paris and did a lot of directing in theater here. He's now back in Romania, where he's head of the Romanian Film Commission, and he's directed his first film in many, many, many years. All of the other films that he had done before he was forced to live in exile were confiscated, and he's now directed this extraordinary film called *The Oak.*

Interviewer: Can you finish the story about Tennessee Williams and *Crève Coeur*? How did you move from *A Streetcar Named Desire* to *Crève Coeur*?

Knight: He said, "I've written this little play for you." Barbara and Maureen and I read it, because that's who he wanted to do it—Maureen Stapleton, Barbara Baxley, and me. After we read it, Tennessee said, "Are you all going to do it?" Maureen said, "No." Tennessee said, "Why?" She said, "Because Shirley's got all the cookies." She was quite right; my part was better. So she didn't do it. Tennessee was such a dear soul. I don't quite know what to do except tell stories about him.

Interviewer: That's fine.

Knight: When we were doing the play in Charleston, South Carolina, which is where we did it before we took it to New York, we stayed in a beautiful old hotel. David Merrick was producing the play. David Merrick and Tennessee and I were walking into the lobby, and there were these two older southern ladies who evidently had a little hearing problem, because they talked very loudly to one another. One woman said to the other, "Look. Oh my God, that's Tennessee Williams." And the other one said, "Don't be ridiculous. He's been dead for years." And Tennessee went over to her and said, "Not quite yet, honey. Not quite yet." Afterwards, I thought about that. I was talking about it with Charlotte Moore, who was also in the play with me, and I said, "Why did they say that?" Then I thought that our awareness of the kind of woman that Tennessee wrote about has been with us for so long that of course she thought he was dead. Then I went further and said, "Our whole view of that part of the country is based on Tennessee and Faulkner and Eudora Welty." Later, when I did *Glass Menagerie,* we were going to have dinner, my husband and I and Tennessee. He said, "Is it all right if I bring Rose?" His sister, Rose, was visiting. I said, "Of course." He said, "You'll see. It'll be all right. You'll be able to have dinner with her because it's quite unusual to have a meal with someone who thinks she's the Queen of England." She didn't really say anything. Of course, one knows that Rose had a lobotomy and about the tragedy of that dear woman.

Interviewer: One gets so fascinated by the whole Tennessee Williams mystique.

Knight: Yes, he was a wonderful man. I was very fortunate to know him. He did a really curious thing. A man was writing a book about him. This was about three months before Tennessee died. They were walking around New Orleans, and Tennessee said, "I'm going to buy some presents for all the actresses that I like." So he bought these little gifts for Geraldine [Page] and myself and Elizabeth Taylor and Barbara Baxley, people he'd worked with and loved. After he died, this gentleman brought me a little box. It was like a little Godiva chocolate box. Tennessee called me a witch, because I'm always able to say, "Well, that's what's going to happen." I predict things. In this box were all these strange things that reminded him of me. There was one of those fortune-telling fish, those little things that lie in your hand. I wear glasses all the time; there were some glasses that were a keychain. There was a picture of the Madonna. There was one earring that was like an Egyptian hiero-glyphic thing. Isn't that curious? He gave all these other little weird things to all these other women too. He was just a dear person, as well as, I think, probably our finest playwright. I'm allowed to say that, aren't I?

Interviewer: Sure. Speaking of movies, Francis Ford Coppola wrote a role for you in *Rain People,* right?

Knight: Yes, he did. That was extraordinary. I had won a prize at the Cannes Film Festival, and he was there with another film. He came up to me and said, "I'm going to write a film for you." I thought, "Oh yes." People say this; I believe it. Then six months later he knocked on my door and said, "Here's the script. Let's go make it." So we did.

Interviewer: While you were making the film, did you have any input in terms of the dialogue that you spoke?

Knight: Yes. The unfortunate thing was that originally Rip Torn was sup-posed to do the role in it, but he quarreled with Francis. Then Robert Duvall did it. I suppose that was fortunate; he was very good. But he couldn't ride a motorcycle and Rip could, and that was rather important to the story. Yes, we improvised a lot, and he would take down dialogue; but he's very much his own man. You're part of it; that's wonderful, but you're not the boss.

Interviewer: Did you ever come up with a line on your own that actually ended up in the movie?

Knight: Oh yes, several.

Interviewer: Of course, the playwright in closest proximity to you is your husband, John Hopkins. This is a very interesting relationship for a lot of rea-sons. What is it like living with your professional collaborator? Does he write his plays on his own and then say, "Here they are"? Or do you go back and forth and have little workshops right there at home?

Knight: Oh no. He writes whatever he's into at that time. Most of his work is very serious. He wrote a play called *Next of Kin,* which Harold Pinter di-rected, that was done at the National Theatre in England. That was a play that was actually written for me to do that I didn't end up doing because I wasn't British. Then he wrote a play called *Absent Forever* that I did do.

Interviewer: For public television?

Knight: We did it on public radio, and Gerald Freedman directed it at the Great Lakes Shakespeare Festival in Cleveland. We're going to do it again, actually. Then there was *Losing Time* that I did in New York with Jane Alexander. He wrote that for Jane and me because Jane had done another play of his called *Find Your Way Home* on Broadway; so he wrote *Losing Time* that the two of us did. That play was difficult for people to deal with because of the subject matter. It was about a woman who had been sexually assaulted and then goes to her friend who's gay. My goodness! In Europe they loved it. It's still running; it's been running there for something like ten years. People fainted when we did it in New York, and one man had a heart attack. We caused riots and everything. I love it when things like that happen, because when I did *Dutchman* years ago, that was a play that people got upset about too. The John Birch Society picketed us when we did *Dutchman* in Los Angeles, and they were very upset. There was a line in the play toward the end, just before I kill Al Freeman Jr., where I said, "I've had enough." About ten or fifteen times during the run, somebody in the audience would stand up and say, "So have I!" and leave. Can I tell a quick story about *Losing Time*?

Interviewer: Sure.

Knight: Harold Clurman was a critic at that time, and he came to review the play. My daughter Sophie was ten years old or so then, and she has always been an outrageous child. We didn't have a baby-sitter for her, so she came to the theater this particular night. To keep her busy, Jane suggested that she usher. Someone told her that Harold Clurman, this man she was ushering into his seat, was a critic. So she said to him, "I can't come and see this play because it's much too dirty, but I hope you like it anyway."

One night a woman stood up in the middle of the second act, when I was doing a scene with Tony Roberts, and shouted at us, "This play is blank, blank, blank." Bad word. I stood there and stopped, and she just kept shouting and carrying on. Finally, somebody had to come in to take her out. She said, "I'm not leaving without my friend." But her friend said, "I want to stay and see what happens." This rabbi was in the audience, and he went over to the woman and said, "Look, we'd like to see the play, so. . . ." Meanwhile, we're just standing onstage. The rabbi started having a philosophical discussion with her. He said, "I think Mr. Hopkins is after something here. If you saw his play *Find Your Way Home,* you would know he was a moralist—so maybe you should stay and see." She said, "No, I'm not staying. I'm leaving." She was not happy. Finally, she was ushered out and the rabbi said, "Okay, Miss Knight, you can go on now." It was wonderful. I love things like that!

Interviewer: Can you talk a little bit more about the experience of working on *Dutchman*—about the racial tensions that are inherent in doing a project like that?

Knight: I'll tell you a couple of rehearsal stories. Al Freeman Jr. is very fastidious with his clothing. He always wears really nice clothes; he doesn't wear jeans or anything like that. The woman in the play, Lula, eats apples, and

Burgess Meredith was directing the play. I was getting sick from eating so many apples, so I said to Burgess, "Can I eat an orange today instead of an apple? I'm really getting sick from all these apples." He said, "Sure." So I ate an orange, and after I'd eaten a bit of the orange, I was coming up on this speech where I say, "Do the gritty grind, like your ol' rag-head mammy." And I squeezed the orange all over Al. Well, he had a fit. He stopped and said, "You wouldn't do that! She can't eat an orange! She can't squeeze this on me! She can't do this! I can't stand this!" This was because Burgess immediately wanted to keep it in the play, of course. This little voice at the very back of the audience who was watching the rehearsal, Mr. Baraka, said, "She'd do worse than that, man. She'd do worse than that." So we kept it in. It was hard to do, yes.

Acting is interesting because it's like a catharsis. I haven't had to go through therapy because you utilize so much of yourself, at least in the kind of acting that I do. There's really only one kind of acting as far as I'm concerned, and it's not careful. It's not what I call "English acting." The English audiences love comfortable acting. They like to be able to sit there and go, "Oh yes, I know that emotion." But they don't like to be penetrated. I like to scare people to death. Otherwise, I don't understand how you reach that center of them. I think acting is dangerous and there's only one pure state of acting, and that is when you do not know what you're going to say next. You don't know what you're going to do next. You don't know what the other person is going to say or do next. Of course, you do; but you cannot be in the state of knowing or expecting or anticipating.

I used to be friends with a wonderful ballet dancer named Edward Villella of the New York City Ballet. Do you remember him? I think he was an extraordinary character actor–dancer. I once said to him, "How do you achieve what you achieve, because what you are doing is different than what the other dancers are doing?" He said, "Well, first of all, I learn all the steps technically. I work months and months and months and I learn all the steps." I said, "Okay, like playing the piano. You learn it and then you forget it?" He said, "Yeah. And then I find a psychological reason for absolutely every move I make." This was a revelation to me because what it did to his dancing was that everything had another impetus. He said, "And then I forget that too, and I forget the steps, and I just exist in the moment." That's what it is when it's wonderful.

I was very fortunate, because the first Broadway play I ever did was *The Three Sisters*. Olga was played by Geraldine Page, and Masha was played by Kim Stanley. Barbara Baxley was in it; so were Robert Loggia, George C. Scott, Luther Adler, and Tamara Daykarhanova. It was just an extraordinary cast. One night I felt like I didn't do it well or something and I was weeping offstage. Geraldine came to me and said, "You know what happened, don't you?" I said, "What?" She said, "You liked what you did yesterday, so you tried to do it again—and that's absolute death." It's true. You can't fall in love with yesterday; you have to be in today. It's like life, isn't it? It's a continual process, and I think that's why I'm so fascinated with it at this stage in my life, because it keeps changing. I keep doing other things. I would never compare myself to Mr. Blake, but he did, after all, write poems and paint. So I guess I'm allowed to.

Interviewer: You have also devoted a considerable amount of energy to political projects. Would you mind talking about your experiences as you traveled around the country for a year and a half doing *The Depot,* the one-woman play about the nuclear threat, which Joanne Woodward directed? Did Joanne Woodward travel with you? What sort of interaction did you have with the audiences? Did they give you any evidence to suggest that you had affected their thinking?

Knight: Absolutely. First of all, I have no patience with anyone who says they're not political. I don't care who it is. Everyone is political. If you buy a postage stamp, that is a political act. If you send your children to school, that is a political act. If you pay your taxes, that is a political act. We live in the world, and there are things that are wrong. It's absurd not to deal with them, don't you find? Some actors who are public figures will say, "Well, I'm not really political," and I just want to go POW! *The Depot* happened because Joanne and I were tired of giving bad speeches. We thought it would be much better if somebody wrote something, because we were, at that time, both of us, working a lot with the Center for Defense Information. We decided to do this piece about a woman who became politically aware. Joanne directed it, and I played the woman. It was written by Eve Ensler, a wonderful young writer. It was about a woman who suddenly gets annoyed at all the money being spent on things like the MX missile or the B-1 bomber. She doesn't really know what they are, but she knows that they're spending an awful lot of money on these things, and, as a result, other things that should be happening aren't. She has a wonderful line in the play where she says, "You know, if there is somebody up there looking down, he's saying, 'Look at these odd people. They keep making all these things they don't need and they don't make things they do need.' It only takes two hundred nuclear missiles to blow up and destroy the entire world. Only two hundred and we have fifty-seven thousand." It was that kind of play—wonderful and very funny. She was a funny character.

We would do it a lot for schoolchildren. One day, there were sixth graders or seventh graders, and Joanne said something like, "So what do you think this is about? Why do you think the Russians keep making more weapons and the Americans keep making more?" This little boy said, "Well, it's like if I have a G.I. Joe and my friend has two G.I. Joes. I want my mom to go out and get another G.I. Joe. Then if he has a tank, I want it." He totally locked in to what we were talking about, understood it, and hopefully was made aware. One night, a young man who was going to go into the army afterwards said, "I'm not going to join the army now." I thought that was incredible. I was very pleased.

I don't think you can, in life, do something because you feel something will come from it. I don't think you can look for rewards. When I talk to young people who want to be actors, I talk to them about food and I say, "Look. You must decide right now"—and I think this applies to everything—"what your food is going to be. If your food is going to be that you want to be famous or you want to make a lot of money or you want people to give you prizes, and that's going to be your food and what sustains you, don't do this. Because you will starve to death. If it does happen, any of those things, they happen once, maybe for five minutes, and then they go away. So you'd better decide that the reason why you're doing this is because you want to do it and just the act of doing it sustains you. You must decide that that is your food, that that is your joy, that that is your commitment to it. Otherwise, it's nonsense." It's dreadful what has happened to the art of acting in this country. It's really tragic. I don't like to dwell on things that are negative, but most people haven't a clue what the real art of acting is anymore. They really think that Patrick Duffy is an actor. Bless his heart, I'm sure he's a very sweet person— and there are many others. When that is what's presented to you constantly, then when somebody actually does act, it's such a shock, you think, "Oh, that can't be what it is." The level is so bad. It's like if you listen to what my husband calls "children's music," you'd be very confused by Bartók, wouldn't you? If you listened to Dire Straits or whatever all the time, it would be very difficult for you to hear good music.

Interviewer: As you've mentioned earlier, you have a daughter, Kaitlin, who is working as an actress. What did you tell her about the art of acting?

Knight: I told her not to do it! She got a part in *Kiss Me, Kate* at her school and she called home and said (before that she was going to be a social worker, I think, because she was always helping everybody, or a nurse or something like that), "I decided, Mom, I'm going to be a singer. I'm going to be an actress." I said, "Uh, no." I said to my husband, "Okay, I'm going to go see her in this musical, and if she is anything less than wonderful, I'm talking her out of this." I go up and I see this kid come out—she has nothing to do with me. She's wonderful. I think, "Oh no!" I went home and I said, "She's wonderful. We're just going to have to let her do this." He said, "You're her mother. I'm going. I'll talk her out of it." I said, "Okay." The next weekend we both go, he sits next to me, she comes out and sings her first number, sashaying around the stage, and he turns to me and says, "Ah, she's wonderful." There was no hope. But the other two have been saved. My other two daughters are not in show business; they are not actors. I just didn't want her to have to go through the pain of it. Because even if you are successful, it's hell.

Interviewer: Let's talk a little bit about New York versus the rest of the country. Obviously you've worked in New York, on Broadway and off Broadway, and in regional theater. Is New York theater dying?

Knight: Yes. Again, it depends on where you're starting from. If your goal is to make money, New York is a very difficult place to start from because what happens there isn't based on what the quality of the work is, but rather more on spectacle. We're just going to have to kill Trevor Nunn; that's all there is to it. I don't mean that, but you understand what I'm saying. It's the more smoke, the bigger sets, and the more this and the more that; again you see what happens. It's a tremendous confusion because people will go to that and they will think they are being satisfied, but they are not. We only have two things that help us to understand the human condition. One is art and one is religion. That shows us the best of us, the worst of us, where we can go, what we can learn and benefit from. If suddenly all we see is spectacle, and if twenty hours a day the food that we get from television is *Rescue 911* and people talking about absolutely the worst aspects of the human animal on endless Oprah Winfrey–type shows, eventually we will have a race of people totally devoid of humanity. You'll be so inured to it, you'll be deadened. I think it's what people like Aldous Huxley in *Brave New World* were writing about and thinking about then. It frightens me very much. I write President Clinton a letter every week. I even wrote Ross Perot. I wrote him a very short letter. I just said that I thought that he was politically naive and intellectually primitive.

Interviewer: Do you ever write to theater critics?

Knight: I don't read them anymore. When I was very young, I really was upset if anyone said I was not perfect. You know how you are when you're young. I got this review in the *New York Times* which said, ". . . and Shirley Knight has to be seen to be believed." I thought it was terribly rude. I was in my kitchen, and I was so angry I threw a glass on the floor and a piece of it flew up and stuck in my leg. Not only did it hurt, it bled a lot, and I had to go to the hospital and have stitches. I decided right then and there I was not going to worry or care about critics anymore because I would lose my whole body. I could bleed to death. Oh dear, that was terrible. I also have a scar on my hand. This is a wonderful Method-acting story. May I tell a Method-acting story? In *Three Sisters*, directed by Lee Strasberg, one night a glass had broken and a piece of it had fallen on the floor. I knew that Kim Stanley was going to come and kneel at my feet in the very next scene, and I knew that she might kneel on this piece of glass. So being a good person, I picked up this piece of glass and I held it in my hand. She decided to do the scene very differently. She came and knelt at my feet and, for some reason or another, took my hand and grabbed it and was acting her heart out. She sees blood running out of my hand—what an actress!—she opens my hand, looks at it, takes her handkerchief, and wraps it around my hand. She takes out the piece of glass;

she's holding it. It was wonderful. Two stitches, nothing major—not nearly as bad as the leg. The critic was much worse. I did write a critic once who criticized my accent, and it was supposed to be a Kansas accent—so I was really furious. This was years ago. I did write him and tell him, "I'm from Kansas and you're not from Kansas and you don't know."

Interviewer: Speaking of Kansas, can you talk for a couple of minutes about how you emerged from Kansas and found your way to Broadway?

Knight: Oh my goodness. This is a long story. Are you sure you want this boring story? Okay. I was raised in a very, very small community outside Hutchison, Kansas. Hutchison is in the very middle of Kansas, and if you go about thirty miles north of Hutchison, you come to a town called Lyons, which has about 4,500 people. If you go eight miles east of Lyons and a half mile north, you come to this teeny-weeny place, Mitchell, that has thirteen houses, one school, one church, and one depot (the train doesn't stop there anymore). I went to a two-room schoolhouse, and when I first started, there were only two people in the first grade, myself and Donnie Ray Hall. They put us into the second grade, and my brother was in the second grade. It made him furious because then I was at school in the same grade with him, even though he was older, for the rest of our school days. I had two teachers. I had Mrs. Rhodes for grades one through four and Mr. Rhodes for grades five through eight. By the time you hit the fourth grade, you were so bored, you couldn't wait to get to Mr. Rhodes. Anyway, they were very nice people.

What made me? My mother's family are very interesting, very musical. My mother sang and played the piano. My grandfather played the cello. My grandfather and grandmother were from England and quite cultured. My father's family is totally opposite, more *The Grapes of Wrath*. I started singing from the time I was very young. My sister and I sang every Sunday at church and at every wedding and funeral. I was always going to be a singer. My mother had wanted to be an opera singer, and we listened to the opera every Saturday on the radio. I think that's how it all began. I went to a university in Enid, Oklahoma, a Christian church university, because it was the only one I could get a scholarship to. I started studying music. Then when I was about eighteen, a junior in college, I went to see Maria Callas in concert, in Kansas City. You know how, when you're that age, you just make decisions so quickly? I sat there and I said, "I will never be that good." I was so arrogant, I said, "If I can't be that good, I'm not doing it." I immediately decided I was going to be George Eliot instead; so I changed my major to English and literature and started writing. I got a job writing, because I always had to work. That was before my father discovered oil, but that's another story. In the house that I was raised in, we had no plumbing, of course. The one thing in my life that was extraordinary was visiting my aunt Opal, who lived in town, because she had two things that were amazing: indoor plumbing and store-bought bread.

Anyway, to make a long story short, I started studying English, and I was working at a newspaper, because I had transferred to Wichita University. I was working as an assistant society editor for the *Wichita Beacon*. They had a magazine there called *Theatre Arts* that I would read every time it came in. I was fascinated. There was a course that you could take, a summer acting course; and I thought, "I bet I could do that. That would be interesting." So I took this summer course at the Pasadena Playhouse. That was sort of the beginning. But then I was still going to go and get a master's degree, because I was determined to be George Eliot. I had a month before I was to go to UCLA to get a master's degree. My course at the Pasadena Playhouse had finished, and I couldn't afford to go to Kansas for the month, and anyway I didn't want to, because I finally—I was nineteen—had seen the ocean and I wanted to look at it a little more. At any rate, I heard about this place called the Hollywood Studio Club where you could stay for $17.50 a week, room and board. This was in 1959. I applied there and I got in and I thought, "I'll just be in this place until I go to school."

They put me together with this woman who was, to me, the most amazing, sophisticated, extraordinary person I had ever met in my life. Her name was Jo Anne Worley, and she was my roommate. I learned so much from her; I was straight out of Kansas. She said, "I'm going to NBC to do an audition. Do you want to come along? Maybe you'll see Milton Berle or something." I said, "Absolutely." This is a true story. It doesn't happen this way anymore. We went to NBC. She went in, she had her audition, she came out, and the man said, "Okay, you're next." I said, "Oh no. I'm just here with my friend." And the man said, "Well, you're very right for this, so why don't you come in and read?" I said, "Okay." So I went in, and I read for this part of a sixteen-year-old unwed mother. This was a perfect part for me, because I looked ten years old. Evidently, I did quite well, and he said, "Have you done anything?" I said, "No, just college plays." He said, "I'll keep you in mind." It was for a show called *NBC Matinee Theater*. It was a different play done live every day. They called me the next day and said, "The actress that we wanted to do this can't, so we're going to take a chance with you." It was a leading part. Michael Landon played the guy that got me pregnant, and Marsha Hunt played my mother.

I did the show and an agent saw it and took me on, and then he got me into an acting class. Jeff Corey was my teacher. In my class were Sally Kellerman, Bobby Driscoll, Dean Stockwell, Jack Nicholson, and Robert Blake. We decided to put on a play together. We put on *Look Back in Anger,* and I played the wife. People came to see it, and I was offered a movie contract. Then I did my first movie, *The Dark at the Top of the Stairs,* and I was nominated for an Oscar. This all happened within about eight months. It doesn't happen that way anymore. In those days, you went into something because you were gifted. Now it's different. People watch television and they say, "I could do that." Then they go and do it. There are thousands of people, and for them to wade through all these people to find the gifted people is very hard. The gifted people sometimes get lost in the shuffle, I think.

Interviewer: You have done quite a bit of television. Recently, you had a continuing role on *thirtysomething*. What was that like, working with an established ensemble of actors?

Knight: Actually, I did the second show in the series, so it wasn't established yet. The writer-director, Ed Zwick, hired me because, I guess, he just wanted to. When I got there, he said, "Oh my God, you're too young. You're this, you're that." I said that it would be okay, and we went off and grayed my hair, put lines and stuff like that. I had a great time playing that part. I know what this woman is like. She's like my aunt Ruth. I enjoyed it. I did it that year, and then I did it two years later. It was very interesting, because Ed said to me, "I'm really sorry we haven't had you back more. However, there are so many regulars and we have to give them so much to do." The character that I played would take over. She was so big, she would take over; so they couldn't have me very often.

Interviewer: Why don't we have more people writing quality scripts for television, like Dennis Potter in England—or like Rod Serling and Reginald Rose in the fifties in this country?

Knight: The answer is very sad. In the fifties and sixties when all the extraordinary American writers were writing for television, you were able to do a television play without a lot of censorship. Now, unfortunately, the censorship is in the form of endless people who feel that they have something to contribute. Someone will write something and every day, literally, on every television show you do, they'll come in with green pages, yellow pages, pink pages, blue pages, turquoise pages, orange pages—because every day some executive or some secretary or somebody rewrites it. Someone says, "Well, we can't do this. We can't say that." Endless. Great writing always has an incredible poetry. Dennis Potter had a wonderful voice. Tennessee had a wonderful voice. You can't minimize the writing like that and expect it to survive. It might actually have been a good script, but by the time they finish it, it's awful. My husband is a British writer, and he was just honored this past year by the British Film Institute and also the BBC for his work. He wrote an extraordinary quartet of plays called *Talking to a Stranger*. He only writes for British television, because he knows that it will be done the way he wrote it. In American television—he's tried several times—it does not survive. It's tragic. If anything is good on American television, it is nothing short of a miracle if it survives. Usually it will be on something like PBS, occasionally on the cable channels, although that's going now too. By censorship, by the way, I don't mean necessarily censorship in the sense of "You can't say this or do that." I mean censorship in the sense of artistic censorship—censorship of poetry and ideas.

Interviewer: What about the differences in technique and approach between stage acting and movie acting? Do you think a person who's successful in one medium can be equally successful in the other?

Knight: The thing about acting in film and television is, if it's all you do, you never get better as an actor. It's what I call *coitus interruptus.* You are just beginning your pursuit of this character. You are just starting some kind of semblance of ideas and thoughts and lines and everything else, and that's what they print. That's what ends up in the film. As a result, people who only work in films become crazy people, because they never go through the process, which is a very long one. It takes a very long time to be good at it. I did *Kennedy's Children* for nine months. After about, I would say, the seventh month, in San Francisco, I said, "I've got it. I think I understand this person." I did Blanche in *A Streetcar Named Desire* twice, two different productions, because I hadn't finished my work. The first time I did it, I did it for about three months, and I wasn't finished. I didn't have it yet. I don't know how people only do films.

The thing about films is that you can make anything look interesting, because it's isolated. You can make it look significant. You can photograph a glass and say, "Oh, that means something." In the theater, you are on your own. You have to, as they say, come up with the goods. You also have to have an instrument, a vocal instrument. You can hear me down the road. No one has ever said, "Could you speak up, Shirley?" In terms of the technique, it's exactly the same. There are people, because they don't know any better, who say things like "Well, you act differently in films because it's smaller." It's not true. It's almost the opposite. You can get by with things in a film that are simply technical things that you could never get by with in the theater. People would say, "She's overdoing it a bit."

Interviewer: Aside from your husband, what current playwrights do you admire?

Knight: John Guare wrote a play for me, too, which was very good, called *Landscape of the Body.* I like his work very much. Unfortunately, that play wasn't a success. It should have been; it was a wonderful play. I like David Mamet. I like Harold Pinter, of course. I like his writing very much.

Interviewer: Any women?

Knight: Any women? I think Marsha Norman is good, don't you?

Interviewer: Sure.

Knight: I like her work.

Interviewer: *'Night Mother.*

Knight: Yes, interesting. There are probably some that are wonderful that I haven't seen or worked with.

Interviewer: Is there a role that you'd like to play that you haven't played?

Knight: Yes, there are several actually. I'd like to do *The Seagull*. And I'd like to do another Shakespeare. The problem with Shakespeare is all the good parts are men's. Lady Macbeth is sort of a good part, I guess; maybe I'll do that. There's an Ibsen play I'd like to do. Maybe I'm too old now, but I'd sort of like to do *Rosmersholm*. I think that's kind of a nice part. *Mother Courage*. It's time we did that again, isn't it?

Nathan Lane

Nathan Lane was born in Jersey City, New Jersey, on February 3, 1956. He made his off-Broadway debut in A Midsummer Night's Dream *in 1978 and his Broadway debut as Roland Maule (with George C. Scott) in* Present Laughter *in 1982. Other theater roles include Prince Fergus,* Merlin *(1983); Harry,* Love *(1984); Tony Lumpkin,* She Stoops to Conquer *(1984); Toad,* The Wind in the Willows *(1985); Pompey,* Measure for Measure *(1985); Nick Finchling,* The Common Pursuit *(1986); Harvey Wheatcreft,* Claptrap *(1987); Stanley,* Broadway Bound *(1987); Jonathan Bolton,* The Film Society *(1988); Mandy,* The Lisbon Traviata *(1989); Henry McNeil,* Some Americans Abroad *(1990);* Hugh Gumps, *Bad Habits (1990); Sam Truman,* Lips Together, Teeth Apart *(1991); Mr. Brink,* On Borrowed Time *(1991); Nathan Detroit,* Guys and Dolls *(1992); Max Prince,* Laughter on the 23rd Floor *(1993); Buzz Hauser,* Love! Valour! Compassion! *(1994); Pseudolus,* A Funny Thing Happened on the Way to the Forum *(1995; Tony Award); Davis Mizlansky,* Mizlansky/

Zilinsky, or "Shmucks" *(1998)*; *Sheridan Whiteside,* The Man Who Came to Dinner *(2000).*

He has appeared in the films Ironweed *(1987),* Joe versus the Volcano *(1990),* The Lemon Sisters *(1990),* Frankie and Johnny *(1991),* He Said, She Said *(1991),* Life with Mikey *(1993),* Addams Family Values *(1993),* The Lion King *(1994),* Jeffrey *(1995),* The Birdcage *(1996),* Mouse Hunt *(1997),* The Lion King II: Simba's Pride *(1998),* The Best Man *(1999),* Popcorn *(1999),* Get Bruce *(1999),* At First Sight *(1999),* Isn't She Great *(2000),* Titan A.E. *(2000),* Trixie *(2000), and* Love's Labour's Lost *(2000).*

On television, he has been in Valley of the Dolls *(1981),* One of the Boys *(1981),* Alice in Wonderland *(1983),* The Wizard of Oz in Concert: Dreams Come True *(1995),* Timon and Pumbaa *(1995),* The Boys Next Door *(1996),* Merry Christmas, George Bailey *(1997),* Encore! Encore! *(1998), and epid-sodes of* Mad About You, Frasier, *and* Inside the Actors Studio.

This interview took place on October 10, 1997.

•——————————————————————•

Interviewer: You grew up in northern New Jersey, and you came to New York to go to the theater. Is that how you really got interested in theater?

Lane: Well, that came later. My brother Dan, who was a teacher, started taking me to plays very early on. If he would bring a class to New York to see a play, he would bring me along. He also really started me as an actor, because he came home one day when he was in college and said, "Would you like to do a play?" I said, "I don't know." And he said, "Well, you're going to do one. I volunteered your services." Some friends of his were putting on this play by Frank Gilroy called *Who'll Save the Plowboy?* and they needed a little boy in the second act. So I did this play; I can remember the actor bringing me onstage piggyback. I remember coming in and seeing the audience, and I remember people were laughing a little bit; but the thing I was most upset about was they had their opening-night party and they told me I had to go home. I was very indignant that I couldn't go to the opening-night party. I kept saying to my brother that this is wrong, I should be there; I'm in the cast and I should be at the party. That was my biggest concern.

Interviewer: How old were you?

Lane: Ten, I think. And that's still what I really care about the most, what's the opening-night party going to be like. So that's where it started.

Interviewer: Were you really interested in theater from that moment on, or did it take a while?

Lane: I don't know whether it formulated in my mind that maybe this is what I could do with my life as a career, but certainly it intrigued me. Then when I was in school I did a play, *Around the World in 80 Days,* and I played the French servant, the Cantinflas role in the movie. There was a scene where Indians were attacking a train and I had this little suitcase which I hid behind, and it got a big laugh. I remember that very vividly, and being very excited by that. It was sort of a little improvisation that worked; and I think that probably was when I was bitten by the bug, as they say.

Interviewer: Is that what appealed to you, do you think, about being on-stage, that you were doing something that could get a response?

Lane: I think initially, yes—I think the fact that it was laughter.

Interviewer: It was always comedy at that point, then? The kind of response that you could immediately elicit was to be funny. Had you seen yourself as a funny person as a young child? Did your parents say, "He's such a funny little kid," or something like that?

Lane: I would sort of perform. I remember my family encouraging me to get up and do impressions, and I remember I would get up and do those cliché impressions of stars; so I was like this little bad lounge act as a kid. I would get up and do impressions and make people laugh. I also think of it as a very classic defense mechanism of being funny because I was overweight as a child. Before anyone made fun of me, I would make a joke.

Interviewer: How did you get from *Around the World in 80 Days* to the professional theater?

Lane: Well, after high school I was supposed to go to St. Joseph's College in Philadelphia. I had a drama scholarship. On the day of registration, I went in to talk to someone in the registrar's office, and they said that I owed them several thousand more dollars because I had a student loan and a government loan and the drama scholarship. We had no money at all, and I was thrown by that. I was with my brother and my mother, and I remember saying to them, "I'm concerned about this." Then my brother uttered the fateful words: "Well, no one says you have to go to college right now. You could take a year off and work, and then go." So I said, "Okay, that's what I'll do." I went and got my bags out of the room and went into show business—not right away. First I had a job for a few months as a bail interviewer at the Seventh Precinct in Jersey City. I did the paperwork for the court clerk to determine whether someone should be released on their own recognizance. Why I was qualified to do this, I'll never know! But I somehow got this job from some odd family political connection. I was interviewing people who had just been arrested. Then, three months later, I went to work with this non-Equity theater company that I had worked for the summer before, doing a couple of musicals. They were putting together a children's show for the Bicentennial that was coming up— a musical revue about the history of New Jersey, called *Jerz.*

Interviewer: This was where?

Lane: In New Jersey at a little theater company called the Halfpenny Play-house, a little non-Equity theater-in-residence at Upsala College in East Orange, New Jersey. We had a lot of bookings for schools all over New Jersey—grammar schools, high schools, colleges. We would go out and perform this show every day. That was a great learning experience. It was my first paying job, doing this little children's show. Then I worked a lot in non-Equity summer stock and dinner theater and eventually made the decision to move to New York at the end of 1977. So I became a struggling New York actor. Eventually I did get my Equity card through a children's show again, produced by the same company but now under an Equity contract; it was a musical about the metric system. There was the possibility of the United States going metric, so they did a musical about the metric system—and that's how I got my Equity card.

Interviewer: From a history of New Jersey to a musical about the metric system—the story of your career.

Lane: That's right. Frightening stuff.

Interviewer: Had your brother taken you to a Broadway show before you did *Around the World in 80 Days* in grade school? Do you remember your first Broadway show?

Lane: Yes. I don't know if he did it before or after. The first Broadway play I saw was *Black Comedy, White Lies* with Geraldine Page and Michael Crawford, and then he took me to see *Butley* with Alan Bates. It was kind of heavy for a youngster. We went to a matinee, and I remember my brother said, "He's going to have to do this again at eight o'clock, you know; he does the show again." I couldn't fathom how he could ever go through what he had just gone through again that evening. See, already I was objecting to matinees—at an early age.

Interviewer: The pattern was set—parties yes, matinees no.

Lane: Opening-night party, no matinees. He took me to see *Hair,* I remember, on my thirteenth birthday. Then I saw *Hello, Dolly!* with Pearl Bailey. I remember she went up on her lines and stopped and ad-libbed with the audience and was very funny. Then at the end of the show she came out and did a club act; she came out and sang a couple of songs and talked to the audience. The cast had to stay onstage with her, so I thought it was very entertaining for the audience but slightly cruel for the cast.

Interviewer: When you were seeing these plays and musicals, did you envision yourself doing this sort of thing?

Lane: I don't know. It was just very exciting—the whole process: the ritual of walking into the theater and sitting down, and the lights going down, and sitting there in the dark, and if it was a musical, hearing the overture. Everything about it was exciting to me and made me want to be a part of it. I wanted to join in.

Interviewer: Is it still exciting, now that you do it eight times a week?

Lane: Absolutely. Even during *Forum,* they would start that overture, which begins with these big notes coming in, and it would slightly strike fear in my heart. I would think, "Do I have the energy to go through this again?" So yes, it still is exciting.

Interviewer: Do you still get the rush from the audience?

Lane: Oh, absolutely, especially with a show like that. I remember the first time, I came out and the reaction was so strong—you certainly feel, "I can't let them down now; I've really got to do this the best I possibly can," because it was such an outpouring of affection. It's kind of overwhelming and gratifying and frightening all at the same time.

Interviewer: How do you as an actor maintain the energy level? How do you come on every night and do exactly the same thing—or try to do exactly the same thing? Is it training or experience or what?

Lane: Yes, it's partly experience and training, and also you never know what the audience is going to bring, and that affects you. Especially if you're in a long run, things change. You go through a period—usually it's in cycles—where it does start to become a job, so you have to try to keep it fresh. I remember doing a matinee of *Laughter on the 23rd Floor* and coming out and thinking: "I really hate this performance that I'm giving; I hate what I'm doing. I'm not going to do anything; I'm going to throw it all out and start almost from scratch and see what happens, see where it goes, and I'll do whatever pops into my head." I was playing this very volatile character who was drinking and on drugs, so it could withstand a bizarre choice here or there. It was very freeing. Some of it was better, and I realized that maybe I was working too hard in certain places. But when you're in a long run, you can do that, as long as you're not throwing the other actors or doing something that would disrupt their performance or hurt them in some way. It's also what makes it exciting.

Interviewer: In that case, did you retain some of that in future performances?

Lane: Oh, absolutely.

Interviewer: Can you give us a specific change that you made, or was it just a bunch of small ones?

Lane: Well, in that particular play one of the problems we kept having was how to introduce that character. We all felt, Neil Simon, Jerry Zaks, and myself, a certain amount of pressure that I come on and it be funny in some way. It was such a buildup. They talk so much about him and then finally he arrives. You feel, "I'd better live up to what they've been talking about." They would say, "He's a comic genius, and he's tortured and he takes drugs and he's a drunk"—and what do you do? How do you live up to that? In a sense, you can't. We kept thinking, "Oh my, why are they not laughing right away?" Neil rewrote it so many times, and then you realize you have to allow the audience to take you in and see who you are before they can understand what the character's humor is about. The other problem was that the character was not as verbal as the other characters, who were all joke writers and who all had their very specific senses of humor and would come on and be very, very funny. Then the star of the show comes on and it turns out he's this kind of inarticulate guy, but a lot of the comedy was about what he's going through and his emotions and the physicality of it and his eccentricities. It just needed time to settle and for them to take you in; so we certainly came to that realization. Then I also realized: "Don't do anything." That's always good advice in acting. You should have an action, but sometimes you should trust that you come out and say the lines, and if they're good lines, it'll work. I also realized he was someone who's very upset about the network but he's also had this long night of drinking. He's been shooting at things at his home, with a shotgun. I realized that the fact is that he's totally exhausted, he has this huge hangover, even though he's seething about the network; so what was actually the funnier choice was for him to come on slightly dazed. He's trying to keep up an appearance when he shows up, but he's in a slight coma. It worked much better.

Interviewer: At what point in the run did you make this change?

Lane: It was a matinee, and it was after we had been running a few months.

Interviewer: And that didn't affect the other actors?

Lane: Well, it did in some ways. It took them by surprise, some of it did. But also, the nature of the role was they never knew what he was going to do because he was so volatile. So suddenly everyone was really paying attention because they thought, "Oh, who knows what he's going to do?" At least they expressed to me that it was very exciting, because they said, "We really didn't know what you were going to do next," which is a bit of a risk to take. But it certainly made it a lot of fun that day to be onstage and to take some chances and trust that they would be there with you.

Interviewer: I'm sure you've heard this from many people. You give the appearance of making it up as you go along. It's terrific for an audience. There's something dangerous about it.

Lane: That's the highest compliment.

Interviewer: On the other hand, what you're saying is that you're not making it up as you go along.

Lane: There's also a certain amount of trust with the people who are on-stage, several of whom I'd worked with before; so I know that they're not going to be thrown by something a little different.

Interviewer: How do you achieve, insofar as you know how you do it, that sense that we get as an audience that you're making it up? Is that the result of tremendous calculated craft, or is it a talent you have inherently to some extent?

Lane: I think it's a little bit of all of that. It's partly craft and experience and having the confidence and the freedom to experiment a bit; but then it comes after a long time of acting too. Sometimes you can go too far, and I think that's healthy. There are going to be days when you've got to shake things up, I think. I think anyone would tell you honestly that there are days when you go to the theater and you really don't want to be there. As much as you love what you do, you just don't want to be there; or you've got things on your mind and you've got to put all that aside. But sometimes you can use some of what's going on to your advantage. You get through it with a certain amount of technique that you can rely on, and then I think it really is about what, again, an audience brings to the table. They are like another character in the play, so that will sometimes infuse the entire thing and will take you where you didn't think you could go that day. I've gone out and thought, "Okay, I have to do eight performances a week and today—not that I'm not going to give them a good show—I only have so much energy and this is what I'm going to do. I've got to relax a little, don't push." Then I get out there and the audience is from heaven, and suddenly you would go to the ends of the earth for them. There are so many things you think about as you're doing a show eight times a week—about having to conserve a certain amount of energy because you're doing two shows. Then suddenly that will all go out the window if it's a great house and they're there to have a good time. It changes everything.

Interviewer: I read somewhere that an opposite thing was happening to Eddie Bracken and he ended up playing his lines to you in the second row. Is that true?

Lane: Yes, I went to see a production of *Forum* at the Paper Mill Play-house. Eddie Bracken was Pseudolus; it was a very small house, and it was a matinee. I was laughing hysterically. I thought it was great; I thought he was hilarious.

Interviewer: You were a kid?

Lane: At the time, I was living in New York, so I was in my early twenties. I was laughing and laughing, and he finally just started to play the whole show to me. When he had to talk to the audience, he would address me: "Do you believe this?" That made it all the more enjoyable.

Interviewer: Now that you're an actor, you understand why he did it—because you were feeding him, just the way you're saying an audience can feed you.

Lane: Sure. It kept it alive for him that I was laughing it up. It was funny.

Interviewer: Which of the roles that you've played on the stage so far has been the most challenging for you, either right from the start or as it developed onstage?

Lane: Let's see. Well, *The Film Society;* that was a difficult character. In the last scene of *The Film Society,* the character has a three-page monologue about the killing of a cow. His father made him watch the killing of this cow and then it all led to him firing these two people. I had become the headmaster of the school, and I had to fire these two people I loved very much. I remember it was an incredibly difficult transition. It was a play I really enjoyed doing but I found very difficult. I think also of the plays I've done with Terrence McNally. He always writes something that's really interesting and challenging for me because, I think, he's always believed that I'm capable of doing it. It's not always just the comedy. In *Love! Valour! Compassion!* really at the very last minute he wrote this scene where I had this breakdown about who was going to be there for me when I died. He's a character who is HIV positive, and he has a relationship with someone who is dying of AIDS, and he's frightened. It's what's going on underneath all the humor; this guy is actually really scared. It was incredibly powerful; but he believed enough in me as an actor that I could pull it off.

Interviewer: He wrote that scene later?

Lane: Yes, it was really just before we went into the theater. He said, "I think something is missing for you in the third act. What do you think it is?" And I said, "I think it's probably what's going on underneath all of the jokes about musical theater. What is he hiding? It may be that musical comedy is this theme in the character. Life isn't like a musical comedy. It may be as basic as that." Then he went off and he wrote this incredible scene. I remember the director, Joe Mantello, calling me and saying, "He's written this wonderful scene; I hope you like it." I came in the next morning and read it and just cried because it was so moving.

Interviewer: In Terrence McNally's case, he's written some of the plays with you in mind. Have you similarly in other cases taken a role in the shaping of the play through rehearsals? The way you describe that situation, in a sense you were a part of the creative team putting it together. Is that a typical situation for you?

Lane: Well, it is with Terrence. He's incredibly collaborative and really wants your input. If you make a suggestion and it's good, he takes it and runs with it and then creates something spectacular. Also because we've had a history, I feel comfortable enough to say that to him. Basically he's said, "I want to create things for you and work with you." I think that's very rare, and it's something that I treasure about the whole experience with him. Then there are times when you don't feel comfortable enough. With Neil Simon, I idolized him, and it was very hard for me to say if I thought something needed some work. I couldn't bring myself to tell him that because I didn't know him as well and he'd always been a hero to me.

Interviewer: Do you think the character and the production suffer a bit when you as an actor don't have that kind of input?

Lane: Well, I don't know.

Interviewer: Let me turn it around. Is it better when you can have that kind of input?

Lane: I think it helps. Not that you want to tell him how to write the play; but sometimes when you're in the middle of it and doing it, you have this other perspective that can help them—because you're coming to the material fresh and they've been living with it for a while. Some writers can be very protective about not wanting to change anything; but if people are open to talking about it, then I think it's always healthy.

Interviewer: If you're not comfortable saying the line, you're not going to be as good saying that line.

Lane: I always go out of my way to give them what they've written. I hate actors who say, "I don't think my character would say that." Unfortunately, the author thought so; so why don't you try it, try to make it work. Then if something doesn't feel comfortable or if it feels like it's not consistent, you can say that, as long as you're not indulging yourself.

Interviewer: When somebody sends you a play—and you're in a position now where people send you things—what makes you be interested in doing a role, at this point in your career?

Lane: I think it's always about good writing, no matter where it comes, whether it's the movies or television or the stage. That's what I'm always drawn to. As far as a role or a character, you try to do something totally different from the last thing you've done, or you're looking for some sort of a challenge. I think if it scares you a little about doing it, then it's probably a good idea to do it. You should keep testing yourself. It would be easy to get comfortable and just say, "I can do a variation on the same character over and over and make a nice living." But I think you have to keep testing yourself and pushing yourself to try different kinds of things. At this point, I would love to come back to the theater and do something serious, something that wasn't an out-and-out comedy.

Interviewer: I read somewhere that you want to do the older brother in *Long Day's Journey into Night,* Tom in *The Glass Menagerie,* or Richard III. Is that accurate information? That sort of covers it, doesn't it?

Lane: Yes, that's pretty good. That would be a pretty good rep season! Well, sure, I've always loved those characters. At a certain point, you get too old for some of them, but yes.

Interviewer: Why those three?

Lane: The older brother in *Long Day's Journey:* I just have always felt that I would be good in that role. I have an understanding of it and, having come from a dysfunctional Irish Catholic family myself, I think I have some insights. And Tom in *The Glass Menagerie:* it's just such a beautifully written character, funny and very touching, and it's one of my favorite plays. But I may be getting a little long in the tooth to do that, although I remember seeing Rip Torn do it with Maureen Stapleton and he was slightly older than she was. And Richard III: I don't know; I always throw that in because it's the character actor's Hamlet, but you'd have to find a way of doing it. I think the last sort of really acclaimed one was Antony Sher, who was on crutches; he had this whole spider imagery that he used, and he was incredible.

Interviewer: What about Simon Gray's comment to you about great comics or great comic actors or something along those lines?

Lane: We were out one night in a bar and he said, "Nathan, I think you can either be a great comic or a great actor, but you have to decide which." And he said, "I think you should be a great actor." I thought, "What the hell does that mean?" But I sort of knew what he was talking about. It's always a battle between the need to be funny and to be liked by an audience and just playing the role.

Interviewer: Has it affected your choices?

Lane: Sure, I think so. I think he recognized in me this ability to come on and be funny, to be funny in many different ways and to make an audience laugh, and that it can be a trap to fall into.

Interviewer: But aren't there two parts of that trap? There is your part of it and there's the producer's part of it. Is a producer at this point likely to offer you the role of James Tyrone Jr.? Is the audience going to accept Nathan Lane in that role?

Lane: Right. Sure. There's now sort of a built-in expectation that I'm going to be funny.

Interviewer: But how do you, who know you could do James Tyrone Jr., deal with that? Do you automatically now say to people who want you to do the funny roles, "I don't want to do that now for a while," and wait for somebody to give you a chance at a more serious role? Is that how you control your career at this point?

Lane: Sure, you have to be willing to say no, until the right opportunity comes around—because it would be easy just to do Pseudolus over and over again.

Interviewer: Is there any difference between doing a musical and doing a play, in terms of the actor's skill and preparation, or is it all just acting?

Lane: It is all just acting. I think there's a little bit of a prejudice about musical theater, that it's less dramatic stuff and doesn't require the same kind of skill. I think in some way it's more demanding because all the same rules of acting still apply but also just technically you have to be in very good shape; it demands a lot of energy. Vocally it's much more demanding usually, so I think it's much harder. Also, for it to work, especially with the new musicals, there are so many elements involved. That's why there's only a handful of great musicals, because very rarely does it all come together and seem like one piece.

Interviewer: What about the difference between film work and stage work?

Lane: I think it's the same instincts. I think in some ways film is a little more difficult because you don't just show up and go from the beginning to the end as we do in the theater, where you're in control. You're doing things out of sequence, and ultimately it's the director who's in control. He goes into an editing room and puts it all together and you just hope for the best. I went to see *Boogie Nights* the other evening, which is really terrific, and I was watching Julianne Moore, who plays this actress in the "adult film industry," as Burt Reynolds puts it. She's a drug addict and she wants custody of her child and the father doesn't want her to have the child because she's out of control; and then you see this one scene and they cut to her and she's standing against a wall and she's sobbing, just sobbing. I was watching it and thinking, "That is so hard to do; because you show up, you prepare, and then they say, 'Go lean against the wall and cry your eyes out.'" It's not like you've been doing a play and it builds up to that particular scene. So I do find that that's a skill that really takes time to develop in film. In the theater you have a little more of an advantage because you live through the whole thing from beginning to end, and you also have an audience there to communicate to.

Interviewer: What about in terms of comedy? One of the clichés always mentioned is how much smaller things are in film because the camera is right on top of you. As a comic actor, do you have to scale down your performance for the camera?

Lane: Yes, they say that. But then there's Jim Carrey, who scales up. But yes, I think that is true. You have focus by virtue of the fact that the guy with the camera is in your face. As they say, it's all in your eyes, and you can think something and it comes across on screen. Working with Gene Hackman in *The Birdcage* you couldn't even see what he was doing, and then you'd go sit in the dailies and watch him and you'd say, "Oh my God, it's all there. He's so brilliant." Then there are people who are just big, like Bette Davis, and yet you still believe it, because it's all truthful; it's just a larger size.

Interviewer: What are some theater performances that you've seen that you've most admired?

Lane: Linda Lavin in *Broadway Bound* was really incredibly moving, and I'll always remember her.

Interviewer: What was it about that performance?

Lane: I don't know. It made me so emotional. I was so moved by her. Every time I saw her, I got emotional. I don't know why. I'll discuss it in therapy later! I thought she just captured that woman. She was always cleaning something and she had this cloth with her a lot. She finished this very emotional phone conversation with her mother, she put the phone down, and then she absentmindedly wiped the phone, the top of the phone. I'll always remember that. What else? I loved Janet McTeer in *A Doll's House.* That was a very controversial performance. I know people who just hated the production and thought she overpowered it and was extremely over the top. I thought she was just great. I loved what she did—the bravery of it and the commitment to it. I thought she and the man who played Torvald were sensational, and I thought the end of the play was just devastating.

Interviewer: Talk a bit about the actor-director relationship. What are some of the different ways you've worked with directors? What works for you and what doesn't?

Lane: John Tillinger is a director I've worked with a lot with Terrence McNally; he actually cast me in *The Film Society*, the Jon Robin Baitz play. He just offered me the part and didn't ask me to audition, just said, "I'd like you to do this," and I was very impressed that he would just offer me the role. He believed so much in me as an actor, maybe more so than I did myself. He gave me that opportunity to do something that was not just a comedy. There's humor to it, but it was also a very serious play. And again I had him to thank for suggesting me for *Lisbon Traviata*; he said, "What about Nathan Lane?"— which was odd because they were looking for someone older. John Tillinger creates a really wonderful atmosphere; you feel utterly free to try anything, and he's also a terrific editor. Then I worked with Gene Saks; he and I got along very well, and I liked him a lot. My favorite thing was that he would try to point something out to you and he would act it out for you. He's a wonderful actor, and I said to him, "What would be better than us doing the play is if you came out in a tuxedo and just read the play, because it's far more entertaining." That's how he directed; he would act it for you, and you'd go, "I see, okay. I get it." And he was very funny, too, a very funny man.

Interviewer: What about an actor-director relationship that didn't work for you—or have you been lucky?

Lane: I've been very lucky. I always got on my report card, "Works well with others." So I haven't really had that much of a problem with directors. I tend to get along. Or if it doesn't work, then I can take care of myself, which is what sometimes you have to learn how to do. You have to learn to direct yourself. I'm trying to think of all the directors I've worked with. Jerry Zaks is someone who has a very, very clear idea about what he wants to do, and yet with someone like me over the years a great deal of trust is there, and a friendship, so he will allow me to try things. Now we don't even have to discuss it, we know each other so well, and I feel free enough with him to suggest things. I think of something—not just for me—and I might take him aside and say, "Why don't you try this?" And he feels comfortable enough with me to do that because we've known each other for so long and we've worked on so many things together. But he's a very strong director, and you have to come in and have done your homework, because he's got forty ideas for every idea you have. He's incredibly imaginative and fun to be around. I worked on *The Birdcage* with Mike Nichols, who again is someone who really knows what he wants but who doesn't really say all that much. We rehearsed for three weeks, like a play, and he kept stressing, "Always remember to hold on to his humanity, and don't forget who he is as a person as opposed to just the flamboyance." He said, "We can always get laughs, but the humanity is the most important thing." Mike is just the smartest person I know. He's like God, but more charming.

Interviewer: What about the actor-actor relationship? Where does that work and where doesn't that work? Along these lines, every time I go to the Circle in the Square Theatre I'm drawn to a photograph of George C. Scott with his arm around your neck—from *Present Laughter.* He gave you your first big break, didn't he? And in that case he was both actor and director, wasn't he?

Lane: Yes, I owe him everything. *Present Laughter* was my Broadway debut, and to make it with George C. Scott was unbelievable to me. He was an acting hero of mine, and he was so generous to me and supportive. I remember he actually asked me to do some crazy things and I thought, "Well, this will really be going out on a limb with this performance." I was a little nervous, but he could have asked me to jump off the Brooklyn Bridge and I would have done it. We had a great relationship onstage and off. I think he loved actors.

Interviewer: Had he seen you in something or heard about you?

Lane: No, I just walked in and auditioned. I remember he laughed a great deal and was very charming. They called two days later and said I had the part, and I was shocked. I didn't think I would get it, because it was such a wonderful role; I thought they would find a name person to do it.

Interviewer: What do you look for in another actor when you're onstage, and what do you want from another actor onstage?

Lane: Well, I think you want someone who's talented and who's present and focused and giving their all—as they would expect of me. It helps if they have a sense of humor, a sense of fun, and they enjoy what they do. Ultimately, I think it's also got to be fun. It really helps.

Interviewer: Have you ever wanted to direct? Can you see yourself as a director?

Lane: People say to me that I should direct, I guess because I have a lot of opinions. But I haven't so far. I would be really nervous about doing something like that, so maybe I should try it. I don't know; maybe at some point I would direct a play, maybe one I felt comfortable with.

Interviewer: When you go to see a play, do you think you view it as an actor, or do you think you view it from the outside, as a director might?

Lane: Even when I'm in a play, I always have been able to look at the over-all piece and say, "How do I fit into this, and what is my job in this particular play?" It's not just all about me; I see the whole picture. So yes, I think I do have that sort of director's sense; but whether I would do it or not, that's still unknown.

Interviewer: What is your feeling about theater critics? Do they ever help you? Are they a hindrance? Do you ignore them?

Lane: I think it's a love/hate relationship. When I was starting in the theater, there were some critics who were extremely helpful to me. Not so much what they had to say about the performance, but just that they were noticing me. I think it certainly made people more aware of me, because they would say, "Even though the play didn't work, Nathan Lane was very good." I remember Mel Gussow in particular was someone who was incredibly helpful to me. Mel Gussow was the one who wrote a wonderful review of *The Lisbon Traviata*, which was the show that put me on the map. Then he wrote a whole article about character actors in New York, and I had just gone into *Some Americans Abroad* at Lincoln Center and had done *Bad Habits* and *Lisbon Traviata* just before then, so he was talking about the variety of roles I had played. Those kinds of things, I think, were really incredibly helpful to my career, and so I'll always be grateful.

Then, as Mickey Rooney once said to me, "They build you up to knock you down." It's a cycle. They write a lot of nice things about you and then they become familiar with you. It's like a marriage; they get sick and tired of you. It was interesting with *Forum*. I started to read things that were negative about me and I felt like, "Fellas, what happened?" I read several things from different people, not just New York critics, saying something bothered them about the fact that when I came out at the opening of the show I received this huge ovation. To my mind, just psychologically, it seemed as if it was taking away some of their power. They want to be the ones to discover you and tell people what you're about. They love to discover people, and that has an effect. I remember one critic criticizing me for not doing something more challenging; and I thought, "Okay, maybe it's time to take a little break from the theater. Let them miss me a little." People can be hurtful; John Simon does it on a daily basis. I don't know whether they think you're not aware of that or that you don't pay any attention to it (some people don't); but sure it hurts, especially if they just say something about your physicality or whatever they think you are. Sure it hurts. I take it personally. I'm sorry. I'm funny that way. I do. So yes, it does have an effect. Certainly in retrospect, with certain plays, if you look back you say, "I certainly understand what they were talking about with the play; maybe it wasn't my finest moment." But somehow, once they get to know you better, it becomes a little personal in some ways.

Interviewer: When you look at the New York theater, are you pessimistic about it? Are you optimistic about it? You're at that point in your career now where you're doing a lot of film work. You're apparently not reading a whole lot that really makes you want to come back to the theater right away. What is your sense of what the possibilities are for you as a serious actor in the New York theater?

Lane: I would tend to think that I would try to do something maybe a little more serious off-Broadway or at somewhere like the Manhattan Theatre Club, where you can take that risk because they have subscribers and it's a limited engagement. I certainly would want to return to the theater. I was reading a *New York* magazine article about all these young film actors who are now living in New York and that this is the place to be. You're not supposed to live in Hollywood; this is where young actors like Parker Posey and Billy Crudup, who are up-and-coming stars, are living. And I think, when they were in nursery school, I was the one living here refusing to go to L.A.! I'm really getting old; and so yes, I do want to explore the other options now—with film and television—and see where that leads. It really would have to be something special at this point to go back into a long run. Because it is a year of your life usually, especially with a Broadway play.

Am I pessimistic about it? I think the theater is always going to survive and it's always going through changes. To be honest with you, yes, sure I'm pessimistic about it. Broadway is safer and safer, especially with Disney coming in. You fear these huge theme park shows and then they surprise you with something like *The Lion King,* where they have a very imaginative director who took some risks with the material. I think it's harder and harder; but I can remember reading an interview with Tennessee Williams saying, back in 1954 I think, that there was no room for the serious play on Broadway anymore. So this is not a new problem; it's just that now financially everything is out of control. It's so expensive to produce and so expensive to go to the theater. I do tend to be a little pessimistic about it. They say, "Where are the new musicals coming from?" Deep down I think, with the rare exception, we're not going to have those great musicals that we all know and love. That's it: we got them and there aren't going to be many more. Every once in a while, they'll come along; *Ragtime* is really a wonderful show. The guys who wrote those shows are gone, with the exception of [Stephen] Sondheim or [John] Kander and [Fred] Ebb; but it gets harder and harder for them to be produced because it's so expensive.

Interviewer: Suppose a regional theater came to you with a role that you have always wanted to play, would you think of doing that?

Lane: Sure, absolutely.

Interviewer: Elsewhere, you've been asked about heroes and you talk about Jackie Gleason and Laurel and Hardy. Anyone else? You didn't mention Chaplin; is that because it's so obvious?

Lane: Chaplin? I admire Chaplin and what he was able to do, not only as a performer but as a director. I can't say he doesn't make me laugh, because he has, but—I don't know, he didn't really make me laugh from the gut. Laurel and Hardy really make me laugh from the gut. I don't know why that is. It's so personal, what makes somebody laugh.

Interviewer: Are your heroes mostly the comics?

Lane: I think so. Sure, absolutely. Woody Allen was a big influence. I love listening to his old stand-up comedy albums. And Nichols and May. It does tend to be comedy people.

Interviewer: There's a wonderful scene in *The Birdcage* when Robin Williams asks you to walk like John Wayne. That was one of the most incredible things I've ever seen because of all the emotions you managed to get into that walk and still capture John Wayne. How did you do that?

Lane: I just tried to walk like John Wayne. I remembered the French film, and I remembered what Michel Serrault did. It was nothing like John Wayne, and I remembered his lover says to him, "No, that's Miss John Wayne you're doing." I said to Mike, "Should he just be totally unable to do anything that resembles John Wayne?" And he said, "No, no, really try to walk like John Wayne." So I just tried to do that swaggering walk in clogs and toreador pants.

I thought that would speak for itself. That was the last day of shooting. We were outside; it was July in Miami Beach, and it was sweltering. In fact, the script supervisor passed out from the heat. It's a long scene, and Robin and I both sweat a great deal. I remember it was particularly hard and was a key scene in the movie. It was not easy. It was slightly emotional, too, because we knew once we finished this scene, we were all going to say good-bye and go our separate ways. So it was interesting to play that wildly funny scene with all that going on—which is another reason why moviemaking is hard. You really have to shut it all out and concentrate.

Jason Robards

Jason Robards was born Jason Nelson Robards Jr. in Chicago, Illinois, on July 26, 1922. He trained for the stage at the American Academy of Dramatic Arts and with Uta Hagen. His stage debut was in Out of the Frying Pan *in Rehoboth Beach, Delaware, and his Broadway debut was in* The Mikado, *both in 1947, the same year he played the rear end of a cow in* Jack and the Beanstalk *for the Children's World Theatre in New York City. Other roles include Ed Moody,* American Gothic *(1953);* Hickey, The Iceman Cometh *(1956 and 1985);* Jamie, Long Day's Journey into Night *(1956);* Hotspur, Henry IV, Part 1; *Polixenes,* The Winter's Tale *(both at the Stratford Shakespeare Festival, Ontario, Canada, 1958);* Manley Halliday, The Disenchanted *(1958; Tony Award); title role,* Macbeth *(1959);* Julian Berniers, Toys in the Attic *(1960);* William Baker, Big Fish, Little Fish *(1961);* Murray Burns, A Thousand Clowns *(1962);* Quentin, After the Fall *(1964);* Seymour Rosenthal, But for Whom Charlie *(1964);* Erie Smith, Hughie *(1964);* Vicar of St. Peter's, The Devils*

(1965); Captain Starkey, We Bombed in New Haven *(1968); Frank Elgin,* The Country Girl *(1972); James Tyrone Jr.,* A Moon for the Misbegotten *(1973); James Tyrone Sr.,* Long Day's Journey into Night *(1975 and 1988); Cornelius Melody,* A Touch of the Poet *(1977); Martin Vanderhof,* You Can't Take It with You *(1983); Cooper,* A Month of Sundays *(1987); Nat Miller,* Ah, Wilderness! *(1988); Jacob Brackish,* Park Your Car in Harvard Yard *(1991); Andrew Makepeace Ladd II,* Love Letters *(1993); Hirst,* No Man's Land *(1994); Andy,* Moonlight *(1995); and Mr. Rice,* Molly Sweeney *(1996).*

He made his movie debut in The Journey *(1959). Among his films are* By Love Possessed *(1961),* Tender Is the Night *(1961),* Long Day's Journey into Night *(1962),* Act One *(1964),* A Thousand Clowns *(1965),* Any Wednesday *(1966),* A Big Hand for the Little Lady *(1966),* Divorce American Style *(1967),* Hour of the Gun *(1967),* The St. Valentine's Day Massacre *(1967),* The Night They Raided Minsky's *(1968),* Once upon a Time in the West *(1969),* The Ballad of Cable Hogue *(1970),* Julius Caesar *(1970),* Tora! Tora! Tora! *(1970),* Johnny Got His Gun *(1971),* Pat Garrett and Billy the Kid *(1973),* All the President's Men *(1976; Academy Award),* Julia *(1977; Academy Award),* Melvin and Howard *(1980),* The Legend of the Lone Ranger *(1981),* Max Dugan Returns *(1983),* Something Wicked This Way Comes *(1983),* Laguna Heat *(1987),* The Good Mother *(1988),* Dream a Little Dream *(1989),* Parenthood *(1989),* Quick Change *(1990),* Storyville *(1992),* The Trial *(1993),* Philadelphia *(1993),* The Paper *(1994),* Little Big League *(1994),* Crimson Tide *(1995),* Beloved *(1998),* The Real Macaw *(1998), and* Magnolia *(1999).*

For television he has done For Whom the Bell Tolls *(1959),* The Iceman Cometh *(1960),* One Day in the Life of Ivan Denisovich *(1963),* F.D.R.: The Last Year *(1980),* Haywire *(1980),* Sakharov *(1980),* The Long Hot Summer *(1985),* The Atlanta Child Murders *(1985),* Johnny Bull *(1986),* The Last Frontier *(1986),* Bright Lights, Big City *(1988),* The Christmas Wife *(1988),* Inherit the Wind *(1988),* The Perfect Tribute *(1991),* Mark Twain and Me *(1991),* Chernobyl: The Final Warning *(1991),* The Adventures of Huck Finn *(1993),* Heidi *(1993),* The Enemy Within *(1994),* Journey *(1995),* My Antonía *(1995), and* Going Home *(2000). He has also appeared on* Alcoa Hour, Studio One, Philco Television Playhouse, Suspense, Armstrong Circle Theatre, Goodyear Playhouse, Westinghouse Presents, *and* Omnibus.

He was elected to the Theater Hall of Fame in 1979 and received the Kennedy Center Honors in 1999. Robards died on December 26, 2000.

This interview took place on November 1, 1993.

Interviewer: Let's go back a bit and talk about your stage debut in Rehoboth Beach, Delaware, in a play called *Out of the Frying Pan.*

Robards: Yes, that's right. That was my first—for an audience of eight.

Interviewer: What do you remember about it?

Robards: I think the play was about an actor, and I think I played a bad actor. I remember Tom Poston was in it; he was one of the bosses of the company. The play was a thing they did in summer stock often and also at the American Academy quite a lot. I'd been on the stage of the American Academy in their examination plays, but it was not the same as going on for people who were paying for it. They seemed to like it. It was a light comedy about a bunch of out-of-work actors; that was very good for us because we all were!

Interviewer: And your New York debut was in a thing called *Jack and the Beanstalk,* where you played the back end of a cow.

Robards: That's right. I played the hind end of the cow in *Jack and the Beanstalk.* They sell her for the bean that makes the beanstalk, so she comes in very early. I was also the stage manager. They put me in the rear end because they didn't trust me to do the eyes and the head in the front end. I was in there with someone else; it was a woman who was very bossy—and I had to follow her. Being inside the suit was terrible. I crawled out of the suit and then stage-managed the rest of the show—played records, did music, and those sorts of things. Anyway, the farmer that bought us walked up to the cow and said, "I'm afraid we're going to have to sell you, Bossie," and he did. He sold us and we left. Thirty-five years or more later, I was in *You Can't Take It with You* in New York on Broadway, and this same actor who played the farmer in *Jack and the Beanstalk* played a G-man in *You Can't Take It with You.* In the role, he said, "I'm arresting all of you and this and that for setting off fireworks in this place," and he turned to me on opening night and he said, "And I'm afraid we're going to have to sell you, Bossie." That was Page Johnson, my friend, who nailed me to the wall.

Interviewer: We'll get on to some of the more substantial roles, of course, in a minute; but talk a bit about your training at the American Academy of Dramatic Arts.

Robards: It was a wonderful training at the American Academy. My father went there in 1910. In his class were Guthrie McClintic, Edward G. Robinson, William Powell. Spencer Tracy went there later. It was very good training in the theater. You got theater history, you got makeup, you got dance and sword-fighting, you had play analysis, you had Greek drama. You had voice, of course, the patterns of voice and speech. Best of all, you had plays. You were onstage rehearsing. First you started out with just one actor, and eventually you ended up doing an entire play, with an audience by the way, not just doing them in class. That was the most valuable thing. We had the old Carnegie Theatre, which is now a movie house, but then it belonged to the American Academy. It was part of the Carnegie Hall building, and it was a 350- to 400-seat theater. We had our own sets, and we just kept doing plays. That was of great value. It was fabulous. If they booed you off the stage, whatever, at least you got out there.

Interviewer: Is that the sort of thing you'd recommend to others? How does one break into this business today?

Robards: Isn't it strange? My father was an actor and he broke into it in 1910 or 1911 and he said, "You know, in those days we had theaters all over the country. We had no radio to bother us." Then when I went into the theater, in 1946, he said, "How do you break into the theater nowadays? You've got radio, television, movies." Television was just coming in then, but you had movies. Now I say the same thing to you. It was easy for us then. How do you do it *today* when everyone wants to be an actor or in the business? Even people that are lawyers want to be in this business. Everybody somehow wants to be involved. We see a lot of people who graduate with business degrees who want to get into the theater or movies because there's a big home entertainment business. I feel that as an actor, again I'm talking for me, the way you last, or try to last, is by knowing what's going on in the theater. The playwright, the audience, and the actor form a triangular frame that goes into something else and becomes another life, another understanding. That can help you immensely. Say you have to go run in and do a television thing where you do this scene now and do that one later—or a movie. That can help you very much, having that kind of theater background.

Interviewer: And can you imagine a time twenty-five years from now when you'll look back on today as the good old days? It's happened each time, hasn't it?

Robards: I think so. We don't know where the technology's taking us; that's another thing. I don't know. We may not even need actors.

Interviewer: A pretty scary thought. Let's talk about the actor's process. Are you an "inny" or an "outy"? Actors seem to work either from the outside in, externally, or from the inside out.

Robards: I would, I suppose, say the outside is the thing that makes your insides work, because you have to look at a script. You just can't get up and start acting. You can do improvisation for only so long and then it becomes quite boring. I guess certain people can do that, can gab away on talk shows and all that. I think that you have to look at the script and then move in and see what the piece is about, what the theme is, what the characters are doing. You have to obey the rules of the character, not the rules that you think. You can't say, "Oh, I don't feel this way. I wouldn't do that." It has nothing to do with you in that respect; it has to do with the character and how he behaves in the piece.

Interviewer: Can you think of a production or a role where you got a block but, when the hat or some other external was right, you then understood the character?

Robards: Oh, you mean props?

Interviewer: Right.

Robards: No, costume and makeup all help tremendously, but I think the better you know the script, the more you know the words until finally it ceases to be words on a page or verbs or whatever you've learned by, then the creative process starts. You've got to be out there; it's got to be in front of people and they tell you: we've shared something. It's hard, you can't put your finger on it, it's an agreement. If it happens back and forth, we know where we are. We know where the humor is, we know where the passion is. It's another sense that tells you that; it's like you're split in a number of pieces every time. That is from preparation, relaxation, and concentration. Then it begins to get out of itself and become an event, a stage life. It's two and a half hours. When I played the Scott Fitzgerald part in *The Disenchanted,* I couldn't live real life that way and die at the end. Stage life is a whole different life. It's a magic of its own, and this is what we strive for—where time is broken. As Ralph Richardson said, "It's eight o'clock. It's time to dream; this is when we dream." I hope I have nightmares, by playing serious parts. It's true, you do shatter time.

Interviewer: The first serious part which brought you to prominence was *The Iceman Cometh* in 1956 at the Circle in the Square, where you played Hickey. I understand that you had to convince José Quintero that you were right for the role. Tell that story.

Robards: I had seen *The Iceman Cometh* in 1946 when I was at the American Academy. Students at the American Academy were invited as a preview audience to go to see it, about five hundred of us, and I've never forgotten it. Not that it was so tremendously well done, but I remember James Barton's face and his hat, this guy who was playing the part of Hickey. It stuck in my head, though the play did not realize itself. Ten years later I was on my way to a radio show I was doing in New York, and a fellow actor, James Greene, was selling papers on the corner of Hudson and—I believe it was Montague Street. I was on my way to a radio gig, buying my paper to get on the subway, and he said, "José's doing *The Iceman.* Did you know that?" José had directed me in *American Gothic* at the Circle three years earlier. Suddenly everything came to me. That was it. I had to be in that play. I had never read the play, but I knew I had to go to see José. So I ran over to the Circle, and I didn't go to the radio show. I never got hired on that show again! José said, "I'm not reading you for the part of Hickey. That's an older fellow. I'm thinking of Franchot Tone or Howard Da Silva. Willie is the part you should play." I said, "No, I don't want to play that. I only want to play Hickey." So he said, "Well, I'll have to ask you to read, which I don't usually do." So I said, "Okay," and I went home and I looked at it, and I read for him later that afternoon. I did part of the monologue, the speech which leads up to it, and he said, "Now do some of the funny parts up front." I read the scene with him, and he said, "Okay, so long, I'll let you know by six o'clock tonight." Then he called me up and said, "You can do it." So that was how it started—with that play and with O'Neill.

Interviewer: And over the years, you and José Quintero have worked together many times and have a special way of working together. Talk about the actor-director relationship with you two.

Robards: It's wonderful with him because he takes the play split second by split second and goes through it and does it in such a supportive way. He doesn't let you do things that don't work for the play or that he feels wouldn't fulfill the moment. He won't let you fall on your face, in other words. He's the best support that anyone ever had, and we have a sort of a secret language. He looks at me to move there or to do this or, if that doesn't work, move later. He says, "You know what to do here," and I say, "Oh yeah," and he says, "And you know you know." I say, "I do know what I'm doing. That's right." What I do is I study the part a little more.

Interviewer: Is it confidence-building that he's doing for you?

Robards: Maybe so, because now of course he hardly has to talk about anything.

Interviewer: When you do something that he doesn't think is quite right, then what?

Robards: He says it's wrong, we must start over. When we started *Iceman,* by the way, I was doing a *Studio One,* a live television show in those days, and I did not attend the first few rehearsals. We only had two and a half weeks. He said, "Don't worry about it. You don't come in anyway till an hour into the first act, so you can finish that TV show." He knew I needed the money; we were getting five dollars a week for rehearsal and twenty-five dollars a week to play. I came back the second week and he said, "All right, we're starting from the beginning." I said, "What happened?" He said, "I did it all wrong. I just saw a run-through of what I'd done with these actors"—there were, I don't know, seventeen of them—"and it's all wrong. I tried to impose my 'great talent' on the playwright, and I was all wrong. I saw it and saw that it was terrible." So we started all over again, and it was wonderful.

Interviewer: That alone suggests a director of competence, to be able to admit he was wrong.

Robards: With the monologue, I only ran it twice before opening night. I ran it in a dress rehearsal and in a preview. He said, "Start off up by the bar, then just go down right when you say, 'So I beat it to the Big Town,' then go around behind Cora when you talk about getting venereal disease, then move center for this, then go back up in the bar area and finish it off." And you know, somehow that's what I did, and it went over great. But I knew the words, see, that was it.

Interviewer: Like a football coach diagramming a play.

Robards: That's right. He did *Moon for the Misbegotten.* We did it in Washington, and we had played it in Lake Forest, Illinois. We came to New York, where we had five previews, and he said, "You know, that whole section with you and Colleen. I'm going to move it all stage left and make a pavanne out of it. I don't want to move it over around here, it dissipates." So that's what he did; we changed that about three nights before we opened.

Interviewer: Obviously, if you're going to have faith in a playwright, Eugene O'Neill is the right one to have faith in. But in 1956, when you did *Iceman* for the first time, that was really bringing O'Neill back. How was it that his reputation had waned?

Robards: I don't know what happened after that *Iceman* in 1946. There was a ten-year hiatus for him in which none of his plays were done. Maybe a college might have done the sea plays or something, but none of his plays were in production, except in Sweden. That's why he gave Sweden *Long Day's Journey* and *Hughie.* Then O'Neill died and we didn't hear about him. I remember that José and his partner in the Circle, Lee Connell, picked *Iceman,* and all the people that had anything to do with the business end of it said, "You're going to close the theater with this show. The playwright is dead; nobody wants to see this kind of stuff. You might as well forget it." He went ahead with it. The seat man from Roger Stevens put some seats in the Circle that people could sit in for five hours, and we went ahead with it, against the advice of our own people, and it went through the roof. Mrs. O'Neill then came down to see it and gave José *Long Day's Journey into Night* to do in America. So we went right from *The Iceman*—I did, and José, and Ted Mann—into doing *Long Day's Journey.* It was about a three-year stretch there I had with O'Neill's plays.

Interviewer: And suddenly audiences wanted to see O'Neill's plays?

Robards: Then they wanted to see them. Carmen Capalbo and Stanley Chase did *A Moon for the Misbegotten,* with Franchot Tone and Wendy Hiller and Cyril Cusack. O'Neill's plays were being done and revived, and it's never stopped actually. I just finished doing *Hughie* again. Thirty years after doing *Hughie* with Jack Dobson, we did it at Trinity Rep in Providence, Rhode Island, for the thirtieth-anniversary production. The play went over incredibly. I don't mean by that that the Providence audiences are suckers or anything, it's just that it went over beautifully—because of our age and our knowledge of the play, I guess. The years dropped away from our lives, and we became those characters.

Interviewer: It is interesting how you have gone back to certain plays that you did when you were perhaps too young, and you feel that now you have more strength to do them.

Robards: I felt that way, in a way. Part of the performance in the original *Iceman* was that I was only thirty-four and the guy should have been in his fifties, married for twenty-five years. The guy who kills his wife at fifty is a much more tragic thing than a guy who's thirty-four. So he's out drinking and sleeping with a lot of girls at thirty-four, so what? It's different. I had a lot more energy at thirty-four than I did at sixty-four, but nevertheless I found other things in it when I played it thirty-two years later. I blacked my hair. I lost a little weight.

Interviewer: And a similar thing has happened with *Hughie*?

Robards: Yes. The age brought something to it. And the age brought tragedy in the relationship between Hickey and his wife. The tragedy remained and enabled him to deny. Those phrases are all very pertinent in that play. I never knew it until I hit on the monologue from *Iceman* as a thing for alcoholism at the Mayo Clinic. That monologue was a teaching tool. I'm not trying to say that it cured people from drinking or anything. I'm just saying I suddenly realized he's in denial. In so doing, he kills her, saying he loves her.

Interviewer: In 1958, you won a Tony Award for *The Disenchanted*.

Robards: Yes.

Interviewer: And what interests me is that you appeared onstage with your father.

Robards: That's right, I did.

Interviewer: What was it like, acting with him?

Robards: The best! He was the best, he was wonderful. I was on a raked stage for the first time, too, and he said, "I'll show you how to use this stage." Then every time I looked at him, he was two feet upstage of me!

Interviewer: You were both trained at the same academy.

Robards: Same academy, same teachers.

Interviewer: Were you similar actors?

Robards: He was better, though. He was much better-looking. I'm sorry that he gave up on the stage and went to the City Gruesome, that's Hollywood, and stayed there and did not come back. Budd Schulberg and I talked about having him play my best friend in *The Disenchanted,* and we got him to come back, and he was absolutely wonderful. I saw him onstage when I was eleven and was mesmerized. That was in a production out in Los Angeles. But I wish I'd seen him at his peak, when he was onstage in New York.

Interviewer: One of my favorite roles of yours is Quentin in Arthur Miller's *After the Fall*. Arthur Miller was very coy about how autobiographical the role is. In your mind, were you playing the fictional version of Arthur Miller?

Robards: Well, it was a very strange thing about that. I had made a promise to Robert Whitehead, who started the Lincoln Center Repertory Company. He said, "I need to have your promise—you and Maureen [Stapleton] and Gerry Page and David Wayne—that a few of you will be in this company. I don't know when we're going to get it aligned, but we're going to have a repertory company in New York. We haven't had one since Eva Le Gallienne died." I said, "Sure, count me in." He said, "We don't know what play we're going to do." By the time five years came around and we did actually start, there were only a few of us left—David Wayne and Hal Holbrook and Ralph Meeker and a few of us were around—and we had a whole new company. Faye Dunaway was one of the young actresses in the company; she played a small part, a nurse, in *After the Fall*.

Anyway, Miller came to the first reading. We were going to do three plays: *After the Fall; But for Whom Charlie,* an S. N. Behrman play; and O'Neill's *Marco Millions.* I was in two of them. I was not in *Marco Millions*. But *After the Fall* was only one act when we went into rehearsal; it didn't have a second act. I thought it was about the blacklisting and bad faith and lack of honor that happened in those days, and I found that very interesting. And about the breakup of a marriage, by the way, whatever happens in a marriage—someone else comes along, you don't know why you're staying. That was the end.

Interviewer: That's the first act.

Robards: It was wonderful. The next thing I know, we're into another character. This happened after about three weeks of rehearsal; we rehearsed for eight weeks. After about three weeks, he brought in the second act. It was all about what seemed to be Marilyn Monroe. I said, "Well, this is about Arthur." He said, "Oh no, it's not me, and that's not Marilyn." Barbara Loden was playing the part. The director, Elia Kazan, and Arthur said, "Come up to Arthur's apartment," at a hotel over on 23rd Street where he stayed, the Chelsea, "and we're going to have a little dinner and make some cuts. We need cuts. We're running for over four hours." I was out there talking the whole time. I said to Kazan, "What if I have to go to the bathroom? I'm never offstage." He said, "All right, tell you what. I'll cut a piss hole in the floor behind the stairway." The minute they said that I never had to go to the bathroom!

Anyway, it was long! We thought we were going to do cuts at Arthur's apartment, but that didn't happen. Suddenly, a wigmaker, a costumer, a negligee maker, and a makeup artist showed up, and they started making Barbara up in another room of Arthur's hotel suite. I'm sitting there with Kazan and I said to him, "What's going on?" And he said, "I don't know." Barbara appears half an hour later, and she looked just like Marilyn. I said, "How can he say that this isn't her?" And I got a little upset and I left. I almost left the production at that point too. I had some misunderstandings with the playwright. But I didn't; I stuck with it. I felt there was some wonderful stuff in it, but I was quite uncomfortable with it. It was incomplete. It didn't follow to where it was going, it went into a whole other thing. I didn't mind the Holocaust and all those things it brought up; it was this whole other area.

Interviewer: But your performance clearly was not an impersonation of Miller?

Robards: No, no, not at all.

Interviewer: And yet there was an essence there.

Robards: I guess there was. I'll tell you what happened. We did this show and we had some wonderful humor in it. Barbara and I had some wonderful stuff together before things got bad. And so did Mariclare Costello, and David Stewart, and Ralph Meeker, who played Mickey. You had to have this balance of levity and seriousness. The minute that we closed, Arthur took over the play to direct the road company. Chuck Aidman, who played my part on the road, told me this. He said, "We went to rehearsal and Arthur said, 'Now we're going to get out all those laughs that Jason and Kazan put in the play. We're cutting all that stuff.'" I never saw that production, but it wasn't the laughs that were out of character. It was genuinely funny. There were some funny and cute things that happened, dear things that happened in the play too. The flirtation and the relationships with his friends earlier—but they were gone. So I wasn't happy with that play.

Interviewer: You've played a variety of real people and fictional versions of real people—Ben Bradlee, Dashiell Hammett, Howard Hughes.

Robards: Lincoln four times.

Interviewer: What do you do to research these people?

Robards: Not much. Howard Hughes is a good example. Howard Hughes is Howard Robard Hughes. His aunts were named Loomis; my grandmother's maiden name is Loomis. My father's name is Robards, and I said, "I don't need to do any research on this." I didn't do any research on him. I got a letter from Terry Moore, who had been a close friend of his in his later years. "I don't know how you got this," she said, "but you captured him better than he himself did." I don't know how it happened. It wasn't anything I planned, I was with a wonderful director, Jonathan Demme; it was one of his early films. He saw the truth in the situations we were in. It wasn't a long part, and I had an actor that I had a great deal of fun working with, Paul Le Mat. I couldn't help laughing with him a lot.

Interviewer: I'm interested in some of the roles that you've created, how you as the actor can help to shape the play. Take something like *Toys in the Attic*.

Was that something that you recall changing much in rehearsal based on your input?

Robards: That's a very difficult play, and other actors didn't do well with it. Dean Martin didn't do well at all with it, but that was a movie and a different situation. It's a very tough play to do. I think an actor can bring something to it, maybe innocence. Also there's the chemistry of the people you're with. Here we had Maureen, my old friend Maureen Stapleton whom I've known since she was a kid, Anne Revere, Irene Worth. You get that kind of a cast together, and you get a good playwright like Lillian Hellman, and something happens. You could change the cast, just one element of it, and all of a sudden it starts to teeter. This is the ability of a great director. Eighty percent of the work is casting. Casting can bring that extra thing you're talking about. It can change a play and help it. With *Toys in the Attic,* I thought we were dying in Boston. So did everybody else; the backers and Elliott Norton took Lillian aside. Norton was a critic there, and they had a long, long conversation about this play and what was wrong and how it could be helped—in performance, mostly, not so much in dialogue, because she didn't change much. Sure enough, we pulled it off. What we thought was a disaster in Boston turned into the best play of the year in New York, and the only straight play, by the way, that lasted the entire season—which in a way was a forerunner to what's happening now. It's a visitor's sort of strange theater now in New York. It's a shame that we can't support a serious theater. I guess off-Broadway we can.

Interviewer: Even that's getting to be like the old Broadway, very commercial. Before we start assuming that you're solely a man of heavy drama, let's talk a bit about *A Thousand Clowns.* Had the playwright, Herb Gardner, and the producer, Fred Coe, seen you do comedy before?

Robards: No, I don't know that they had. I was in stock for years and I used to do a lot of light comedy. People used to say, "He is a light comedian."

Interviewer: Out in the hinterlands?

Robards: Yes, in these stock companies that were all around the country. Anyway, I had been doing that kind of stuff off and on. I was in *Toys in the Attic,* and the stage door at the Hudson Theatre was on 45th Street right next to the Palace Bar & Grill. The Palace Bar & Grill was a great hangout for actors. Everybody hung out there. Bell Telephone Hour conductor Donald Voorhees hung out there, A. J. Liebling was there; it was a great place. So we'd go there right after the show. I was sitting in a booth one night after the show with Irene and Maureen and Percy Rodriguez, and a guy walks in and throws a script at me—this kid about twenty-five-years-old—and says, "I want you to do this." I said, "Oh, go away kid, you bother me."

Interviewer: That happens to you a lot, I bet.

Robards: It was Herb. I put the script on the table and I said, "Oh, I'll take it home and read it." It was Herb's *A Thousand Clowns.* It took us two years to get it on, and then Fred Coe got involved. Fred was able to raise the money to get it on. I had worked for Fred in the old live television days; he was the producer of some of the live television shows, and I'd done a couple. I guess he assumed that I was the guy to do this. Maybe he thought, because of *Toys in the Attic* or something else that I had done, that I could bring something to this part. They didn't want just a comic. It doesn't work that way. It's got a lot more to it. And of course, the great thing about it was the great writing of Herb Gardner. I think it is the best play he's written. It's really a wonderful play.

Interviewer: It was a wonderful performance. Do you ever think that maybe Murray Burns is sort of a comic flip side of some O'Neill characters?

Robards: You know who said that? Jules Feiffer said Herb is our flip side of O'Neill. That's interesting, isn't it? I never thought of that. Now you brought that up, and now I remember what Jules said. I did mostly serious roles for two years; and when you get a comedy part, or if you think it's a comedy part, you say, "Oh, this is not for me." But you get a laugh and it's like a racehorse, you just take off—and there it goes. You try to get a laugh on everything, and the whole play goes down with it. After two weeks, Fred said, "Come over to the office at noon tomorrow. I want to talk to you." I went over to the office. Herbie Gardner was there, and they laid me out about this very thing of going for the laughs and wrecking the real story. That play is really about this young boy and his uncle, and the love of the girl, and the idea of trying to form a life in that day and age, which, as you know, was the sixties. Of course, I was angry as hell. I went to the theater that night and I told Sandy Dennis, "You're not going to see the wonderful performance. I'm going to play this serious tonight." She said, "Oh, the hell with them; play it the way you want." But I didn't, I listened to them.

Interviewer: And it was gangbusters.

Robards: And it went—yeah!

Interviewer: After all the towering O'Neill roles, do you really think, like so many people say, that comedy is harder?

Robards: Yes. Well, it's really not comedy. Comedy is just a flip side to drama. It's got to be believable and real, and it's not all gags. Any time you create a character it's difficult to get those things—whether comedic or dramatic—that are flat on that page.

Interviewer: So you don't have one slot for drama, one for comedy. You're doing work.

Robards: No. Take it out of there, make it behave in a way that is understandable to the audience that's in there. It's a question of make-believe. Acting is make-believe. Otherwise, we would have a new Desdemona every night. It's make-believe, and the better we make-believe, the better the audience makes-believe. They know they're out there; they hear the sirens going or the guy who coughs in the audience. Yet they make-believe, they pull, they stay with us. That's what it's about. We get so much "real" here nowadays. You see too many killings, too many love affairs, doing the actual union of things. I don't understand that. I think it takes away from the intellect, the creativity, the romantic.

Interviewer: In Washington, during the first year of the Kennedy Center, you did *The Country Girl,* with Maureen Stapleton and George Grizzard. Tell us a little about that production. What comes to mind?

Robards: John Houseman called and said he wanted me to do Frank Elgin in *The Country Girl,* the drunk actor who tries to get back into combat. I had done Ralph, the dresser, in a production with Sidney Blackmer and Judith Evelyn, with Steve Hill playing his old part—on the subway circuit in New York. We played it traveling around.

Interviewer: What was the subway circuit?

Robards: It was all the theaters in the boroughs: the Bronx, Brighton Beach, Brooklyn, Queens. It was a different city then.

Interviewer: You didn't have to go into Manhattan, did you?

Robards: No, but it was a great thing in the summers. I always watched Sidney Blackmer, who was playing Frank Elgin. Old Sidney was all right at this thing. He had a lot of ham in him and yet he had a lot of truth in him, and I liked that combination. So when John called, I said, "Fine"; but the thing I remember about our first rehearsal was we got everybody together and he said, "You're all absolutely marvelous. You don't need any directing. Just go ahead and do the play." So we did; he got up and moved us around and that was about it. Anytime anything went wrong, he'd say, "That's no good; go back to the original, go back to the original." But John was a wonderful producer. He really did a job on the Eisenhower Theatre at the Kennedy Center—great lighting, great sets; all that was terrific.

Interviewer: Then, a few years later, in a production of *Long Day's Journey into Night,* there was a director named Robards.

Robards: Oh, well, that was a mistake.

Interviewer: You did say of that production, "I muffed it up." What did you mean by that?

Robards: Roger Stevens, my dear old friend, in the Bicentennial year, 1976, had promised this production to the University of Michigan, to the Kennedy Center, and to the Brooklyn Academy of Music. Those were the three dates.

We were going to have José direct, and I was going to play the old man for the first time. I'd played one of the sons, and I was going to play the old man. José couldn't make it, and Roger and I were talking and I said, "Well, I'll take care of this. I know the play. At least I'll get them up and move them around"—and I did. But I hadn't cast it right, and I really messed it up. I did not cast well at all. Another problem was that it's a family. There's a lot of love in it, and we didn't have that in this cast, except maybe Zoe Caldwell and I. The other thing was that I found I could get it up and move it around, but I could not go out front once we began performing and be the sounding board that was needed. I was standing on the stage.

Interviewer: Your eyes needed to be out there.

Robards: Yes, they did. George C. Scott can do it; he's incredible and he can do that. Larry Olivier did it in *Henry V,* but on the screen—so it's a little different. It's very difficult for somebody playing the father in the play not to be out front. Fortunately we got José in for a week; he flew up from the islands and came in for just a week. Then we got Harold Clurman, which was the best thing that ever happened. It really leveled us out.

Interviewer: Do you want to get back to directing? Does that interest you?

Robards: No, I found I'm not a good director. I want to act out all the parts. You can't do that. If I could get rid of this acting, then I'd be all right.

Interviewer: We don't want you to get rid of that acting! How do you choose a role? What is it that you have to find when you read a script?

Robards: I was thinking of the last one I did, which you very kindly helped us with in Baltimore, *Park Your Car in Harvard Yard* by Israel Horovitz.

Interviewer: Not enough, obviously.

Robards: No, I think we made a big jump when you and Dick Coe came in. This is what theater should be about: we all help one another in these ways so we can do something that the audience enjoys. Actually, we got four months out of that, in a show that I thought might go down in very short order. What attracted me to it was Judith Ivey. I liked the play in a way, and yet I knew something was wrong with it; but how many parts do you get anyway, anymore? At my age, there's only one part left, Lear. Otherwise you play bits, small guys. But the idea of working with Judy and with Bob Whitehead, and Bob wanted to do it. Bob had worked on the play when it was first done in New York with Buzz [Burgess] Meredith and Ellen Burstyn. It was done in an off-Broadway house. He had taken for granted a lot of the stuff and put it together in a different way and worked with the playwright, Israel Horovitz, on it. By the way, in the whole process of working on that play, we never did the same script for more than two days before Israel changed it again or Zoe Caldwell, who directed it, changed it or somebody did something to it. Four days before we opened the play, we did four performances of the same play in New York, in the previews.

Interviewer: It must have felt like a luxury.

Robards: Oh boy! And you have a paying audience; that's the thing. If you go out and do a bad job for a paying audience, that's not good. We wanted to give them our best. We didn't want to be stumbling around in stuff that's been thrown in because of a whim. Israel had many whims.

Interviewer: You mentioned the *L* word.

Robards: Love?

Interviewer: No, Lear.

Robards: Oh, Lear.

Interviewer: In preparing for tonight, I went over ten years of interviews with Jason Robards, and in each one he said, "I'm going to do Lear. I'm just a couple of years away. I'm almost ready for it now."

Robards: I've got to get either Anthony Page or Michael Langham to do it. That's my move now.

Interviewer: So the deal is, if you could get Michael Langham to direct it, you'd do it?

Robards: Yes, I would.

Interviewer: We're going to get this down and hold you to that.

Robards: Michael and I did Hotspur in *Henry IV, Part 1,* and I loved playing for him. And I love Anthony Page. I've always wanted to do it, ever since I played FDR for him.

Interviewer: What appeals to you about the role of Lear, and why do you think you can play him?

Robards: You know what appeals to me about it? It's the last leading part a man my age can do. That's it. I mean, I don't know anything about him, if you want to know the truth. Once I take the play and start sitting and talking a little bit, maybe to the director, or think about it a little more, I might be able to give a more in-depth answer, an intelligent answer. I'd like to see if I can make it through without dropping dead of a heart attack. You have to have so much breath for it. Paul Scofield once told me, "Jason, you've got to do this before you're forty. It's such hard work." He was about thirty-eight. I was going to do it once and we were casting for a small Cordelia. I understand that they had someone else carrying her on. Who did it recently? He had someone carry her on. Bob Stephens over in London. Robert Stephens just did it over at Stratford in England, and he had someone carrying her on. But that's a tough part.

I don't know, I just want to do it because I think it'll require me to act, require me to think. Quit doing some of these silly pictures that I do in order to stay alive.

Interviewer: You have other roles that you want to get to? Others on a list?

Robards: I don't know anymore what I can pull off. I don't know how I pulled off *Hughie*. The guy's supposed to be fifty and I'm seventy-one. They said it didn't matter. Somebody wrote in a review that nobody even thought of it. Maybe I could pull something off. Maybe in the world of make-believe, you see, we could pull off anything. I could dye my hair, put the juvenile makeup on, lose ten pounds, and I might be able to cut a few rugs. If I could do a musical I would, but I don't know what to do.

Interviewer: There was a little musical bit in *Booth Is Back in Town*.

Robards: There was, and it ended up collapsing on us. My wife and I went on a fund-raising thing through Texas with that play, trying to get money to do it. It fell by the wayside. It was about Junius Brutus Booth going on the road with his son Edwin, who was seventeen at the time. It was about their life, the family life, and the touring, and a disaster that occurred. Back in those mining days, they played a lot of mining camps too. But with the music and the play, I don't know why it never worked. It had a lot of wonderful stuff. It was eventually done; Frank Langella did it as a straight play with Austin Pendleton, up in Williamstown; but that's the last I heard of it. I thought it could have been a wonderful thing. It never had a director.

Interviewer: Doing a movie like *The Night They Raided Minsky's* with singing, did that make you want to do a full-fledged musical?

Robards: No. In high school there was a guy and I who used to play instruments together. We put on a show one night for Father and Son Night at the Boys' Club. He wrote some stuff and we sang. We played guitar and something good happened. I thought, "Gee, I could really get in a musical and sing my head off." That was it. At that point, I never even thought about going into plays.

Interviewer: At one point, you were supposed to be writing a book about your work on the plays of O'Neill. Did that get abandoned?

Robards: There's still plenty I could say, maybe twenty-five or thirty thousand words. I would start the book with rehearsals of *Iceman* and through that go into my personal life at the time, then go into *Long Day's Journey* and go into my childhood, parallel with the plays. Then *Moon for the Misbegotten* when I'd been drinking and how that almost killed me, how Jamie chose death and I didn't. I found I was writing a psychiatric tome and nobody but out-of-work actors and psychiatrists would buy it. However, I found out there were more of those than I knew! But I shied away from it.

Interviewer: What's the next time we'll see you onstage?

Robards: Christopher Plummer and I are going to appear in a revival slated to run at the Roundabout in New York, Harold Pinter's *No Man's Land*. We don't know what it's about; we'd be happy to have anyone tell us. But we're very excited. The author is coming for the first week of rehearsals, and he himself has played it in London the past season—and he doesn't know what it's about. And if he did, he wouldn't tell anyone. Ralph Richardson played it in New York and they asked him, "What is it? What do you do? What is this play?" And he said, "I have a secret life which I live in the nights and I'm not telling you what it is." He hadn't the vaguest idea what it was about! I asked Nigel Hawthorne and he said, "I don't know what it's about. Play everything for the moment as if it were completely real. That's the only thing I can tell you."

Interviewer: So your doing it is about getting up onstage with Chris Plummer?

Robards: Oh, that's great. Yes, I think that's one of the real reasons I'm doing it, to work with Chris again. I first worked with Chris when he came down from Canada and we did a number of live shows on television. The last one we did was *A Doll's House* with Julie Harris. Then I was the first American to work in the Stratford company, Stratford, Ontario, and we were friends; but we have never worked together since. I've always wanted to.

Interviewer: Talk a little bit more about your inner feelings concerning O'Neill and playing in his plays—and about alcoholism and the Irish.

Robards: Well, oddly enough for some reason, for me O'Neill is like a road map that I really understand—where those highways are going and those side streets that you read in the script. Once I had great doubts in one of his plays, in *Moon for the Misbegotten*. I said to José, "You know something, this is a Freudian soap opera; everybody knows it." I was wrong. Once it was on its feet, it began to behave; we began to behave in the play, and it was entirely different. I've done the later plays mostly. *Iceman's* very clear. *Long Day's Journey's* terribly clear to me—exactly where it's going, where the breaks are, almost to the point of where the breaths are. Transitions stand out, and O'Neill's very helpful. I found his stage directions are almost as important, if not as important, as the dialogue. People say, "Cross them out. He's just talking too much." I don't believe that. I think the more you look at them, the better.

The thing about alcoholism is that I was playing alcoholics. Years ago, I did the Scott Fitzgerald thing, *The Disenchanted*, and I did Jamie. I never thought I had any problem with it, because I wasn't pissed onstage or any of that stuff. Except once, but that was the end. If you do that, then you're finished. It was only later, in fact during *Moon for the Misbegotten*, when I had a choice of ending my career or living and I chose to live. I found that a very important step. As a matter of fact, the alcoholic behavior became clearer in the later plays. When I did *A Touch of the Poet,* it seemed to be getting simpler, understanding everything.

Interviewer: The teetotaler could play an alcoholic better.

Robards: Yes. Freddie March used to say to me, "If you need a drink, I've got a bottle hidden in the dressing room. You take a shot before you come on." I only did that a couple of times. The British seem to be able to do it all the time. You go into a British dressing room and they have it there between acts. "Have a little Naval Mixture," Ralph Richardson used to tell me when we were doing *Long Day's Journey.* We were both in the navy; grog was something the British served in the morning. So we'd be shooting—and "Time for a little Naval Mixture": rum and water straight down. You see, they're able to do that. Somehow we have this Calvinistic guilt in this country. You can't drink. They bar even beer in the commissary at Warner Brothers. Taboos sometimes hurt us more. I'm part Irish. I'm Irish, Welsh, Swedish, English, so I don't know where the Irish gets in. It does get in. I'm married to a fabulous lady whose name is O'Connor, so that helps very much. While some of the parts are Irish, O'Neill and Fitzgerald, there are others that one plays that aren't Irish parts.

Interviewer: Do you have trouble distancing yourself from O'Neill? He's such a distressing person to spend time with. With his characters, can you simply take off the makeup and go home, or does it stay with you?

Robards: When I played Hickey in the 1956 *Iceman,* I really was terrified. We'd hang out afterwards; we were all denizens of the bar. We'd done the play in the Village, we all lived in the Village. We went down to the docks and we drank beer on into the night, or four in the morning. Or we'd hang out at Julius's. Peter Falk was in that play; he was a bartender and he tried to get behind the bar at Julius's. We played football in the street; we always hung out. It was hard to lose, hard to lose. I then got into Jamie in *Long Day's Journey.* Fredric March was pretty much like my father, his contemporary; they looked very much alike when they were young. Florence Eldridge was my mother, and we were almost a family. I was drinking, not drinking onstage, but I kept on, not being the guy who went to the whorehouses and all that, but I couldn't get rid of the character for a while after the show. I'd go over to Dinty Moore's, go over to the Palace, and hang out and then finally go home to sleep at three or four in the morning. It really affected me—two years of it, that is—not all the time, but sometimes it really got to me. It's partly my own bad behavior, but it's also living that every night, trying to peel that onion every night. When I played *Hughie* the first time in the 1960s, I was staying at all those terrible hotels—like he did. I used to stay in a hotel in New York called the Van Rensselaer Hotel. It was on 11th Street and University Place, and they always would put me up there. I'd go into that room—it had steel doors on it, and when you checked in at three or four in the morning, you'd sit down on the bed and the door would clang shut like a jail cell! My father said to me,

"You know, that hotel," he said, "I've been down there. The next thing you know Pat O'Brien is going to come in and give you the last rites"—in reference to a James Cagney picture [*Angels with Dirty Faces*].

Interviewer: Other than staying in better hotels, how did you learn to divorce yourself from the character when you were offstage?

Robards: Well, I somehow had to keep on making a living and having children and trying to see to them. I think you have to eventually grow up. It was very difficult, very difficult. It wasn't until I was in my fifties that I was able to grow up.

Interviewer: When you were playing *A Thousand Clowns*, did you go off to the docks?

Robards: No, I did not. But they worried about me. In fact, I've never missed a performance in my life, and that's the proof, as James Tyrone says in *Long Day's Journey*. We had a very big camaraderie in New York. We'd all hang out at Downey's or Frankie and Johnny's—Bob Preston, Chris Plummer, anybody who was in town. For the acting community, our day began at four in the afternoon when we got ready to go to the theater. Our cocktail/dinner hour was one in the morning. The restaurants stayed open and we'd go back after the show, and then we'd go to bed at four or five in the morning and sleep the next day. It was sort of an endless summer, shall we say. But there were a lot of wonderful actors and wonderful friends. Nowadays actors won't tell other actors where to look for a job. Then, everybody was telling you: "Listen, I didn't get this thing. Run down there; Josh Logan's casting, maybe you'll get it," or Jimmy Greene would say, "Go down to see José, he's doing casting." Nobody does that anymore, everybody's against one another.

Interviewer: More cutthroat?

Robards: Much more cutthroat. I had some friends, Walter Matthau and James Karen, who had a stenciled sheet of job opportunities in the theater and sold it for twenty-five cents to broke actors. Unbelievable. I was in the fifty-two/twenty club, which means you get twenty dollars a week for fifty-two weeks. To spend twenty-five cents meant a lot to me. I bought this thing; it later became *Actor's Cue,* a paper you look in to see who's casting. They put jobs in there. I went down for "Wanted: Man for this part"; it was in a lumber warehouse. And the guy is angry as hell. He says, "There's 300 people who've come down here! What the hell is going on here?" And Walter and Jimmy got the job! They sold that sheet to Lucille Lortel, and she made *Actor's Cue* out of it.

Interviewer: It's worth mentioning that it is in some of your comedy roles that you have most moved audiences—for example, in *Parenthood,* where you played Tom Hulce's father.

Robards: It was a comedy, in a way. Steve Martin played the other son, and that had more comedic elements in it, I think. The father was a grump, but here's what happens when actors help a role—as we were talking about. Tom Hulce is great. He and I had just finished a picture together before that, and we were so happy to be working together again. Ron Howard said, "I thought these scenes were going to be harder; I've been doing them all in one or two takes. Something's wrong. I don't know how I'm going to do it any better—with you and Tom." It's just something inside; we knew it worked for us. It's very funny how those things happen.

Interviewer: Because of your pessimistic comments about the unhappy state of the Broadway theater, I wonder if you saw *Angels in America* and how you felt about it. Did you feel it was a ray of hope?

Robards: A ray of hope? No, not at all. I've heard all the jokes and seen all that stuff for forty years. Listen, I did the first homosexual play ever done in New York, *Big Fish, Little Fish,* and it had a lot more to say about relationships and understanding. I did a film called *Philadelphia* which has much more to say than *Angels in America.*

Interviewer: What's the last thing that you saw on the stage that you liked a lot?

Robards: *The Madness of King George.* I saw it in London, and when it got here we saw it right away when it was in Stanford. Nigel [Hawthorne] said it's cut down a bit from London, but I just thought it was overwhelming. I loved that. It was beautiful.

Interviewer: Do you ever get involved in the playwriting process when you create a role?

Robards: Well, I've been working with dead playwrights so long. I think a little bit with Israel Horovitz. I didn't really tell him. I can't write. With playwrights that have been around, I don't get in the process, no. Things may change, but we usually leave it in the hands of the director, who is sort of representing you and the playwright and the producer. We can say things, and they may take them to heart, but really it's up to the people out there to choose, in a way, what the play has to say and to make us understand it.

Interviewer: You hear about it more in film. On a set does one often say, "I don't think the character would say this, I think I'll say it this way"?

Robards: A lot of bad actors do it that way, but I don't listen to them. I try not to. When you get a film that is a vehicle for somebody, that's when you find this happening more. They order people around on films: "I don't do this, I don't do that. Why have you got this here? I'm not coming on the set until you get rid of it." Everybody else stands around. Now, that's different. I don't know about that. I've been very lucky in doing work with good people and rehearsing well.

Interviewer: Could you share some comments on the 1983 revival of *You Can't Take It with You,* where you played Grandpa Vanderhof? Tell us a little about putting that together.

Robards: Ellis Rabb, who's a wonderful director and friend, called up and said, "Look, we've got four weeks out at the Paper Mill Playhouse in Jersey. Have you got four weeks to do *You Can't Take It with You?* We'll just get a lot of friends together and do it." I said, "Sure, I'd love to do it." He said, "Let's get Liz Wilson." We got Colleen [Dewhurst]; she wanted to come in. We had a wonderful time. It was sort of a labor of love. We did the thing at the Paper Mill, and Kitty Hart and Anne Kaufman, the daughter of George Kaufman and the wife of Moss Hart, came backstage and said, "Look, if you'll continue, we can go down to Washington with this." I said, "Well, I don't want to put you people out of a job and I need one myself, so let's go to Washington." So we did. Then they said, "Let's go to New York. We can get in up there." So we went into the Plymouth. We stayed together as a labor of love; it was a lot of people who cared a lot. Ellis was wonderful, just terrific in the direction of that play. He had us do a very interesting thing. Once we learned our lines, he said, "Now let's all go as fast as we can. Don't even let the person finish a sentence." We ran the whole play in about thirty-five minutes. He said, "Now that's what I want. That's the pace this has to play at." It was not it exactly, but by taking us way over to the other side of it, we then played it and played it, whoosh.

Interviewer: You would think that what the director would be concentrating on was the humanity of the characters.

Robards: That was the casting. We were all old friends who loved one another. That was what it was. Everyone, even down to the guy who said, "I'm afraid I'm going to have to sell you, Bossie."

Maureen Stapleton

Maureen Stapleton was born Lois Maureen Stapleton in Troy, New York, on June 21, 1925. She attended Siena College and trained for the stage with Herbert Berghof. She made her stage debut as Sarah Tansey in The Playboy of the Western World *in 1945. Her other stage roles include Isis,* Antony and Cleopatra *(1947); Miss Hatch,* Detective Story *(1949); Emily Williams,* The Bird Cage *(1950); Serafina,* The Rose Tattoo *(1951; Tony Award); Elisabeth Proctor,* The Crucible *(1953); Bella,* The Emperor's Clothes *(1953); Anne,* Richard III *(1953); Masha,* The Seagull *(1954); Flora,* 27 Wagons Full of Cotton *(1955); Lady Torrence,* Orpheus Descending *(1957); Aunt Ida,* The Cold Wind and the Warm *(1958); Carrie,* Toys in the Attic *(1960); Amanda Wingfield,* The Glass Menagerie *(1965); Karen Nash, Muriel Tate, Norma Hubley,* Plaza Suite *(1968); Beatrice Chambers,* Norman, Is That You? *(1970); Evy Meara,* The Gingerbread Lady *(1970; Tony Award); Georgie Elgin,* The Country Girl *(1972); title role,* The Secret Affairs of Mildred Wild *(1972);*

Juno Boyle, Juno and the Paycock *(1974); Fonsia Dorsey,* The Gin Game *(1978); and Birdie Hubbard,* The Little Foxes *(1981; Tony Award).*

Her films include Lonelyhearts *(1959),* The Fugitive Kind *(1959),* Vu du pont *(1961),* Bye Bye Birdie *(1963),* Airport *(1970),* Plaza Suite *(1971),* Summer of '42 *(1971),* Interiors *(1978),* Lost and Found *(1979),* The Runner Stumbles *(1979),* Reds *(1981; Academy Award),* On the Right Track *(1981),* Montgomery Clift *(1983),* Cocoon *(1985),* The Cosmic Eye *(1985),* Heartburn *(1986),* The Money Pit *(1986),* Made in Heaven *(1987),* Nuts *(1987),* Sweet Lorraine *(1987),* Cocoon: The Return *(1988),* Doin' Time on Planet Earth *(1988),* Liberace: Behind the Music *(1988),* Passed Away *(1992),* The Last Good Time *(1994),* Trading Mom *(1994),* Addicted to Love *(1997), and* Wilbur Falls *(1998).*

For television, she has been in What Happened? *(1952),* Track of Fears *(1955),* No License to Kill *(1957),* All the King's Men *(1958),* For Whom the Bell Tolls *(1959),* Riders to the Sea *(1960),* The Betrayal *(1962),* One Drink at a Time *(1964),* Save Me a Place at Forest Lawn *(1966; Emmy Award),* Among the Paths to Eden *(1968; Emmy Award),* Mirror, Mirror, off the Wall *(1969),* Tell Me Where It Hurts *(1974),* Queen of the Stardust Ballroom *(1975),* Cat on a Hot Tin Roof *(1976),* The Gathering *(1977),* Arthur Miller on Home Ground *(1979),* The Gathering, Part II *(1979),* Letters from Frank *(1979),* The Fan *(1981),* Electric Grandmother *(1981),* Little Gloria . . . Happy at Last *(1982),* Alice in Wonderland *(1983),* Johnny Dangerously *(1984),* Family Secrets *(1984),* Sentimental Journey *(1984),* Private Sessions *(1985),* The Thorns *(1988),* Auntie Sue *(1989; Emmy Award),* Lincoln *(1992),* Miss Rose White *(1992),* Last Wish *(1992), and episodes of* Road to Avonlea, The Equalizer, B. L. Stryker, Naked City, *and* Car 54, Where Are You?, *as well as* Alcoa Hour, Philco Television Playhouse, *and* Goodyear Television Playhouse.

She was elected to the Theater Hall of Fame in 1980.

This interview took place on July 13, 1995.

●────────────────────────────────────●

Interviewer: It would be interesting, just to get us started, to talk about how you developed an interest in theater. You grew up in Troy, New York, and the sources that I've read indicate that your family was not particularly interested in theater—or were they?

Stapleton: No, no, they weren't. I just went to the movies all the time. That's what I was crazy about, movies. I don't go at all anymore—I look at the old ones—but anyway, that's what started me, really, was wanting to be in the movies. Everything I read and everything I heard said that the best thing to do would be to study acting and go to New York and try to get on the stage.

Interviewer: Not as an end in itself but as a means of getting into movies?

Stapleton: Yes, so I went to New York, went to school, did all those things like everybody else, and made the rounds.

Interviewer: But your ultimate aim was to be in the movies when you first came to New York?

Stapleton: Yes, I think that was really it.

Interviewer: When did that change?

Stapleton: It never really changed; it just happened.

Interviewer: Now, when you first came to New York, you studied with Herbert Berghof, didn't you?

Stapleton: Yes. I studied very briefly with someone named Frances Robinson Duff, but that was very brief; and then somebody told me about the New School and Herbert Berghof, and I went there. Later he opened his own school and hired Mira Rostova, a wonderful teacher. And then I worked at Herbert's school for a while—as his secretary.

Interviewer: How did you go from Berghof to the Actors Studio?

Stapleton: Well, there was quite a while in between. I went at night to the New School because I had to work in the day. During the summer of 1945, Herbert got a lot of his students from both the Neighborhood Playhouse and the New School (he also taught at the Neighborhood Playhouse, I think, which was Sandy Meisner's domain)—we each put in $150—and had a stock compay. We were not Equity; we all chipped in, and we put on plays in Blauvelt, New York. Then, when I came back, I still went to school, made the rounds, did all those things everybody else does, and finally I got a job.

Interviewer: Is that when you did the Guthrie McClintic show?

Stapleton: Yes, Guthrie gave me my first three jobs actually. What was the first one? Oh yes, yes, *The Playboy of the Western World*! I'm not sure; I think that was 1946. And then *Antony and Cleopatra* with Miss Cornell and her last tour of *The Barretts of Wimpole Street*.

Interviewer: What sort of a director was McClintic?

Stapleton: I adored him, I just adored him. Anybody who would give you your first three jobs you're going to adore!

Interviewer: Was he a good director for a beginning person like yourself? Did you learn a lot from him?

Stapleton: Well, they had a way, Mr. and Mrs. McClintic; you learned without knowing you were learning. You learned backstage manners. You never talked backstage while other actors were doing their job. I understudied in both *Playboy* and *Antony and Cleopatra;* he would have on the board when you were to come in for rehearsals. You didn't just come and stay all day. I've never seen it done this way since either. If you were going to have understudy rehearsals, you were due at, let's say, 1:30 to 3:30 or whatever it was. Your time was specified.

Interviewer: He was very well organized. In other words, you never just sat around when you were there. You were working, and when he was finished with you you would leave.

Stapleton: Yes.

Interviewer: What was it like working with Katharine Cornell?

Stapleton: I adored her, I adored her. She was a lovely lady in every way; she was tremendously gracious to everybody. She was terrific.

Interviewer: How did your association with the Actors Studio come about?

Stapleton: Some friends of mine, Monty Clift and Kevin McCarthy, were friends of Bobby Lewis, who was starting the Actors Studio with Elia Kazan in 1947. Actually I belonged in the beginners' class because I hadn't done that much, but these friends of mine recommended me to Bobby Lewis, who ran the advanced class. That was a great time, the first two years.

Interviewer: When you look at the list of the people who were in that class with you, it was just an incredible group, wasn't it?

Stapleton: Yes, yes!

Interviewer: Were you aware when you were part of that group of how talented those people were?

Stapleton: Oh yes. I had seen a lot of them already. I had seen their work in the theater, and I knew it didn't come much better than that.

Interviewer: It was Eli Wallach and Anne Jackson . . .

Stapleton: Yes, Eli and Annie, Karl Malden, and Monty Clift. An actress I'm crazy about, Julie Harris, was in Kazan's class. And E. G. Marshall.

Interviewer: Julie Harris was in the beginning class! And then Marilyn Monroe was at the Actors Studio, too, wasn't she?

Stapleton: That was much, much, later, in the fifties.

Interviewer: Was that Actors Studio experience how you got involved with Williams and with *The Rose Tattoo*?

Stapleton: Yes, because Cheryl Crawford, who was the producer of *The Rose Tattoo,* was one of the starters of the Actors Studio. She wasn't a teacher, Cheryl, she ran things, and she was going to produce *The Rose Tattoo* by Tennessee Willliams. I guess they read everybody in the world. I think Eli and I read about fifteen times for it; you felt by the time you got the job like you had already been playing it for two weeks! I remember that, after about the twelfth reading, Eli was cursing and saying, "I'm not going to do this again. Why don't they make up their minds?" I said, "Eli, we'll read again and you'll read again. Just simmer down." It was driving him crazy!

Interviewer: And you always read with him? In other words, they were already considering the two of you together to see how you worked?

Stapleton: Yes, we read together.

Interviewer: By then you knew each other pretty well. Do you think that contributed to the success of casting you two together?

Stapleton: No, you can be immediately at home with another actor that you may not know at all when you start to work.

Interviewer: Is the opposite true, too, that someone you may know very well you may have difficulty with onstage?

Stapleton: I suppose that could be.

Interviewer: You've acted many, many times now with Eli Wallach. Do you feel particularly comfortable with him?

Stapleton: Yes, because when you're working with a good actor half your work is done for you. You just look at them and they are there.

Interviewer: Is that when you first met Tennessee Williams, when you got involved in *The Rose Tattoo*?

Stapleton: Yes, that was the first time I met Tenn.

Interviewer: Over the years, you became very close, didn't you?

Stapleton: Oh yes, yes.

Interviewer: Would you say he was an actor's playwright?

Stapleton: Oh my lord, yes. He just gives you so much. It's just that there's so much. I don't know how to describe it. It's difficult for me to say it in words, but you have a plateful.

Interviewer: Did he participate pretty fully in the rehearsal process?

Stapleton: Oh, he was always there; but most playwrights discuss with the director what they feel is wrong or right or how they want it to go. They don't come to the actors. The actors deal with the director.

Interviewer: Did you feel that Williams was very sympathetic to the actors during rehearsal?

Stapleton: Oh yes. But once he and his friend whom I adored, Frank Merlo, went to Europe while *Tattoo* was running. They were gone a couple of months, and while they were gone during the run I found this moment that I thought was so great—a tiny little thing. I just loved it. There's a scene where Serafina blows out the candle in front of the Virgin, in front of the vigil light, on the prie-dieu. Immediately after I blew it out, before I ran out the door, I grabbed the statue and kissed it. I had first blown it out in a rage and I ran out of that place. It was one of those things where actors sometimes would come back and mention that particular moment. When Tenn and Frank came back, they were coming to see the play and we were going out afterwards to get something to eat; they came back and it was all very happy. I kept waiting for Tennessee to say something, and as we're going out of the door of the dressing room, he said, "Oh, Maureen, what are you doin' slobberin' all over the Virgin?" And I said, "Slobbering all over the Virgin? Tenn, I thought . . ." He said, "No, no, no, honey. Blow out the candle and get out of there; she wouldn't do that." So there went my one great moment that I'd thought I found!

Interviewer: What was it like working with Harold Clurman?

Stapleton: I loved Harold, of course. He was like all good directors. They steer you right, they keep you on course, they give you room.

Interviewer: You've also done two of Neil Simon's comedies, haven't you?

Stapleton: *The Gingerbread Lady* wasn't a comedy; it had a lot of funny stuff in it, but it was a serious play.

Interviewer: What about *Plaza Suite*? Neil Simon has said that the problem with *Plaza Suite* was that when he and Mike Nichols first did it, they had to take the laughs out of it because there were so many laughs in it that people weren't stopping to hear the serious part. What was working with Mike Nichols like?

Stapleton: Pure heaven! There's a story about *Plaza Suite*. We'd been running about four months or something, and there was one laugh that was huge. It was built in, it was solid, it was there all the time, and one night I didn't get it. Gone! I was stunned. George C. Scott, who was the leading man, and I tried everything. He tried helping me; I tried every which way, but I couldn't get it back. So I called Mike Nichols, our director, and I said, "Mike, I don't know what to do. I've tried everything. I lost the laugh on whatever the line was that's surefire, and I can't get it back. Would you please come and watch and tell me what to do?" So Mike did; he came back after the first act, or whatever act, I think it was the first act. He said, "Take the second half of the sentence an octave lower." Okay, that sounds very technical, which it was. The next night I took the last half of the sentence an octave lower, and back came the laugh like gangbusters. George winked, we went on, and I still don't know why I lost it or how it came back, but it did.

Interviewer: I just want to throw out a couple of other names and see what your response to them might be. What about working with Jason Robards?

Stapleton: Oh, of course. That's what I'm saying. I've been so lucky in the other actors and actresses. Half your work is done. Just look at them and they're it!

Interviewer: Without using a name, what is the difference between working with Jason or George or someone like that and someone who isn't as good as they are? What happens to you as an actress when you get out onstage with somebody like that?

Stapleton: You're not as good. You're not as good as when you're playing with them. I don't know why. I don't know why offhand.

Interviewer: Is it that you feel very secure with someone like Jason or Eli? You're in good hands.

Stapleton: Yes.

Interviewer: Is that story about you and Marilyn Monroe at the Actors Studio true, that you did a scene together from *Anna Christie*?

Stapleton: Yes, we did.

Interviewer: Was she good?

Stapleton: Oh God, yes, she was terrific! We started out doing something else. Lee Strasberg had us doing something from Noël Coward. Now, I loved Noël Coward. I loved to watch Noël Coward; I loved him, and I love his work; but I can't do it. There is some technique or something you have to have that I didn't have. We rehearsed it a few times and finally I said to Marilyn, "I can't do this; let me find something else for us." So I picked *Anna Christie*, and the first time we read it I thought she was terrific. I said, "There, don't you feel better? Isn't that great?" She said, "I don't feel any different." I said, "You must, it's so terrific." Anyway, we just kept rehearsing *Anna Christie*, and she was worried about remembering the lines. She knew them, so the night before we were going to do it I said, "You know, lots of times at the Studio people who are worried about the lines put the script on the table and have it there; and if you have to refer to it, it's there." She said, "If I do that now, I'll do that forever, and I don't want to." I said, "Okay, but sometimes when I'm having a hard time learning a part I write it out in longhand, write my part out, and something about it helps me remember, if I'm having trouble with the learning." Well, we finally did it. We rehearsed a long time, too, but she was quite wonderful in it, knocked everybody's socks off, and I was so proud.

Interviewer: Do you think she would have been a good stage actress?

Stapleton:　If she had wanted to, oh yes. She was terrific.

Interviewer:　But wasn't that one of the few times she ever did a scene at the Studio? Didn't she mainly come as a spectator and just sit and watch?

Stapleton:　Yes.

Interviewer:　Who from your early years or later on were the biggest influences on your career? Was there anybody that really made a difference when you were coming along?

Stapleton:　I don't think so. Like everybody else, it was just people that I loved to see and still do love to see. I'd go anywhere to see Julie Harris and Colleen Dewhurst and Zoe Caldwell. I love watching them. Julie always wipes me out, and Colleen did too—and Zoe. I don't know; I just love watching them. I love to watch Kim Stanley.

Interviewer:　What was Kim Stanley like as a director? You did *Waiting for Godot* with her, didn't you? That must have been something!

Stapleton:　I didn't know what the hell it was about when I originally saw it with Tom Ewell and Bert Lahr. Kim called me; she was in New Mexico at the College of Santa Fe. She said, "Maureen, would you come down and do a play with my students which I'll direct?" I said, "Kim, I'll do anything you want," and she said, "I want to do *Waiting for Godot.*" I said, "Kim, could we go back to where you said, 'Would I come down to . . . ?' " I truly never got it, but we did it! I said, "I saw it, I don't understand it, I've never understood Beckett, I don't connect." She said, "I understand it." I said "Okay, lady, Okay."

Interviewer:　What was she like as a director?

Stapleton:　Oh, she's terrific!

Interviewer:　Now, this is the kind of question that you might have great difficulty with; it's the hardest kind of question for an artist to talk about. How do you prepare to do a role? When you read a play and you decide you're going to do it, what do you do?

Stapleton:　What you have is the script, and you just read it over and over and over again. I don't know how to say it, but if there's outside research that you have to do you do that separately. Certain accents, like a French accent, I would have to practice with somebody who could teach me how to do a French accent—or a British accent, which I don't come to easily. You'd have to do that work separately till you had an accent that was proper.

Interviewer:　What about when you did Emma Goldman? Did you do a lot of research on Emma Goldman?

Stapleton: Oh lord, yes. I read her autobiography; it was two huge tomes. All those people at that time were Communists or anarchists, I forget, all kinds of isms. They all thought that their anarchism was better than Communism, but when it came to a war they were all united. Remember that story about how Emma Goldman's beau went to Pittsburgh and shot at, was it Andrew Carnegie?

Interviewer: Her beau's name was Alexander Berkman.

Stapleton: Yes, he shot him four times or stabbed him twice or something; and the guy lived. Was it Carnegie?

Interviewer: I think it was Henry Clay Frick.

Stapleton: This guy that did it was put in jail for fourteen years, and when he came out he wrote a book about his life in the American prisons. Emma Goldman, who was a friend of Jack London's, sent it to Jack London to write the foreword for the book. At the end he compliments the book in print and then he says there are certain things he didn't agree with and how the anarchists were not good people. He said they had all these flaws, and he said any guy that can't think straight can't shoot straight. Goldman was so enraged she never used his foreword and never spoke to him again! But one thing about those anarchists or Communists or whatever they were, they were humorless, absolutely humorless people. After I read the autobiography, I thought that I just wanted to put that out of my mind. All I can do is what's in the script. I wanted to forget everything I read, because you've got to do what's there on the paper, not what you read in books. I just tried to forget what I read about her. At first I thought it would help, but not in that particular case. It might not be true in some other.

Interviewer: Did you have much contact with Lillian Hellman when you were doing *Toys in the Attic* in 1960?

Stapleton: Oh, sure. I had known Lillian before from way back.

Interviewer: What was your sense of her?

Stapleton: I adored her. We had great screaming fights all the time, not serious fights. I'd be at her apartment a lot. I said to her once, "I'm like your token dummy." She'd have the president of Yale and Lenny Bernstein and this one and that one. We had a deal. Once a year, I would take her out to dinner to the restaurant of her choice so she couldn't bitch about anything afterwards. She would pick it; I'd get a limousine and take her to wherever she wanted to go. She had to pick it because I didn't want to hear any bellyaching later about how I took her to this awful place—but I enjoyed it.

Interviewer: What about theater critics? Do you read the critics?

Stapleton: Of course, when I was young. I always read them for years. I remember there were a few actors who said they didn't read their reviews, and
I couldn't conceive of it, when I was young. How could you not? Then, much,
much later on, I stopped reading them. I'd read them later after the play
closed, because if anybody says anything derogatory that's all you remember.
You don't remember any of the good stuff; you only remember something
somebody didn't like about you, and it's very hard to go out night after night
with that ringing in your ear. You can't; I couldn't, anyway.

Interviewer: Did you ever learn anything from a critic?

Stapleton: No, you only listen to the director; you can't listen to anybody
else.

Interviewer: Have you ever had any interest in directing?

Stapleton: No.

Interviewer: Why not?

Stapleton: Well, it's like anything. Either you want to do that and you study
to do that or you don't. Just because you've been around a lot of directors
doesn't make you a director. You can't be a brain surgeon by hanging around
with brain surgeons. You've got to study it separately to do it, but I've never
had any desire to.

Interviewer: Do you think you would have been any good at it?

Stapleton: No, I don't think so. I couldn't teach either. You have to have a
desire to do it, to want to do it, to learn how to do it. I can't teach. I can do
questions and answers, but I couldn't teach.

Interviewer: In connection with the difference between acting onstage and
in films, you have a story about George Seaton directing you in *Airport.*

Stapleton: Oh, well, we were doing the scene at night of the woman running into the airport frantically trying to find her husband, to see if he's there.
When we first shot it, I looked frantically for my husband, and George Seaton
said, "Cut." He came over and he said, "Maureen, this is in Cinemascope,
and when you turn your head that frantically, on camera it looks like you're
crazy almost to the point of comedy. You can't do it that fast." He told me to
look at a face but to take the time to make sure it wasn't my husband. He gave
me a way of doing it that slowed it down.

Interviewer: Do you see any fundamental difference in acting "serious" theater and doing comedy? When you as an actress prepare for a role that you are
aware is comic, is there any difference in the preparation?

Stapleton: I don't think so. I've never found it different yet. You do the same
things. Acting is acting whether it's comedy or tragedy; it's the same process.

Interviewer: Do you find acting difficult?

Stapleton: Oh, I don't know. I've never thought about it. It's hard. In the theater, it's a different discipline. If you have a big part you have to be sure that your energy level is high. It's a new audience every night, and you can't say on Thursday, "Oh, you should have caught me Monday, I was in good shape then."

Interviewer: Do you think as an actor you've been pretty aware of when you had a good night and when you had a bad night?

Stapleton: Not so much. You try to keep it the same.

Interviewer: Is there a role in theater you've not played that you wish you'd played?

Stapleton: No.

Interviewer: You've never said, "That's a role I'd really like to play"?

Stapleton: No, because years ago when I first came to New York and I was in Frances Robinson Duff's class, there was a girl in the class who wanted to play Saint Joan so badly that it was frightening to me. She scared me so I thought, "If that girl doesn't play Saint Joan she'll kill herself." It's hard enough to get a job when you're starting out, but to give yourself the extra added burden of wanting to play Saint Joan, or having to play Saint Joan! I thought, "I don't want to have anything that I've got to do or any part that I've got to get. I'll take what comes." Do you remember Simone Signoret? She was a great girl, wonderful. Anyway, I had known her in New York, and we got to be in each other's company quite a bit. I was in America, and she was here, and she had some friends who wanted to produce *Sweet Bird of Youth.* I had seen Geraldine Page do it. There wasn't anything left to do. If you see a part and it's not well done you think, "Oh, I could do that." But Geraldine Page owned that store, and it was still fresh in people's minds. By the time I did the revival of *The Glass Menagerie,* it was like twenty-five or thirty years after Laurette Taylor; but this was shortly after *Sweet Bird* had closed. So Simone is telling me about her friends, and I said I could never do that, not after just having seen Geraldine, and Simone gave me this lecture about how an actor's an actor and you should do whatever it is and if it's a good part you do it no matter what. She just went on and on, and I said I couldn't do that. Anyway, much, much later we're in New York, we're having lunch or something, and some people came over. I don't speak French, I don't understand French, but I got the picture; it was *Sweet Bird of Youth* again. These men had wanted her to do it in Paris, and she had turned it down. I got that much; so after they left I said, "Did you turn down *Sweet Bird of Youth* in Paris?" And she said, "Yes." I said, "Why? Why did you turn it down?" And she said, "For the same reason you wouldn't do it in London." And I said, "And you gave me that lecture! You SOB! Telling me how I should do the part—you made me feel so guilty." I always loved that.

Interviewer: I've always wondered, with *Reds,* how Warren Beatty integrated the interviews with the real people. Did he shoot those scenes separately from the movie? All those people weren't around the film, were they?

Stapleton: No, he did interviews and didn't use them. I saw four hours of the most marvelous stuff that he never used. He only used little pieces. After I saw the real people talking, I said, "Oh my God, you don't have to do the movie. Just show that." It was just marvelous.

Eli Wallach
and Anne Jackson

Eli Wallach was born in Brooklyn, New York, on December 7, 1915, studied at the University of Texas (B.A.) and the City College of New York (M.Sc.), and trained for the stage at the Neighborhood Playhouse and the Actors Studio. He met his wife, Anne Jackson, in an off-Broadway production of This Property Is Condemned *in 1946. He made his Broadway debut as crew chief in* Skydrift *in 1945. Other Broadway stage roles include* Cromwell, Henry VIII *(1945);* Diomedes, Antony and Cleopatra *(1947);* Stefanowski, Mr. Roberts *(1949);* Alvaro Mangiacavallo, The Rose Tattoo *(1951; Tony Award);* Kilroy, Camino Real *(1953);* Sakini, Teahouse of the August Moon *(1955);* Bill Walker, Major Barbara *(1956);* Willie, The Cold Wind and the Warm *(1958);* Berenger, Rhinoceros *(1961);* Ben, The Tiger, *and* Paul, The Typists *(1963);* Milt Manville, Luv *(1964);* Charles Dyer, Staircase *(1968);* Ollie H. and Wesley, Promenade, All! *(1972);* General St. Pe, The Waltz of the Toreadors *(1973);* Peppino, Saturday, Sunday, Monday *(1974);* Mr. Frank, The Diary of Anne Frank *(1978);*

Alexander, Every Good Boy Deserves Favour *(1979); Leon Rose and Gus Frazier,* Twice Around the Park *(1982); Stephen,* The Nest of the Wood Grouse *(1984); David Cole,* Café Crown *(1988); Noah,* The Flowering Peach *(1994); Mr. Green,* Visiting Mr. Green *(1997); himself,* Tennessee Williams Remembered *(1999); and Sid Garden,* Down the Garden Paths *(2000).*

He made his movie debut in Baby Doll *(1956). Among his other films are* The Lineup *(1958),* The Magnificent Seven *(1960),* Seven Thieves *(1960),* The Misfits *(1961),* Adventures of a Young Man *(1962),* How the West Was Won *(1962),* The Victors (1963), Act One *(1963),* Genghis Khan *(1965),* Lord Jim *(1965),* How to Steal a Million *(1966),* The Good, the Bad, and the Ugly *(1967),* The Tiger Makes Out *(1967),* A Lovely Way to Die *(1968),* MacKenna's Gold *(1969),* The Adventures of Gerard *(1970),* Cinderella Liberty *(1973),* The Deep *(1977),* The Sentinel *(1977),* Movie Movie *(1978),* Winter Kills *(1979),* The Hunter *(1980),* Nuts *(1987),* Tough Guys *(1988),* The Godfather, Part III *(1990),* The Two Jakes *(1990),* Night and the City *(1992),* Mistress *(1992),* Article 99 *(1992),* Smoke *(1995),* Too Much *(1996),* The Associate *(1996),* Uninvited *(1999), and* Keeping the Faith *(2000).*

On television he has appeared in The Baby *(1953),* Shadow of a Champ *(1955),* The Outsiders *(1955),* The Plot to Kill Stalin *(1958),* For Whom the Bell Tolls *(1959),* Hope Is a Thing with Feathers *(1960),* Tomorrow the Man *(1962),* The Poppy Is Also a Flower *(1966; Emmy Award),* A Cold Night's Death *(1973),* Indict and Convict *(1974),* The Pirate *(1978),* The Pride of Jesse Hallam *(1981),* The Wall *(1982),* The Executioner's Song *(1982),* Anatomy of an Illness *(1984),* Murder: By Reason of Insanity *(1985),* Embassy *(1985),* Christopher Columbus *(1985),* Our Family Honor *(1985),* Something in Common *(1986),* Rocket to the Moon *(1986),* Impossible Spy *(1987),* Vendetta: Secrets of a Mafia Bride *(1991),* Legacy of Lies *(1992),* Teamster Boss: The Jackie Presser Story *(1992),* Vendetta II: The New Mafia *(1993),* James Dean: A Portrait *(1996),* Clark Gable: Tall, Dark, and Handsome *(1996),* Naked City: Justice with a Bullet *(1998), and* The Bookfair Murders *(2000).*

He was elected to the Theater Hall of Fame in 1988.

Anne Jackson was born Anna June Jackson on September 3, 1926, in Allegheny, Pennsylvania. She attended the New School for Social Research and trained for the stage with Sanford Meisner at the Neighborhood Playhouse and with Herbert Berghof and Lee Strasberg at the Actors Studio. She made her stage debut as Anya in The Cherry Orchard *in Wilmington, Delaware, in 1944 and her Broadway debut as Guest in* The Cherry Orchard *in 1945. Her other Broadway and off-Broadway stage roles include Frieda Foldal,* John Gabriel Borkman *(1946); Judith,* The Last Dance *(1948); Nellie Ewell,* Summer and Smoke *(1948); Margaret Anderson,* Love Me Long *(1949); Hilda,* The Lady from the Sea *(1950); Louka,* Arms and the Man *(1950); Coralie Jones,* Never Say

Never (1951); *Mildred Tunner,* Oh, Men! Oh, Women! (1953); *The Daughter,* The Middle of the Night (1956); *title role,* Major Barbara (1956); *Daisy,* Rhinoceros (1961); *Sylvia,* The Typists, *and Gloria,* The Tiger (1963); *Ellen Monville,* Luv (1964); *The Actress,* The Exercise (1969); *Molly Malloy,* The Front Page (1969); *Ethel Rosenberg,* Inquest (1970); *Mother H. Doris and Joan J.,* Promenade, All! (1972); *Madame St. Pe,* The Waltz of the Toreadors (1973); *Mrs. McBride,* Marco Polo Sings a Solo (1977); *Mrs. Frank,* The Diary of Anne Frank (1978); *Natalie Garrilovna,* The Nest of the Wood Grouse (1984); *title role,* The Madwoman of Chaillot (1965); *Anna Cole,* Café Crown (1988); *Esther,* The Flowering Peach (1994); *Charlotte,* Mr. Peters' Connections (1998); *herself,* Tennessee Williams Remembered (1999); *and Stella Dempsey,* Down the Garden Paths (2000).

In the movies, she has been in So Young, So Bad (1950), Tall Story (1960), The Tiger Makes Out (1967), The Secret Life of an American Wife (1968), How to Save a Marriage and Ruin Your Life (1968), Dirty Dingus Magee (1970), The Angel Levine (1970), Lovers and Other Strangers (1970), Zigzag (1970), Nasty Habits (1976), The Bell Jar (1979), The Shining (1980), Sanford Meisner: The American Theatre's Best-Kept Secret (1984), Sam's Son (1984), Funny (1989), Funny About Love (1990), *and* Folks! (1992).

On television, she has appeared in 84 Charing Cross Road (1975), The Family Man (1979), A Private Battle (1980), Blinded by Light (1980), Leave 'Em Laughing (1981), A Woman Called Golda (1982), Out on a Limb (1987), Everything's Relative (1987), Baby M (1988), Rescuers—Stories of Courage: Two Women (1997), *and episodes of* Philco Television Playhouse, Goodyear Television Playhouse, Worlds Beyond, *and* Law and Order.

She received the Lions of the Performing Arts Award in 1987.

This interview took place on December 2, 1996.

• ——————————————————————————— •

Interviewer: I'd like to start by asking you both how you got into the theater. Eli, I know you were born in Brooklyn, went to school in Texas, and then probably gravitated back to New York. When did your interest in theater begin?

Wallach: When I was four. I always wanted to be in the theater. My bed was always the Sahara Desert, and I was always in the Foreign Legion, being shot, crawling across the desert, bleeding. My mother would say, "Come eat," and I'd say, "Look, Ma! Look! I'm bleeding!" So I've always wanted to act. Now I get paid for it.

Interviewer: How did you actually get into the theater?

Wallach: There was a long pause. Everybody in my family were teachers. I was destined to be a teacher, so I took a master's degree at City College in order to teach in New York. I took the teacher's exam with about two thousand others. I think forty-two passed. I was in the majority. I realized that someone up there loves me, so I got a scholarship to an acting school called the Neighborhood Playhouse School of the Theatre. Tony Randall was in that class. For the senior dance project, under Martha Graham's tutelage, we did some of *Look Homeward, Angel*. At one point, a man stood on a chair and pointed at me and said, "Uncle Sam wants you!" Five months later, Uncle Sam had me. I was in the army as a medical soldier, and an officer, for five years. When I got out in 1945, I said, "Broadway, here I am!" I met Anne the next year, and that started our life together.

Interviewer: All right, now let's get Anne to that point. Tell me how your interest in theater began, and how you got to the point where you met Eli.

Jackson: I think I was four. I'm pretty sure I was four. My sister, my older sister who really wanted to be an actress, taught me to sing a song. I was tone-deaf, and she decided I would do a poem, which was about having red hair and the evil of having red hair. I took my bows and got my applause, and then I went and hid in the cellar of my home and couldn't come out—but I went back and did it again and again and again, mind you. That's an early memory. I think that that's what most actors will talk about—that need to act as very young children. Then when I got older, after high school, I went into the John Golden auditions. That got me started. I went to the Neighborhood Playhouse after that. I got a scholarship with Sanford Meisner, and then I got a job with Eva Le Gallienne; I played Anya in *The Cherry Orchard* on tour in 1944.

Interviewer: Then you met each other in an off-Broadway production of Tennessee Williams's *This Property Is Condemned*, right?

Jackson: Yes.

Interviewer: Was that the first close-to-Broadway experience for both of you?

Jackson: Yes. I played a thirteen- or fourteen-year-old, and he was supposed to be a fifteen-year-old. When he came to audition, he came in uniform. I said to the producer-director, Terry Hayden, "Terry, isn't he too old to play the part?" Because all the other kids who were reading for it came and did broken voices; that's how they read it. She said, "Well, we're having Eli Wallach." I said, "Which one was he?" And she said, "The one who just left, in the uniform." Well, the rest is history.

Interviewer: There were some parts he wasn't too old for, right?

Jackson: No, because after he began to rehearse the play, he looked like a kid of fifteen. It shows you what acting can do.

Interviewer: I want to ask you both: has that combination of terror and excitement that Anne described at age four ever left? Is it still both frightening and exciting to get out there, or is all the terror gone?

Jackson: No, it's more so. It gets to be more so, the terror.

Wallach: You know, we're at a stage where we go into a room now and think, "Why did I come in here?" I'm about to do a play this winter, *Visiting Mr. Green,* that I did this past summer. There are only two people in the play, and it lasts two hours. I'm always terrified that there's no prompter. I once did a play where there was a young boy who was Polish who was the prompter— and I forgot my lines. He said, in a very thick Polish accent, " 'When you can'; your line is 'When you can.' " I said, "What?" No, there is a certain amount of terror on the stage. It's the most daring and dangerous of the media. I'm not talking about television, where they can cut now. We used to do live television; that was exciting too—and frightening. One time I played a boxer. My father used to listen to the radio, and at the end of a prizefight, they'd put the microphone in front of the fighter—because there was no television then. And the fighter would say, "Hello, Ma. Hello, Pa. I won." So I did a prize-fighter on television, and I did the fighting sequence, I ran to the phone afterwards, called my father, and said, "Well, Pop, what'd you think?" He said, "You couldn't say hello?"

Interviewer: I think you mentioned somewhere that Kilroy in Tennessee Williams's *Camino Real* was one of your two favorite roles. Is that true, and if so, why? What was it about that role?

Wallach: Kilroy was a character during World War II. He was Everyman; he was every young soldier in danger. In the play Tennessee Williams writes that he has a heart as big as the head of a baby, and it's about to break.

Jackson: And it's solid gold.

Wallach: And it's solid gold. It was just a glorious experience for me. Actors don't often get great roles to play, but this was one I got.

Interviewer: What was it about it, beyond the big heart and the excitement of working with Williams?

Wallach: Well, it's Tennessee's fantasy, his phantasmagoric dream. It takes place below the border, where all the legends are assembled in a little village: Camille, Don Quixote, Lord Byron, Casanova. And into this group comes this young sailor.

Jackson: What does it mean, Camino Real? It means real road, or real path?

Wallach: The Royal Highway.

Jackson: The Royal Highway. It's done as a comic strip about death and dying. The garbage men come and pick up the bodies and wheel them off. You find yourself laughing and crying.

Wallach: I love one little thing that Tennessee put in. The young man says to a stranger in the square, "It's good to see you." And the man says,

"Why?" He says, "A normal American in a clean, white suit." And the man says, "My suit is pale yellow, my nationality is French, and my normality has often been subject to question." Then the man says, "Why don't you clean up? Why don't you take a shower?" The boy says, "Well, I would if I could find the Y." And the Frenchman says, "What is the Y?" The man says, "It's a Protestant church with a swimming pool in it." That's Tennessee at his best.

Interviewer: What's a favorite role for you, Anne?

Jackson: Do you mean one that I've done?

Interviewer: Yes.

Jackson: I think the Madwoman of Chaillot. I'm so fickle, though. It's the last one that I did as an older woman.

Interviewer: That has some of the same quality as *Camino Real.* It has that same free, open, phantasmagorical aspect to it.

Jackson: Yes. The wonderful part about that play is the fantasy of changing the world by getting rid of all the evil in it. Isn't that what we'd all love to do?

Interviewer: Somewhere I read you also liked your role in *The Master Builder.*

Jackson: Oh yes!

Interviewer: Why?

Jackson: I didn't do that professionally. I did it at the Actors Studio with Rod Steiger. Hilde Wangel was a strange, marvelous character who was sending the Master Builder up, up, up to the highest steeple. It's a wonderful role, and a wonderful play—all about the power of youth and her sexual power over the master builder.

Wallach: We had a great time together spending a year doing a play called *The Waltz of the Toreadors.* We put our two daughters in it. One of the hardest lines I had to say as they ran across the stage was "My God, aren't they ugly!" At the end of Act II, I choke my wife, who is bedridden in this play. She drives me crazy and I start to choke her. The usher came backstage and said, "A couple were going up the aisle, and the wife said to the husband, 'Do you think he killed her?' And the husband said, 'I hope so.' "

Interviewer: Now, that's good acting!

Jackson: Well, talking about Giraudoux's *Madwoman,* Ibsen's *The Master Builder,* and Anouilh's *The Waltz of the Toreadors: The Waltz of the Toreadors,* in my opinion, is one of the really beautifully constructed plays. *Madwoman* you really have to work hard for, because there's that long scene at the beginning where the Madwoman just listens to the men debate about oil and greed. With the Ibsen, you'd always have to do your own kind of paraphrasing, because the translation was awkward. *Waltz* is written and translated beautifully.

Interviewer: What attracts you to a role now? Eli, what attracted you to the role in the new play that you're going to do in Florida?

Wallach: Well, I got a taste of something. I did a play by Arthur Miller three seasons ago called *The Price,* and I played an old man. I've gone through all the ethnic stages. I've been Mexican bandits, half-breeds, Okinawans, Greeks, Italians. I'm in my old Jewish phase now. I was fascinated with that Arthur Miller role, Gregory Solomon. The new play by Jeff Baron, *Visiting Mr. Green,* had a lot of the elements of that old man. He's alone, he's depressed, his wife has died, and yet there's something bright and gutsy about him. The author put in something I told him my father used to say. My father used to say, "Do you know Jacob Adler?" I'd say, "Yes." He says, "The greatest actor in the world. He played King Lear. Do you know King Lear?" I'd say, "Yes." He said, "He played the Jewish King Lear. Everybody else played him in English; he played him in Yiddish. And he broke your heart, that man. He could make you laugh, he could make you cry. And he didn't die quick. It took him half an hour." So I find that this man takes half an hour to die, and I love doing the part.

Interviewer: What about you, Anne? What attracts you to a role now?

Jackson: I like comedy, and I like blood and thunder, I find. Eli and I did a very interesting project called *The Masques of Melancholia* with Richard Chamberlain. It was an industrial show that we did in New Orleans. *The Masques of Melancholia* relates obviously to tragedy—depression, melancholia, and suicide. The drug company that makes Prozac had put up the money, so our audience was two thousand psychiatrists. Can you believe this? We did excerpts from all these great plays and literature. We did a scene from *Hamlet;* I played Gertrude, Eli played the king. We did a reading from *Madame Bovary.* I did Medea at the end; I want to tell you, that makes you feel very good.

Wallach: It makes you feel tall.

Jackson: I'll tell you what is wonderful about it. In real life, we say, "Oh my God, I wouldn't be in her shoes," or you say, "Oh my God, don't even ask! That poor person, that poor woman." As actors, we say, "Guess what I'm going to play? A woman who kills her children to avenge her husband." And the response is "Wow, you are going to do Medea!" Everybody else is excited that we get the chance to go where angels fear to tread. We go to those places where we say, "Ohh, don't talk, don't speak. I can't imagine." And the actor has to say, "What's going to happen to me if I imagine that? Where is that going to take me?" That's what we all strive to do as artists. We say, "The playwright had to go to those dark places." The painter, the musician, and the writer all go there. That's what art is about. And we love the experience!

Interviewer: The obvious next question is, how do you get there? How do you prepare yourself for specific roles? Has that changed from your first performances to now?

Wallach: Well, we learned never to criticize one another. I did once. We did a play called *Rhinoceros,* with Zero Mostel. It was a wonderful production, a brilliant, strange, phantasmagoric play about people turning into rhinoceroses—except one man who defies it. Annie did a certain gesture in the play, and I said to her, "Are you going to do that, actually do that?" She said, "It's something I've worked on, and I'm going to do it." And every critic picked that thing out and praised it; so from then on I keep my distance.

Jackson: But it doesn't stop me from criticizing. Do you know what is interesting? When I was going to do Medea, I had seen Judith Anderson do it, and I had seen Zoe Caldwell do it. I thought, "Oh gosh, how am I going to work on that?"—having seen these two really great actors do it. But what happens to the actor is that, when you begin to go to those places, to imagine what it is that you have to dredge up to do that, it comes from you; and you no longer think in terms of Judith Anderson or Zoe Caldwell, because you're not thinking in terms of acting. You're finding the place where you have to say what that would be like. There are times when I have said, "I could kill him. I could kill him." I unfortunately am a very jealous woman. In interviews on television, when Eli used to go away and do movies, and he would be playing with all these famous actresses, Merv Griffin used to tease me about it. He'd say, "Who is Eli working with now? He's not with Marilyn Monroe, is he?" He would give me that look. Eli was doing a film with—who's the lovely French actress?

Wallach: Jeanne Moreau.

Jackson: Yes. Merv Griffin said, "Oh, I understand Eli is in England. He's doing this film, and he has a bedroom scene with Jeanne Moreau. How do you feel about that?" And I said, "Well, I'll tell you how I feel about it. I'm jealous, but Eli is a very sensitive man. I say to him, if he is unfaithful to me and I find out about it, I won't touch a hair on his head; but I will kill the woman. And I don't think he would put any woman in that danger."

Wallach: Well, I'll tell you, mentioning Jeanne Moreau: there was a scene we had in this movie where I was an army sergeant, and we're in her château, and there's a bombardment going on. I'm in the bed, and she's in a corner whimpering like a wounded bird. I pull the covers back, and she gets into the bed with me.

Jackson: You see?

Wallach: Wait, wait. In the morning, my arm was across her breast, and she wakes up and she thinks it's her husband. Now, I'll tell you what I did. I had them put a tattoo on my arm with a rose and a heart; and in the middle it said ANNE.

Interviewer: And she's still alive?

Jackson: Yes, Jeanne Moreau is still alive.

Interviewer: I know it's difficult for actors to talk about how they work on a role. Do you and Eli work on roles similarly or differently? When you do something together, do you work together away from the rehearsal at all? Do you talk about it?

Jackson: Yes, we do. We do talk about it. I learned a lot from Eli. When I used to work, I wasn't able to learn the lines until I more or less knew where I was going with the part. It wasn't about that for me. Since I've been working with him for a while and have watched him work, I now learn the lines almost by rote, so that I can get them out of the way. And then I explore where they have to go. I think that's the way Eli works.

Wallach: Yes, basically, that's the way.

Jackson: But the difference is that I would sometimes get ahead of him in terms of the emotional input into a play. He would know the lines and he would kind of go through it. Then, I don't know, there came a point where he would get way ahead of me, because I was not sure if this choice or this commitment was right—and then I would have to catch up. I don't think that now, technically, we have had that problem in the last ten years or so, because I've learned that lesson; I learn the lines. Learn your lines. I teach that to my students. Learn the lines. To perfection. Don't change an author's lines.

Interviewer: What role has working with directors played in your life? Both of you have worked with some of the great directors of the modern theater—Kazan, Mike Nichols, lots of others. What made Kazan such a good director, Eli?

Wallach: He understood that drama is conflict. He'd work it out so that he'd tell one actor, "Go onstage and make friends. I don't know. Each person does it differently. I'm not going to tell you how to do it. Just go onstage and make friends." He would tell all the other actors, "Don't go near him. He has body odor." You would get a conflict going, and it's a game. Children do it. We were playing with our grandchildren yesterday. When they're playing games, grandparents get rather impatient with the kids. Annie got angry with them, and she had a trial. I used to have a trial with our own children. I'd say, "All right, each one gets a chance to speak, and I'm the judge; and then I will issue the sentence." She did that with the grandchildren. Each one got their sentence. Some directors wind you up and push you in, and some leave you alone. In films, mostly, the actor is left alone, because there are other technical aspects that come into play. What's on the screen is not determined by the actor; it's determined by the editor, the printer, and the producer—all those other people.

I once did a movie in Italy with an Italian man who was not an actor; he had one arm. He said to me, "I don't like Americans." I said, "Why?" He said, "I lost my arm in the war." I said, "I didn't do it." The director came over to him—he was not an actor—and said to him, "I want you to count from one to ten angrily." So the man's looking at me, and I guess thinking about his arm and all that. He said, "Uno, due, tre, quatro, cinque, sei." Then they dubbed in words when they put it on the screen, and he was great. I spent my whole career learning about acting, and I'm worried because I can never reach what this man reached alone—just by counting! So you never know what a director will do. Leone said to me in a movie, a western called *The Good, the Bad, and the Ugly*, "I don't want you to put your gun in a holster." I said, "Where do I put it?" He says, "You have the rope around your neck, and there's the gun." I said, "I know, it dangles between my legs, right?" He says, "Here, when you want the gun, you twist your shoulders, I cut to your hand, there's the gun." I said, "Show me." He put the gun around his neck, he went like this, it missed his hand and hit him in the groin. He said, "Keep it in your pocket." So you never know what a director's going to do.

Jackson: George Abbott was considered by Method actors as "one who gives you line readings." And that was the worst. Well, we worked with Abbott when he was in his eighties, and he was marvelous. He did what Eli describes Kazan as doing with the actors. It really amazed me to see him do it. I was having a little bit of trouble. I played the Carole Lombard part in the play *Twentieth Century*, the actress, and I had to make an entrance on a train. The woman playing my maid was very popular on a television commercial. She did something about the beef in meat or something. She was adorable, cute, chubby, and English. And she loved to act, as we all do. So she would come on the stage, into this little compartment, and search in her pocketbook for a tip for the porter. She'd make sure that he got downstage of her so that she could show that she was giving the money, and then it took a long time for her to get out of the room. Unfortunately, I would have to wait in the doorway in one of these star entrance poses. She would be in my way. But Abbott caught it. Each time I came in, she was ad-libbing, "And there's for you, porter, and blah, blah, blah." So George came up on the stage—he was six foot four and handsome, even at eighty—and he said, "Now, dear, when you come in—" and she said, "Oh yes, Mr. Abbott, oh yes?" He said, "I want you to do something in the hall before we see you. I want you to take out the money for the porter. Because I want you to come in and I want you to get in that room so that you can fix it up for Miss Jackson before she comes on. I want you to get rid of him as fast as you can. And you know something, we don't mind seeing your back. It's so expressive." "Well," she said, "ooh, yes, Mr. A." What a dear way he had, not to say to one actor,

"Don't upstage the other" or "Don't do that." He just told her what the character's job was. He gave her the incentive to do it.

Interviewer: Evidently Mark Twain, after a performance, used to stay up all night thinking about where he got the laughs., Do you make adjustments in performances because of the audience? Do you take the play home with you and talk about it?

Wallach: Sometimes you get a laugh and it's unplanned. As a young actor, I was in a play with Annie called *Androcles and the Lion,* with a famous old actor named Ernest Truex. He did a lot of movies too. I came offstage one time and said, "Oh, I get a great laugh there." He looked at me and he said, "You do?" I said, "Yes." And the next performance, I didn't get a laugh, which was his way of saying, "Listen, don't be such a hotshot. There are other people on the stage, and they help you get the laugh." We spent a year with Charles Laughton doing *Major Barbara* by Shaw, and he taught us a lot.

Interviewer: What was it like acting onstage with Charles Laughton?

Jackson: He was big. I had some trouble with the play because the conflict between Barbara and Undershaft has to do with morality and religion and socialism. There's a real confrontation that they have in that poverty scene. Of course he was the star of the production, he was larger than I am, had a wonderful voice, and I must say he was quite a brilliant actor. I had replaced Glynis Johns, who had left to go to Hollywood. We were doing this scene and he said to me, "You know, Barbara is a lady, and she never makes fists, and she doesn't frown, and she doesn't this and she doesn't that." I was standing like a moron. Well, anyway, I broke out of my straitjacket one night. I just broke out. I couldn't take it anymore. So when we had this confrontation, I broke out of the staging, I did everything. I just went to town, like a mad thing. This was after having played the part for about three weeks. Before that I was getting anxiety attacks because I was pushing everything down. As the young people say, I just let it all hang out. When he got to his poverty speech, he really intoned, "Poverty is the worst of sins." He was going on, and I was carrying on with my lines. We finished and I thought, "Well, I'm going to be fired, and I don't care. I don't care." So when I'm passing his dressing room, his dresser said, "Oh, Mr. Laughton would like to see you, Miss Jackson." So I go into the dressing room, and I wasn't even scared. I really wasn't. I guess I was resigned because I just had felt so good about doing what I did. He looked at me through the mirror, and his hair was all plastered down by now because he was sweating after having done that scene. There was a line in the play where he says to his son who finally stands up to him, "You have earned your latchkey." I go into the dressing room, and he looks at me and he says, "You have earned your latchkey. That's what I meant when I said to you that this is Greek drama." I thought, "Why didn't you say it like that?" But it was a wonderful lesson I learned.

Interviewer: What's a role, Eli, that you've never played that you would love to play still?

Wallach: For years, Sidney Poitier and I said we're going to do Othello and Iago.

Jackson: Which part are you going to play?

Wallach: It became a response that I automatically gave, but I never did it. I got a little crack at it when we did these *Masques of Melancholia.* I did Lear. I had a good time doing Lear.

Interviewer: Would you like to do that sometime?

Wallach: Oh yes, I would. I don't know if you saw Al Pacino's *Looking for Richard.* It was a distinguished movie. He did Richard and he got clobbered by the critics, and he said, "I'm going to figure a way. I'm going to do it." Why are Americans afraid of Shakespeare? Because the people speaking English now are not speaking it the way they spoke Shakespeare in those days. Kevin Kline in the movie is interviewed and says, "I took my girl, we went up in the balcony, and I saw an English production of *Hamlet.* I didn't understand a damn word. I made out with my girlfriend." Shakespeare is seemingly an insurmountable obstacle for American actors; but American actors bring to it a kind of passion and guts that's there in the play.

Jackson: So does Paul Scofield.

Wallach: Yes, he does.

Jackson: He doesn't play it the way you're describing a lot of English and a lot of Americans. Paul Scofield, as the Ghost in *Hamlet:* Is that a memorable performance?

Wallach: Wonderful.

Interviewer: Anne, what's a part that you've not played that you'd like to play?

Jackson: Oh, there are so many, but I'm too old for them. I would have liked to have played Cleopatra, both the Shaw Cleopatra and Shakespeare's Cleopatra, and put on the dark makeup and all that stuff. I would love all that. I think I would have liked to have played that wonderful part in *The Trojan Women.*

Interviewer: You both were in a number of Tennessee Williams's plays. What role did he assume when these plays were in rehearsal? Did you communicate with him directly or through the director? Were you conscious of his presence during the filming of *Baby Doll,* Eli?

Wallach: Well, *Baby Doll* was the first screenplay he ever wrote, and he didn't want to bother with close-up, medium shot, traveling shot; he didn't understand the language of filmmaking. After the first eight pages of the script were written, he said, "Oh, the hell with it, I'm writing this as I see it." He didn't bother any of us. It all went through Kazan.

Interviewer: What about with the plays?

Wallach: I did *The Rose Tattoo*. I played Alvaro Mangiacavallo. We were in Chicago, and he couldn't figure out an ending for the play. Every night he'd come in with a new ending—until one night he found it. "Voilà," he said, "I got it!"

Jackson: Is it true that Kazan had told him to please give it an uplifting ending? I think it was Kazan. I think Kazan didn't want to do the play at first.

Wallach: Kazan didn't direct *The Rose Tattoo*.

Jackson: I didn't say that. I said that Kazan told Tennessee to finish that play on an upbeat, not to write it as a tragedy. Tennessee did, and that was one of the things that made it into such a charming, lovely, romantic play. Tennesee did an interesting thing. Eli and I did *The Glass Menagerie*—as odd as that may seem, because neither one of us is right physically for the roles. I played Laura. It was a part that, when I saw the play, I knew I could play. Nobody else knew it; I had red hair and freckles, and I was always being cast as a feisty ingenue. But I knew I could play it because that girl was my mother. Laura was like my mother. I wanted to do it, and so when we were asked to do something in summer stock and they said, "What's your favorite play?" I said, "I've always wanted to play Laura in *The Glass Menagerie*." My agent said, "You're crazy. That's not even the leading part. They tell you you can do anything you want to do and you want to do Laura?" I said, "I want to do that." Eli said that he would do Tom, and I wanted Steve Hill to do the Gentleman Caller. We wanted Shirley Booth to do Amanda, but Shirley said, "I can't do it. I see Laurette Taylor in it, and I just can't." So, to make a long story short, Jo Van Fleet did it with us. Tennessee would come to rehearsal and he would change lines. He'd say, "Oh, I just had a wonderful idea. Oh, I love it, I love it!" Tennessee had the most marvelous personality, and he was the most adorable hypocrite in the world. Whatever you were playing, you were the best that's ever done it. He would say, "Oh, I just love what you do. I love it!" Boy, that made you want to go on and do more of the same. But I felt, "My God!" This was fifteen or twenty years after the play had been done on Broadway, wasn't it, Eli?

Interviewer: He was still working on it.

Jackson: It was in the early sixties, and he was still working on it! It was lovely.

Interviewer: What are some of the memorable stage performances that you have seen over the years?

Jackson: I can tell you that I saw Paul Scofield do *Time Remembered,* and I've never forgotten his performance. He played the prince, and he made me cry when he did the speech about all the Sundays that he had. Of the women, one never forgets Laurette Taylor in *The Glass Menagerie;* I think that was one of the first plays I ever saw. I was a student at the Neighborhood Playhouse, and we used to sneak in and see it. I'm not sure that some of that wasn't also because of Sandy Meisner's description of what a great performance that was and saying that young actors had to see it. But I don't think so; she was just incredible.

Wallach: Alfred Lunt in *The Visit* I thought was wonderful. Marlon Brando in a play called *Truckline Café* was brilliant. *Streetcar Named Desire;* the whole production was wonderful. You retain these. People see us years and years later and they remember vividly. Television, dramatically now, is kind of a wasteland. Television in the afternoons is a freak show: "I slept with my sister's boyfriend." I don't know.

Jackson: Darling, I think that, recently, Uta Hagen's performance and Zoe Caldwell's performance in their respective plays were as good as it gets in the theater. I think that Frank Langella gave a memorable performance in *Present Laughter;* I think he's wonderful.

Interviewer: Hasn't the theater changed a lot since the forties? Or is it a cliché to talk like that?

Jackson: Yes, it has; but I don't think it's changed for the worse.

Interviewer: Really?

Jackson: No, I don't.

Wallach: I spent two years, every night, in the theater with Henry Fonda in *Mr. Roberts.* The tickets were $4.80. Now it costs an arm and a leg to go to the theater.

Jackson: But do you think that the theater has changed that much?

Wallach: Well.

Jackson: Speak up, Eli!

Wallach: I'm trying to give a deep answer.

Jackson: No, he goes right to the economics. Do you notice that? He would come out onstage and look to see how many were in the audience.

Wallach: I'll tell you an economics joke. I get mail all the time now. I played one episode of *Batman* when it was a TV thing. My kids used to say, "Oh Dad, do *Captain Kangaroo!*" or "Dad, do *Batman.*" So I did Mr. Freeze on *Batman.* I think I got $350 for the episode. Two weeks ago, they signed Arnold

Schwarzenegger to play Mr. Freeze in the movie *Batman* for $25 million. I think I've been doing the wrong thing all these years. Anne suggested I lift weights!

Interviewer: You just came along at the wrong time.

Jackson: It's not about that, Eli. It's not about money. You'd be crazy to come into this profession thinking you were going to make money.

Wallach: That's true.

Interviewer: What you're saying, Anne, is that you don't think the quality of the theater has changed in that time. You still can see a thrilling performance today. That's what you mean when you say it hasn't changed.

Jackson: I think so, but the unfortunate part of it is that the theater is rarer. There aren't as many plays; the playwrights go off to California, I guess. Although David Mamet, who I consider a very fine playwright, is hanging around and doing both mediums.

Wallach: We didn't go because Truman Capote said, "Every year you spend in L.A., you lose two points on your IQ."

Interviewer: Anne, you did *The Cherry Orchard* when you were about eighteen, and then some thirty years later you did it again, in a different role. Did your attitude toward the play change in any significant way?

Jackson: Well, it's what I explained before. I thought, "How am I going to do that?" I'll always see Le Gallienne in that role; she was absolutely beautiful as Madame Lyubov. I was her Anya. But once I got into that other place, it was a whole different experience. The hard thing for me about playing that woman was the lover she had in Paris that she wanted to go see and be with and all of that. That was a little difficult for me for a while. That's where I really had to do some work. Somebody—it was an actress at the Actors Studio, somebody very good; I'm sorry I don't remember her name—said, "I find that when I work on a part I say, 'I don't have to work on that; I have that. I don't have to work on that; I have that.'" She meant that you understand certain aspects of a role; they come naturally to you. It's almost like typecasting. It was not easy for me to understand that kind of frivolity in that Russian woman. That didn't come easily to me, so that's where I had to work. The death of the little boy, on the other hand, I just had to mention and, I don't know why, but that set me off immediately into an emotional understanding of the woman—but not the lover.

Interviewer: Eli, do you operate somewhat that same way with a role? Are there certain parts of it that are harder for you to do, or do you deal with it as a totality?

Wallach: I've learned more and more—as you mature in the craft, you begin to say, "Leave it alone." It's been posited there, some of it, and if you pinch it, it'll happen. I'll never forget, Anne Bancroft had been doing a play, *The Miracle Worker*, for two years, and they invited a Japanese company to talk at the Actors Studio. This man's name was Yushikawa Number 62; he was the sixtieth generation. He'd been playing this role for years. Anne said, "I've been playing Annie Sullivan for almost two years, and there are times when I just haven't got any emotion. What do you do?" He said, "Well, what we say on the stage is so moving, the audience is moved; and when they're moved, I'm moved. I don't get moved first." She said, "But what if nothing comes?" He pinched himself and he said, "Make it come." I think that's what's happening. People say, "How do you do the same play over and over again?" We don't. The difference is that the audience changes each night. They have a different character. They've got colds, it's income tax time, it's Easter. "Is the car parked? Did I leave the lights on?" All that's going on, and there's a difference. Sometimes you hate them. Sometimes you say, "Oh my God, what a lovely evening we're going to have." That doesn't happen in any other medium. It doesn't happen on television or in the movies.

Interviewer: And that's what sends you back to the theater all the time, isn't it?

Wallach: Yes.

Jackson: And that's what hopefully sends you *to* the theater.

Interviewer: Of course. Anne can't kill anybody in *The Misfits* because they're all dead now, so, Eli, you can talk about that movie safely. What was that experience like? There's been so much written about that film and what was going on at the time in the lives of all of the actors.

Wallach: I'll never forget, Anne and I spent an afternoon with Clark Gable around the swimming pool. Do you remember? He never talked about movies with us or with me. He talked about his stage experiences, about the theater. He had gone to California in a play called *The Last Mile,* and he had a contract to come back to the theater in New York. He called the producer in New York and said, "I've just been offered a contract out here to make movies." The producer said, "How much they going to pay you?" He said, "Six hundred dollars a week." And the producer said, "Stay out there!" He never came back.

Interviewer: Did it seem as if he regretted it?

Wallach: I don't know. That was a tormented experience. I don't know how many people have seen *The Misfits,* but it came at a time when Marilyn's marriage to Arthur Miller was breaking up, when Clark Gable's wife was pregnant and he was excited about having the baby. He never saw that child; he died ten days after we finished the film.

Jackson: Paula Strasberg was on the set with Lee Strasberg visiting, so that there were all kinds of tensions and pressures. I think that Arthur was appalled by Paula's coming and coaching Marilyn. Eli has told me this, but I saw it with my own eyes as well: John Huston was absolutely the gentleman and knew exactly how to handle everybody on that film. Marilyn was so ill at that time. We had become friendly with her. She had baby-sat for us at one point. When I went to California that time, I by this time had three children. She loved our son, Peter; she'd put him on her lap, and he was a terrible little flirt at four. I brought all three of my children to the set, and we had said hello to Clark Gable. My kids didn't care about him; they didn't know anything about him. Then we walked over to say hello to Marilyn. She saw me and she turned her head and ran into her trailer. I was so hurt; I thought, "Why would she do that? Why is she angry at me?" I didn't realize until much later what that must have been for her, to have me coming with my three children and my husband. She by this time was divorcing Arthur and had had two miscarriages. We had seen her right after one of the miscarriages, before she had gone to England. She had been out in East Hampton. We'd socialized with her, but you never got palsy with Marilyn; she wasn't a girlfriend. She was a man's friend; that's what her thing was.

Interviewer: It became a quite good movie, which is amazing when you think of what must have gone on.

Jackson: Marilyn was quite good in it. She was beautiful in it. I thought all of the acting in that film was way above average for a film.

Interviewer: To return to *Rhinoceros* for a minute, was Zero Mostel as big a personality offstage as on?

Jackson: He was a bit of a troublemaker. He was also an artist, a painter, and I brought him some pictures that our son had done. Peter was about twelve, and he had done a picture of a dragon with fire coming out of its mouth. It had the coloring of a tiger with reddish fur and green eyes. There was another one that was a long portrait of a man who I guess was Frankenstein, with the green face and hands, and he was in a suit. I brought Zero these, among others, and he looked at the one of the dragon. He said to me, "That's a portrait of you." I said, "Really?" He said, "That's you. Do you ever chew your son out?" Zero was going to an analyst at the time! Then he said to Eli, "And that's you, Eli." Eli said, "What? Frankenstein?" He said, "Look at the hands. See how sweet the hands are. That's you." So we went up to our dressing room and I said, "Oh my God, we have to hang our portraits—by our son."

Wallach: That play deals with one man resisting turning into a rhinoceros, and Zero was not the man. At the end of the play, my character continued to resist turning into a rhinoceros.

Jackson: You were the only good one in the whole bunch.

Wallach: Yes. Everyone who adapts, conforms, bows, obeys, who doesn't make waves, becomes a rhinoceros. That's what Ionesco was saying. In terms of fascism or Nazism or Communism, you have to have individuals. Zero, in the ten-minute scene we did, literally turned into a rhinoceros, without leaving the stage and without putting on any makeup. We just saw a production of *Rhinoceros* recently where the actor went offstage and came back with little pieces of makeup on, but that wasn't what Zero did. I said to Zero, "Your skin looks strange." He said, "Brrrr," and he chased me all around the room. I opened the bathroom door and he went in; I slammed the door and locked it. And then his head came through the door, right through it, and the audience jumped out of their seats. People came to the theater to see a man turn into a rhinoceros. That was Zero, bigger than life. If he didn't like your necktie, he always carried scissors, and he'd cut it off.

Interviewer: When you do two shows on Wednesdays and Saturdays, how do you bring yourself back up for the evening performance if it's a particularly tough role?.

Jackson: A surgeon recently gave Eli a new hip. I asked him, "How many of these operations do you do?" He said, "Sometimes four or five in a day."

Wallach: Tell them what Picasso said.

Jackson: I'll tell you what Picasso said. This is all going to relate to your question. It was reported in Picasso's obituary that he went into his studio every day, age ninety or whatever he was, at eight in the morning and stayed until five at night. An interviewer said, "How do you do that? How do you stand in front of the easel all those hours?" He said, "When I go into my studio, I leave my body outside." In a sense, that's what actors have to learn to do. We get our rest, but we leave our troubles and our bodies, in a sense, outside—and we inhabit the play again. It's what we're trained to do.

Wallach: I was playing an Oriental in a play in London. The afternoon performance started at five and was over at about seven-thirty. At eight-fifteen the curtain went up again for the second time. It was very hard, but you learned to do it. If you're going to run a mile you don't suddenly burst out; you time it.

Jackson: We saw Siobhan McKenna, who was a very great Irish actress, do *Saint Joan* in England. She went from four in the afternoon until six-thirty, and at seven she went on and did it again. We had to do it when we went to England and did the two one-act plays that we had done in America. That's like doing four plays back to back. Remember, Eli?

Wallach: We've done a lot of one-acters, just the two of us; they're terrible.

Jackson: It's hard when you don't have other actors who are picking up some of that energy and expending some of it on the stage.

Interviewer: Have the two of you ever done a musical?

Wallach: Are you kidding?

Interviewer: No.

Wallach: Joshua Logan, the great director, asked me to audition for a musical he was going to do. I said, "What is it?" He said, "*South Pacific.*" I said, "I can't sing." He said, "No, no, don't worry about that. Just get up on the stage and read." Sitting in the audience in the dark were Rodgers, Hammerstein, and Joshua Logan! I came out on the stage and read and they said, "Very good. Now sing." Anne had warned me. The pianist came running up and said, "What key?" I didn't know one key from another, but I whispered to him, and he went back to the piano. I took an imaginary coin, put it in an imaginary phone, dialed, and sang, "Hello, I'll be down to get you in a taxi, honey, you'd better be ready by half past eight." I hung up and said, "I can't do it. I've got butterflies in my stomach, I can't do it." They said, "We'll get you a real phone next time."

Interviewer: Eli, you have done a wide variety of roles, but the public seems to think of you as the Bandito in *The Good, the Bad, and the Ugly.* Why do you think that is?

Wallach: I don't know. I think on my tombstone it's going to say THE UGLY.

Jackson: I won't allow that, Eli; if you predecease me, I won't allow that.

Wallach: Many, many people saw that movie. I once got a trip to Israel with my son to work one day in a movie. It was one of those kung fu movies. I took it to have the trip. This is my character: I'm in a huge cauldron in the desert. The hero comes running up to the cauldron and says, "Can I help you?" I said, "Why?" He says, "You're in the cauldron." I said, "I put myself in there." He said, "Why?" I said, "The thing between my legs has been giving me so much trouble I'm dissolving it. Take a look." He looks in. I said, "What does it look like?" He says, "It looks like a raisin." I said, "It's working! Climb in!"— and he runs away. I get more mail about that masterful performance. You never know.

Interviewer: Eli, you have a story about doing *The Teahouse of the August Moon* on Broadway.

Wallach: I was on a percentage with that show, so I used to look through the curtains to see how many people were in the audience. Half the part was written in Japanese, which I memorized. One night, I looked through the curtain and there were four Japanese men in the front row. I was terrified. So the captain says to me—I was the interpreter and I translated—"All right, tell them there will be rice for everyone." All I could remember was "The school will have five sides like the Pentagon." So when he said, "Tell them that there will be rice for everyone," I said, in Japanese, "The school will have five sides like the Pentagon." The Japanese in the front row were going crazy. They couldn't contain themselves. The captain said, "Tell them we'll clean the village. There'll be no trouble here. You'll have laundry." I said, "The school will have five sides like the Pentagon."

Interviewer: It was a completely different play for them.

Wallach: Marlon Brando's father came to see me once in my dressing room, while I was getting made up. I had no eyebrows because I used to soap them out and paint eyebrows on. His father came in and said, "I have bad news for you. Marlon is going to play your role in the movie." I said, "Well, I have one caution for him. This play was written by an American, and it deals with his imagination of what these Okinawans are like. Marlon should play it in a theater for a month just to get the feel of it." The director was not right for the movie, and it didn't work out.

Interviewer: What was Brando like as a stage actor? You never acted onstage with him, did you, Eli?

Wallach: Once. At the Actors Studio.

Interviewer: What was he like at the Actors Studio?

Wallach: He was an imp, a troublemaker. We once did a little scene, practicing an improvisation. I said, "Listen, I'm an FBI agent looking for drugs. I come into your apartment and I'm looking for drugs. You stay outside, give me a minute to look around, and then come on. It's your apartment." He said, "Okay." So I come in. I'm looking under the table and the door opens—this is thirty-five, forty years ago—and he says, "What the f—— are you doing here?" I said, "Watch your language." That kept feeding him. He said, "I don't give a goddamn, you son of a bitch." I said, "The landlord told me that the apartment was for rent." He said, "The landlord didn't. He's deaf and dumb. He couldn't talk to you." He would do these things. Finally, he pushed me. I said, "Don't push, just don't push." I wasn't playing a scene anymore. He picked me up and threw me out of the room. When I came back, I was angry as hell, and he started to laugh—and I was criticized because I didn't find the drugs in the apartment!

Interviewer: Do you feel, like so many people, that he was a great loss to the theater, that he would have been capable of great stage performances?

Wallach: Without question. But that was his choice.

Jackson: I agree. It isn't a question of whether he was a great loss or not. You have to want to do it. There are so many actors who want to do it. Yes, he was a great actor; he still is a great actor. So was George C. Scott, so was Walter Matthau. Walter Matthau was a really extraordinary actor.

Interviewer: But when you say about an actor, as you can say about all of those people, that they're great actors in film, isn't that different from saying they are great stage actors?

Jackson: But, my darling, we don't have a stage. It's wonderful that Paul Scofield is doing film now so that people can see what a fabulous actor is. You see it when you see *The Crucible*. His thought onscreen is simply marvelous. He does what every actor tries to train to do, which is to think the character's thoughts. You read his mind on the screen.

Wallach: I'll tell you how we are. Once we had a real fight and I got so mad I went in the bedroom and slammed the door, and I couldn't get out. Now she's terrified, because I have a bad temper. So she called the super to come up.

Jackson: I called the super and I said, "Send somebody up. Mr. Wallach has slammed the door and he can't get out of the bedroom." When the fellow came up, I got hysterical. I started to laugh because he said, "Hey, is anybody in there?" I said, "My husband is in there." Wham, he opens the door. Now Eli's got to come out, right? I ran out into the hall. I said, "If he sees me laughing, I'll be murdered."

Interviewer: Have you ever done a play which you really didn't understand?

Jackson: I will tell you what John Gielgud said. When Eli and I were doing the play *Luv,* Sir John Gielgud was doing *Tiny Alice*—and we had gone to see it. I was most anxious to find out from Sir John what that play was about. But I'd better tell you what happened before that. In *Luv* there was a scene where I tell Alan Arkin that I don't love him anymore and that I want my husband back. My husband was played by Eli. Alan sits on my lap, and I'm sitting facing the audience. Alan sits crossways on my lap and he moans and groans, and the audience screams with laughter. He says to me, "I love you, Ellen." I say, "No, just a minute." He says, "I didn't know anything was the matter with our marriage." I say, "What did you think I was doing in the bathroom all night?" That was my line. He says, "I don't know, I don't know." And I say, "I asked you a question, Harry. What did you think I was doing in the bathroom all night?" Evidently, there was a man in the audience whose wife ran in the bathroom and cried; so this man, when I said it the second time, got absolutely hysterical. I knew that I had to say it again; but he laughed so loud and so strangely that everybody around him was laughing, and Alan started to laugh. Alan was facing upstage, and I was looking at the audience. You get it? I said, "What did you think I was doing?" The man fell on the floor, out of his seat. Alan is laughing so hard he's bouncing, and I say to the audience, "Oh, I'm so sorry. Let's get it out of our systems. Let's all laugh." And we all laughed; so we're over it, and we go on with the scene.

Now it's Eli's entrance. He comes on the stage in this sou'wester, soaking wet; he had fallen into the river. He comes on, he's blowing water out of his mouth. He comes across the stage, throws his lips upward, looks at me and says, "Amateur!" I break up again; I can't help it. Eli is in a fury. The curtain comes down and he says to me, "I'm reporting you to Equity." He leaves the stage and is calling the stage manager. I was terrified, and Alan had run off the stage and up the stairs to get away from him; we're both terrified. So now Eli and I have to meet Sir John Gielgud for lunch between shows for dinner! So I think, "Oh my God, I don't know if he's going to come or what's going to happen, but I'd better get over there fast." So I get over there and I say to Sir John, "Sir John, I don't know if Eli is coming." He says, "Why?" I said, "I broke up on stage. Did you ever break up onstage, Sir John?" And he said, "Good God, no, I'd be too frightened. But Larry [Olivier] was a terrible giggler." Anyway, that's a long roundabout way to get to your question, but I'm going to answer it. I said to Sir John at that meeting, "What is *Tiny Alice* about?" He said, "Oh good God, I don't know. I haven't got a clue!"

Index

Blau, Herbert, 161
Blinded by Light (television), 240
Blithe Spirit (Coward), 40
Blood Knot, The (Fugard), 143, 148
Boesman and Lena (Fugard), 55, 66, 143, 147
Boogie Nights (film), 198
Bookfair Murders, The (television), 239
Booth, Shirley, 250
Booth Is Back in Town (Pendleton), 220
Born Yesterday (Kanin), 154
Bosco, Philip, 134
Bostonians, The (film), 22
Boys from Syracuse, The (Abbott, Rodgers, Hart), 124
Boys Next Door, The (television), 189
Bracken, Eddie, 194
Branagh, Kenneth, 104
Brand, Phoebe, 60
Brando, Marlon, 37, 103, 158, 251, 257
Breathing Lessons (television), 108
Brewster McCloud (film), 157
Brewster's Millions (film), 21
Bridge of San Luis Rey, The (television), 21
Bright Lights, Big City (television), 206
Brighton Beach Memoirs (film), 41
British actors, 3–4, 249
British Film Institute, 185
Broadway Bound (N. Simon), 188, 199; television version, 21
Broadway theater, vi–viii, 75
Brooklyn Academy of Music Theatre Company, 128
Brother Rat (Monks and Finklehoffe), 90
Brown, Arvin, 86, 159, 164
Brown, Richard, 154
Brown, Rita Mae, 174
Browne, Winifred M., 3
Bruce, Carol, 116
Brustein, Robert, 139, 162
Brute Force (film), 21
Bryer, Jackson R., xvii–xviii
Buck and the Preacher (film), 56
Bucks County Playhouse, Pa., 41
Buckskin (television), 173
Bump in the Night (television), 173
Burnt Offerings (film), 108
Burr, Raymond, 157
Burstyn, Ellen, 218
Burton, Richard, 36
Bus Stop (film), 108, 123
But for Whom Charlie (Behrman), 205, 213
Butley (Gray), 191; film version, 22

Butterflies Are Free (Gersh), 40, 43, 47, 107, 108; film version, 108
Butterfly (film), 157, 170
By Love Possessed (film), 206
Bye Bye Birdie (film), 227

Cabin in the Sky (Root, Duke, Latouche), 90, 93
Caesar and Cleopatra (G. B. Shaw), 249
Café Crown (Kraft, Brill, Hague), 239, 240
Caldwell, Zoe, 1–19, 85, 218, 233, 245, 251
California Suite (N. Simon), 71, 83
Call to Remember, A (television), 41
Callas, Maria, 183
Camilla (film), 21, 22, 34
Cameron, James, 148
Camino Real (T. Williams), 22, 238, 242, 243
Cannibali, I (film), 173
Cannon, J. D., 148
Capalbo, Carmen, 211
Capote, Truman, 252
Captive Heart (television), 56
Carnegie-Mellon University, 125, 126–127
Carney, Art, 103
Carnovsky, Morris, 60–61
Caroline? (television), 71
Carrey, Jim, 199
Carried Away (film), 89
Case of Libel, A (television), 71
Cass Theatre, Detroit, Mich., 89
Cat on a Hot Tin Roof (television), 227
Cat People (film), 56
Cats (Eliot, Rice, Lloyd Webber), 146
Caucasian Chalk Circle, The (Brecht), 22, 156, 161
Cay, The (television), 144
CBC, 16
Cemetery Club, The (Menchell), 108, 118–119
Century of Cinema (film), 22
Century of Women, A (television), 41
Chamberlain, Richard, 244
Champions: A Love Story (television), 173
Channing, Carol, 118
Chaplin, Charlie, 203
Chase, Stanley, 211
Chekhov, Anton, 44–45. *See also titles of works*
Chernobyl: The Final Warning (television), 206
Cherry Orchard, The (Chekhov), 5, 21, 22, 48, 135, 143, 175, 239, 241, 252

Tempest, The (Shakespeare), 21, 85, 143
Tender Is the Night (film), 206
Tennessee Williams Remembered (T. Williams, Wallach, Jackson), 239, 240
Texas Trilogy (P. Jones), 82
That Championship Season (film), 157
That Man of Mine (film), 55
That Secret Sunday (television), 71
theater. *See* avant-garde theater; Broadway theater; dinner theaters; Greek drama; nonprofit theater companies; off-Broadway theater; regional theater; repertory companies; stock companies; summer theaters
Theater Company of Boston, The, 43
theater critics. *See* critics
Theater Hall of Fame, 21, 22, 56, 89, 108, 144, 206
Theatre-by-the-Sea, Matunuck, R.I., 127
Theatre Guild, New York City, viii
There Was a Crooked Man (film), 21
These Men (M. Simon), 2
They've Taken Our Children (television), 89
Thicker than Water (television), 89
thirtysomething (television series), 185
This Property Is Condemned (T. Williams), 126, 238
Thornton, Billy Bob, 152
Thorns, The (television), 227
Thousand Clowns, A (Gardner), 205, 216; film version, 206
Three Men on a Horse (Holm and Abbott), 20, 73, 121
Three Sisters, The (Chekhov), 1, 20, 22, 48, 50, 70, 124, 161, 172, 179, 182
Threepenny Opera, The (Brecht, Blitzstein, Weill), 160
Tiger, The (Schisgal), 238, 240
Tiger Makes Out, The (film), 239, 240
Till the End of Time (film), 173
Tillinger, John, 86, 199
Time and the Conways (Priestley), 22
Time Remembered (Anouilh), 251
Time to Dance, A (film), 56
Timon and Pumbaa (television), 189
Timon of Athens (Shakespeare), 167
Tiny Alice (Albee), 258
Titan A.E. (film), 189
To Be Young, Gifted, and Black (television), 41, 56
To Dance with the White Dog (television), 21, 22, 33, 34
To Kill a Clown (film), 40

To Save a Child (television), 173
To Wong Foo, Thanks for Everything (film), 41
Tommy (Townshend), 121
Tomorrow the Man (television), 239
Tone, Franchot, 211
Tongue of the Bird (McLaughlin), 124
Tony Awards, xi, 2, 11, 21, 22, 40, 43, 71, 88, 89, 108, 124, 143, 144, 172, 188, 205, 212, 226, 227, 238
Too Far to Go (television), 41
Too Good to Be True (television), 89
Too Much (film), 239
Too True to be Good (G. B. Shaw), 107
Toomer, Jean, 68
Tora! Tora! Tora! (film), 206
Torn, Rip, 177, 197
Touch of the Poet, A (O'Neill), 206, 222
Tough Guys (film), 239
Toys in the Attic (Hellman), 205, 215, 226
Track of Fears (television), 227
Tracy, Spencer, 123, 207
Trading Mom (film), 227
Traitor, The (Wouk), 107
Travis Logan, D.A. (television), 71
Trial, The (film), 206
Trinity Rep, Providence, R.I., 211
Triumph over Disaster (television), 71, 108
Trixie (film), 189
Trojan Women, The (Euripides), 249
Trouble with Women, The (film), 89
Truckline Café (M. Anderson), 37, 251
Truex, Ernest, 248
Truth about Women, The (film), 89
Turner, Lana, 90
Twelfth Night (Shakespeare), 21, 40, 44, 131, 135
Twelve Angry Men (television), 21
Twentieth Century (Hecht and MacArthur), 247
21 Hours at Munich (television), 173
27 Wagons Full of Cotton (T. Williams), 226
Twice Around the Park (Schisgal), 239
Two for the Seesaw (Gibson), 95
Two Jakes, The (film), 239
Typists, The (Schisgal), 238, 240

Ultimate Betrayal (television), 108
Union Theatre Repertory Company, Melbourne, Australia, 1
Under Siege (television), 71
Uninvited (film), 239
Uninvited, The (television), 173

About the Editors

Jackson R. Bryer is a professor of English at the University of Maryland. He is the editor of *The Playwright's Art: Conversations with Contemporary American Dramatists* (Rutgers, 1995), *Conversations with Lillian Hellman, Lanford Wilson: A Casebook,* and *Conversations with Thornton Wilder* and coeditor of *Selected Letters of Eugene O'Neill.*

Richard A. Davison is a professor of English at the University of Delaware. He has published three books on Frank, Charles, and Kathleen Norris and more than sixty articles in such journals as *Modern Fiction Studies, North Dakota Quarterly, Modern Drama, Journal of Modern Literature, American Literary Realism, American Literature, Studies in American Fiction, Hemingway Review,* and *Playbill.* He is writing a study of the New York theater in 1958.